WATER AND SACRED ARCHITECTURE

This edited book examines architectural representations that tie water, as a physical and symbolic property, with the sacred. The discussion centers on two levels of this relationship: how water influenced the sacredness of buildings across history and different religions; and how sacred architecture expressed the spiritual meaning of water.

The volume deliberately offers original material on various unique contextual and design aspects of water and sacred architecture, rather than an attempt to produce a historic chronological analysis on the topic or focusing on a specific geographical region. As such, this unique volume adds a new dimension to the study of sacred architecture. The book's chapters are compiled by a stellar group of scholars and practitioners from the US, Canada, Europe, Asia, and Africa. It addresses major aspects of water in religious buildings, such as rituals, pilgrimage, water as a cultural material and place-making, hydro systems, modern practices, environmental considerations, the contribution of water to transforming secular into sacred, and future digital/cyber context of water and sacredness. All chapters are based on original archival studies, historical documents, and field visits to the sites and buildings. These examinations show water as an expression of architectural design, its materiality, and its spiritual values. The book will be of interest to architects, historians, environmentalists, archaeologists, religious scholars, and preservationists.

Anat Geva, PhD, a registered architect in Israel and Associate Member of the AIA, is a Professor Emerita of Architecture at Texas A&M University, and the College of Architecture Outstanding Alumni. She taught design; history/design of sacred architecture; history of building technology; and historic preservation. She published many articles and three books: *Frank Lloyd Wright Sacred Architecture: Faith, Form, and Building Technology* (Routledge, 2012); *Modernism and American Mid-20th Century Sacred Architecture* (Routledge, 2019); and *Israel Architecture as an Experimental Lab for Modern Architecture: 1948-1978*: with Inbal Ben-Asher Gitler (Intellect Books, 2020). Geva's forthcoming book *The Architecture of Modern American Synagogues (1950s–1960s)* is currently in press (Texas A&M University Press). She also has an extensive record of editorial work: being a co-editor of *Arris*, and founder and co-editor of *Preservation Education & Research*. She is a recipient of several awards and research grants including the prestigious *James Marston Fitch National Award* for innovative research in historic preservation.

WATER AND SACRED ARCHITECTURE

Edited by Anat Geva

LONDON AND NEW YORK

Designed cover image: Photo by Pixabay from Pexels: https://www.pexels.com/photo/water-drop-photo-220213/

First published 2023
by Routledge
4 Park Square, Milton Park, Abingdon, Oxon OX14 4RN

and by Routledge
605 Third Avenue, New York, NY 10158

Routledge is an imprint of the Taylor & Francis Group, an informa business

© 2023 selection and editorial matter, Anat Geva; individual chapters, the contributors

The right of Anat Geva to be identified as the author of the editorial material, and of the authors for their individual chapters, has been asserted in accordance with sections 77 and 78 of the Copyright, Designs and Patents Act 1988.

All rights reserved. No part of this book may be reprinted or reproduced or utilised in any form or by any electronic, mechanical, or other means, now known or hereafter invented, including photocopying and recording, or in any information storage or retrieval system, without permission in writing from the publishers.

Trademark notice: Product or corporate names may be trademarks or registered trademarks, and are used only for identification and explanation without intent to infringe.

British Library Cataloguing-in-Publication Data
A catalogue record for this book is available from the British Library

Library of Congress Cataloging-in-Publication Data
Names: Geva, Anat, 1947- editor.
Title: Water and sacred architecture / edited by Anat Geva.
Description: Abingdon, Oxon : Routledge, 2023. | Includes bibliographical references and index.
Identifiers: LCCN 2022048977 (print) | LCCN 2022048978 (ebook) | ISBN 9781032415901 (hardback) | ISBN 9781032415895 (paperback) | ISBN 9781003358824 (ebook)
Subjects: LCSH: Water and architecture. | Sacred space. | Water--Religious aspects.
Classification: LCC NA2542.8 .W372 2023 (print) | LCC NA2542.8 (ebook) | DDC 714--dc23/eng/20230114
LC record available at https://lccn.loc.gov/2022048977
LC ebook record available at https://lccn.loc.gov/2022048978

ISBN: 9781032415901 (hbk)
ISBN: 9781032415895 (pbk)
ISBN: 9781003358824 (ebk)

DOI: 10.4324/9781003358824

Typeset in Bembo
by KnowledgeWorks Global Ltd.

Let anyone who wishes take the water of life as a gift (Revelations 22:17)

CONTENTS

Acknowledgment   *x*
Contributors   *xi*

Introduction: Water and Sacred Architecture   1
Anat Geva

PART I
Rituals   11

1 Beyond Baptism: Incorporating Water as a Primary Symbol in Contemporary Roman Catholic Church Architecture   13
Roberto Chiotti

2 Water and Ritual *Wudu* (Ablutions) in Canadian Mosques   29
Tammy Gaber

3 *Chattri* and *Kund*: The Architecture of Kusum Sarovar, Govardhan, India   41
Amita Sinha

4 Sacred Water Architecture for Every Jew: Rabbi David Miller and DIY Mikvah in Charleston, South Carolina   52
Barry L. Stiefel

PART II
Water as Material Culture and Place Making   67

5 Architecture, Water, and the Sacred in the Sanctuary
   of the Great Gods on Samothrace, Greece   69
   Andrew Farinholt Ward, Jessica Paga, and Bonna Wescoat

6 Roman Waterscapes, Architecture, and Religion:
   Notions of Sacrality and Sensory Experience   84
   Dylan K. Rogers

7 Purifying the Stupa: Symbolism of the Lotus in
   Buddhist Architecture   98
   Di Luo and Gerald Kozicz

8 The Sacredness of Water and Place: African and Diasporic
   Religious Cultural Encounters   113
   *Peter F. Adebayo, Christopher S. Hunter,
   and Oluwafunminiyi Raheem*

PART III
Environmental Impact   131

9 The "Sacred" Architecture of Anupam Mishra's Water-Culture   133
   Ricki Levi

10 Sacredness in the Presence and Absence of Water:
   The Case of Stepwells in Ahmedabad, India   148
   Priyanka Sheth

11 Tethering Buddhism to Climate Change: Lessons from
   the Ladakhi Ice Stupa   165
   Carey Clouse

PART IV
Water Systems   181

12 Hymn to the Waters: *Anāhitā* in Ancient Persian Architecture   183
   Stephen Caffey

13 Tower and Temple: Re-sacralizing Water Infrastructure
   at Balkrishna Doshi's GSFC Township   199
   Daniel Williamson

14 Geothermal Systems and Religious Ethics: Frank Lloyd Wright's
   Unity Temple, and First Unitarian Society of Madison 215
   Joseph M. Siry

PART V
Modern Practice **231**

15 Sacredness and Water in Contemporary Japanese Architecture:
   Reinterpretation of Ancient Traditions 233
   Galia Dor

16 Baptistries in Marcel Breuer and Associates' American
   Catholic Sacred Spaces 247
   Victoria Young

17 Strength in Weakness—Daoist Waters and the Architecture
   of the Xinjin Zhi Museum 262
   Ariel Genadt

Epilogue: The Expression of Water in Virtual Sacred Architecture:
The Case of a Virtual Baptism 279
Nesrine Mansour

Index 292

ACKNOWLEDGMENT

Water and Sacred Architecture

Anat Geva Editor

Editing this volume was an exciting and challenging project. The call for chapter proposals on water and sacred architecture attracted more than 40 scholars from around the world (USA, Canada, Europe, Africa, Central and South Asia). Following a review process, only 18 papers are included. These chapters address how water and sacred architecture are expressed in various religions (e.g., Christianity, Islam, Judaism, Buddhism, Hindu, Daoism, Shinto, Zoroastrianism); during different time periods in history (e.g., from ancient times to modern); and in different parts of the world. Though the articles are so diverse, they all focus on the underlying theme of the book–water and sacred architecture.

The uniqueness of this book is attributed to all authors who contributed to this volume. I thank all of them. It was a pleasure working with each of them and to be engaged in reviewing and revising their projects. Their essays enriched the scholarship of the book and its professional level. I also thank the reviewers and the copy-editors for their constructive comments, which strengthen the book.

I deeply thank my husband Dr. Nehemia Geva for our invaluable discussions, his encouragement, critique, and mostly his love. With gratitude to my children, their spouses, and my grandchildren for their support and for serving as my light.

Finally, many thanks to Routledge, their Senior Publisher Francesca (Fran) Ford and her team for publishing the book.

CONTRIBUTORS

Peter F. Adebayo is a Professor and former Head of the Department, History and International Studies, University of Ilorin, Kwara State, Nigeria. He was a 2003 Fulbright Scholar at the New York University's prestigious Multinational Institute of American Studies (MIAS), where he successfully completed a certificate course on 'Civilization of the United States of America.' In 2005, he won the Advanced Research Fellowship Program Award from the Council for the Development of Social Science Research in Africa (CODESRIA), where he researched on Lebanese returnees from Nigeria to Miziara and Juway, respectively. He is currently preparing a full-length monograph entitled: *From Peddlers to Industrialists: The Lebanese in Lagos, 1890-1980.* Adebayo has published widely in both highly reputable local and international journals.

Stephen Caffey, PhD is an Instructional Associate Professor in the Department of Architecture at Texas A&M University, where he currently serves as director for the MS in Architecture and PhD in Architecture programs. His research focuses on art and architectural histories, visual and spatial literacies, virtual heritage, and the history, theory, and practice of design thinking and design process. He has authored and co-authored a number of articles and book chapters, the most recent of which address notions of urban space in heritage conservation initiatives in Isfahan, Iran, and the appropriation of private space for public sacred rituals in Yazd, Iran.

Roberto Chiotti, OAA, FRAIC, LEED AP, CAHP. In addition to obtaining his professional architectural degree in 1978 from the University of Waterloo, Canada, Roberto Chiotti completed his Master of Theological Studies degree at the University of St. Michael's College, the University of Toronto in 1998 with a specialty in Theology and Ecology obtained through the Elliott Allen Institute for Theology and Ecology at St. Michael's. He is a founding principal of Larkin Architect Limited, a Toronto-based firm specializing in the design of sustainable sacred space for parishes and religious communities, mostly within the Christian tradition. He also currently serves on the board of directors for the Architecture, Culture, and Spirituality Forum. In addition to his teaching appointments, Roberto has been invited to speak on the topics of liturgical design, sacred space, eco-theology, and the architectural response to the ecological crisis at universities, colleges, and conferences throughout North America and abroad.

Carey Clouse is an Associate Professor in Architecture and Landscape Architecture at the University of Massachusetts, Amherst. She holds a post-professional degree (SMArchS) in Architecture and Urbanism from the Massachusetts Institute of Technology and a BArch from the University of Oregon. Clouse is the recipient of a Fulbright-Nehru Senior Research Fellowship in Ladakh, India, and the Enterprise Rose Architectural Fellowship in New Orleans, LA. Clouse's research addresses climate change adaptation, with particular attention to the small-scale, DIY, ground-up interventions initiated by engaged citizens. In an effort to bolster interdisciplinary research and learning at UMass, she teaches in both the architecture department and the landscape architecture regional planning department (LARP).

Galia Dor, PhD is a multi-disciplinary lecturer of Chinese and Japanese philosophy, aesthetics and architecture; she received her M.A. and PhD from the department of East Asian studies in Tel Aviv University, in which she has taught courses on Chinese and Japanese philosophy and architecture'; prior to the Humanities, she had studied for a B.Sc. and M.Sc. in the life sciences, researching animal behavior and evolution. Her PhD explores the metaphorical significance of gates in ancient Chinese philosophy, architecture and material culture. Her forthcoming book with SUNY Press is (temp.) titled *Instrumental for Actualized Life: A Correlate Interpretation of gates in ancient China (and beyond)*.

Tammy Gaber, PhD is a Director and Associate Professor at the McEwen School of Architecture, Laurentian University (Canada), which she joined as founding faculty in 2013. Dr.Gaber completed a federally funded research project which led to her recent book from McGill Queen's Press, *Beyond the Divide: A Century of Canadian Mosque Design* and has published on gender and architecture with a chapter in the forthcoming *Global Encyclopedia of Women in Architecture*. Dr.Gaber has also published chapters on vernacular and regional architecture in *Habitat: Vernacular Architecture for a Changing Planet* and *Diversity and Design: Perspectives from the Non-Western World*, and has two chapters in the forthcoming *The Religious Architecture of Islam*. In 2019 Dr. Gaber won the *Women Who Inspire Award* from the Canadian Council of Muslim Women and in 2020, she was awarded Laurentian University's *Teaching Excellence Award* for a Full-time professor.

Ariel Genadt, PhD is an Architect and a Lecturer at the University of Pennsylvania. His research and teaching focus on construction techniques and their potential expression of environmental and cultural aspects of places. He further specializes in modern architecture in Japan and has published scholarly articles on these topics in *EAHN, ACADIA, JSAH, docomomo,* and *CIRICE,* among others. He holds a PhD in Architecture (U.Penn), an M.Arts (Architectural Association, London), and a B.Arch (Technion, Israel). He was a JSPS Fellow at Tokyo University (2012), and a visiting scholar at the Fondazione Renzo Piano, Genoa (2013). He has curated the exhibition *Critical Abstractions - Modern Architecture in Japan* (2018), and was Associate Curator of the exhibition *Building in China* (2021), both at the University of Pennsylvania's Architectural Archives Gallery. Genadt has collaborated as an architect on a wide range of buildings and urban design projects in Asia, Africa and Europe.

Contributors **xiii**

Anat Geva, PhD, a registered architect in Israel and Associate Member of the AIA, is a Professor Emerita of Architecture at Texas A&M University, and the College of Architecture Outstanding Alumni. She taught design; history/design of sacred architecture; history of building technology; and historic preservation. She published many articles and three books: *Frank Lloyd Wright Sacred Architecture: Faith, Form, and Building Technology* (Routledge, 2012); *Modernism and American Mid-20th Century Sacred Architecture* (Routledge, 2019); and *Israel Architecture as an Experimental Lab for Modern Architecture: 1948-1978*: with Inbal Ben-Asher Gitler (Intellect Books, 2020). Geva's forthcoming book *The Architecture of Modern American Synagogues (1950s–1960s)* is currently in press (Texas A&M University Press). She also has an extensive record of editorial work: being a co-editor of *Arris*, and founder and co-editor of *Preservation Education & Research*. She is a recipient of several awards and research grants including the prestigious James *Marston Fitch National Award* for innovative research in historic preservation.

Christopher S. Hunter, PhD was born and raised in Dayton, Ohio. He holds a Bachelor of Architecture from the University of Cincinnati as well as a Master of Science and a Ph.D. in Architecture both from Texas A&M University. His research focus is the study of the design and construction of early African American church buildings built from 1800 to the 1920s. Chris has presented a number of papers on his research as well as made presentations to academic as well as church audiences. Chris is currently an Assistant Professor of Architecture at Mississippi State University, where he teaches various design studios as well as lectures on the history of architecture from the late 18th century to the present.

Gerald Kozicz, received his PhD in architecture at Graz University of Technology (TU Graz) in Austria. Since 2005, he has led six stand-alone research projects funded by the Austrian Science Fund (FWF). He has more than twenty years of field research experience in Asia, and his study on the Buddhist and Hindu art and architecture in the Western Himalayas involves the extensive documentation and digitization of the local cultural heritage sites. Kozicz has published more than forty articles and book chapters on Indo-Tibetan art and has given invited talks and conference presentations in Europe, Asia, and the United States. He has taught courses on architectural history, hand drawing, and landscape architecture at the University of Vienna, Humboldt University of Berlin, and TU Graz.

Ricki Levi, PhD is an Assistant Professor and Assistant Dean for International affairs at the Jindal School of Environment and Sustainability (JSES), O.P. Jindal Global University, Sonipat, India. She received her doctoral degree at the Department of Environmental Studies, Porter School of the Environment and Earth Sciences, Faculty of Exact Sciences, Tel Aviv University. Her dissertation topic is "Environmental Gandhi," where she researches Indian Environmentalists such as Anupam Mishra, Vandana Shiva, and Rajni Bakshi as Gandhian environmental practical interpretations. She has a Philosophy and South-Asian studies degree and an M.A. thesis on "Time and Temporality in Indian Buddhism (Theravada)," both from Tel Aviv University. The results of her study in India were presented at conferences and workshops in Israel, India, and Germany. They were also published in a peer-reviewed journal, *Transcience: A Journal of Global Studies,* and as chapters in two scholarly books: *Global Water Ethics: Towards a Water Ethics Charter* and *Epistemologies of Water in Asia.*

Di Luo is Chu-Niblack Assistant Professor of Art History and Architectural Studies at Connecticut College. She studies Chinese wooden architecture, the building traditions of Asia, and the application of digital technologies to art history, urban studies, and the preservation of cultural heritage. Before joining Conn, Luo taught at Wake Forest University, the University of Pittsburgh, and the University of Southern California. As a trained architect, she previously worked as an architectural designer and modeler in Los Angeles and Beijing.

Nesrine Mansour, PhD, is an Assistant Professor of Architecture at South Dakota State University where she teaches design, sacred architecture, history, and theory. She holds a Certificate in Digital Humanities and is the 2020/2021 research fellow with the Center for Theological Inquiry at Princeton conducting research on Religion and the Built Environment. With a background in environmental design, she has experience with architectural daylighting systems working on a project awarded by the Environmental Protection Agency. Her research investigates the intersection of architecture, religion/faith, and digital media. She merges architecture scholarship with social sciences research methods and the digital humanities. She uses empirical methods and digital ethnography to assess the effect of virtual sacred architecture on spiritual experiences (i.e., virtual sacred spaces in games, websites, digital applications, etc.). Her research examines the intersection of sacred architecture, lighting design, communication and mass media, religious studies, and psychology. She studies the phenomenon of digital religion and its impact on sacred architecture, using both empirical and theoretical methods.

Jessica Paga is an Associate Professor of Classical Studies at the College of William & Mary. She received her PhD from Princeton University and her BA from Smith College. Her research interests include Greek and Roman architecture, architectural history, ritual theory, and Greek epigraphy. She has published widely on matters related to Athenian architecture, including *Building Democracy in Late Archaic Athens*, published with Oxford University Press in 2021, and "Contested Space at the Entrance of the Athenian Acropolis," in *The Journal for the Society of Architectural Historians* in 2017. At Samothrace, where she has worked since 2012, Jessica is a senior archaeologist and architecture specialist.

Oluwafunminiyi Raheem was a Research Fellow at the Centre for Black Culture and International Understanding (CBCIU), Osogbo, and currently a doctoral student at the University of Ilorin, both in Nigeria. He currently teaches at the Osun State University, Osogbo. His research interest intersects themes such as African cultural history, heritage studies, political and social history, and contemporary popular culture. He has published several articles and chapters in learned journals and books in these areas, respectively. His recent publication is titled: Not Your Color, Not Your Size, Not Your Spec': Marching against Market Harassment and Molestation in Nigeria," in Msia Kibona and Wunpini Mohammed (eds.), African Women in Digital Spaces: Redefining Social Movements on the Continent and in the Diaspora, Dar es Salaam: Mkuki na Nyota Publishers, 2023. Raheem is currently researching the Yoruba context of holy wells in Ile-Ife and Ondo, southwest Nigeria, and the collections in the Ulli Beier Archive at the CBCIU, Osogbo.

Dylan K. Rogers is currently the Postdoctoral Scholar in Classics at Florida State University, and he has previously taught Roman art and archaeology at the University of Virginia (2019–2022) and served as the Assistant Director of the American School of Classical Studies at Athens (2015–2019). He is the author of *Water Culture in Roman Society* (2018) and the co-editor of the volumes, *What's New in Roman Greece?* (2018) and *The Cambridge Companion to Ancient Athens* (2021), along with articles on Roman fountains, sensory archaeology, wall painting, and mosaics.

Priyanka Sheth is an Architectural Designer and Researcher currently working in New York. She is a co-author of the book *Stepwells of Ahmedabad: Water, Gender, Heritage* (Calmo, 2020). She co-curated exhibitions on stepwells at the Kanoria Centre for Arts and Gandhi Memorial Museum in India and Yale University and the Cooper Union in the United States. Her recent contributions were published in *Archives of New Traditional Architecture* (University of Notre Dame, 2022) and *Constructs* (Yale School of Architecture, 2021).

Amita Sinha is a former Professor in the Department of Landscape Architecture at the University of Illinois at Urbana Champaign (1989–2018) and has taught in the Department of Architecture and Regional Planning, IIT Kharagpur and the Humanities and Social Sciences Department at IIT Gandhinagar in India. She is the author of *Landscapes in India: Forms and Meanings* (University Press of Colorado, 2006; reprinted by Asia Educational Services, 2011) and *Cultural Landscapes of India: Imagined, Enacted, and Reclaimed* (University of Pittsburgh Press, 2020), editor of *Landscape Perception* (Academic Press, 1995), and co-editor of *Cultural Landscapes of South Asia: Studies in Heritage Conservation and Management* (Routledge, 2017). She was a Senior Fulbright Researcher at the Indian National Trust for Art and Cultural Heritage (INTACH) in New Delhi in 2009 and is the recipient of the Fulbright-Nehru Academic and Professional Excellence Award Fellowship in 2018–2019.

Joseph M. Siry, PhD is a Professor of Art History and William R. Kenan, Jr. Professor of the Humanities at Wesleyan University. His books are *Carson Pirie Scott: Louis Sullivan and the Chicago Department Store* (University of Chicago Press, 1988); *Unity Temple: Frank Lloyd Wright and Architecture for Liberal Religion* (Cambridge University Press, 1996); *The Chicago Auditorium Building: Adler and Sullivan's Architecture and the City* (University of Chicago Press, 2002), which won the 2003 Society of Architectural Historians' Alice Davis Hitchcock Book Award; *Beth Sholom Synagogue: Frank Lloyd Wright and Modern Religious Architecture* (University of Chicago Press, 2012), which was a finalist for a 2013 National Jewish Book Award, Visual Arts Category; and *Air-Conditioning in Modern American Architecture, 1890–1970* (Pennsylvania State University Press, 2021). His work has been supported by the National Endowment for the Humanities, Graham Foundation for Advanced Studies in the Fine Arts, and the Mellon and Getty foundations.

Barry L. Stiefel, PhD is an Associate Professor in the Historic Preservation & Community Planning program at the College of Charleston. He is interested in the preservation of Jewish heritage, as well as how the sum of how local preservation efforts affect regional, national, and multi-national policies within the field of cultural resource management and heritage conservation. Dr. Stiefel has published numerous journal articles and books, including *Jews and the Renaissance of Synagogue Architecture, 1450–1730* (Routledge, 2014).

Andrew Farinholt Ward, PhD received his Doctorate from the Institute of Fine Arts, New York University, and is currently with a Visiting Assistant Professor in the Department of Art History at Emory University. Andrew is the Supervisor of Excavations for the American Excavations Samothrace, and the Field Supervisor for the IFA-NYU and UniMi Excavations at Selinunte. His research interests include "colonial" contact between Greek and other ancient cultures and site formation processes in Greek sanctuaries. At Samothrace, Andrew's research is particularly focused on the ravines and broader water system of the Sanctuary of the Great Gods.

Bonna D. Wescoat is the Director of the American School of Classical Studies at Athens, Samuel Candler Dobbs Professor of Art History at Emory University, and Director of Excavations, Sanctuary of the Great Gods, Samothrace. Her books include *Samothrace; excavations conducted by the Institute of Fine Arts of New York University: Vol. 9, The Monuments of the Eastern Hill* (2017); *The Temple of Athena at Assos* (2012); *Architecture of the Sacred: Space, Ritual, and Experience from Classical Greece to Byzantium* (eds. B. D. Wescoat and R. Ousterhout, 2012); *Samothracian Connections; Essays in honor of James R. McCredie* (eds. O. Palagia and B. D. Wescoat, 2010). In addition to archaeological work on Samothrace, Wescoat's international collaborations include the FACE Foundation-sponsored French-American collaboration, "Architectural Networks of the Northern Aegean," and the Getty-sponsored Connecting Art Histories program, "Beyond the Northern Aegean: Architectural Interactions across Northern Greece, Macedonia, Thrace, and the Pontic Regions in the late Classical and Hellenistic Periods."

Daniel Williamson, PhD teaches the history of art and architecture at the Savannah College of Art and Design. He holds a Master in architectural history from the University of Virginia and a Ph.D. in art history from the Institute of Fine Arts-New York University where he wrote a dissertation entitled "Modern Architecture and Capitalist Patronage in Ahmedabad, India: 1947-1969." He is currently preparing a book manuscript on the same topic and has recently published articles on Brutalism in the United States and the architecture of market reform in Colonial Bombay.

Victoria M. Young, PhD is a Professor of Modern Architectural history and chair of the Art History Department at the University of St. Thomas (MN). She currently serves as President of the Society of Architectural Historians. Her 2014 book, *Saint John's Abbey Church: Marcel Breuer and the Creation of a Modern Sacred Space*, explored how the relationship between Breuer and Associates and the Benedictines shaped mid-20th-century Catholic space. She has published extensively on the Abbey Church, most recently comparing the role of concrete as its building material with the work of Voorsanger Mathes Architects in their design for the precast concrete chapel at the National World War II Museum in New Orleans. Young's current research examines how the sacred is created in the settings housing the three versions of William Holman Hunt's "The Light of the World" - chapel, cathedral, and art gallery.

INTRODUCTION

Water and Sacred Architecture

Anat Geva

The cover of the book describes a drop of water falling into a body of water[1] and expresses the book's spiritual metaphor of water as the Ocean of God, where "each individual is a drop of water. Together, we are an ocean."[2] This shows the tremendous role of water as cultural material and place-making in myth and spirituality. As such, water's intangible virtues represent the sacred values of heaven, earth, and hell. These beliefs and water's physical attributes underly the idea to devote a book to water and sacred architecture, *"With only scant amount of water and spirited design, all water in the world can be called to mind"* (Moore & Lidz 1994: 15).

The aim of this edited volume is to analyze and illustrate the interwoven relations between water and sacred architecture. This special relationship unfolds in the book through two main inquiries. The first focus is on how water, as a universal tangible element and yet a spiritual concept, influences the sacredness of buildings—across religions and geographical locations. Second, the book illustrates how sacred architecture expresses the spiritual meaning of water. The volume's chapters offer original material that introduces various unique faith and design contextual aspects of this relation.

Sacredness of water and its materiality is already evident in the perception that it is one of the four universal elements (water, earth, fire, and air) that are believed to construct the universe (Geva 2012). This perception is drawn from the Bible story of the Creation as described in the book of Genesis. The description includes each of the element's functions and their interwoven attributes in creating the cosmos. *Earth* represents "the element of life that surrounds us" (Geva, 2012: 19) and is a symbol of stability, permanence, and materiality. As an element "[o]ld enough to give you dreams" (Snyder 2008),[3] it has unique spiritual traditions that often are worshiped in their own right. *Fire* is associated with light and heaven on one hand but with hell on the other. It is often worshiped as an object of admiration and awe; *air* is a key to human existence, a dynamic element that frequently is associated with heaven; *water* represents the liquid state of the energy of life; It is essential to human survival, purity and fruitily (Geva 2012). Its fluid and still substance can appear as ice, liquid, and steam. The state of water impacts its physical movements as well as its spiritual inspiration from freezing to running through rivers, from bursting out from underground to falling from mountains, or calm waters in lakes or pools. Flooding is another water condition, which is portrayed as an evil force (see Leonardo da Vinci's 1517 drawing of water from his Deluge series, Moore & Lidz 1994: 18).

DOI: 10.4324/9781003358824-1

The strength of water is drawn from the descriptions of the separations among the four universal elements in the process of the Creation. The body of water was first separated from the sky (air) "Let there be a vault between the waters to separate water from water," (Genesis 1:6-8); and then it was separated from the land (earth) "Let the water under the sky be gathered to one place, and let dry ground appear" (Genesis 1:9-10). These separations were part of the transformation of the formless and empty cosmos into the world – the universe. More so, it points to the world's horizontal and vertical axes. These axes create the universe order, sacred geometry, shapes, and symbols, to which Frank Lloyd Wright referred as nature's "clean integrity in the terms of living" (Wright 1958/1992: 228). Similarly, Japanese architect Hiroshi Sambuichi wrote that wind [air], water, and sun [fire] are his inspirational universal elements in creating the ideal architecture (Sambuichi, 2016: 9). Thus, translating the elements and the universe's axes into sacred architecture shows how their combination creates a sacred three-dimensional space in the image of the world – the *imago mundi* (Mann 1993). The example of the Taj Mahal in Agra, India (1631-1648)[4] shows the combination of the axes that are highlighted by water. The calm water pool in front of the main elevation represents the horizontal axis as it leads the visitor toward the building, while the reflection of the elevation in the water of that pool enhances the vertical axis showing the domical monument. Thus, water can appear as a calm mirror pool creating horizontal and vertical axes. Water gushing down from the mountains is an additional form of creating the vertical axis. For example, the site of the Seiganto-ji Temple and its red pagoda, stand in front of the Nachi Falls in Wakayama, Japan. The 436.35 feet (133 meters) Falls is the highlight of the Kumano Kodo pilgrimage route.[5] The background scene of the Temple exemplifies the role of water in creating the vertical axis of the place.[6] The combination of the landscape and the Temple and its pagoda exhibits the sacred verticality of both the water and the temple showing water as material culture that transforms nature and the sacred building onto a set of beliefs and places.

Out of the four elements, water is the one specified as sacred since "the Spirit of God was hovering over the waters" (Genesis 1: 2), and often it is considered as one of God's Dwelling (Mirsky 1976). In the New Testament water is described as essential to the physical and mental human existence "The water that I give will become in them a spring of water gushing up to eternal life" (John 4: 14). Water is also mentioned in the gospel, "… unless a man is born of water and of the Spirit, he cannot enter the kingdom of God…" (John 3: 1-6). These quotes and the symbolic meanings of water are part of the myth developed about water. It is a purifier of mind and body, and a transitional entry to the sacred realm. It is mentioned 722 times in the Bible and thirty times in the Quran, where water is associated with paradise. Examples include abundant water as a symbol of fertility and youth "Let anyone who wishes take the water of life as a gift" (Revelations 22:17). However, it should be noted that water is also associated with a catastrophic, dark, mysterious, and cold evil force. See, for example, the flood story of Noah's Ark in Genesis Chapters 6–9: "For my part, I am going to bring a flood of waters on the earth, to destroy from under heaven all flesh in which is the breath of life; everything that is on the earth shall die;" and the flight of the Israelites from Egypt, where they had to cross the Red Sea (Exodus Chapters 14–15). Despite the catastrophic events, they all ended with hope and freedom. Other positive examples show the Biblical love stories where most are centered around water (e.g., the meeting of Isaac and Rivka around the water well; and Jacob and Rachel; or the story of David and Bat Sheba that is associated with bathing). Additional uplifting stories related to water appear in the New Testament when Jesus turned water into wine (John 2: 1-11) or walked on water (Matthew 14: 22-33). As such, water became the core of various myths, beliefs, and sacred attributes of the holy.

Indeed, during antiquity the role of water was pronounced by the Sumerians, Babylonians, Egyptians, Greeks, Persian, and Romans as responsible for the creation of the universe (Salimi et al, 2016). For example, in ~762BC, Homer, the Greek poet saw the creation of the world as impacted by the *Okehanos*—Ocean, and its marks on the universe (Homer, trans. 2018). The Greek philosopher Thales of Miletus (c. ~ 624BC–546BC) looked at water as the essence of all matters that impacted the world's creation, with the earth floating on a vast sea (Aristotle, trans. 2018). As part of Japanese water's mythology, the Shinto faith and mythology of the 8th century manifest their benevolent divinity of water worshiping Suijin – the God of Water.[7]

The strong role of water as developed through time is best summarized in the poem "Little Things" by American poet Julia Carney (1845):[8]

> *Little drops of water*
> *Little grains of sand,*
> *Make the mighty ocean,*
> *And the pleasant land.*
> *So the little moments,*
> *Humble though they be,*
> *Make the mighty ages*
> *Of eternity.*

Water became a universal concept across faiths and around the world. It is an object of praying and part of various rituals. It often serves as a core of worship with deep faith symbolism that is expressed in the sacred building. Such is the dramatic case of architect Tadao Ando's Church on the Water in Japan (1985). Ando set a large concrete cross into the water in front of the sanctuary glass wall.[9] He employed water as the "embodiment of the spirit" to "transform the site as experienced from both the threshold of the water and the belvedere above" (Frampton 2010: 105). In this case, the architect highlights the relationship between water and architecture by illustrating the tangible features of water (e.g., the pool of water around the church) and its spiritual meaning in reflecting the cross. Thus, water enhances the sacred.

Another pertinent example where architectural detail enhances the sacredness of water, is Architect Mario Botta's church of Sant Giovanni Battista in Mongo, Switzerland (1992). Botta designed an open drain as part of the church's tilted glass roof. The water is channeled underneath the church's bells that hang above the drain. Thus, the architect enhanced the tangible element of water with a religious spiritual element of the bells.

The interwoven physical and spiritual meaning of water can also be observed when it serves as a threshold and a tangible barrier between the outdoors and the interior. In this capacity, water directs the worshiper from the profane to the spiritual realm. Across faiths and cultures, separation from the mundane is one of the major spiritual characteristics that enhance the sacredness of the house of God (Geva 2012). Examples include, but not limited, the MIT Chapel designed by architect Eero Saarinen in 1955. The cylindrical chapel is set in a mote filled with water that surrounds the building's base. The worshiper needs to cross over the water to enter the chapel and leave behind the outside world (Siry, 2019: 282-3, Figures 14.5; 14.7). In Frank Lloyd Wright 's proposed design for Taliesin Unity Chapel in Wisconsin in 1958, two water pools are located as boundaries of the sacred path (Geva 2012: 27, Fig. 1.8). In this case the journey from the mundane to the sacred realm is defined by water. Thus, he attempted to separate the chapel from the secular world. Architects like Tadao Ando and Loius Baragan used water as a threshold to distinguish between the secular profane and the spiritual place in public and domestic architecture. Such is Ando's design of the Museum of Modern Art in Forth-Worth, Texas (2002), or Loius Baragan's home (Casa) in Mexico City (1948) where water surrounds the structures and separates them from the outside. Moreover, the water reflects the buildings, absorbs their shadows, and emphasizes their depth.

The concept of water as a physical and psychological threshold is also manifested by using water as a purifying ritual, where worshipers prepare themselves for the sacred. Water in the purification process serves as the physical material for washing/bathing to purify the body; and as a spiritual element that purifies the soul and washes the worshipers' sins. Purification rituals are based on washing either the hands/feet in daily prayers; while at other times, it requires a full immersion once a week, or during special events. In mosques, for example, worshipers are expected to perform a purification ritual called *Wudu*[10] before entering the sacred. This ablution procedure calls for the design of water features that vary from simple functional faucets to elaborated decorative basins and fountains which are located usually at the mosque's entrance courtyard or in washrooms set aside.

Purification rituals are also performed inside the house of worship such as in churches with Christian holy water fonts and Baptismal. The ritual of Baptism can be performed either by sprinkling water on the worshiper's or baby's forehead, or in other cases by immersing in water (e.g., the Jordan River). This ritual is not only a symbol of purification but also a sign of being accepted into Christianity. The font is a vessel containing holy water, which is generally placed near the entrance of a church for the worshipers to dip their fingers into the holy water and make the sign of the cross over themselves. With that, they reconnect with that mysterious and foundational experience of receiving the sacrament of baptism.[11] Additional examples of modern fonts are Mario Botta's 1990s designs in Sant Giovanni Battista in Mongo, Switzerland, and in the Holy Pope Giovanni XIII Church in Seriate, Italy. The design of each of the fonts is completely integrated into the sanctuary. One is based on the white and gray marble of the church, and the other is built from the church's red and texture of Verona stone. As such, this design integrates the ritual into the sanctuary and becomes part of the structure and its sacredness.

Purifying rituals are also conducted in special structures separated from the main building. In the Japanese Shinto tradition of Temizuya (hand-water), there is a separate place where worshipers can cleanse their bodies and minds before entering the shrine. In Jewish traditions, a *Mikvah* is built as a separate structure where the worshiper fully immerses in water once a week in addition to washing hands before praying. Women are required an additional immersion to purify themselves once a month after menstruation. In modern times, this separate building often is built as part of a synagogue complex (Geva, 2017).

Water is also used to reflect light and to serve as an acoustical barrier. Frank Lloyd Wright's proposal for the Memorial to the Soil Chapel, Wisconsin (1936) included an outdoor pool behind the interior choir area (Geva 2012: 22, Fig. 1.2). He used water to reflect the light behind the choir and into the chapel. Moreover, he used that pool as an acoustical barrier blocking the outdoor everyday life noises to focus on the choir sounds. The use of water for acoustics also appears in Frank Lloyd Wright's proposal of the Steel Cathedral in New York City (Geva, 2012: 22; 64, Fig. 2.3.1). In this design, which was never realized, Wright attempted to unite all Christian denominations under one roof by creating a pyramid structure with all chapels located around a core of a water feature installed in the middle of a sunken center at the entrance level. The fountain would throw water 1000 feet high in the air and be illuminated by a reflection of countless light rays from the pyramidal roof (Geva 2012). As such, when worshipers would enter, they would be exposed to soft light reflected by the water, and to sounds of water that would divert background noises and "metaphorically [would] lift the spirit toward heaven"

(Geva 2012: 223). Thus, the sounds from the entrance or one chapel would not disturb the sounds from the central lobby or one chapel to the others (Geva 2012: 223).

The water mote surrounding Saarinen's MIT chapel is not only a threshold before entering the sacred, but also enhances the light and acoustics in the chapel. Light is reflected from the water into the interior through lower arched openings (Siry, 2019: 284, Figure 14.8). The water blocks the outdoor sounds and enhances the chapel's interior acoustics quality, which was created by using wavy walls of bricks inside the chapel.

Across faiths and cultures, water is perceived as a prime material and is considered as a material culture element within the context of each faith. Material culture is an aspect of culture grounded in the built environment and defines its relation to a specific culture and set of beliefs.[12] It reflects the relation of water as a tangible element with its intangible implications (see Chapter 8). An image of water running on a stone wall exhibits a tangible liquid material that becomes part of the wall expressing water as a prime material. It also may transfer the wall into a spiritual and mythological realm of a sacred place, or sacralize a secular building or part of it. A contemporary example is the water running over a brick wall in Xinjin Zhi Museum in China, designed by architect Kengo Kuma in 2010 (see Chapter 17). This aspect of water as culture material shows how water enhances sacred architecture.

The need of water for its physical essence and spiritual attributes called for the development and establishment of systems to control and manage waters across the world. These techniques help in enhancing the sacredness of water and the built environment associated with it. Most of the publications about managing waters focus on protecting the built environments and landscapes from extreme water conditions like rising waters, or droughts. Since the systems' developments depend on a specific region and its environmental conditions, changes in geography and climate trigger new techniques and adaptations in urban planning, architecture, and landscapes. This book is unique in focusing on these developments as related specifically to sacred architecture. It covers some of the developments through antiquity and modern times.

This edited volume is organized into five parts following this Introduction on Water and Sacred Architecture and ending with an Epilogue: The Expression of Water in Virtual Sacred Architecture: The Case of a Virtual Baptism. The common thread of all the chapters is the investigation of the relationship of water and sacred architecture and the manifestations of water as a tangible and intangible element that enhances architecture.

PART I is entitled *Rituals* and includes four chapters that focus on rituals related to water and their expressions in sacred architecture in the context of various faiths: Christianity (Catholics), Islam, Hinduism, and Judaism.

Chapter 1 in this part, "Beyond Baptism: Incorporating Water as a Primary Symbol in Contemporary Roman Catholic Church Architecture" by Architect Roberto Chiotti analyzes church contemporary interior elements of baptism in contemporary architectural designs. Examples include the author's recent design proposals that express the seamless integration of the biblical/mythical and scientific/empirical origins of creation. These projects focus on the significant contributions of "eco-theology" that address the ecological crisis.

Chapter 2, "Water and Ritual Wudu (Ablutions) in Canadian Mosques" by Tammy Gaber analyzes the Muslim ablution ritual of *Wudu* as being expressed in two mosques in Canada. The shift of ablutions to interior spaces in Canadian mosques, is a response to the colder climate context and to the diasporic complexities of mosques design in the west.

Chapter 3 entitled "*Chattri and Kund*: The Architecture of Kusum Sarovar, Govardhan, India" by Amita Sinha relates to Hindu myths about water as expressed in pilgrimage temples from the 18th-century in the Braj region, India. The attraction of pilgrimage is based on the myth of the divine transcendence made immanent in materiality of *chattri* (pavilion) and the waters in the *kund* (tanks).

The last chapter in this part (Chapter 4), "Sacred Water Architecture for Every Jew: Rabbi David Miller and DIY Mikvah in Charleston, South Carolina" by Barry L. Stiefel introduces the water rituals performed in Judaism in a *Mikvah* a special bath for purification. Stiefel describes the 1910s idea by Rabbi David Miller from Oakland, California of building a *Mikveh* by yourself at home. A non-popular concept that is supposed to encourage every Jew to use the *Mikveh* as an important part of water rituals.

PART II of the book is entitled *Water as Material Culture and Place Making* and includes four chapters. Water in all four chapters is investigated as a material culture within the context of each faith. As mentioned before, material culture is an aspect of culture grounded in the built environment. Thus, it reflects the relation of water as a tangible element with its intangible implications that may define a place. The first three Chapters examine archeological findings related to water and the sacred from Ancient Greece, Ancient Rome, and Afghanistan. While the last chapter exemplifies how water as cultural material in West Africa was transformed as place-making in the US by enslaved people.

The first chapter (Chapter 5) in this part, "Architecture, Water, and the Sacred in the Sanctuary of the Great Gods on Samothrace, Greece" by Andrew Farinholt Ward, Jessica Paga, and Bonna Wescoat investigates archeological findings in Samothrace, Greece. The chapter illustrates water as a powerful force that "guided the initiate's kinesthetic experience and thus was central to the transformative efficacy of the cult" during wet and dry months.

Chapter 6, "Roman Waterscapes, Architecture, and Religion: Notions of Sacrality and Sensory Experience" by Dylan K. Rogers shows how symbolic and sensory experiences with water make a building sacred. The chapter includes examples that illustrate water as adding new meanings within spaces such as healing sites, imperial exhibit places, and as a symbol of the divine and thanks offerings.

Chapter 7 is entitled "Purifying the Stupa: Symbolism of the Lotus in Buddhist Architecture" by Di Luo and Gerald Kozicz. It explores the sacredness of the water flower—the lotus. The lotus serves as a metonym for paradise and a symbol of purifying the Stupa, which is the core of Buddhist temples. The authors provide archeological evidence of lotus pedestals, lotus tiles, and lustration rites in Tapa Sardar, Afghanistan.

The last chapter (Chapter 8) entitled, "The Sacredness of Water and Place: African and Diasporic Religious Cultural Encounters" by Peter F. Adebayo, Christopher S. Hunter, and Oluwafunminiyi Raheem shows water's role in place making. The authors demonstrate how the powerful rituals associated with water in West Africa (Nigeria) were carried by the slaves onto America and transformed into a new place. Furthermore, the chapter describes how those rituals influence the design of black churches in the south of the US.

PART III of this volume is entitled *Environmental Impact* and includes three chapters. These chapters examine the religious markers inscribed into the landscapes by climate change and its impact on different parts of India.

The first chapter (Chapter 9) in this part entitled "The 'Sacred' Architecture of Anupam Mishra's Water-Culture" by Ricki Levi examines the philosophy of Anupam Mishra (1948–2016) about water. "Mishra was a Gandhian environmental researcher and activist" who called for the revival of the Indian traditional water-harvesting systems in modern times. The chapter provides Mishra's analysis of water harvesting systems and the sacred as found in India's driest state the desert region of Rajasthan.

Chapter 10 entitled "Sacredness in the Presence and Absence of Water: The Case of Stepwells in Ahmedabad, India" and authored by Priyanka Sheth. It focuses on the changes caused by the drying of sacred wells in the region of Ahmedabad, in west India. It investigates the question of whether the absence of water triggers changes in the spiritual aspects of those wells. The findings demonstrate that the physical changes in water supply not necessarily impacted the spiritual rituals, pilgrimages, and beliefs associated with water. However, the changes in the climatic conditions generated different solutions to manage water and in return impacted the design of houses of worship and their details.

The last chapter in this part (Chapter 11), "Tethering Buddhism to Climate Change: Lessons from the Ladakhi Ice Stupa" by Carey Clouse illustrates the phenomenon of melting Buddhist ice stupas located in the dry desert region of Ladakh in north India. It analyzes a recent experiment of Buddhist adaptations of new practices to express local sacred architecture and overcome their loss of ice stupas due to climate change and thus loss of water resources.

PART IV of the book focuses on *Water Systems* and illustrates different examples of hydro techniques during history and modern times. The three chapters of this section demonstrate the ingenuity of people during different times and at various locations in harvesting, channeling, and preserving water.

The first chapter of this part, Chapter 12, "Hymn to the Waters: Anāhitā in Ancient Persian Architecture" by Stephen Caffey analyzes pre-Zoroastrian and Zoroastrian belief systems and how water serves as the core of the Anāhitā Temples. It shows water as an architectural feature articulated through the innovative ancient Persian *qanat* system. The *qanat* is a canal system that channels waters from the mountains to the Persian Desert Plato.

Chapter 13, "Tower and Temple: Re-sacralizing Water Infrastructure at Balkrishna Doshi's GSFC Township" by Daniel Williamson looks at the work of Pritzker Prize-winning architect Balkrishna Doshi. In his projects, Doshi developed modernism as a synthesis between Indian traditional culture and modern times that used water as enhancing the secular to become sacred. There, a secular dam and water towers become sacred as they harvest and contain the region's source of life.

The last chapter in this section (Chapter 14), "Geothermal Systems and Religious Ethics: Frank Lloyd Wright's Unity Temple, and First Unitarian Society of Madison" is authored by Joseph M. Siry. These cases follow the studies of water systems as part of hydrologic research and sustainable design. Siry shows that religious values of sustainability are considered stewardship to God, especially in preserving sacred architecture.

PART V of the book is entitled *Modern Practice* and includes three chapters. The chapters investigate modern/current practices and interpretations of water as part of sacred buildings. All show the transformation and inspiration of traditional water aspects as a feature in modern sacred architecture.

The first chapter in this part, Chapter 15, is entitled "Sacredness and Water in Contemporary Japanese Architecture: Reinterpretation of Ancient Traditions." The author Galia Dor looks at water as a major segment of modern Japanese sacred architecture. There, water serves as a threshold—a gate to enter the sacred realm. Dor examines the traditional Japanese rituals as related to water, their interpretation in the design of modern Temples, and their impact on secular structures to become sacred.

Chapter 16, "Baptistries in Marcel Breuer and Associates' American Catholic Sacred Spaces" by Victoria Young explores the role of water in the designs of Baptistries by modern architect Marcel Breuer and Associates following the Second Vatican Council. Three case studies are presented in the chapter to illustrate the renewal of the sacraments during the 1950s and early 1960s. The architects created a modern Catholic baptistery typology to showcase the meaning of the holy water and their interpretation of the Second Vatican Council.

Chapter 17, "Strength in Weakness—Daoist Waters and the Architecture of the Xinjin Zhi Museum" by Ariel Genadt introduces Architect Kengo Kuma's design of Xinjin Zhi Museum in Chengdu, China. The chapter shows how the museum from 2010 is a gateway to the Daoist sacred site of Laojun Shan. The author analyzes architect Kuma's writings and shows Kuma's allusions to water formations. Genadt relates them to concepts from the Dao De Jing and the Zhuangzi scriptures. The author focuses on the museum's design expressions of water as a physical material in its various stages and on its spiritual and mythological realm related to Daoism.

The final part of the book is its *Epilogue: The Expression of Water in Virtual Sacred Architecture: The Case of a Virtual Baptism,* authored by Nesrine Mansour. Rather than providing a summary of the various aspects of the chapters in this book, Mansour introduces us to the future of sacred architecture. She claims that sacred architecture follows the new field of digital religion and the development of cyberspace in the form of virtual architecture. Apparently, the virtual may enhance the sacredness of the space and create spiritual experiences (Mansour, 2019). The epilogue critically surveys the very little research conducted on water and sacred architecture in the virtual world that became part of our life. Mansour exhibits a case of virtual baptismal rituals showcasing water in sacred virtual reality.

As a whole, the book's parts and their chapters illustrate the various solutions to the use of water in relation to sacred architecture across different religions in various places in the world. Water is described as a tangible and intangible feature that enhances the architecture and its sacredness. It challenges designers to cater to rituals and holy meanings and forces people to look for sustainable solutions to overcome environmental changes. These solutions become part of the stewardship to God. As such, the book highlights the similarities of the use of water as a fundamental universal element of the creation and the essence of life, which enhance the sacredness of the built environment.

Notes

1. The image's source: https://www.pexels.com/photo/water-drop-photo-220213/
2. A quote by the Japanese poet Ryunosuke Satoro (1892–1927). https://inspyreapp.com/author/15753/ryunosuke-satoro. Accessed August 2021.
3. Gary Snyder's poem "Earth Verse" online: https://www.mindfulnessassociation.net/words-of-wonder/earth-verse-gary-snyder/ Accessed July 2021.
4. The Taj Mahal, India was inscribed as an UNESCO's World Heritage Site in 1982.
5. Nachi Falls and the Pagoda of Seigantoji Temple https://jw-webmagazine.com/the-best-scenic-waterfalls-nachi-falls-a96da3b685a0/ Accessed July 2021.
6. https://www.japan.travel/en/spot/971/ Accessed December 2021.
   In 2004, it was listed as a UNESCO World Heritage Site along with other locations, under the name "Sacred Sites and Pilgrimage Routes in the Kii Mountain Range".
7. https://www.worldhistory.org/Shinto/ Accessed August 2021.
8. I introduce part of Julia Carney's poem "Little Things" from 1845. https://www.famlii.com/little-things-poem-julia-carney/ Accessed July 2021.
9. For an image, please visit https://www.archdaily.com/97455/ad-classics-church-on-the-water-tadao-ando
10. *Wudu* video is shown online: https://www.pbs.org/wnet/religionandethics/2016/11/23/february-12-2016-wudu-islamic-washing-prayer/29054/ Accessed July 2021.
11. https://spiritualdirection.com/2014/09/15/why-are-holy-water-fonts-at-church-doors-why-bless-ourselves-with-holy-water Accessed December 2021.
12. https://www.sciencedirect.com/topics/nursing-and-health-professions/material-cultur Accessed June 2022.

References

Aristotle. *Metaphysics*. Translated by John H. McMahon (New York, NY: Dover Publications, third edition 2018).

Frampton Kenneth. "The Secular Spirituality of Tadao Ando" in Cavarra Britton Katla (ed.) *Constructing the Ineffable: Contemporary Sacred Architecture* (New Javen, CT: Yale University Press, 2010), 96–111.

Geva Anat. *Frank Lloyd Wright's Sacred Architecture: Faith, Form, and Building Technology* (London & NY: Routledge, 2012).

――――――. "Immigrants' Sacred Architecture: The Rabi Baal Hanes Synagogue in Eilat, Israel" in Mohammad Gharipour (ed.) *Design and Identity: The Architecture of Synagogues in the Islamic World* (Edinburgh, Scotland: Edinburgh University Press, 2017), 271–292.

Homer. *The Iliad & The Odyssey of Homer*. Translated Alexander Pope (Farmington Hills, Michigan: Gale ECCO-A devision of Cengage, 2018).

Mann A. T. *Sacred Architecture* (Rockport MA: Element Books LTD, 1993).

Mansour Nesrine. "Virtually Sacred: Effect of Light on the Spiritual Experience in Virtual Sacred Architecture" *PhD Dissertation* (College Station, TX: Texas A&M University, 2019).

Mirsky Jeanette. *Houses of God* (Phoenix edition) (Chicago, IL: University of Chicago Press, 1976).

Moore Charles and Lidz Jane. *Water and Architecture* (New York, NY: Harry N Abrams Publishers, 1994).

Salimi Aysegul Yurtyapan, Salimi Amineddin, and Pilehvarian Nuran Kara. "Position of Light and Water in Architecture and Philosophy of Art." *The Turkish Online Journal of Design, Art and Communication - TOJDAC* (April 2016 Special Edition): 58–67.

Sambuichi, Hiroshi. *Sambuichi and the Inland Sea* (Tokyo, Japan: TOTO Publishing, 2016).

Siry Joseph M. "Tradition and Transcendence: Eero Saarinen's MIT Chapel and the Nondenominational ideal" in Geva Anat (Ed) *Modernism and American Mid-20th Century Sacred Architecture* (London: Routledge, 2019), 275–295.

Snyder Gary. *Mountains and Rivers Without End* (Berkeley, CA: Counterpoint Press; 2nd edition, 2008).

Wright, Frank Lloyd. "Is It Good-Bye To Gothic?" *Together Magazine* (May, 1958); reprinted in Brice Pfeiffer (ed.) *Frank Lloyd Wright Collected Writings* (New York, NY: Rizzoli International Publications, Vol. 5, 1992), 227–233.

PART I
Rituals

1

BEYOND BAPTISM

Incorporating Water as a Primary Symbol in Contemporary Roman Catholic Church Architecture

Roberto Chiotti

The creation story shared by the Abrahamic religions – Judaism, Christianity, and Islam, begins with the Spirit of God, in darkness, hovering over the waters (Genesis 1:1-2 RSV). There is nothing else, just water, and as the creation story unfolds, everything, including the heavens, the earth, the sea creatures, the birds, the animals, and finally humans emerge from this one powerful life-giving source. It is thus appropriate that water participates as a potent archetypal element and tangible symbol of transformation in the sacrament of baptism, the primary rite of initiation into the Christian faith.

This chapter is written not from the perspective of an architectural historian, but rather, from that of a student of theology who is also an architectural practitioner engaged in the design of sacred spaces. It is structured as three interrelated parts. First, there is a brief introduction to the scriptural roots of baptism. Next is a guided meditative visualization employing hermeneutics to interpret the historical roots of the baptistery and baptismal font designs and their contexts. It highlights the architecture and ornately decorated mosaics of the Neonian Baptistery in Ravenna, arguably the most impressive baptistery to survive from the Early Christian period (Wharton 1987: 358). Part three of the chapter explores some recent sacred space designs by the author's firm Larkin Architect Limited, featuring unique contemporary expressions for baptismal fonts in addition to other creative ways in which water is incorporated beyond baptism. They reveal themes such as Christian Eschatology, the seamless integration of the biblical/mythical and scientific/empirical origins of creation, and the significant contributions of eco-theology toward addressing the ecological crisis. Individually and collectively, these opportunities for incorporating water as a primary symbol in recent Roman Catholic church and chapel architecture in Canada represent tangible, meaningful forms of catechesis[1] that engage the senses, provoke reflection, and invite transformation.

Christian Scriptural Roots for Baptism and the Transformative Power of Water

The scriptural roots for baptism can be found in the Old and New Testaments (Wagenfuhr 2020). Leviticus 15:16 talks about immersing into water for cleansing from sins. It continues to mention that this ritual should also apply to garments and skin. Through the rite of baptism, a ritual cleansing took place that prepared the Israelites for a new exodus (Spivey & Smith 1989: 65). The physical cleansing is accompanied by spiritual cleansing as well. The prophet John the Baptist, who appears at the beginning of the New Testament's Gospel appeared in the wilderness to preach a baptism of repentance for the forgiveness of sins, "To prepare the way of the Lord" (Mark 1:3-4 RSV). Mark goes on to say that all the people of Judea and Jerusalem came to be baptized in the Jordan River and confess their sins, as though the entire nation was undergoing mass repentance (Mark 1:5 RSV). Furthermore, John declares that this baptism by water would be completed by one who would baptize with the Spirit (Mark 1:8 RSV), and as such, John's act of prophecy indicates that the Spirit's appearance is imminent.

> In first-century Judaism the Spirit, which was the enabler of prophecy, was thought by many to have departed Israel with the last prophets (Haggai, Zechariah, and Malachi) and was expected only in the last days (Acts 2:17-22 & Joel 2:28-32). As John clearly points to the approach of another, Jesus, he also foreshadows an irruption of the end of time, the time of the active Spirit.
>
> *(Spivey & Smith 1999: 66)*

Jesus suddenly appears to be baptized in the waters of the river Jordan by John the Baptist. Upon his emergence, Mark shifts to cosmic language, describing that the heavens opened up and the Holy Spirit descended upon Jesus like a dove, followed by the voice of God proclaiming the baptized Jesus to be His beloved Son with whom He is pleased (Mark 1:9-11 RSV). Baptism thus serves as the defining initiatory cosmic event in which the "Son of God" is designated (Spivey & Smith 1989: 65), the Judaic prophecies of a coming messiah are fulfilled, and Jesus receives his commission to metaphorically lead God's people to a new exodus through his own radical ministry of love and salvation.

For Christians, Jesus is often characterized as "life giving water." This understanding is biblically based on the story of the Samaritan woman who comes to draw water from Jacob's well beside which Jesus is seated. She is confused when Jesus asks her for a drink since culturally, "...Jews have no dealings with Samaritans" (John 4: 7-9 RSV). When she questions him about his request, Jesus replies, "If you knew the gift of God, and who it is that is saying to you, 'Give me a drink,' you would have asked him, and he would have given you living water" (John 4: 9-11 RSV). Jesus goes on to compare the water of the well, which can only quench thirst temporarily, to the water that he will give them, from which one will never thirst again. He also alludes to the Christian precept that belief in Jesus will result in everlasting life. "The water I shall give him will become in him a spring of water welling up to eternal life" (John 4:13-15 RSV).

Through Jesus, water is bestowed a cosmic significance beyond its trans-cultural use in ritual cleansing. In the initiation right of baptism, it has transformative power in and of itself to ritually assist the transition from one's life preceding baptism to become sanctified afterwards as a follower of Christ. Historian of religions, Mircea Eliade describes the significance of rites of passage in the life of religious man:

> Initiation rites, entailing ordeals and symbolic death and resurrection, were instituted by gods, culture heroes, or mythical ancestors; hence these rights have a superhuman origin, and by performing them the novice imitates a superhuman, divine action.
>
> *(Eliade 1987: 187)*

Through the sacrament of baptism, it is understood that faithful catechumens "die to sin and are reborn to new life in Christ" (NCCB 2000: 26). Consequently, the design and location of baptismal fonts in Catholic Church architecture throughout the past two millennia have reflected their physical, practical, and transcendent role as a primary liturgical center associated with Christian sacred space.

The Orthodox Baptistery at Ravenna as Archetypal Precedent

The Orthodox Baptistery represents an archetypal example of early Byzantine Christian Baptistery and Font design. It was constructed as a separate building in relation to the Basilica of Ursiana in Ravenna, Italy, in the late 4th to early 5th century by Bishop Ursus (Thompson 2019: 1). A few generations later, Bishop Neon replaced the wooden roof with a masonry dome, redecorating the interior with mosaics. Therefore, it is often referred to as the Neonian Baptistery (Wharton 1987: 358). Understanding the baptism ritual in relationship to its architectural context demonstrates how the design and decoration of a baptismal font and baptistery building are informed by the sacrament's liturgical and theological traditions. Indeed, a reciprocal dialogue exists between the sacred spatial container and the ritual liturgical action that unfolds within. Each informs the other, and in concert work together to dramatically enhance our understanding.

Let us begin with a guided visualization: accompany me as an adult catechumen, sometime during the 5th century, on our way to the Neonian Baptistery at Ravenna. We go to receive the sacrament of baptism followed by participation in our first Eucharistic celebration within the worship space of the adjacent Basilica. We have obtained our sponsors and prepared for the initiation rite through fasting, rigorous catechetical teaching, and exorcisms, and participated in the preparatory rites during the Lenten period before the bishop and the worshipping faith community leading up to Easter. We now find ourselves on the very Eve of Easter, Holy Saturday, deemed to be the most appropriate moment to die and be reborn in Christ (Wharton 1987: 361). Even though infant baptism is becoming popular, we chose to put off baptism until maturity like the scores of other neophytes gathered with us tonight as we join the sacred procession moving in contemplative silence toward the baptistery. It is a separate structure given over to this single purpose only, thereby emphasizing the significance of the rite in which we are about to partake (Wharton 1987: 361).

Like most baptisteries throughout Italy built during the 4th and 5th centuries, it is octagonal in shape (Wharton 1987: 359). This sacred geometry reflects the belief that seven of its sides recall the seven days of creation with the eighth side representative of Christ's resurrection (Thompson 2019: 2). We wait outside and watch as the bishop as primary celebrant, accompanied by his priests and deacons, enter the baptistery. They precede the procession of baptizands in order to first exorcise the font and deliver an invocation and prayer to ensure the sanctity of the waters and the presence of the Holy Trinity.[2] As we approach the eastern door garbed in our white robes, we chant Psalm 32:1 and hear our voices proclaiming the words "Blessed is the one whose transgressions are forgiven, whose sins are covered," as we eagerly anticipate experiencing this phenomenon of faith (Spinks 2006: 95).

Once inside the voluptuously open interior of the baptistery, we notice the motif of the number eight replicated in the eight Roman columns that support the arcade and the eight windows within the dome high above. At this point, we are facing west, the direction of the setting sun, the direction associated with darkness and the devil (Thompson 2019: 3). Encouraging us to renounce the power of sin, we are confronted with relief sculptures within the stucco panels flanking the windows that depict scenes from the Old and New Testaments representing the promise of the triumph of Christian faith (Wharton 1987: 362). We can just make out an image of Christ giving the law to his disciple Peter in the presence of Paul, and Christ trampling the Devil. Flanking these images are Jonah in the whale and Daniel in the lion's den, metaphoric references to God's power over evil, and serve as visual reminders of His eternal promise granted to us as followers of Christ through our baptismal covenant (Thompson 2019: 3).

Upon renouncing the Devil, we turn 180 degrees toward the east altar niche, and find ourselves perfectly oriented to view Christ in the image of his baptism exquisitely executed in the finest mosaics within the central medallion at the apex of the dome above us (Fig. 1.1). Jesus is depicted naked, standing up to his waist in the waters of the river Jordan with the Holy Spirit descending upon him from the heavens above, transmogrified into the familiar image of a dove. He is flanked on the left by John the Baptist who is seen pouring water from a dish over the head of Jesus, and on the right by the personified river Jordan, the gaze of both fixated on Jesus, the central character of this narrative scene. Christ looks straight ahead, gazing down upon us, as though He were personally welcoming each one of us into his heavenly kingdom, made more potent by the circular mosaic cornice with egg-and-dart molding, which creates the illusion that we are looking through a hole in the dome roof directly into heaven above (Deliyannis 2014: 99). We can see the candlelight reflected and amplified in the brilliant gold

FIGURE 1.1 Ravenna, Neonian Baptistry interior, view of dome seen by observer oriented to southeast
Photo: Robin Jensen

mosaics within the molding framing Christ's baptism, making it appear as though they are the very source of radiant divine light.

Just below the illusory aperture, within a contrasting background of deep blue mosaics festooned with mosaics depicting garlands of white and gold cloth, we observe another indication of the interaction between us and the heavenly realm above. Led by Peter and Paul, the twelve apostles, dressed in ornately decorated robes carrying crowns, gaze down upon us in solidarity as though also welcoming us into their heavenly kingdom (Thompson 2019: 7). One might suspect that the crowns are meant for us, but we soon realize that they are likely meant either for Jesus or perhaps to honor the bishop responsible for decorating the baptistery (Weitzmann 1979: 660 cf. Weinryb 2002: 49). In the four lunettes that line the lower level of decoration are four biblical passages with water as a motif to emphasize the transformational powers of water during the baptismal ritual (Thompson 2019: 7).

The font is circular in form, which traces the dome directly above. As Jesus is baptized, so are we, and through this ritual, our connection to him as new followers is affirmed. One at a time, we disrobe before descending into the font, its depth, and circular shape reminiscent of a tomb.[3] We are fully immersed in the water three times; the first time in the name of the Father, then the Son, and finally the Holy Spirit. Each time, we symbolically descend with Christ into a watery grave only to rise up again in new life with Him (von Simson 1987: 114). We emerge, don the white robes again, and continue our journey to the northwest niche where we await our turn to have our feet washed by the bishop. Engaging in this ritual, the bishop models the sacramental humility that Christ demonstrated by washing the feet of his apostles before the Last Supper (Wharton 1987: 365). Our baptismal service is then concluded with the bishop anointing us with holy oil to seal our faith and empower us with the Holy Spirit to live in faithful dedication to our new life in Christ (Wharton 1987: 364). Finally, in joy and celebration, we proceed from the Baptistery to the Basilica, where we enter triumphantly, "resplendent in white in the illuminated night" (Wharton 1987: 365), and are welcomed by the community of believers to participate in our first Eucharistic celebration together.

Having "experienced" the ancient precedent of the Orthodox Baptistery at Ravenna, we turn to some recent examples that are inspired by the traditional design and yet seek to expand the use of water and its references as a powerful element within contemporary Catholic church and chapel architecture.

Contemporary Examples that Explore the Power of Water Beyond Baptism

The Loretto Christian Life Centre Chapel, Niagara Falls, Canada

The font at the renovated chapel of the Loretto Christian Life Centre in Niagara Falls, Canada must be analyzed not as a stand-alone liturgical element, but rather as part of a Gestalt whole that defines the chapel's transformation from a patriarchal, insular space buried deep within the convent, to a feminine, inviting, contemplative environment for worship and prayer that is fully integrated with the convent and retreat center's geographical context, history, and the mission it serves.

Built in 1870, the center is situated in close proximity to the crest of the Horseshoe Falls, arguably the greatest natural icon of "living water" in North America. The original chapel's design and location ignored this unique relationship, turning its back to the falls with no

FIGURE 1.2 Loretto Christian Life Centre chapel's font by sculptor Russell Baron
Photo: David Drake

reference to its greater context as sacred place. The transformation is signaled the moment you arrive on the second floor of the convent. The sight and sound of liturgical sculptor, Russell Baron's font alerts us to that greater context, drawing us inextricably toward the chapel, the "sacred heart" of the center (Fig. 1.2).

As sacred space, the renovated chapel is accessible to all. The sequence of doors that once interrupted a visitor's passage through the halls leading to the chapel is gone. Rather, gently curving, textured glass panels that recall the color, form, and shape of the Horseshoe Falls on a sunny afternoon invite you first to pause at the font. Distinct from a parish church, the sisters do not offer the sacrament of baptism at their chapel. Instead, the font serves another purpose, inviting the visitor to engage their sense of sight, hearing, and touch to reflect upon and integrate new perceptions into the transformative power and meaning of the sacrament.

An inner glass bowl effervescently overflows re-circulated water into an outer shell. Lined in metallic copper leaf, it creates a resonant chamber that serves to magnify the sound of flowing water, a microcosm of the formidable torrent of water that cascades over the cataract just outside the center on its perpetual journey from Lake Erie to Lake Ontario and onward to the Atlantic Ocean through the Gulf of the mighty St. Lawrence River. This outer shell, lovingly hand-crafted of Winterstone (a clay-like sculpting medium), is egg-shaped, resting gently upon a piece of natural limestone reminiscent of the layered stone walls of the gorge that, for millennia, has been carved by the power of the falls. Upon closer examination, one discovers that the terra-cotta-colored surface depicts representational art in the form of relief sculptures. The viewer will recognize prehistoric sea crustaceans, different species of fish that

Beyond Baptism 19

can be found today swimming in the waters of the Great Lakes, sea birds that make their home on the distant coastal shorelines of Canada, and the form of a breaching humpback whale that describes the uppermost portion of the font. Individually and collectively, these images remind us of the emergence of all life from the primordial seas and invite us to seamlessly integrate the mythic Genesis creation story with the 4.5 billion years of evolutionary narrative required for it to unfold in reality. In this way, the font draws upon the ancient symbolism of the womb from which all life emerges in addition to recalling that the sacrament of baptism itself is symbolic of procreation, rebirth, and new life in Christ.

After pausing at the font to reflect upon and integrate a broader understanding of the baptized Christian's covenant with God, a potential shift in spiritual orientation to prepare for the sacred mysteries of the liturgy is prompted by the visitor's required physical shift in orientation, a full 90-degrees to the left. However, the convex curve of another textured glass wall bars entry, once again causing the visitor to pause as they discern the form of a cross, the details of its carved surface obscured by the glass that forces yet another 90-degree shift in orientation back toward the right. A gap between the curve of the textured glass and the concave curve of an adjacent plastered wall invites visitors to continue their pilgrim journey toward Christ by metaphorically accompanying His passion, walking contemplatively past a series of 14 identical wall-mounted sconces, each containing a lit candle representing the traditional 14 Stations of the Cross that depict Christ's Passion and Death on a cross before finding their place within the peaceful embrace of the chapel (Fig. 1.3). Each physical shift and spatial context demarcate an important threshold, a metaphorical line in the sand that

FIGURE 1.3 Loretto Christian Life Centre chapel's transformed worship environment
Photo: David Drake

distinguishes the divine presence of the sacred realm within from that of the external quotidian order. Paradoxically, these same thresholds afford the very point of transition from one realm into the other (Turner 1979: 22).

The details of the cross previously obscured by the textured curving glass are now revealed from within the worship environment. One notices that it is fashioned from an actual cedar tree, the remains of tangled roots providing tentacles of support. It has been further enclosed within the "flesh" of the Winterstone sculpting medium. The elements of earth, air, fire, and water are carved from the cross at the four cardinal directions of the circle that define its particular form. Together with the representation of the seasons within the bands of the circle itself, the carvings embrace and echo the richness of this ancient Celtic symbol to acknowledge and pay homage to the Irish roots of the sisters.

The chapel's form departs from the rectangular box of its predecessor. Instead, what emerges recalls the shape and symbolism of the font - asymmetrical, egg-shaped, and womb-like, a place to be in touch with the divine mother, the creator God, the "word made flesh" (John 1:14 RSV). The stained glass that visually insulated the original chapel environment from its context has been removed to invite in the sun's warming rays and to open up vistas of the surrounding trees and lawns where the Loretto Niagara Community's foundress, Rev. Mother Theresa Dease is laid to rest. Like the font, the liturgical furnishings illuminate the sacred memory of Rev. Mother and her five sister companions who sailed from their motherhouse in Rathfarnham to begin their mission in the New World back in 1847. It also commemorates Archbishop Lynch who thought there should be a place of prayer adjacent to such a wonder of nature and accordingly, allocated this site overlooking the Falls to Mother Teresa Dease for a convent and school in 1861.

But the chapel design also celebrates a deeper history, one that predates the story of the sisters' arrival, and even our own human story. It celebrates the story of prehistoric creatures that left their imprint in the limestone used to build this edifice, of the plunging water of the nearby cataract, and of the primeval forest that once lined its shores. The chapel design provides a different catechetical environment, one that is designed to illuminate the connection between the story of Christian salvation and the story of the earth's biology/geology/ecology, between the good of religion and the good of all God's creation.

Mary Mother of God Roman Catholic Church, Oakville, Ontario, Canada

The design and location of the baptismal font for the Mary Mother of God Roman Catholic Church in Oakville forms an integral component of the worshiper's physical and metaphorical pilgrim journey toward Christ. They are informed by the guidelines for the design of worship environments approved and promulgated by the National Liturgy Offices in Canada and the US. Outside the entrance doors to the church, an exterior piazza inscribed with concentric circular paving stones defines a generous outdoor gathering space that serves to demarcate the initial transition from the quotidian world to the sacred realm of the worship environment within. It is here, within the sacred circular geometry, that congregants receive their palm branches for the Palm Sunday liturgy and where the Paschal candle is lit to begin the Saturday night Vigil service of the Easter Triduum Liturgy, the most significant event in the Christian liturgical calendar.

Oversized central doors demarcate the ceremonial entrance from the outdoor gathering space, an important threshold designed to represent Christ as the gateway to salvation. Beyond these doors, the narthex or lobby space of the church is where the hospitality ministers and

FIGURE 1.4 Mary Mother of God Church view of baptismal font from the narthex
Photo: David Drake

the presiding priest welcome those who have arrived to participate in the sacred mysteries of the liturgy. It is also the liturgical space where the infant, parents, and godparents gather to initiate the sacrament of baptism. From here, another pair of oversized ceremonial doors, directly opposite the exterior doors, upon opening, reveal the baptistery and its font located on the axis with the altar (Fig. 1.4). Its prominent location reminds those already baptized to recall their own initiation into the community of faith every time they enter the worship space for the Eucharistic liturgy. They pause momentarily to dip their fingers into the Holy Waters of Baptism to anoint themselves before continuing to their seats and as per the guidelines, there is ample space surrounding the font to emphasize its significance as a primary liturgical center and to accommodate those participating in the sacrament of baptism (Boreskie and Schaefer et al. 1999: 24). To draw further attention to the font as a liturgical center, a round skylight, in combination with a conical aperture in the ceiling, appears to flood the font with divine, heavenly light.

Like many of its ancient antecedents, the egg-shaped plan of the font is inspired by traditional designs throughout history that emphasize the symbol of both womb and tomb (Fig. 1.5). The end of the font nearest the entry doors from the narthex is dominated by a rough-hewn, egg-shaped granite rock, quarried from the nearby geological formation known as the Canadian Shield. The curvilinear sweep of a gently ascending limestone curb terminates beside the granite to support the Paschal candle and provide a permanent location after its lighting at the Easter Vigil. In compliance with the guideline's requirement to facilitate infant baptisms (Boreskie & Schaefer et al. 1999: 26), a shallow circular bowl is carved into

FIGURE 1.5 Mary Mother of God Church view of baptistery
Photo: David Drake

the granite's flattened top, from which re-circulating bubbling water flows through four channels carved at the cardinal points into the adult immersion pool below. This detail recalls the river flowing out of Eden as a source of life-giving water for the garden that splits to become the Pishon, the Gihon, the Tigris, and the Euphrates spreading forth to nourish the four corners of the earth (Genesis 2: 10-14 RSV).

In compliance with the guideline's requirement to facilitate adult baptism (Boreskie & Schaefer et al. 1999: 26), the immersion portion of the pool accommodates three steps below the surface of the water, leading down toward the overflowing granite rock. The pool is lined with mosaic tiles, a simple contemporary expression of the decorative mosaic tiles used in ancient baptisteries such as the one in Ravenna. The steps reference the three days from the time of Jesus's Good Friday death on the cross to his Easter Sunday resurrection. As the adult catechumen steps down into the font, she symbolically dies to sin, and through immersion in the water, is re-born to new life in Christ. As the baptized Christian emerges from the font, she must turn around to face the altar, focused and ready to complete her initiation through the sacraments of Confirmation and the Eucharist. "… [the font's] power is the power of the triumphant cross; and baptism sets the Christian on the path to the life that will never end, the "eighth day" of eternity where Christ's reign of peace and justice is celebrated" (NCCB 2000: 26).

This understanding is made visible as we turn from the font toward the altar, through the glazed wall behind to the verdant garden terminating at its enclosing wall beyond, from which

FIGURE 1.6 Mary Mother of God Church view of altar with waterfall fountain above in garden wall beyond
Photo: David Drake

abundant water pours (Fig. 1.6). This design references the Christian Eschatological belief in the City of God, the New Jerusalem, with "…the river of the water of life, bright as crystal, flowing from the throne of God and of the Lamb, through the middle of the street of the city; also, on either side of the river, the tree of life with its twelve kinds of fruit, yielding its fruit each month; and the leaves of the trees were for the healing of the nations" (Revelation 22:1-2 RSV). Thus, the sacred Christian scriptures begin and end with the powerful symbol of water, reminding us of its essential life-giving role, both physically and spiritually.

The baptistery area is framed on either side by a reconciliation room or confessional, a separate space exclusively given over to the Sacrament of Reconciliation. Despite the transformative grace acquired through the Sacrament of baptism, it was understood that because of our human nature, the baptized remain vulnerable to sin and the possibility of estrangement from Christ. The Sacrament of Reconciliation recognizes and addresses this need for a continual process of conversion throughout the Christian's mortal life by providing an ongoing opportunity for the baptized to confess their sins, be repentant, and receive absolution by the priest as the way to become reconciled to self, Christ, and their faith community. This understanding is directly informed by the passage in scripture that describes the moment when the risen Christ appears to his disciples on the evening of Easter Sunday and says to them:

> "Peace be with you. As the Father has sent me, even so I send you." And when he had said this, he breathed on them, and said, "Receive the Holy Spirit. If you forgive the sins of any, they are forgiven; if you retain the sins of any, they are retained."
>
> *(John 20:21-23 RSV)*

This location of the reconciliation rooms in close proximity to the baptismal font, at the entrance to the worship space, reinforces the understanding of both initiation into the Christian community of faith and the ongoing mechanism for restoring the grace received through the Sacrament of baptism.

St. Gabriel's Passionist Parish, North York, Ontario, Canada

In 1998, the Passionist Community of Canada decided to provide a new legacy for St. Gabriel of the Sorrowful Virgin, a Roman Catholic parish in North York which they had served for over 53 years. The design mandate was to replace an existing 500-seat deteriorating facility that had become prohibitively expensive to operate and maintain, with a new 750-seat "green" church facility that would not only reduce energy costs but also establish a link between the sacredness of the gathered community of faith and the sacredness of the earth. As such, the new church constitutes a dramatic departure in the design of sacred space. It has been conceived to embody the eco-theology of the Passionist Father Thomas Berry and his belief that we must work toward establishing a mutually-enhancing, human-earth relationship (Berry 1990: xiii). Father Berry asserted that our best hope for living in a more sustainable and ecological age would lie in our ability to articulate a new cosmology based not upon an anthropocentric view of the human as primary but instead upon a biocentric understanding of the earth as primary and the needs of the human as derivative (Berry 1990: 21). The challenge then was to re-examine the design of traditional church architecture through the lens of Berry's teachings. Every design decision had to be carefully considered in order to incorporate the contributions of eco-theology in a tangible, realistic, and meaningful way while still providing an acceptably familiar and faithful worship setting for the traditional sacramental liturgies to unfold.

In contrast to most churches that are inwardly focused and employ stained glass to create an other-worldly liturgical environment, the entire south façade of the worship space at St. Gabriel's is glazed with clear glass (Fig. 1.7). This glazed wall was designed in order to passively harness the winter sun's energy. It extends the sacred space of the worship area into the sacred space of the garden beyond, emphasizing that when we gather to worship, we do so within the greater context of creation the primary revelatory experience of the Divine (Berry 1990: 120). The remaining three walls of exposed concrete serve as a constantly changing canvas for the dynamic play of natural light admitted and filtered through colored-glass panels created by artist, David Pearl, which have been integrated into a continuous perimeter skylight. Dichroic-coated reflectors, mounted perpendicularly on the wall just below the skylight, further fracture and animate sunlight that enters the worship space. In effect, the cosmos shape the liturgical environment and participates in the ritual action of the liturgy. Similarly, time also takes on a cosmic dimension as the sun traverses the sky above. Seasonal influences on the sun's intensity and inclination together with daily weather conditions ensure that no two Masses will be set in an identical liturgical environment.

The pews, re-claimed and re-furbished from the original church, are arranged antiphonally in the new 750-seat worship space. The facing rows embrace a sacred north-south axis that begins in the south garden and terminates at the north wall of the nave with the tabernacle. The original church's re-furbished and transformed marble ambo and altar are situated along this sacred axis. Likewise, the marble baptismal font has been re-designed to flow with "living water." In contrast to the traditional placement of the font at the entrance to the nave (as in the Mary Mother of God church), the font is located adjacent to the south wall of glass (Fig. 1.8).

Beyond Baptism 25

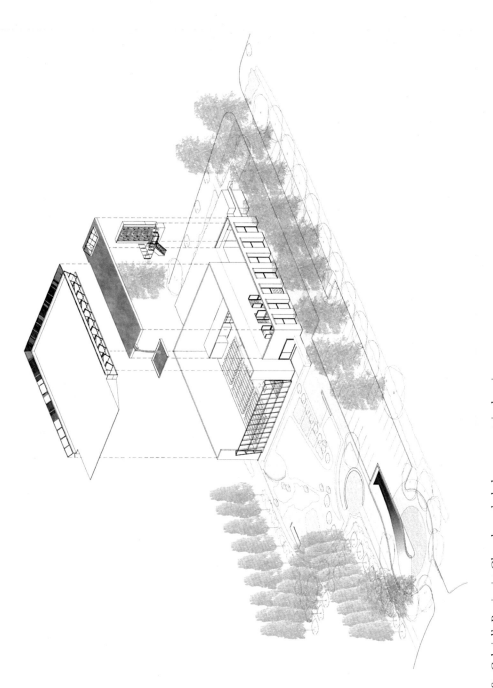

FIGURE 1.7 St. Gabriel's Passionist Church exploded axonometric drawing
Photo: Author

FIGURE 1.8 St. Gabriel's Passionist Church baptismal font
Photo: Author

The garden as a backdrop beyond the glass wall emphasizes that when we are baptized into the faith community, our baptism also consecrates us for the sacred earth community.

Inside, the narthex is terminated at the north end by a sky-lit "living green wall" (Fig. 1.9). Water running over the roots of the living wall's tropical plants conditions and purifies the air of the narthex and worship space. The enzymes in those roots process the volatile organic compounds and other atmospheric pollutants while the water provides natural humidification during winter and de-humidification in summer. Parishioners coming up from the underground garage are drawn into the light by the "living wall" and are reminded of their baptismal covenant by the sound of its purifying waters. They are also reminded of how the rainforests serve a crucial role in earth's climate.

At the opposite end of the narthex is a framed view of an outdoor water feature that harvests rainwater from the roof to support plant life within a constructed wetland below, a macrocosmic version of and reference to the font (Fig. 1.10). Potable water usage throughout the church facility and grounds is significantly reduced by a highly efficient drip irrigation system for the garden, the waterless urinals, dual low-flush toilets, and low-flow fittings on all sinks. This helps to complete the narrative that underscores the irony of holding the precious natural resource of water as a primary religious symbol while willfully contributing to its ongoing degradation. Incorporating these and other sustainable design strategies such as passive solar heating and cooling, the use of local materials, the dramatic use of natural light in combination with colored glass skylights, and mechanical systems modeled after natural earth systems, contribute to the understanding of early scriptural teachings that emphasized

Beyond Baptism 27

FIGURE 1.9 St. Gabriel's Passionist Church "Living Wall"
Photo: Author

FIGURE 1.10 St. Gabriel's Passionist Church roof scupper and constructed wetland
Photo: Author

the sacredness of all creation and not just the sacredness of humankind. The new building as a sacred space presents a Gestalt whole, and like the medieval cathedrals of Europe, becomes itself a form of Catechesis, engaging the senses and inviting transformation.

In summary, each of these three contemporary examples builds upon the 2,000-year-old tradition of liturgical norms and theology associated with the Christian initiation rite of baptism while embracing a more comprehensive narrative that grounds them in the 21st century to address the relevant issues of our time.

Notes

1. "catechesis" is used here to describe religious instruction given to both a catechumen in preparation for baptism and to the baptized as part of their ongoing faith development.
2. Wharton cites the ancient writings of Bishop Ambrose, Sacraments: 4.1.1-2 as her source.
3. The current font is octagonal and dates from medieval times. The ancient one several meters below serves as its foundation. According to Wharton (1987: 363), the original font was circular in plan but nothing more can be said of it. In many parts of the early-Christian world, baptizands were naked for immersion and anointing. For a more fulsome discussion with citations, see Wharton (1987: 362–363).

References

Berry, Thomas. *The Dream of the Earth*. San Francisco: Sierra Club Books, 1990

Boreskie, Michael & Schaefer, Mary M. et al. *Our Place of Worship*. Ottawa: Publication Services, Canadian Conference of Catholic Bishops, 1999

Deliyannis, Deborah Mauskopf. "Ravenna and the Western Emperors, AD 400-489." *Ravenna in Late Antiquity*. Cambridge: Cambridge University Press, 2014

Eliade, Micea. *The Sacred and The Profane, The Nature of Religion*. New York: Harcourt, 1987

Mauck, Marchita. *Shaping a House for the Church*. Chicago: Archdiocese of Chicago, Liturgy Training Publications, 1990

Spinks, Bryan D. *Early and Medieval Rituals and Theologies of Baptism: From the New Testament to the Council of Trent*. Aldershot, England: Ashgate, 2006

Spivey, Robert A. & Smith, D. Moody. *Anatomy of the New Testament, A Guide to Its Structure and Meaning, Fourth Edition*. New York: Macmillan, 1989

The Holy Bible. *Revised Standard Version Containing the Old and New Testaments with the Apocrypha/Deuterocanonical Books*, Expanded Edition. London: Collins, 1973

The National Conference of Catholic Bishops (NCCB). *Built of Living Stones: Art, Architecture, and Worship*. Washington D.C.: United States Catholic Conference, Inc., 2000

Thompson, Mary. "Building Baptism: Theology and Ritual in the Structure and Interior Decoration of the Neonian Baptistery of Ravenna." *Relics, Remnants, and Religion: An Undergraduate Journal in Religious Studies*: 4, no.1 (2019), Article 4

Turner, Harold W. *From Temple to Meeting House, The Phenomenology and Theology of Places of Worship*. The Hague: Mouton, 1979

von Simson, Otto Georg. *Sacred Fortress: Byzantine Art and Statecraft in Ravenna*. Princeton, N.J.: Princeton University Press, 1987

Wagenfuhr, Rev. Dr. G.P. "History and Sources of Baptism." *Baptism and Theology Resources - ECO Theology Series*, Standing Theology Committee, (January 2020): 3–10

Weinryb, Ittai. "A tale of Two Baptisteries: Royal and Ecclesiastical Patronage in Ravenna." *Asaph*, no. 7 (2002): 41–58

Weitzmann, Kurt, ed., *Age of Spirituality: Late Antique and Early Christian Art, Third to Seventh Century*. New York: Metropolitan Museum of Art, 1979

Wharton, Annabell Jane. "Ritual and Reconstructed Meaning: The Neonian Baptistry in Ravenna." *The Art Bulletin*: 69, no. 3 (September 1987): 358–375

2
WATER AND RITUAL *WUDU* (ABLUTIONS) IN CANADIAN MOSQUES

Tammy Gaber

Gardens through which running waters flow beneath
(The Qur'an)

This phrase describing water within the environment of Paradise is repeated in the Qur'an thirty times.[1] Throughout the holy text, there are descriptions of the four-fold gardens divided by intersecting rivers (Qur'an 55: 49-77). *Janna* is the Arabic word for garden, and Paradise is described as the plural, *Jannat* (many gardens). For a religion born in the desert, the importance of water is emphasized in the imagined Paradise resplendent with vegetation, which served as both an ideal and a contrast to the harsh existing conditions. Additionally, water is an activated component of worship in the form of required ritual washing prior to prayer. The tenants of ablutions, or *wudu* as is it called in Arabic, are laid out clearly in the Qur'an with thrice repeated motions of washing parts of the body prior to prayer (Qur'an 4:43, 5:6). During this process the individual is transitioning into a state of contemplation and setting an intention of cleansing both the body and the mind. In historical mosques, *wudu* was conducted in specially designed fountains located in exterior or semi-exterior spaces. These ranged from simple spouts along the exterior walls of the mosque to elaborately designed radial fountains with stools in courtyards. In many of these historical examples, the *wudu* area was surrounded with embellishments in the form of epigraphy, decoration, or planting of vegetation that emphasized the transitory nature of *wudu* which connects to prayer and a vision of Paradise.

In contemporary mosques, especially those located in colder climates, *wudu* facilities have become a part of washroom facilities for practical reasons. Additionally, this move to washrooms has allowed for more privacy as these spaces are separated by gender. In Canadian mosques, which have a history of almost a century, *wudu* areas in washroom facilities most often included specifically designed furniture or built-in elements (Gaber 2022).

Three examples to be examined include the first extant mosque in Canada, Al Rashid, constructed in 1938 in Edmonton; the new Al Rashid mosque constructed to replace it in 1982; and the Noor Cultural Centre, which has a Muslim prayer space (2008). The latter was converted from the former Japanese Canadian Culture Centre in Toronto that was originally constructed 40 years prior. In all three of these sacred spaces, the design of the *wudu* area

DOI: 10.4324/9781003358824-4

encapsulates the contextual conditions of the time and is foregrounded in the architecture prior to entering the worship space. Examination of the *wudu* areas is conducted through analysis of the spaces and the social history to underscore the contemporary and Canadian design approaches of ritual washing before Muslim prayers. Not embellished in the same manner as historical mosques, the dedication of *wudu* spaces in Canadian mosques do demonstrate the increased and consistent effort to design purpose-built *wudu* areas that are comfortable, adapted to the cold weather, and appropriately adjacent to prayer spaces.

Wudu and Designs in Historical Mosques

"O those who have believed! When you stand up for the formal prayer, then wash your faces and your hands up to the elbows and wipe your heads and feet up to the ankles." (Qur'an 5:6)

Given the original context of the faith in the harsh, hot and arid, climate, the use of precious water is an added signifier to the importance of physical cleansing and contemplative purification to frame intentions before each of the five daily prayers. Though the established norm is that Muslims perform *wudu* with water prior to each prayer, there is a provision in the Qur'an that if water is not available, an abbreviated version of *wudu* may be conducted with sand in a ritual called *tayammum*, "and you find no water, then aim at getting wholesome, dry earth and wipe your faces and hands with it" (Qur'an 4:43, 5:6). The presumption was that sand was easily available and abundant in the surrounding desert context.

The earliest mosques, such as the one the Prophet had constructed in Medina (622 CE) did not originally have an architecturally designed area for ritual washing (Creswell 1979: 13–15). Early examples of constructed areas for *wudu* include fountains in the 8th century Great Mosque in Aleppo, Syria, and the Great Mosque of Cordoba, Spain (Creswell 1979: 146–147). In the centuries that followed, mosques throughout the Islamic world included designed areas for the ritual *wudu* ranging from interior to exterior located fountains.

The Umayyad Great Mosque in Aleppo constructed in 715 CE (burned in 962 and rebuilt in 1090 CE) is one of the earliest mosques that included a large fountain for *wudu* (Creswell 1979: 482–483). Located in the center of the courtyard, the *wudu* fountain was surrounded by vegetation-themed mosaics on the walls of the exterior of the mosque "like a waterhole at an oasis." (Hillenbrand 1994: 22–25). The connections to Paradise Garden at Aleppo were further reinforced with colorful paving stones arranged in a pattern similar to four-part gardens referenced in the Qur'an (55: 49-77). The Great Mosque of Cordoba, constructed in 785 CE and enlarged several times in the following centuries included a prominent courtyard (Creswell 1979: 146–147). By 987 CE the courtyard comprised a third of the enclosed mosque area, and was planted with a grid of fruit-bearing citrus trees, and included three *wudu* fountains (Creswell 1979: 146–147). This garden has been planted continuously since the beginning of the 9th century until the present day (Ruggles 2008: 90). The three *wudu* fountains were ingeniously fed with rainwater from the prayer hall roof. The water was collected in an underground tank and then pumped up with an animal-powered wheel that both irrigated the fruit trees and fed the *wudu* fountains (Ruggles 2008: 90–91) (Fig. 2.1). The transitional space of the courtyard, surrounded by a living Paradisiacal Garden, phenomenologically emphasized the ritual of *wudu* and served to prepare the worshipper for the contemplative state of prayer within the mosque.

Dedicated *wudu* fountains in the center of large courtyards preceding prayer halls were found in mosques throughout the Islamic world, including the rectilinear fountains found in 11th–14th century mosques in Isfahan, Iran, and in 13th–15th century mosques in Fez,

FIGURE 2.1 Courtyard at the Great Mosque in Cordoba, Spain, with three wudu fountains surrounded by a grid of fruit-bearing citrus trees
Photo: Author

Morocco (Hillenbrand 1994: 102–104; Bloom 2020: 181–263). Circular *wudu* fountains were commonly found in 17th-century mosques in Lahore, Pakistan, and Delhi, India (Korbendau 1997: 38–41). Throughout Mamluk Egypt, the 14th–16th *madrasas* (religious schools) and mosques included *wudu* fountains in the center of the courtyards often with permanent stone stools framed within an octagonal and domed structure with important scripture, such as at Sultan Hassan madrasa and mosque in Cairo (Gaber 2015) (Fig. 2.2).

The architectonic centralized location of the *wudu* fountain in the sacred spaces coupled with the textual references emphasized the act of intentional cleansing and purification in the transitional space of ablutions prior to prayer. Similarly, Ottoman mosques throughout the

FIGURE 2.2 Wudu fountain in the central courtyard of the Sultan Hassan mosque and madrasa in Cairo, Egypt
Photo: Author

empire often included *wudu* fountains in the center of exterior courtyards, allowing for physical and metaphysical transitions to enter the sacred space (Necipoğlu 2007). Some exceptions such as the 14th century Ulu Cami in Bursa, Turkey have the *wudu* fountain in the center of the interior prayer hall. The expansive Süleymaniyea complex mosque in Turkey, from 1548–1559 CE, includes water taps placed on the exterior west-façade of the mosque for *wudu*, in addition to the central fountain in the courtyard (Necipoğlu 2007: 207–210; Kuban 2010: 133–139). Dedicated wooden clogs were kept at the entrance of most of the historical mosques to accommodate the movement from the *wudu* areas to the prayer hall. Many extant mosques still continue this practice for worshippers to keep their feet clean when moving between the ablutions area to the prayer area, as outdoor shoes are left at the entrance of the mosque.

Historically, the amount of surface elaboration and symbolism included in *wudu* areas was limited, as it was a transitional zone between the outside world and the inner sanctum of the prayer space. Examples such as the epigraphy located on the dome of the *wudu* pavilion at Sultan Hassan madrasa and mosque in Cairo, Egypt, the planted courtyard at the Cordoba Mosque in Spain or the surrounding gilded mosaics at the Great Mosque of Aleppo, Syria are all exceptional. When surface elaboration was included in *wudu* spaces historically the allusions were always to some aspect of Paradise: in word, landscape, or art.

Wudu in Contemporary Diaspora Mosques

The number of diaspora Muslims globally has increased in the past two centuries with Muslim communities forming throughout the world. Diaspora Muslim communities have formed mosques and prayer spaces in borrowed and converted spaces and in purpose-built constructions. The earliest mosques in the "West" include the Shah Jahan Mosque in Woking, United Kingdom constructed in 1889 (Saleem 2018: 21), and the Mosque and Muslim Institute in Paris constructed by the French government in 1922–1926 to honor North African citizens who fought alongside France in the world wars (Holod & Khan 1997: 228). The earliest mosques in the United States were temporary structures (since destroyed) constructed by Muslim Africans forcibly enslaved in the 1700s (Haddad & Smith 2014: 15). Beyond the "West," the first permanent residence of Muslims in Australia dates back to the mid-1800s with the influx of camels brought in initially by Colonial British expeditions who also brought in the camel drivers, "cameleers" from Afghanistan, North India (now Pakistan) and Baluchistan (Jones & Kenny 2017: 9). As a result, many mosques were constructed throughout Australia.

The creation of mosques by the Muslim diaspora globally since the 18th century have served not only as places of prayer but also have become important hubs of community and centralized gathering beyond sacred rituals. Thus, these mosques architecturally included programming beyond the prayer hall and came to include multi-purpose spaces for social and religious gatherings, educational spaces, sometimes kitchen areas, and expanded washroom facilities, which interiorized *wudu* areas (Gaber 2022). Although not architecturally celebrated with emphatic and decorative design, the inclusion of *wudu* areas in interior washroom facilities has two-fold benefits: it allows for private and discreet gendered areas where women are more comfortable performing *wudu*, and it accommodated practically the colder climates often found in diaspora communities.

The examples of contemporary mosques examined in Canada generally demonstrated negligible use of surface elaboration or symbolism. This is in part due to the location of *wudu* spaces within washroom spaces which are generally not decorated. Additionally, the *wudu* spaces in Canadian mosques, like the majority of the mosque space (except the prayer hall orientation niche- *mihrab* areas), were often restrained and minimal in surface elaboration following general design aesthetics influenced by the prevalent Modernist buildings in cities, such as Toronto, with minimal embellishments (McClelland & Stewart 2007). The design of *wudu* areas in mosques across Canada did tend to include similar built-in stool areas with spouts and water run-off channel. Measured drawings and guidelines for *wudu* furnishings are not included in building code standards but are illustrated in resources such as *Building Type Basics for Places of Worship* (Roberts and Daly 2004: 176–177).

Wudu at Al Rashid Mosque, Edmonton, Alberta, Canada

The 1871 census in Canada counted 13 Muslims, which grew to 300 Muslims in 1911 (Husaini et al. 1999). The first Muslims in Canada created spaces for worship by gathering in each other's homes and in borrowed spaces until funds were collected to construct the first purpose mosque in the country, Al Rashid Mosque in 1938 (Awid 2010) (Fig. 2.3). In addition to accommodating the community and a range of social activities, the location of the *wudu* area within the heated interiors responded to the very cold temperatures in Edmonton, which can reach −30°C and even −40°C (−22/−40°F) in the winter with significant snowfall.

The entrance foyer of the historical Al Rashid Mosque which led to the main entrance to the prayer hall opened onto two small side rooms. To the left was the staircase leading to the multi-purpose basement space used for social gatherings; to the right was the small room that had a singular *wudu* area – a traditional Canadian ceramic jug and basin on a

FIGURE 2.3 Exterior of historic Al Rashid mosque, Edmonton, Alberta
Photo: Author

FIGURE 2.4 Wudu area at historic Al Rashid mosque, Edmonton, Alberta
Photo: Author

wooden table for washing, that was located in the hexagonal recess beneath one of the minarets (Gaber 2022) (Fig. 2.4).

Running water was not available at the time and the accommodation for Islamic ritual washing in this fashion demonstrated an adaptation of local customs and methods. It is difficult to assume the practicality of the *wudu* facilities for use by the whole congregation. It is possible that these facilities were not used by all members before every prayer and that many worshippers came to the mosque having done their *wudu* at home. The prayer space was used by both genders, without any type of separation for many decades, with women standing behind men (Fig. 2.5). The prayer hall was furnished with large donated carpets.

The renovations and modifications to the mosque over the decades included the addition of: running water, a modern heating system, and washroom facilities for each gender, which accommodated the needs of the whole congregation for *wudu*. However, the shift of ritual *wudu* from a small but celebrated space adjacent to worship hall to basement washroom facilities changed the atmosphere, which was meant to inspire the preparation for prayer and contemplation.

FIGURE 2.5 Prayer hall at historic Al Rashid mosque, Edmonton, Alberta
Photo: Author

FIGURE 2.6 Exterior of New Al Rashid mosque, Edmonton, Alberta
Photo: Author

The historic Al Rashid Mosque could not accommodate the growth of the community and a new Al Rashid Mosque, also called the Canadian Islamic Centre, was constructed in 1982 (Gaber 2022). The New Al Rashid Mosque is a large structure with expansive programmatic spaces including two prayer halls (one for each gender), offices, education spaces, kitchen, social areas, funeral washing facilities, and multipurpose gymnasium (Fig. 2.6). The historic Al Rashid mosque was later moved from downtown Edmonton to Fort Edmonton Historic Park in 1992 and has become a part of the local history. In this museum version of the original spatial arrangement and furnishings were restored (Waugh 2018).

In the historic Al Rashid mosque there was a singular prayer space and one small *wudu* room. Both were not separated by gender. However, in the new Al Rashid mosque, the architect Atta Hai was directly inspired by the Ottawa Muslim Association Mosque in Ottawa, which has a balcony space for women. The all-male board of the new Al Rashid mosque at the time also deemed that a separate and smaller prayer space should be allocated to women (Gaber 2022). The washroom facilities are segregated by gender and each has a section for *wudu* arranged linearly: five built-in pedestals facing water spouts in the wall with a channel for run-off below. The *wudu* areas are finished entirely with ceramic tiles, except the wooden seat on each pedestal (Fig. 2.7). The washrooms with *wudu* areas for men are located at the main entrance on the ground floor, where shoes and boots are left, adjacent to the main prayer area. The main entrance foyer leads, by way of an elevator or staircase, to the first floor where the women's washroom and *wudu* areas are located. It is adjacent to a dedicated coat and boot area and leads to the women's prayer balcony which overlooks the main prayer hall. Specific towels and plastic slippers are kept at the mosque for walking between the washroom and the prayer space so that the feet are not soiled again, and cold on the floor.

FIGURE 2.7 Wudu area at new Al Rashid mosque, Edmonton, Alberta
Photo: Author

The adjacency of the *wudu* areas allows for immediate access to the respective prayer halls and the in-between space functions much like the courtyards in historical mosques as a transition area, preparing each individual for the heightened spiritual atmosphere of worship and contemplation.

In all ninety mosques in Canada examined by the author, *wudu* areas were included in the interior as part of the washroom facilities (Gaber 2022). The majority of mosques, whether built-a-new or in converted spaces included *wudu* in the washroom areas for each gender with built-in stools, water spouts, and a water run-off channel. Very few mosques in converted spaces simply adapted washroom sinks for *wudu*. The *wudu* facilities, such as at the new Al Rashid mosque and at the Noor Cultural Centre included built-in stools, spouts, and channels. Their finished materials are those often found in washrooms (e.g. ceramic tiling). The experience of water for this important ritual has become focused on physical cleansing in an efficient, effective manner in comfortable temperature-controlled atmospheres.

Wudu at the Noor Cultural Centre, North York, Ontario, Canada

The Noor Cultural Centre is located in the former 1963 Japanese Canadian Cultural Centre (JCCC) in North York, Ontario outside of metropolitan Toronto. The JCCC was an important community hub for a Japanese minority community that had historically been marginalized in Canada (McClellan & Stewart 2007: 248). Community member and award-winning architect Raymond Moriyama of Moriyama Teshima Architects designed the space pro-bono and was one of the 75 guarantors of the mortgage on the property (Moriyama 2013). In 2001 when the community had outgrown the space and sold it, a local Muslim, Hassanali Lakhani purchased the building to realize his dream of creating an open and inclusive community center for Muslims and non-Muslims (Gaber 2022). For his vision of the Noor Cultural Centre, he invited the original architect Raymond Moriyama to repurpose the building nearly 40 years after its original construction (Moriyama 2013). The design modifications were minimal and respectful of the aesthetic and the original frugal conception of the building and were completed in 2008. According to Moriyama, Lakhani did not want the project to be called a "conversion" but an alteration to reuse the space and wanted to maintain the innovative minimalist approach of the original building. For example, keeping the original rain chain drains that Moriyama designed in order to drain water from the roof in the most economical manner. As well as

FIGURE 2.8 Exterior of Noor Cultural Centre, North York, Ontario
Photo: Author

leaving Moriyama's original design and use of concrete blocks so specifically that only 11 blocks needed to be cut (Moriyama 2013). This reduced the costs significantly with very little waste. The center is named after the Arabic word *Noor*, meaning "light." The word carries literal and religious meanings with respect to understanding and enlightenment (Qur'an 24:35).

The main, first floor remained a multipurpose space allowing for a variety of community activities. The windows were refitted with wooden latticework that spells out *Noor* and *Allah* in Arabic Kufic script while maintaining the lines of the building and detailing surrounding it. The lanterns at the entryway were similarly fitted with laser-cut panels with the Arabic word *Noor* (Fig. 2.8). The structural walls of the ground space were replaced with columns to allow for an open prayer space and social hall with an adjacent kitchen area. The former martial arts spaces were converted to serve as dedicated *wudu* facilities. The thick wall construction of the building and centralized heating accommodate the winter climates temperatures which, although not as dramatic as in Edmonton, can reach −20°C (−4°F).

The *wudu* areas include three built-in seats and water spouts with a channel for water runoff; all finished with small white square ceramic tiles. These areas are further embellished with a skylight above and a small vestibule for seating, belongings, and towels (Fig. 2.9). The modern minimalistic aesthetic of the building does not include any other decorations or symbols in the *wudu* area. The equality in the allocation of *wudu* spaces for each gender was intentional and paralleled the equal amount of space dedicated in the coat room and the prayer hall. The coat room is housed in the bespoke wooden furnishing created to house footwear, coats, and belongings and is adjacent to the washrooms and the prayer area. In the prayer hall, women pray on the right side and men on the left, separated by a space in the middle, between the prayer rugs allowing for equal access for both genders (Fig. 2.10). Worshippers face the *Noor* embellished window lattice with landscaping behind it. The social space behind the prayer hall is separated by glass doors which can be propped open for expanded prayer

38 Tammy Gaber

FIGURE 2.9 Wudu area at Noor Cultural Centre, North York, Ontario
Photo: Author

FIGURE 2.10 Prayer hall at Noor Cultural Centre, North York, Ontario
Photo: Author

gatherings on special occasions. These glass panels are etched with a verse from the Qur'an, which aptly sums up the purpose of the Noor Cultural Center: "We have created you male and female and made you into nations and tribes so you may know one another" (Qur'an 49:13). Acknowledging equality in the Qur'an demonstrates the need for equal-sized and dignified regular usage of the prayer hall and it is clear washroom facilities were associate with this.

Summary and Conclusion

The integral role of ritual washing with water prior to every prayer was manifested architecturally in mosques and prayer spaces as designated and designed *wudu* areas. Historically, this area was often located outside of the mosque or within a pavilion structure in the courtyard.

The design of these spaces emphasized the sacred role of water and ritual washing through considered location, design, and embellishment of the surfaces with decoration or epigraphy. The use and role of water was a sacred and important resource in the physical cleansing and spiritual purification needed before each prayer. Diaspora communities of Muslims in the 18th century and onwards established communities and worship spaces throughout the world and included spaces for a range of education and social activities. With the expansion of programming and locations within colder climates, the *wudu* facilities shifted and amalgamated with washrooms in most contemporary diaspora mosques. Additionally, this inclusion within washroom facilities also normalized the gendered segregation of ritual washing not documented in historical mosques. Mosque and Muslim prayer spaces in Canada include examples of *wudu* areas embedded within separate washrooms, such as the New Al Rashid mosque and the Noor Cultural Centre. The ennobling of precursor rituals to prayer is important with respect to location, design, embellishment, and finite messages of proportionate inclusion.

Aside from the general proportions published in *Building Type Basics for Places of Worship* (Roberts & Daly 2004), guidelines for the design of *wudu* areas for mosques located in cold climates do not exist. The pattern from the mosques examined in Canada (Gaber 2022) demonstrates that the dedicated spaces for *wudu* are located in washroom facilities and usually have ceramic finishes, built-in stools, and water run-off channels with water spouts in the wall, and heating systems. This arrangement allows for seating as each individual washes the requisite parts of the body prior to prayer. However, at all of the mosques studied, the dimensions of the built-in seating areas did not vary or account for different body sizes or needs. Adjustable seats, areas for storage of personal items, and designed areas for slippers would be beneficial modifications for *wudu* design guidelines.

There is an opportunity for contemporary mosques to include more environmental and sustainable solutions for the use of water from *wudu*, which is generally considered greywater. Potentially, this runoff can be collected for other purposes to be used within the building (toilets) or for landscaping irrigation. Proactive efforts such as the "Green Mosque Initiative" at the Islamic Society of North America in the United States and at the Cambridge Mosque in the United Kingdom highlight such opportunities, in addition, to saving water (ISNA and Ozhisar, 2021). In Canada, the Noor Cultural Centre and the New Al Rashid mosque advocate the reduction in water waste, still, there is a potential to include greywater management in all contemporary mosque spaces. In the Qur'an it is emphasized that Muslims "do not commit abuse on earth" (Qur'an 2:60) and respect the natural environment as guardians – and that, in fact, Muslims are accountable for this to God through their actions. Thus, stewardship to sustainable measures is considered as a stewardship for God.

The spiritual experience in *wudu* areas in contemporary Canadian mosques is much reduced when compared to exceptional historic examples. The interiorized space within washrooms is part of this reason, but also reduced surface elaboration due to design aesthetics that contextually are rooted in Modernist traditions prevalent in the city, has emphasized this. (McClellan & Stewart 2007). Ceramic tiles are generally utilized but not necessarily decorated. Occasionally, special attention has been paid to the design of beautifully day-lit spaces, such as at the Noor Cultural Centre. The *wudu* areas designed in modern mosques in colder climates like Canada have focused on creating functional, comfortable, and effective spaces that allow for the transition to spiritual devotion within the prayer spaces, but lack the special atmosphere preparing the worshiper to enter the sacred area of the mosque.

Note

1. *Qur'an*, 2:25; 3:15, 136, 195, 198; 4:13, 57, 122; 5:12, 85, 119; 9:89, 100; 13:35; 14:25; 16:31; 18:31; 22:14, 23; 25:10, 47:12; 48:5, 17; 57:12; 58:22; 61:12; 64:9; 65:11; 85:11; 98:8

References

Awid, Richard A. *Canada's First Mosque – The Al Rashid*. Alberta: High Speed Printing Edmonton, 2010.
Bloom, Jonathan. *Architecture of the Islamic West*. New Haven: Yale University Press, 2020.
Creswell, K.A.C. *Early Muslim Architecture, Vol.I Part I*. New York: Hacker Publishing, 1979.
Creswell, K.A.C. *Early Muslim Architecture, Vol.I Part II*. New York: Hacker Publishing, 1979.
Gaber, Tammy. *Beyond the Divide: A Century of Canadian Mosque Design*. Montreal: McGill-Queen's University Press, 2022.
Gaber, Tammy. "Paradise Present: The Imagined and Manifested Images of Paradise in Islam" *Faith and Form*. Vol. XLVII, No.3. 2015. 10–16.
Haddad, Yvonne and Jane Smith. Ed. *The Oxford Handbook of American Islam*. New York: Oxford University Press, 2014.
Hillenbrand, Robert. *Islamic Architecture Form, Function and Meaning*. Edinburgh: Edinburgh University Press, 1994.
Holod, Renata and Hasan-Uddin Khan. *The Mosque and the Modern World, Architects Patrons and Designs since the 1950s*. London: Thames and Hudson, 1997.
Husaini, Zohra, Richard Awid, and Khalid Tarrabain. *Muslims in Canada A Century of Achievement*. Edmonton: Arabian Muslim Association, 1999.
"ISNA Green Initiative" *Islamic Society of North America*. https://isna.net/isna-green-initiative/
Jones, Philip and Anna Kenny. *Australia's Muslim Cameleers Pioneers of the Inland 1860s-1930s*. Melbourne: Wakefield Press, 2017.
Korbendau, Yves. *L'Architecture Sacree de L'islam*. Paris: Art Creation Realisation, 1997.
Kuban, Doğan. *Ottoman Architecture*. Woodbridge: Antique Collectors' Club, 2010.
McClelland, Michael and Graeme Stewart. *Concrete Toronto: A Guide to Concrete Architecture from the Fifties to the Seventies*. Toronto: Coach House Books, 2007.
Moriyama, Raymond. "Noor Cultural Centre". Interview with author, 20 November 2013.
Necipoğlu, Gülru. *The Age of Sinan: Architectural Culture in the Ottoman Empire*. Chicago: University of Chicago Press, 2007.
Ozhisar, Hatice. "The UK's First Green Mosque: The Cambridge Mosque" *World Architecture*, 2021. https://worldarchitecture.org/article-links/evhmv/the-uk-s-first-green-mosque-the-cambridge-mosque-.html
Roberts, Nicholas and Leo Daly. *Building Type Basics for Places of Worship*. Hoboken, New Jersey: John Wiley & Sons Inc., 2004.
Ruggles, Fairchild D. *Islamic Gardens and Landscapes*. Philadelphia: University of Pennsylvania Press, 2008.
Saleem, Shahed. *The British Mosque An Architectural and Social History*. Swindon: Historic England, 2018.
Waugh, Earle. *Al Rashid Mosque Building Canadian Muslim Communities*. Edmonton: University of Alberta Press, 2018.

3
CHATTRI AND KUND

The Architecture of Kusum Sarovar, Govardhan, India

Amita Sinha

Water is central to the rich corpus of Hindu myths and essential to all rituals as a purifying element. The wide range of spatial practices involving water has shaped a unique cultural landscape of riverfront *ghats* (steps and landings), *kunds* (tanks edged with steps), and *baolis* (stepwells) in India. This varied typology was a testimony to the munificence of building patrons and ingenuity and skills of artisans. Water structures were key to the urban aesthetics of traditional settlements. Pilgrim towns, where public life revolved around devotional activities, typically have *kunds* in temple complexes in their core and on their periphery circumambulated by devotees. Those on river fronts have long stretches of *ghats* with a temple skyline behind them. The astonishing subterranean architecture of stepwells that evolved in response to water shortage in the hot dry climate of western India is well known and has been extensively written about (Jain-Neubauer 1981; Livingston 2002; Lautman 2017); lesser known and studied are the humbler *kunds*, ubiquitous in the sacred landscape of Hinduism. Their basic form is of a square or polygonal masonry tank with steps leading down to the water, and more elaborate versions would have pavilions, shrines, and temples integrated into their overall structure.

The focus of this chapter is on one particular *kund*, Kusum Sarovar, in Braj, a region in Northern India associated with the childhood and adolescence of the deity Krishna, and spanning three states—Uttar Pradesh, Rajasthan, and Haryana—at a distance of 128 kilometers south of New Delhi. The pastoral landscape of forests, groves, hills, and hamlets through which the holy River Yamuna flows, has hundreds of *kunds*, ponds, and wells, many connected with Krishna's *lilas* (play) and therefore, part of the *ban yatra* (journey through the forests) pilgrimage route (Haberman 1994). Govardhan Hill, where Kusum Sarovar is located, is believed to have been lifted by Krishna on his finger to protect his community from incessant rains and floods (Fig. 3.1). This episode described in Sanskrit texts—*Harivamsa* (1–3 CE), *Vishnu Purana* (5th CE) and *Bhagavata Purana* (late 9th-early 10th CE)—not only established Krishna's supremacy over the rain-god Indra but also clearly communicated his message that the hill with its green pastures where cows graze and which gives them fresh water and fruits, should be worshipped instead of a distant god (Austin 2015).

Among the 23 *kunds* around the Hill, Kusum Sarovar is unique in being part of an architectural ensemble of historic buildings and rooftop gardens. This chapter traces the evolution

DOI: 10.4324/9781003358824-5

FIGURE 3.1 Dan Ghati temple sculpture, Govardhan
    Source: Author

of the landscape from its mythical past of an eternally blooming natural garden to its transformation by the late eighteenth century into a historic monument. Water as a medium of divine instantiation and its purificatory role in physical and moral cleansing is central to this narrative. The built structures and gardens of Kusum Sarovar are analyzed to interpret the principles of composition that give form to water and enable our reading of the monument as a unified ensemble. Kusum Sarovar is a protected monument; however, its significance lies beyond the aesthetic excellence of its historic water architecture.

Lila Sthal (Places of Divine Play)

Kusum Sarovar is part of the network of sacred sites in the northern part of Govardhan Hill, a long low sandstone ridge, seven miles long and barely 100 meters (300 feet) higher than the surrounding plain (Fig. 3.2). Govardhan's groves and ponds were settings of Krishna's playful adventures and numerous sites on the hill attest to his *lila* in their place legends. The hill, popularly known as 'Giriraj' (king of mountains) is perceived as an embodiment of Krishna, of his divine transcendence made immanent in material form. It is considered to be *lila sthal* (place of divine play), his abode (*dham*), and his actual body (Holdrege 2015; Ray 2021); he holds and well as assumes the form of the mountain, as indicated in his names—'Govardhan-dhara', 'Giri-dhari', and 'Giriraj-dharan'—derived from the root *dhr* (Haberman 2015). Textual and visual representations where Krishna is the mountain, worship it as a devotee (*Hari-dasa*), and also stand atop the mountain, show the divine ability to assume many forms simultaneously

FIGURE 3.2 Location of Kusum Sarovar
    Source: Author; drawn by Prerna Jain

FIGURE 3.3 Watercolor from folio of 'Lambagaon' Gita Govinda, Kangra, circa 1825
Source: Los Angeles County Museum of Art

(Austin 2015). Place legends narrated during pilgrimage are about Govardhan and its waters and vegetation transubstantiating into the bodies of Krishna and his companions. These stories are framed within the Hindu worldview which considers nature to be sentient and capable of transmutation between aqueous, vegetal, terrestrial, and anthropomorphic forms (Sinha 1995). The divine immanence in water, vegetation, and stone charges the landscape with energy and is reified in Krishna's *murtis* (statues) in temples.

According to folklore the northern section of the hill was redolent with flowering trees in the Phuspa Van (forest of flowers) where Radha, Krishna's beloved, and other *gopis* (cowherdesses) came to pick flowers to offer to the sun god Surya. The pond received its name 'Kusum Sarovar' (*kusum* meaning flowers; *sarovar* meaning pond) from its verdant surroundings. This was an archetypal landscape of eternal springtime, of blooming flowers, flowing waters, dancing peacocks, and flying pairs of birds, evocative of *shringar rasa* (erotic sentiment). Krishna danced the *raas* (circle dance) with the *gopis* in the autumn full moon night in a forest clearing and dallied with Radha, his beloved *gopi*, in bowers (Fig. 3.3). In earlier devotional poetry and paintings, the *nikunj* (bower) is depicted as an intimate secluded space, framed with vines and creepers, distinct from the forest around it; in later texts, it is ornate with jeweled thrones on marble floors in pavilions (Snell 1998). Rajput paintings and devotional poetry from the sixteenth century onwards narrate episodes of Radha and Krishna meeting, quarreling and sulking, and then reconciling, experiencing love-in-separation (*viraha rasa*). The *nikunj* in these representations is a mysterious inner world of bowers interconnected by pathways in the forest (Aitken 2004).

The landscape of *lila sthal* (place of divine play) is marked by imprints left by Krishna's body, particularly his feet resembling lotus petals (Holdrege 2015). There are many signs of Krishna's trysts with Radha at Kusum Sarovar and its surroundings—a temple (Shyam Kuti) symbolic of the bower and a throne for Radha and Krishna (*ratna singhasan*) in the Ashok Van (grove of ashok trees) where Krishna braided Radha's hair (Fig. 3.4). Nearby are Krishna's feet enshrined as a bodily trace in natural indentations in a boulder (*charan chinha*), a rock that emanates musical sounds when struck (*bajani shila*), and *raas sthali* (place of Krishna's dance with the *gopis*). Ratna Kund marks the spot where the demon Shankhachud with a conch-shaped jewel head crest was killed by Krishna when he attempted to abduct Radha.

The site abounds with legends celebrating transmutations between natural and human/divine forms. The sentience of vegetation is depicted vividly in the episode of *gopis* asking trees and shrubs for Krishna's whereabouts when he suddenly disappears (Smith 2004; Ray 2019). According to folklore, Uddhav, Krishna's cousin and companion, came here to persuade the

44 Amita Sinha

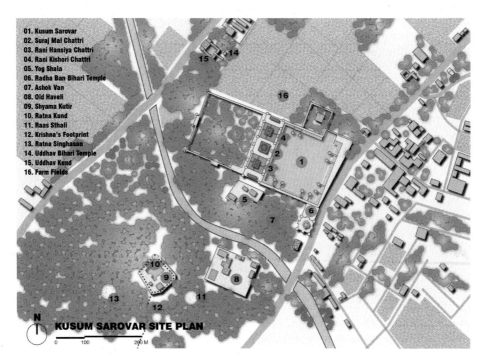

FIGURE 3.4 Layout of Kusum Sarovar
Source: Author; drawn by Heena Gajjar

gopis of the futility of their love when Krishna left for Mathura and to cultivate detachment but instead was converted to their viewpoint that love is supreme (Goswami Maharaja 2007). Uddhav resides here eternally in the grass and shrubs and emerged to join the recitation of *Bhagavat Purana* when Krishna's wives accompanied by his great-grandson Vrajnabh came searching for their husband. This event in the popular imagination is believed to be the first reclamation of memory upon the loss of traces of Krishna's presence in the landscape. Uddhav Kund and a historic *haveli* (mansion) temple with a domed spire are place markers of this episode (Fig. 3.5). About 400 meters southeast of Kusum Sarovar is Narad Kund named after the sage Narad who transmuted into the form of a *gopi* after taking a dip in its waters to be with Krishna. Chaityana (1486–1533 CE), the mystic from Bengal on his visit to Govardhan

FIGURE 3.5 Uddhav Kund and Uddhav Bihari Temple
Source: Author

bathed in Kusum Sarovar, as part of his mission to find and restore the lost *lila sthals*. The sage Astavark who had practiced austerities to obtain *darshan* of Krishna and Radha, left his mortal body, the spot marked by a *shiv-linga* on the eastern bank. The glories of Kusum Sarovar, eulogized in the verses of *Govind Lilamrit* by the sixteenth-century poet Krishnadas Kaviraj are described in place stories narrated to pilgrims when they visit the site during their circumambulation (*parikrama*) of Govardhan (Goswami Maharaja 2007).

Chattri and *Kund* (Memorial and Tank)

The archetypal configuration of temple-*kund* in the *van* is repeatedly found in the cultural landscape of Braj (Sinha 2015). The deity in the temple is an iconic form of divine immanence suffusing the landscape as captured in Krishna's epithet 'Ban Bihari' meaning one who roams the forest. At Kusum Sarovar, however, a magnificent memorial to the Jat king Suraj Mal, instead of a temple, dominates the landscape (Fig. 3.6). Protected by the State Archaeology Department of Uttar Pradesh, it adds a historic layer to the landscape of myth and commemorates a devotee of Krishna who was given the title of *Brajraj* (lord of Braj) as its protector. The pool at Kusum Sarovar had been built into a *kund* in 1675 CE by Bir Singh Deo, the ruler of Orchha.[1] Nearly a century later, Suraj Mal (1707–1763) built a garden around it for his queen Rani Kishori and this site became the place of his cremation as well.

Suraj Mal was an ambitious and powerful king ruling over a large territory that included the Braj region and had become enormously wealthy by plundering Delhi and Agra in the tumultuous period of the Mughal decline (Singh 2001). The Jat farmers had risen to prominence as feudal warlords by building mud forts around their settlements and raiding the imperial route between Agra and Delhi in the late seventeenth and early eighteenth centuries. Suraj Mal had resisted the Afghan Ahmad Shah Abdali's attack on Mathura and Vrindavan in 1757 CE and was a patron of temples, *havelis* (mansions), and memorials in Govardhan and Vrindavan. His queen Rani Kishori had built the Mukut Mukharvind Temple on the banks of a large *kund*–Manasi Ganga– in the center of Govardhan where Suraj Mal had celebrated his victory over Mughal forces by lighting *diyas* (clay lamps) on its waters. Suraj Mal was killed on December 25, 1763 in a battle with Rohillas on the banks of the River Hindon near Delhi. Although his body was never recovered, cremation (with two teeth) was done at Kusum Sarovar as is customary in the Hindu practice of burning the body close to water. Jawahar Singh, Suraj Mal's son, rebuilt Kusum Sarovar in 1768 with three memorial structures to his father and two of his queens, Rani Hansiya and Rani Kishori (Growse 1874) (Fig. 3.7).

The practice of building memorial structures, known as *chattris* (literally umbrellas) by Hindu rulers of Northern and Western India—Rajputs, Marathas, and Jats—was inspired by the grand mausoleums of the Mughal emperors in India following the Timurid tradition. The

FIGURE 3.6 Kusum Sarovar
Source: Author

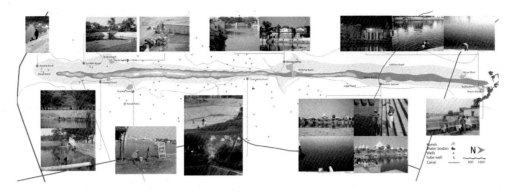

FIGURE 3.7 Manasi Ganga at Govardhan
Source: Author

chattri dome mimics the umbrella, metonymic of religious and political authority in India (Belli 2011). It was therefore an apt symbol legitimizing the successor's claim to the throne and dynastic continuity. The Mughal mausoleums were built in *char baghs* (four square gardens), symbolic of paradise as depicted in the *Quran* (Moynihan 1980). Water channels and pools structured the garden surrounding the cenotaph, dividing it into square or rectangular plots planted with fruit and flowering trees and shrubs. Since Hindus do not bury their dead and there are no mortal remains of the body (except ashes left upon cremation), the borrowed practice of erecting memorial structures does not have the same meaning as in the Islamic tradition of interring the dead in paradisiacal settings. The *chattris* of Kusum Sarovar were built on a 460 feet long terrace above the *kund* as garden pavilions with sunken *char baghs* on either side of Suraj Mal's memorial in the center. Smaller *chattris* of the two queens are located at the intersection of raised pathways in the *char baghs*. Although the image is borrowed from the Islamic concept of tombs in paradise gardens, the *char baghs* have lost their symbolic meaning and are mere ornamental settings for the *chattris*. Their use here and in Rajput royal gardens in northwestern India is an adoption of the quad-partite garden structure without the heavenly connotation (Ruggles 2008). *Chattris* are reflected in *kunds*, adding to their striking visual impression; thus, water is used for an aesthetic effect. The *chattris* overlook the *kund* on one side and on the other, a tree grove in an enclosure with the same footprint as the *kund* (Fig. 3.8).

FIGURE 3.8 *Chattris* at Kusum Sarovar
Source: Author

FIGURE 3.9 *Kund* at Kusum Sarovar
Source: Author

The architecture celebrates the sacred and aesthetic experience of viewing water by framing it and inviting touch. The design vocabulary of water structures evolved to facilitate visual and tactile engagement with the holy River Yamuna in Braj. The riverfront architecture in the pilgrim towns of Mathura, Vrindavan, and Gokul in Braj is dominated by openings such as *jaali* screen windows and pavilions for near and distant views of the river (Sinha and Ruggles 2004). This language was incorporated in designing Kusum Sarovar as a unified composition of buildings and water in which the *kund* is integrated into the complex of raised gardens and rooftop garden pavilions. Its waters are framed from above in the nine smaller outlook pavilions on the edge of the terrace and the *jaali* screens in the *burjes* (piers) extending 60 feet into the water. Steps (*ghats*) around the *kund* enable access to the changing water levels during the year for the ritual dip (*snan*) by devotees that cleanses, purifies, and rejuvenates. The ornate *burjes*, built in pairs on four sides of the *kund* (except on the south-east where there is an overflow basin), interrupt the linearity of *ghats* and are designed with open colonnades and enclosed rooms, submerged during monsoons thus giving a feel for living in the water. The subterranean water architecture is richly embellished with blind cusped arches, *jaali* (screens), and ornamental star-shaped cartouches (Fig. 3.9).

The design vocabulary of Kusum Sarovar is an example of the synthesis of Hindu and Islamic design principles in early premodern India. The architecture of the *chattri* has Indo-Islamic forms such as domes, cusped arches, and tapering columns, fused with curved *bangla* roofs (derived from the Bengal hut). In addition, *chajjas* (projecting eaves for protection from sun and rain) and *jaalis* typical of Rajput architecture appear. Kusum Sarovar shares design features with the Deeg Palace complex, the summer capital of Jat kings, about 14 kilometers (about 9 miles) from Govardhan and on the Braj pilgrimage route. Inspired by Mughal palace gardens, its pavilion-like buildings set in *char bagh* gardens overlook large *kunds*. Deeg palace complex epitomizes the Jat style in architecture—a composite of Islamic and Rajput architectural elements (Chugh and Chugh 2014). The tripartite composition of three *chattris* on the raised platform at Kusum Sarovar is similar to *sawan* and *bhadon* pavilions (named after monsoon months) on either side of Gopal Bhawan overlooking the large *kund* Gopal Sagar at Deeg. This tripartite scheme is derived from the riverfront Mughal garden scheme employed in the Taj Mahal and Khass Mahal in Agra Fort on the banks of the Yamuna in Agra (Koch 2006). The riverfront terrace was a platform for the Taj, flanked by a mosque and its mirror replica, the *Mihman Khana* (guest house), high enough to protect the complex from the

FIGURE 3.10 Fresco in Suraj Mal *Chattri*
Source: Author

flooding river and giving it visibility from the garden below it on the leeward side and the Yamuna. At Kusum Sarovar, the large *kund* substitutes for the river and the *char bagh* gardens instead of being laid out below as they in the Taj, are on the terrace as rooftop gardens but with no water channels or pools.

A strong sense of visual balance and compositional unity is achieved through the use of bilateral symmetry in the layout and repetition of forms at different scales. The high terrace above the *kund* is divided into three squares, two of which are sunken *char baghs* on either side of the raised square. Pavilions with *bangla* and domical roofs create visual axes and reinforce the physical axes set up by pathways in the rooftop *char baghs*. The terraced layout is laterally and longitudinally symmetrical. Domes of different sizes are repeated—the highest and largest one is over Suraj Mal's *chattri*; the next size and height are over the queens' *chattris*; and the smallest ones are over pavilions on the terrace edge. Four small domes around the central dome are interspersed with four cupolas and *bangla* roofs on the three *chattris*—their repetition in different sizes makes for proportional harmony and creates a picturesque effect. Suraj Mal's *chattri* is a 57 feet square pavilion with an inner space enclosed by *jaali* screens with a circumambulatory passage around it. Krishna's feet carved in marble on the floor grace the center of this interior where a cenotaph would be placed in an Islamic mausoleum. Beautiful fresco paintings on the ceiling depict episodes of Krishna *lila*, including his lifting of Govardhan, performing *raas* with Radha and other *gopis*, Suraj Mal venerating Krishna in a *haveli* temple, hunting, and court scenes. These visual representations and the marble feet are place markers of the symbolic appropriation by Krishna of this space, establishing his ever-lasting presence. He is the eternal dweller in the *chattri* dedicated to the memory of his devotee and servant Suraj Mal. Kusum Sarovar is part of an interconnected network of sacred sites, each linked to a specific episode of Krishna's *lila*, and a rest stop on the pilgrim's *parikrama* around Govardhan (Fig. 3.10).

Parikrama (Pilgrimage)

Pilgrimage is advocated within the *bhakti* (devotion) tradition in Hinduism for experiencing the divine immanence in *tirthas* (crossing places or fords), mountains and hills, rivers, and their confluences (Sinha 2006). Mircea Eliade (1958) describes, stone, tree, and water together constitute a microcosm, the first 'sacred place', that reproduces the whole cosmos in religious thinking. The indestructibility of stone, regenerative capacity of vegetation, and purificatory powers and incipient fertility of water combine to create a powerful charge. In Hinduism, this belief constitutes a *tirtha*. Govardhan and the River Yamuna flowing at its foot represent the archetypal hill-water dyad in a *tirtha*. Although the Yamuna changed its course around 1500 CE as revealed in its paleochannels (Ray 2019), the many *kunds* around Govardhan today are significant places on the 21 kilometers long circumambulatory journey (Sinha 2015). Water is believed to be the liquid form of Krishna and Radha and the combined waters of the twin *kunds* at Govardhan—Radha and Shyam, Apsara and Naval—are perceived as symbolic of their union. The purifying capacity of water in its ability to wash away physical dirt and moral sins is evident in the place legends associated with Shyam Kund and Manasi Ganga at the foothill; they are believed to be created by Krishna to expiate his killing of bull-demon Arishtasur and the calf-demon Vatsasur (Goswami Maharaja 2007).

Govardhan *parikrama*, part of the larger circuit of Braj *ban yatra*, is done on foot and by prostrating on the ground to be in contact with the holy soil (*braj raj*). Thus, the pilgrim's body engages through all senses with the embodied landscape of Krishna's *lila-sthal* and feels the divine immanence. *Kunds* in the midst of small settlements are social spaces for singing *bhajans* (devotional songs) and listening to religious discourses by pilgrims and local communities. Pilgrims obtain *darshan* (ritual sighting) of Radha and Krishna *murtis* in the temples located near the *kunds*. They worship stones as *svarups* (essential form) of Radha and Krishna in shrines in the belief that Govardhan's materiality represents the fused love of Radha and Krishna who are essentially one though manifest in two forms (Haberman 2015). Krishna's footprints (*charan chinha*) engraved in stones are lovingly caressed and venerated with flowers.

Kusum Sarovar is a major landmark in the *parikrama* route as well as a tourist stop. The magnificent *chattris* reflected in the waters of the *kund* are very scenic, especially at dusk; they are lit up at night creating spectacular views and enhancing the aesthetic and spiritual experience. Their recently restored frescoes attract many tourists, as well as students of art and architectural history. The ghats and *burjes* of the *kund* are popular spaces for local residents to sing *bhajans* (devotional songs) and devotees dance the *raas* on the terrace adjoining the *kund*. Mundane activities include socializing with friends, fishing, children diving into the water, and splashing. While pilgrims take a dip into the *kund* or sprinkle water on their heads for ritual purification, its ornate *chattris*, *ghats* and *burjes* become spaces for doing *kirtan* (chanting the glories of Krishna) and listening to place legends narrated by the sectarian leaders who organize the *parikrama*. The adjoining sacred sites–Ratna Kund, Narad Kund, Shyama Kuti, and *charan chinha*—are visited by pilgrims as they are walking on the eastern side of the hill. Uddhav Kund, although close to Kusum Sarovar, is a pilgrim stop on the opposite (western) side of Govardhan. The cluster of sacred places invites similar devotional activities; pilgrims offer prayers to Radha and Krishna deities in Shyam Kuti, Uddhav Bihari and Radha Ban Bihari Temples, pour milk, and offer food to Krishna's footprints (*charan chinha*) engraved in the rock, listen to discourses in the forest clearing, and sprinkle water from the *kunds* over their heads. These ritual activities prepare the faithful for envisioning Krishna *lila* around the *kunds* in tree groves and experience *bhakti bhav* (devotional sentiment).

Conclusion

Krishna's lifting of Govardhan proved to be an iconic gesture, celebrated for two millennia as a symbol of the divine child's prowess. Its deeper meaning, Krishna's calling attention to nature's gifts and its life-affirming powers, has become salient in the Anthropocene (Sinha 2014). The pools and groves of Govardhan are memory traces of Krishna *lila*, celebrated in place legends, depicted in visual and textual representations, and are sites of active engagement of the pilgrim with the landscape. A few such as Kusum Sarovar, are historic monuments, that testify to the material wealth of their patrons and the artistic brilliance of their builders. They transformed the pond in the clearing into an architectonic landscape adding historic and spiritual dimensions to places acclaimed in mythic narratives. Kusum Sarovar is an excellent example of a hybrid design vocabulary in landscape and architecture produced by a synthesis of Rajput and Mughal styles in Braj. *Char baghs* are juxtaposed with *ghats* and *burjes*, and bulbous domes with *bangla* roofs to produce composite forms in the monument. Kusum Sarovar set the precedent for Jat kings—Baldev Singh and Balwant Singh who ruled between 1823–1853. They built their *chattris* in Ganga Bagh garden on the northern bank of Manasi Ganga and Randhir Singh's (1805–1823) *chattri* is close by. Thus, the Jat rulers had a significant impact on Govardhan's material heritage.

The environmental health of the cultural landscape depends on the presence of water. The *kunds*' cultural heritage is immense and so is their environmental legacy. They serve dual functions—they are sites of memory and store waters of life that rejuvenate the ecosystem. They have an important role in the traditional system of water harvesting and are centers of community life (Sinha 2015). While Kusum Sarovar is well protected by State Archaeology Department, other sacred sites around it can be better managed by the State Forestry Department. The dense scrub (*prosopos julifera*) can be reforested with a more diverse vegetation palette that includes flowering trees thus conforming to the image of Phuspha Van where Radha came to pick flowers. Trails and interpretive signage will add to the experience of being in a heritage landscape. Although Kusum Sarovar with its picturesque *chattris* is a prominent landmark, it is embedded in a network of sacred sites. This entails its preservation be not stand-alone (as is currently the case) but part of the overall conservation of Govardhan's sacred ecology.

Note

1. https://www.incredibleindia.org/content/incredible-india-v2/en/destinations/mathura-vrindavan/kusum-sarovar.html

References

Aitken, Molly. "The Heroine's Bower: Framing the Stages of Love." In *A Celebration of Love: The Romantic Heroine in the Indian Arts* edited by Harsha Dehejia, 105–119. New Delhi: Roli Book, 2004.

Austin, Christopher. "Lifting the Meanings of Govardhana Mountain: A Review Essay." *Journal of Vaishnava Studies* 23, no. 2 (Spring 2015): 5–26.

Belli, Melia. "Keeping Up with the Rajputs: Appropriation and the Articulation of Sacrality and Political Legitimacy in Scindia Funerary Art." *Archives of Asian Art* 61, (2011): 91–106.

Chugh, Bharat and Shalini Chugh. *Deeg Palace: Its Romance and Wonder*. New Delhi: Niyogi Books, 2014.

Eliade, Mircea. *Patterns in Comparative Religion*. Translated by Rosemary Sheed. New York: Sheed and Ward, 1958.

Goswami Maharaja, Sri Srimad Bhaktivedanta Narayana. *Sri Vraja-Mandal Parikrama*. Vrindavan: Gaudiya Vedanta Publications, 2007.

Growse, F.S. *Mathura: A District Memoir*. Part I. Mathura: Printed at the North-Western Provinces' Government Press, 1874.

Haberman, David. *Journey through the Twelve Forests: An Encounter with Krishna*. New York: Oxford University Press, 1994.

Haberman, David. "Divine Conceptions: The Three Identities of Mount Govardhan." *Journal of Vaishnava Studies* 23, no. 2 (Spring 2015): 27–46.

Holdrege, Barbara. *Bhakti and Embodiment: Fashioning Divine Bodies and Devotional Bodies in Krsna Bhakti.* New York: Routledge, 2015.

Jain-Neubauer, Jutta. *Stepwells of Gujarat.* New Delhi: Abhinav Publications, 1981.

Koch, Ebba. *The Complete Taj Mahal.* London: Thames & Hudson Ltd., 2006. In *A Celebration of Love: The Romantic Heroine in the Indian Arts* edited by Harsha Dehejia, 38-43. New Delhi: Roli Book, 2004.

Lautman, Victoria. *The Vanishing Stepwells of India.* London: Merrell Publishers, 2017.

Livingston, Morna. *Steps to Water: The Ancient Stepwells of India.* New York: Princeton Architectural Press, 2002.

Moynihan, Elizabeth. *Paradise as a Garden: In Persia and Mughal India.* New York: George Braziller, 1980.

Ray, Sugata. *Climate Change and the Art of Devotion: Geoaesthetics in the Land of Krishna, 1550-1850.* Seattle: University of Washington Press, 2019.

Ray, Sugata. "Geoaesthetics and Embodied Devotion in Braj." *Marg: A Pathmaking Arts Quarterly* 73, no.1 (September–December 2021): 47–55.

Ruggles, D. Fairchild. *Islamic Gardens and Landscapes.* Philadelphia: University of Pennsylvania Press, 2008.

Singh, Natwar. *Maharaja Suraj Mal 1707-1763.* Delhi: Rupa Publications, 2001.

Sinha, Amita and D. Fairchild Ruggles. "The Yamuna Riverfront, India: A Comparative Study of Islamic and Hindu Traditions in Cultural Landscapes." *Landscape Journal* 23, no. 2(2004): 141–152

Sinha, Amita. "Nature in Hindu Art, Architecture and Landscape," *Landscape Research*, U.K., 20, no.1 (Spring 1995): 3–10.

_____. *Landscapes of India: Forms and Meanings.* Boulder, Colorado: University Press of Colorado, 2006.

_____. "The Sacred Landscape of Braj: Imagined, Enacted, and Reclaimed." *Landscape Journal* 33, no. 1(2014): 59–76.

_____. "Reclamation of Kunds on Govardhan Hill, Braj." *Journal of Vaishnava Studies* 23, no. 2 (Spring 2015): 101–110.

Smith, Caron. "Footprints in the Dust: The Gopis as a Collective Heroine in the Bhagavata Purana." In *A Celebration of Love: The Romantic Heroine in the Indian Arts* edited by Harsha Dehejia, 38–43. New Delhi: Roli Book, 2004.

Snell, Rupert. "The Kunj as Sacred Space in Poetry of the Radhavallabhi Tradition." *Journal of Vaishnava Studies* 7, (1998): 48–63.

4

SACRED WATER ARCHITECTURE FOR EVERY JEW

Rabbi David Miller and DIY Mikvah in Charleston, South Carolina*

Barry L. Stiefel

Water that is sacred in the Jewish tradition is called מים חיים (pronounced *mayyim hayyim*), which means "living water." Water that is found flowing in its liquid natural state, whether in a stream, lake, or ocean is considered living. This is in contrast to water that is artificially pumped (such as a human-pressurized plumbing or retention system), bottled, or in some other way prevented from moving through the water cycle. According to rabbinic tradition (Caro et al 1961), living water can be slowed, temporarily blocked, dammed, and/or diverted so that it can be used for sacramental immersion purposes. Living water is most commonly used for ritually purifying Jews who have come into contact with something that renders them spiritually unclean and for purifying cooking utensils for *kashrut* (Jewish religious dietary rules).

The structure (such as a pool) and/or place (a building or bathing area) where the living water is temporarily "accumulated" is called a *mikvah* (מקוה). It's first mentioned in the Hebrew Bible ("…a spring or a cistern, a gathering of water remains clean…" / אַךְ מַעְיָן וּבוֹר מִקְוֵה־מַיִם יִהְיֶה טָהוֹר וְנֹגֵעַ בְּנִבְלָתָם יִטְמָא, Leviticus 11:36/וַיִּקְרָא לו)[1] and has been a Jewish tradition for many millennia. Within the Jewish concept of sacred water and architecture, the sanctity lies entirely within the living water. Remove the living water, or the *mikvah* and the ability to house the sacred water, the *mikvah* building loses its holiness. When living water is within a *mikvah* building, it becomes a sacred place, even if it does not appear visually different.

For much of Jewish history, formal *mikvaot* (plural) have been unattainable for the Jewish masses due to prohibitive costs or laws made by non-Jewish government authorities. Most frequently, *mikvaot* were built and maintained by the synagogue congregation and/or a wealthy Jewish family (Hoffmeier 2019). The development and management of *mikvaot* were also often the purview of rabbis who specialized in this form of Jewish ritual infrastructure. According to Rabbi Yosef Caro (1488–1575), one of the most preeminent Jewish legal authorities, the "laws regarding ritual pools are numerous. Wherever an immersion pool is made, it should be under the supervision of a recognized rabbi, great in learning and in piety. If any changes occur therein, no matter how slight, a rabbi should be consulted" (Caro et al 1961, 43). Caro's study on *mikvaot* is still authoritative. Therefore, the idea of a *mikvah* for every Jewish person is an uncommon concept, especially considering that there are not enough rabbis to supervise them all if every Jewish family had one.

---

*In memory of Louis Kirshtein (1926-2021)

DOI: 10.4324/9781003358824-6

During the early twentieth century, Rabbi David Miller of Oakland, California tried to change access by writing economically-minded, do-it-yourself (DIY) manuals for building *mikvaot*. Available in Yiddish and English, Miller offered his manuals free of charge to any Jew that wanted a copy (Miller 1930). Besides North America and Europe, Miller self-reported that his work was known among Jewish communities in Australia, China, India, Persia, and South Africa (Cooper 2011). Miller was of quasi-global importance because of his interest to provide *mikvaot* to Jews of all economic classes, no matter where they lived. This chapter explores the Jewish relationship, conceptions, and beliefs about sacred living water in relation to its vernacular architectural representation as manifested in the *mikvah*. An example of one of Miller's-inspired *mikvaot* in Charleston, South Carolina will also be analyzed. This discussion will center on how sacred architecture expresses the spiritual meaning of water as well as how water influences the sacredness of the building – the *mikvah*.

The *Mikvah*: Space Design and Rituals of Spiritual Purification

According to Jewish architect and *mikvah* user Miriam Hoffman, "[s]acred architecture traditionally serves as a place apart from the profane world wherein worship or rituals are performed, and shared symbolism is expressed. [Unfortunately, m]ikvaot are often treated as an afterthought, an appendage to a synagogue or a communal requirement that must be met, often with little intention or creativity…. These mikveh designs succeed at meeting the *halakhic* [Jewish legal] standards and basic functional needs of a mikveh, leaving the local interior decorator to pick tile and paint schemes."[2] The standards for a *mikvah* are that the bathing space must be large enough to contain enough water for a person to completely immerse themselves without touching the sides or floor. The *mikvah* water must also be from a naturally-occurring source and the *mikvah* must be drainable. The holiness of a *mikvah* is so significant that according to Miller:

> For the purpose of installing a Mikvah in a community, or a private home, it is permissible, and *even commendable* [author's emphasis], that the Holy Scroll [a Torah, the most sacred Jewish ritual object] be sold to raise funds therefor, if no other funds can be obtained. It is a reflection upon, an insult and blasphemy to, the Torah, for the Torah to be found in a community where there is no Mikvah.
>
> (Miller 1930: 440)

In other words, Miller's claim is that a *mikvah* with its associated sacred water has more sanctity than a Torah scroll (a very holy object in Judaism) because immersion in the *mikvah* is needed for spiritual purity, as stated within the Holy Scroll (Leviticus 11:36). The importance of the *mikvah* is its ritual use while its architectural design is secondary.

Mikvah use is central to traditional Jewish family life because among those who use it are married women following the end of their menstruation cycle. The blood from a monthly period is one of several contaminates that necessitate a spiritually scrupulous Jewish person to purify themselves in a *mikvah*. For instance, the woman of a Jewish household is expected to immerse herself in a *mikvah* prior to marriage and when resuming sexual relations with her husband. According to Caro, it "is the duty of every woman whose husband is in town, to perform the ritual immersion at the proper time without delay, in order not to postpone the precept of propagation, even one night" (Caro, et al. 1961: 40). Therefore, spiritual family purity and its maintenance through *mikvah* use is also directly tied to it because the Jewish parents-to-be should be spiritually pure while performing the act of making a child, which is a holy activity (Westheimer & Mark 2020). Because of the importance of *mikvah* use to sex in marriage, Miller's infatuation with family spiritual purity may have originated from his own situation. He never had children, and through his extracurricular work in promoting Jewish families and married life, he may have been trying to live vicariously through others that he could help.[3] Men use *mikvaot* but for other reasons. Before a major holiday or after coming into contact with the dead, and they must also clean themselves prior to immersion. During Biblical times all who entered the inner sanctums of the Jerusalem Temple to give sacrifices had to purify themselves ritually in a *mikvah* before approaching God's presence (Caro, et al. 1961).

The moment before the act of ritual immersion a blessing is recited. During the immersion, the person is not to touch the sides or bottom of the *mikvah* but be free floating under the water's surface. All of this is supervised by a *mikvah* attendant of the same gender (or the spouse) to ensure that the process is done correctly.

Rabbi David Miller (1869–1939)

As a disclaimer, while Miller was incredibly creative and innovative in his vernacular architectural design proposals for economically-affordable, DIY *mikvaot*; the majority of rabbinical authorities today disagree with the manner he proscribed the use of municipal tap water (the technicalities of this use are an aspect beyond the scope of this chapter). Until the 1950s, *mikvaot* that used municipal water supplies was commonly accepted by many Jewish households in the United States. Indeed, Rabbi Aryeh Klapper, Dean of the Center for Modern Torah Leadership, reflects that "Rabbi Miller's ideas for home tap-water mikvaot may or may not have been plausible in his time, and they may or may not have any relevance in our time. But his halakhic [Jewish law] scholarship [especially his designs for mikvaot] deserves respect and consideration,"[4] and this is the focus of this chapter. Furthermore, Miller was not the only rabbi to explore innovative ways to encourage greater *mikvah* use at a time when its usage was waning. Rabbi Yehuda Y. Rosenberg (1859–1935) in Toronto, Canada also developed a Hebrew language DIY manual circa 1920 – *Mikveh Yehuda* – but it was not nearly as widely circulated (Cooper 2014). When rabbis Miller and Rosenberg developed their manuals, they were not aware of each other's work (Rosenberg 1918). Decades lapsed until another book on *mikvah* construction was authored, most significantly by Rabbi Schneur Z. Lesches. In his guide entitled *Understanding Mikvah: An Overview of Mikvah Construction* (2001), he does not seem to be aware of either Miller's or Rosenberg's previous publications. In contrast to Miller and Rosenberg, Lesches asserts that those "who have a private mikvah in their homes are still obligated to assist in building a community mikvah" (Lesches 2001: 33). His book's emphasis is centralized sacred Jewish water architecture in public buildings instead of decentralized vernacular versions in private homes.

Brief biographies on Miller have been written before, most significantly by Levi Cooper a rabbi in Tzur Hadassah, Israel (2011). In summary, Miller was born in what is now Lithuania and studied at *yeshivot* (rabbinical seminaries) in Ruzhany and Slabodka, which are now in Belarus, where he became a rabbi. Miller studied under the renowned rabbi, Isaac Elchanan (1817–1896). As a young adult, Miller immigrated to the United States during the 1890s and worked at synagogues in New York City and Providence, Rhode Island (Cooper 2011). After some years, Miller decided that working as a pulpit rabbi was not for him, thus he resigned from his position and moved to California where he took an interest in construction and real estate. However, living and teaching others about the ways of traditional Judaism continued to be a passion for Miller, including the promotion of *mikvaot* among other aspects of Jewish married life (Cooper 2011).

During the 1910s and 1920s, Miller published multiple editions of *Seyfer Miḳveh Yiśroel* (Miller 1923), a Yiddish language book that explained to lay religious Jews how to make your own *mikvah* on a modest budget. This book was popular and went through multiple editions, including an expanded and updated English language version published in 1930, titled *The Secret of the Jew: His Life - His Family*. As a Jewish public service, he offered his books as "not for sale. [They are] loaned by the author to whomever may be concerned in the subject" (Miller 1930, title page). Because Miller worked in construction and real estate, instead of the formal rabbinate, this put him in an economic situation where he could afford to offer his publications on *mikvaot* to Jewish communities at little or no charge (Miller 1938). Unfortunately, it is unknown how his publications were disseminated, whether by word of mouth or unsolicited outreach. Miller's third and final publication was *The Secret of Happiness: How to Enjoy Life*, completed in the late 1930s and focused on Sabbath observance (Cooper 2011). In some rabbinical circles, Miller's work was highly regarded, including by rabbis Shlomo Elchanan Jaffe (1858–1923, Chief Rabbi of St. Louis, Missouri), Shimon Tzvi Elbaum, and Nissan Telushkin (1882–1970).[5]

Besides being formally educated in Jewish law for rabbinical ordination at well-respected *yeshivot* in imperial Russia, Miller self-identified as "a builder, practiced in construction and engineering, familiar with water-supply systems and their contrivances" (Miller 1930, 336). These qualifications – rabbi and construction engineer – were a rare combination in the early twentieth century. Miller was also an uncommon advocate for Jewish Orthodoxy, where during the early twentieth century religious observances were in decline in North America, and hence an openness for some leniency that rabbinical colleagues in Eastern Europe were not as open to (i.e. they were stricter in the interpretations of mikvah regulations).[6]

The Structure of Rabbi David Miller's Vernacular, DIY *Mikvaot* Architecture

The chapter on "Fundamental Rules of Mikvah" in Miller's *The Secret of the Jew* begins with a discourse on what a *mikvah* is ("an accumulation' of water"), followed by a discussion on the "Quality of Water Required for a Mikvah" and "Qualifying Unqualified Water Under Extraordinary Conditions." It is within these pages that Miller defines from his (minority) opinion on when water is considered *mayyim hayyim*. The issue of contention that Miller expresses is that he does not believe that a water meter qualifies as a "vessel." The majority of rabbis (especially in Europe) disagreed, claiming that the meter de-spiritualize *mayyim hayyim* back into regular water, creating a problem for *mikvah* use (Miller 1930: 330, 340).

The structural aspects of sacred architecture and water begin in the fourth section on "The Quantity of Water Required for a Mikvah." Here, there is a discussion that ties in the dimensions and volume of a *mikvah* so that a person may, "with reasonable convenience, be completely immersed therein, all of the body being covered at one time" (Miller 1930: 344). That approximately a foot of space above the waterline should be afforded for when a person is immersed in the *mikvah* so as not to overflow, recommending a minimum of 24 cubic feet of water. Miller then provides a series of tables and diagrams that illustrate the depth, width, and height of a schematic *mikvah* receptacle, spanning from a rectangular box of 48 × 18 × 64 inches to 66" × 35" × 22", as well as cylindrical from 48" × 38½" to 66" × 31½" and triangular, 48" × 20" × 115¾" to 66" × 40" × 43½ (Miller 1930). From these sections of *The Secret of the Jew*, the reader learns what forms of water are permitted within sacred Jewish ritual baths as well as the quantity of water needed to make them spiritually functional. Miller has also focused exclusively on *mikvaot* for bathing people and not the less common smaller ones for spiritually purifying cooking utensils.

In the following section on "Requirements for the Receptacle – The Mikvah – Containing the Water for Tvilah," Miller directs that "the receptacle which contains the water for *Tvilah*, must not be of a portable nature. It must by all means be built in, set, and permanently attached to the ground or to a building. No ready-made, portable receptacle [such as a bathtub] can be used as Mikvah – even when it is attached to the ground or building" (Miller 1930: 359). Miller also adds in the section "Public Bathing Places for Tvilah" that a "floating bath-house or stationary bathing houses built on the surf – where the bathing is in natural water which, as a rule, does not discontinue in the dry season – and where there are openings at the bottom of the bathing pool… can be used as a Mikvah for Tvilah" (Miller 1930: 361). *Tvilah* (טבילה) is the Hebrew word for a full body immersion. From these sections of *The Secret of the Jew*, Miller has defined where *mikvaot* can be sited, acceptable dimensions, and emphasizes that a bathtub cannot be made into a *mikvah*. Bathtubs are important for washing dirtiness off of one's person in preparation for *mikvah* use, but because they are disqualified as a *mikvah*, immersion in the bathtub does not spiritually purify according to Jewish law. Miller's openness to a floating bathhouse is intriguing – such as a floating ice fishing shanty – but he does not discuss the option further. Instead, he focuses on *mikvah* structures to be assembled within one's private home on dry land. A *mikvah* also does not have to be on or in the ground but can be on a building's roof (Miller 1930).

In the chapter "Simplicity of Mikvah Performance," Miller focuses his proscriptive discussions on the design and building of *mikvaot* as sacred Jewish water architecture. It is in this chapter where he elaborates on the economic bottom line: "any observant Jewish family can make a private Mikvah, at its residence, whether it owns a home or is a tenant, at a material cost within five dollars ($5.00 [$82.00 in 2023]), and a few hours' labor of a handyman. The plans for such a ritual-font are hereinafter described in full… it requires only from six to eight square feet of floor space…." (Miller 1930, 367). Miller wants Jews of all economic backgrounds to have access to their own *mikvah*, and not just the well-to-do. He suggests that *mikvaot* can be installed in any place, including in a dressing room or closet. The necessary, basic components entail constructing a receptacle with a capacity of 24 or more cubic feet of water, a lining to hold the water, a drain at the bottom, and the necessary plumbing for water to fill the *mikvah* (Miller 1930). Miller does not budget for the expense of tools, assuming most people have access to these resources. This chapter is followed by one on "How to Make a Mikvah" (Fig. 4.1), beginning with an illustration of a solitary Jewish man at work in constructing a *mikvah* with a handsaw to show how easy it was. Beneath the illustration is the caption "A sincere Jew installs his own Mikvah at the cost of a few dollars and a few hours' labor…" (Miller 1930: 406). It is an intriguing illustration because while *mikvaot* are associated as a place for women since they (usually) use them more regularly, Miller has charged the making of the *mikvah* to the man of the household and renders it a masculine possession. Through an illustration of what a bare minimum *mikvah* would entail with his proscribed frugal budget, Miller reinforces with the salesman-like caption "A simple home-made Mikvah. It costs less than $5.00. It answers the financial question; solves almost all problems. It challenges the loyalty and the sincerity of a Jew" (Miller 1930: 406). The components of the *mikvah* structure described by Miller are a frame made of lumber and nails on concrete, tile, or metal floor (with details on how to attach the frame to the floor through drilling holes); lining made of roofing paper; an outlet; a step ladder; and instructions for filling and draining the *mikvah* (Fig. 4.2). For a little extra money, the *mikvah* can be finished with a waterproof stain or paint in order to improve its aesthetic

Sacred Water Architecture for Every Jew 57

FIGURE 4.1 "How to make a Mikvah," with a man at work in constructing the family's mikvah
Source: Miller 1930, 406

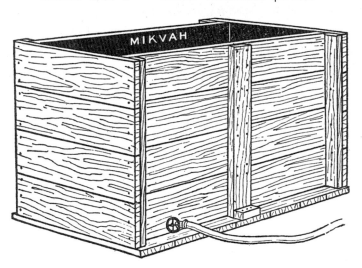

FIGURE 4.2 "Specification for Mikvah – construction and regulations, plan no. 1 – cost within $5.00," illustrating the absolute bare minimum for what can be vernacular Jewish sacred water architecture
Source: Miller 1930, 410

appeal, especially if galvanized sheet metal is used as an additional lining, which Miller highly recommends because it "makes the construction permanent and durable" (Miller 1930: 407). "For occasional and temporary" *mikvaot,* Miller provides instructions on how to make one for short-term use utilizing waterproof canvas and a wood frame (Miller 1930, 404). Temporary *mikvaot* can be foldable, flexible, and collapsible, but he does not provide any illustrations for this kind. Directions are also provided for how to properly move and reinstall the previously described DIY *mikvah,* so a Jewish family can bring it from one house to another when they need to relocate because they should never be without one.

Mikvah's in Disguise: Rabbi David Miller Hides His Architecture

Following a lengthy discussion on how to build your own *mikvah* on a minimalist budget, Miller delves into the siting of the structure within the Jewish home so that it is inconspicuous. No explanation is given, but it's assumed that the presence of a *mikvah* in a Jewish home is not to be public knowledge because of its association with a woman's menstruation cycle, which is a private matter. As mentioned previously, during the late nineteenth and early twentieth centuries, Jewish ritual observance in North America and Western Europe was waning because of declining religious interests.[7] During that time, communal *mikvaot* in New York and other American cities had developed a reputation for being unsanitary due to their overuse and the inability of their managers to adequately keep them hygienically clean (Joselit 1990). Thus, many Jews were not using *mikvoat*. His publication, *The Secret of the Jew,* was a means to stem the tide and increase *mikvah* interest in the private home. The book articulated *mikvaot* as a luxury that the Jewish bourgeoisie should enjoy. Miller's strategy manifests itself most significantly in illustrations where the *mikvah* architecture is camouflaged as household furnishings, such as drawers, refrigerators, and bookcases, and provides more expensive designs for *mikvaot* "harmoniously arranged in a living room" and "installed in a lady's private dressing room, or boudoir" (Miller 1930, 424–425) (Figs. 4.3 and 4.4).

Besides disguising *mikvaot* in plain sight, Miller provides examples of how to hide them in unassuming places, such as in a closet, under a stairway, and in a wall-bed closet. Within a closet, Miller describes how the "Mikvah is very useful and inconspicuous" and the wall-bed closet where "the Mikvah being easily accessible, yet concealed," and "in houses already built, not necessitating alteration or remodeling of the building in any way" (Miller 1930: 440–441). Miller also provides schematic floor plans for *mikvaot* hidden within closets, bedrooms, and bedroom-adjoining bathrooms in single-family houses and apartment buildings (Figs. 4.5 and 4.6).

From his proposal to have *mikvaot* installed within bathrooms adjoining bedrooms, Miller pivots his rhetoric from hiding and disguising them to that of visibly presenting them. He states how *mikvaot* can contribute to "a combination of artistic and religious inspiration" and that "Mikvah can be built into a modern luxurious bathroom" (Miller 1930, 455). He demonstrates his opinion as to what defines the preeminent functional bathroom, which includes a sink, bathtub, toilet, bidet, and – of course – a hybrid shower stall-*mikvah* (Fig. 4.7). Within such a room a Jewish person could get every facet of themselves comprehensively and holistically clean, including their front, rear, and exterior physical and spiritual inner-self.

However, not until Miller's Plan for "A Mikvah De Luxe" does he propose that a *mikvah's* architectural ornaments and placement within the home can be one of prestige and esteem. This is a model Miller argues that "the Mikvah should be treated… as a privilege. The room should be the best in the dwelling, and the mikvah adorned in accordance with its degree of

Sacred Water Architecture for Every Jew **59**

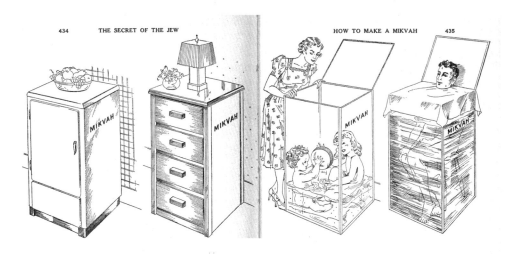

FIGURE 4.3 Rabbi David Miller's illustrations for mikvaot in disguise: a refrigerator (far left) and a drawer (middle left) along with how they could be used for immersion
Source: Miller 1930, 434–435

FIGURE 4.4 Rabbi David Miller's illustrations for mikvaot in disguise within a living room (top) and bedroom (bottom)
Source: Miller 1930, 447

60 Barry L. Stiefel

FIGURE 4.5 Rabbi David Miller's illustrations for hidden mikvaot: a closet (left) and under an under stair closet (right)
Source: Miller 1930, 440–441

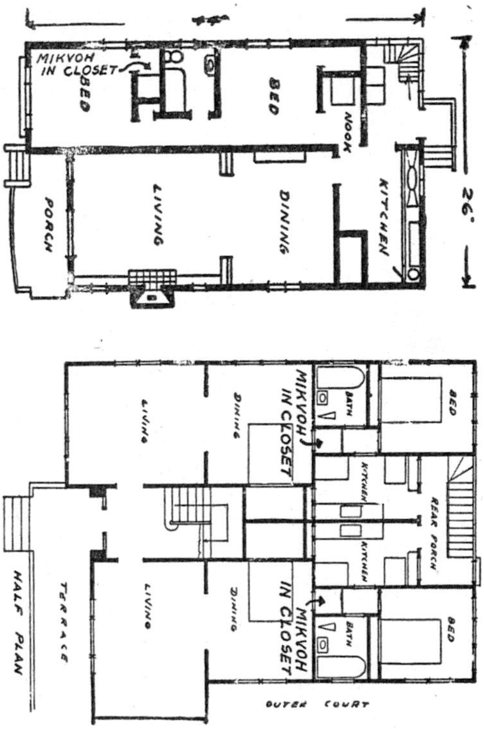

FIGURE 4.6 Rabbi David Miller's floor plans for mikvaot hidden in closets and bedrooms for single-family houses and apartment buildings
Source: Miller 1930, 453

FIGURE 4.7 Rabbi David Miller's illustrations for an ideal modern, luxurious bathroom for a Jewish family with every desired practical furnishing: a sink, bathtub, toilet, bidet, and hybrid shower stall-mikvah
Source: Miller 1930, 455

holiness" (Miller 1930, 458). This *mikvah* is not hidden and takes a very visible place within the room that has been deliberately designed for immersion purposes and no other use. There are no other competing furnishings within this *mikvah* schematic plan. Going a step further is "A Dignified Mikvah: A Shrine" for "those who see beauty in the Jewish religion and find inspiration in the solemn performance of the precept of the Tvilah" (Miller 1930: 457), which is even more architecturally ornamented than the previous plan. This *mikvah* is located at the top of a canopied stage, adorned with a banner that states "This is the Gate of the Lord: The Righteous Shall Enter Into it" (Miller 1930: 457). For the last and final proposed *mikvah* design is "A Sanctuary – A Monument to Family Purity," with no caption of explanation given (Miller 1930: 458). This crowning *mikvah* room illustration is extremely opulent for the early twentieth century, placed in a setting suggesting a secluded sunroom. Miller considers a Jewish family with such a *mikvah* to be noble and has written within the illustration's tile work, "Family Title of Nobility" (Miller 1930: 458) equal to the highest esteemed Jewish nobles of the time such as a Rothschild, Oppenheim, or Montefiore (Fig. 4.8). Considering Miller's previous concerns for economic frugality, he does not acknowledge that families that can afford opulent *mikvaot* are more economically privileged, though this can be assumed through the illustrations provided.

In summary, within *The Secret of the Jew*, Miller covers the full spectrum of how sacred architecture expresses the spiritual meaning of water as valued by Jews in North America and

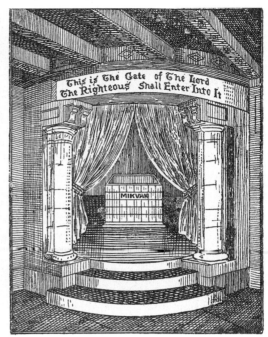

FIGURE 4.8 Rabbi David Miller's illustrations for luxurious mikvah rooms that are to be used exclusively for family ritual immersion purposes in increasing opulent order: "Mikvah De Luxe" (top left), "A Dignified Mikvah: A Shrine" (right), and "A Sanctuary: A Monument to Family Purity" (bottom left)
Source: Miller 1930, 457–458.

Western Europe during the early twentieth-century. With the ritual observance of *mikvaot* on the decline, much of *The Secret of the Jew* has conciliative rhetoric in hope that Jews who are on the fence regarding whether or not to use and have a *mikvah* will decide in favor, especially with Miller's descriptions of how such structures can be built economically and unobtrusively within the private home. The bulk of Miller's rhetoric indicates that it is better to have a plain, vernacular *mikvah* disguised or hidden within a private home than nothing at all, though grand private *mikvaot* at home or within large communal facilities are also possible. Despite the detailed directions for DIY *mikvaot* building on paper, Miller does not cover examples of actually-built *mikvaot* using his DIY manual. Neither is there information available on how many were built. While Miller practiced what he preached he did not provide his own *mikvah* as a case study. His personal mailing address was printed on the page cover of *The Secret of the Jew* – 127 Sheridan Road, Oakland, California – and within the book, he claims to have self-built an extravagant *mikvah* in 1918 according to the directions he shares for $30.00 ($535.00 in 2023). However, not enough information is provided to ascertain which of his design plans Miller used. Moreover, Miller's house no longer exists to study (according to Zillow, an online real estate marketplace company, the building currently standing at this address was built in 1993),[8] but we can glimpse into one intriguing example from early twentieth century Charleston, South Carolina.

Case Study: The Kirshtein Family's *Mikvah* of Charleston, South Carolina

During the early twentieth century there was a residence in Charleston, South Carolina with a private *mikvah* built according to Miller's directions at 43 Radcliffe Street by the Kirshtein family (Stiefel 2017).[9] The brothers "Sammy," Louis, and Sol Kirshtein, and their sister Ruth Kaplan, who grew up at that house from the 1920s through the 1940s claim that their father, Abraham Kirshtein constructed a *mikvah* in the first-floor bathroom of their two-story house. The house was built in 1852, so the *mikvah* followed Miller's directions for an already-built house. Abraham had immigrated from Kaluszyn, Poland in 1920 with a religious background, arriving in the United States, where he settled in Charleston. In Poland, he studied traditional Jewish slaughtering of animals under Rabbi Chaim Soloveitchik (1853–1918) so that he could work as a Kosher butcherer.[10] However, the Jewish community in Charleston was small and the demand for kosher meat was insufficient to make a living strictly through this means of employment. Abraham also peddled and eventually specialized in furniture, ultimately founding Dixie Furniture at 533 King Street in 1946 (Stiefel 2017). Later, Abraham studied at Rabbi Israel Meir Kagan's *yeshiva* in Radun, present-day Lithuania (1838–1933). Oddly, both highly esteemed rabbis Soloveitchik and Kagan discouraged private *mikvah* development that Miller encouraged. Rabbis Soloveitchik and Kagan also opposed using municipal water, whereas Miller had recommended it (Lesches 2001). Abraham was either unaware of his teachers' position on *mikvah* design or more interested in having a private *mikvah* of his own over Soloveitchik and Kagan's opinions (Stiefel 2017). Charleston may have been without a fit communal *mikvah* at this time too, though the more scrupulously religious Jews could have gone skinny dipping at the beach.

For the Kirshtein family's *mikvah*, Abraham used Miller's Yiddish edition of his book, *Seyfer Mikveh Yiśroel* (Miller 1923). The *mikvah* "looked like an indoor pool or hot tub" according to Sammy Kirshtein, with the tile lining and ladder.[11] Near the *mikvah* was a clawfoot bathtub used for sanitary bathing, which was done in preparation before *mikvah* immersion. Based on the description provided by Sammy, it appears that the *mikvah* design that Abraham used was based on Miller's plans in *The Secret of the Jew* (Miller 1930: 454). The only significant difference between the plan and the built *mikvah* is that the bathtub shown by Miller was flush on the ground instead of clawfoot (Fig. 4.9).

Abraham's wife, Edith, used the *mikvah* monthly (Stiefel 2017). Other close family members, especially aunts, also used it. Abraham and other Kirshtein men used the *mikvah* in preparation for important Jewish holidays, such as *Yom Kippur*, the Day of Atonement (Stiefel 2017). In 1940, Edith had begun menopause and the *mikvah* fell out of regular use.[12] Around 1941, Louis requested that the *mikvah* be changed back into a shower stall since he was not fond of "baths," not realizing how exceptional it was to have a private *mikvah* (Stiefel 2017). Since 1997, the house has belonged to Richard "Moby" Marks.[13] When Marks acquired the house, it had been significantly changed on the interior and the entire bathroom with the *mikvah* no longer existed, making it impossible to analyze this space in any further detail (Fig. 4.10).

In Cooper's reflection, private *mikvaot* built using *Seyfer Mikveh Yisroel* or *The Secret of the Jew* are challenging to identify since they were supposed to be convenient to build, and thus made them easy to disassemble. However, the memories of the Kirshtein family are telling in the way that some Jews, such as Abraham Kirshtein, made their own private *mikvaot* to have easier access to sacred water/rituals. Users of Miller's manuals also embedded their homes with a level of holiness through these special baths, which enhanced the tenants' spiritual purity (Stiefel 2017).

64 Barry L. Stiefel

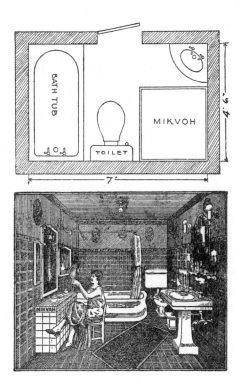

FIGURE 4.9 A rendering and floorplan for a bathroom with a mikvah and other amenities by Rabbi Miller, similar to what appeared at the Kirtshtein House at 43 Radcliffe Street
Source: Miller 1930, 454.

FIGURE 4.10 The vernacular exterior of 43 Radcliffe Street, Charleston, South Carolina, the home of the Kirshtein family during the early twentieth century and where Abraham Kirshtein built a private mikvah according to Rabbi Miller's directions
Photograph by the author.

Conclusion

During the early twentieth century, Miller led a bold initiative to encourage the broader use of *mikvah* when its practice was in decline. His solution was the development of manuals for Jews to make their own *mikvaot* at home. The buildings with *mikvaot* were important holy places as long as they were available and helped make Jews spiritually clean. Within Jewish tradition, beautifying a religious good deed can enhance the spirituality of the act. Thus, this is when Miller encouraged luxurious *mikvaot* in his *The Secret of the Jew*. In a metaphorical sense, Miller advocated for the peculiarity of sacred living water being accessible anywhere as the "secret of the Jew."

Miller's ideas have had little if any impact on contemporary *mikvaot* design. With his passing on the eve of World War II, private *mikvaot* for the masses were simply not on the minds of American Jews. European Jewry was decimated due to the Holocaust, so there were too few who were interested. In Israel, the other major metropole of world Jewry, the government widely developed public *mikvaot* that made it available for all who wanted access.[14] Until the scholarly interest of Cooper emerged in the 2000s, Miller's DIY *mikvah* proposal was largely forgotten. Indeed, this can be observed at Charleston's Brith Sholom Beth Israel synagogue, where the Ruth Kirshtein Kaplan Memorial *Mikvah* Fund supports communal *mikvah* use instead of private DIY examples, like her father Abraham Kirshtein had built. However, with the spread of a DIY movement in architecture and sustainability in the twenty-first century (Broome 2014), Miller's ideas can be inspirational for Jews in the present and future to consider – and they can be mindful of the water meter and tap water complexities in order to navigate around these issues if it is of concern.

Notes

1. "Vayikra - Leviticus – Chapter 11," *Chabad.org*, 2021. https://www.chabad.org/library/bible_cdo/aid/9912/jewish/Chapter-11.htm#v37. Accessed January 6, 2022.
2. Hoffman, Miriam. "Mikveh Design: The Architecture Of A Ritual," *The New York Jewish Week*, June 14, 2017. https://jewishweek.timesofisrael.com/mikveh-design-the-architecture-of-a-ritual/. Accessed September 10, 2021.
3. Safier, Dovi and Yehuda Geberer. "From Kovno to California." *Mishpacha: Jewish Family Weekly*. April 14, 2021. https://mishpacha.com/from-kovno-to-california/. Accessed June 3, 2021.
4. Klapper, Aryeh. "Bathtub Mikvaot and The Curious History of a Halakhic Libel." *Lehrhaus*. June 15, 2020. https://www.thelehrhaus.com/scholarship/7267/. Accessed June 3, 2021.
5. Klapper, ibid.
6. Levine, Yitzchok. "Rabbi David Miller: Forgotten Fighter For Orthodoxy." *Jewish Press*. September 13 2006. https://www.jewishpress.com/indepth/front-page/rabbi-david-miller-forgotten-fighter-for-orthodoxy/2006/09/13/. Accessed June 4, 2021.
7. Ibid.
8. Zillow, "127 Sheridan Road, Oakland, California, 94618," *Zillow*, June 2021. https://www.zillow.com/homedetails/127-Sheridan-Rd-Oakland-CA-94618/24812344_zpid/. Accessed June 4, 2021.
9. The information on the Kirshtein *mikvah* once at 43 Radcliffe Street comes from a personal interview with Sammy Kirshtein, Louis Kirshtein, and Saul Kirshtein, May 15, 2015; phone interviews with Ruth Kaplan and Jeffery Kaplan, May 18 and 22, 2015, and Richard "Moby" Marks, June 16, 2015; a correspondence with Levi Cooper, "Researching a historic *mikvah* in Charleston, South Carolina" (levicoops@gmail.com), May 22, 2015. I am also indebted to Jonathan Sarna of Brandeis University regarding information on Rabbi David Miller and his work about the development of private *mikvaot*.
10. Ibid.
11. Ibid.
12. Ibid.

13. Richard "Moby" Marks is an Adjunct Professor in the joint College of Charleston/Clemson University Graduate Program in Historic Preservation and colleague of the author.
14. Jeremy Sharon, "Two-thirds of mikvaot don't have operating license," *The Jerusalem Post,* October 21, 2020. https://www.jpost.com/israel-news/two-thirds-of-mikvas-dont-have-operating-license-646456. Accessed April 1, 2022.

References

Broome, Jon. 2014. *The Green Self-Build Book: How to Design and Building Your Own Eco-home.* Totnes, UK: Green Books, 2014.

Caro, Y., Ganzfried, S. & Goldin, H. E. *Code of Jewish Law: Kitzur Shulhan Aruh.* Volume 4. New York: Hebrew Publishing Company, 1961.

Cooper, Levi. "D.I.Y. Mivkeh: The Challenge of Encouraging Commitment," *Jewish Educational Leadership,* 9: no. 2 (Winter 2011): 58–63.

———. "Elias Levi: The Rangoon Rabbi." *Jewish Educational Leadership,* 13: no. 1 (Winter 2014): 58–62.

Hoffmeier, James K. *The Archaeology of the Bible.* Oxford, UK: Lion Scholar, 2019.

Joselit, Jenna W. *New York's Jewish Jews: The Orthodox Community in the Interwar Years.* Bloomington: Indiana University Press, 1990.

Lesches, Schneur Z. *Understanding Mikvah: An Overview of Mikvah Construction.* Montreal, QC: Kollel Menachem, 2001.

Miller, David. *Seyfer Miḳveh Yiśroel.* Oakland, CA: D. Miller, 1923.

———. *The Secret of the Jew: His Life – His Family.* Oakland, CA: D. Miller, 1930.

———. *The Secret of Happiness: How to Enjoy Life.* Oakland, CA: D. Miller, 1938.

Rosenberg, Yehuda Y. *Mikveh Yehuda.* Toronto, ON: Y. Yehuda, 1918.

Stiefel, Barry L. "Beyond Synagogues and Cemeteries: The Built Environment as an Aspect of Vernacular Jewish Material Culture in Charleston, South Carolina," *American Jewish History,* 101: no. 2 (2017): 197–236.

Westheimer, Dr. Ruth K. & Mark, Jonathan. *Heavenly Sex: Sexuality and the Jewish Tradition.* New York: NY, 2020

PART II
Water as Material Culture and Place Making

5
ARCHITECTURE, WATER, AND THE SACRED IN THE SANCTUARY OF THE GREAT GODS ON SAMOTHRACE, GREECE

Andrew Farinholt Ward, Jessica Paga, and Bonna D. Wescoat

The Sanctuary of the Great Gods on the Greek island of Samothrace (Fig. 5.1) was sacred to divinities whose secret rites of initiation promised a very particular blessing: protection at sea (Lewis 1959: 226–241). The full identity of these gods remains slippery, but it is certain that they were plural, powerful, and deeply connected to the natural world (Bremmer 2014; Bowden 2010; Burkert 1993; Cole 1984; Lehmann 1998). Their sanctuary, set facing the sea in a declivity carved by torrents pouring down a mile-high mountain range, was defined by the waters that surrounded and flowed through it. These unpredictable natural forces, from

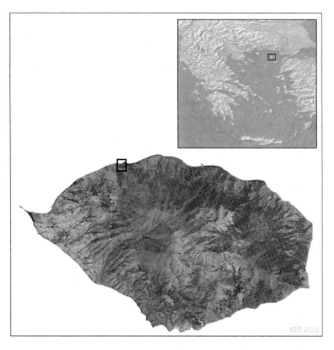

FIGURE 5.1 Map of Samothrace with the location of the Sanctuary of the Great Gods indicated (© American Excavations Samothrace)

DOI: 10.4324/9781003358824-8

the currents that governed access to the island to the seasonal storms that tore through the site, enhanced and magnified the sanctuary's divine aura. Far from treating them merely as natural obstacles to surmount, ancient architects honored and exploited the evocative potential of the deep watercourses in the sanctuary to serve as physical and spiritual passages, creating an environment that married natural and anthropogenic forces in an awe-inspiring expression of sacred energy. With these factors in mind, we examine how architecture and water played off one another to shape the visitors' kinesthetic experience within the sacred space.

While the secret initiatory rites were never divulged, excavation, architectural study, and digital modeling have revealed how the interaction of architecture and water—actual and symbolic—shaped the initiate's kinesthetic experience and thus was central to the transformative efficacy of the cult of the Great Gods (Fig. 5.2). At the heart of such an investigation

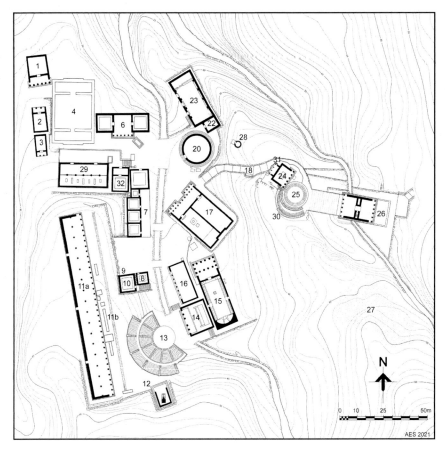

FIGURE 5.2 Samothrace. Sanctuary of the Great Gods. Restored plan of the sanctuary in early 1st century C.E. 1, 2, 3: Unidentified Late Hellenistic buildings; 4: Unfinished early Hellenistic building (Building A); 6: Milesian Dedication; 7, 8, 10: Dining rooms; 9: Archaistic niche; 11: Stoa; 12: Nike Monument; 13: Theater; 14: Altar Court; 15: Hieron; 16: Hall of Votive Gifts; 17: Hall of Choral Dancers; 18: Sacred Way; 20: Rotunda of Arsinoe II; 22: Sacristy; 23: Anaktoron; 24: Dedication of Philip III and Alexander IV; 25: Theatral Circle; 26: Propylon of Ptolemy II; 27: South Nekropolis: 28: Doric Rotunda; 29: Neorion; 30: Stepped Retaining Wall; 31: Ionic Porch; 32: Hestiatorion (© American Excavations Samothrace)

are the two torrents that surged through the sanctuary, converging, along with a third, as they emptied into the North Aegean Sea. In the Hellenistic period (323–331 BCE), architects transformed these water-carved ravines into monuments that concretized the spiritual power of water through human action and memory. When flowing, the water became a full partner in the ritual-architectural matrix. In drier periods, the massive walls defining the watercourses retained a powerful symbolic resonance. The deep channels and limited crossings were physical reminders that water was instrumental to the authority of the Great Gods. Architects deployed buildings, hardscaping, and crossings over these torrents to mediate access to cult facilities, orchestrate view sheds, and create zones of liminality and separation throughout the sanctuary. Intricate schemes moving water to, through, and around buildings crucial to the site's initiation rites emphasize the fundamental role of water in this famed Hellenistic sacred cult.

Water, the Island, and the Gods

The cult of the Great Gods and the rites of its festival, known as the *mysteria*, were predicated on the successful relationship of humans to water. Although enigmatic still today, scholars agree that the Great Gods (*Megaloi Theoi*) were deities with strong connections to the natural world (Blakely 2016; Burkert 1993; Clinton 2003; Cole 1984; Lehmann 1998; Lewis 1959). Ancient references describe a Great Mother figure that commanded wild animals, was worshipped at rocky outcrops and weeping fissures, and was revered as one of the oldest gods of the ancient Mediterranean. Her attendant deities had links to the mountainous landscape of the island, the fertility of the earth, and its many waterways. The *Dioskoroi*, often associated with the Great Gods, were revered by sailors and those navigating by the stars. The Great Gods and their attendants thus had connections both aerial and chthonic, the twin sources of water.

The tension between the protective power of the gods and the elemental forces of the surrounding waters constituted one of the primary sacred relationships around which the sanctuary was configured. Less than 178 km² (69 mi²), Samothrace was dominated by the hulking wooded peak of Mount Saos, which rises 1,611 meters (5,285 feet) above sea level, a worthy vantage for Poseidon during the Trojan War (*Iliad* 13: 10-20). Ridgelines descending from the northern slopes of the mountain flanked the sanctuary to the east and west, funneling waters from winter rains, spring snowmelt, and intermittent powerful storms. The site's rugged topography was shaped by three ravines carved by the resultant seasonal torrents (Baillet, et al. 2021). In antiquity as today, the sudden intensity of storms could swell the torrents and cause catastrophic flooding. Therefore, managing the water required significant thought and investment.

A precondition for anyone seeking the protection of the Great Gods was the sea voyage, both coming to and going from Samothrace (Blakely 2016; Wescoat 2017b). Prospective initiates journeyed to the island between the sailing months of April to November (Dimitrova 2008). Upon arrival, even if the seasonal torrents ran dry, visitors would be reminded of their power by the deep channels that were carved into the land. Vast in scale, primordial in age, and volatile in real time, these watercourses were integral to establishing and maintaining the sacrality of the sanctuary. The three torrent-carved ravines that helped articulate the boundaries and overall shape of the sanctuary were formidable natural features that architects and worshippers respected (Wescoat 2012; Wescoat et al. 2020). While they imposed restrictions on the monumental elaboration of the sanctuary, they also opened avenues for creative architectural design, as Hellenistic architects endeavored to craft a sacred landscape out of and around a naturally evocative one.

The eastern and central ravines particularly stand out for their architectonic status and pivotal role. They were shaped with massive polygonal retaining walls composed of basalt boulders to become monuments in their own right and powerful agents in the human experience of the space. Buildings were positioned in, around, and across these channels, displaying the spiritual force of the water. The integrated and symbiotic relationship between the torrents and the built environment enhanced the sacred experience in the Sanctuary of the Great Gods and facilitated the efficacy of the secret rites.

Building with Water: The Entrance to the Sanctuary

The sanctuary lay west of the ancient city, across a deep ravine that physically and psychologically magnified the separation of secular and sacred spaces. This eastern ravine and the torrent that carved it were thus the first defining features of the sanctuary visitors encountered, and they controlled over a half millennium of its architectural development. The original crossing was rustic—the best place where the torrent could be forded—but its architectural importance was rapidly signaled by the position of the Theatral Circle on its rim (Fig. 5.2, no. 25), as well as the orientation of the buildings and sculptures toward those approaching from the opposite bank (Wescoat 2017a,b), (Fig. 5.2, nos. 24, 30).

With the construction of the Propylon of Ptolemy II (Fig. 5.2, no. 26; Fig. 5.3) in 285–281 BCE the water crossing became an essential part of the architectural fabric (Frazer 1990).

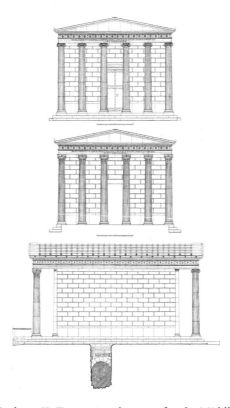

FIGURE 5.3 Propylon of Ptolemy II. Top: restored eastern facade; Middle: restored western facade; Bottom: restored southern elevation (© American Excavations Samothrace)

Architecture, Water, and the Sacred 73

The building's main function was to welcome worshippers into and usher them out of the sanctuary. Given the lack of a permanent wall around the sanctuary, the edifice also served as a physical marker of the metaphysical shift between the sacred and the profane (Wescoat 2017a). To join the building and natural boundary, the builders created an artificial channel with megalithic basalt boulder retaining walls that diverted the natural torrent through a barrel-vaulted tunnel in the western foundations of the Propylon. Among the earliest barrel vaults of the pre-Roman Mediterranean, its walls rested on basalt foundations and were of graduated rustication, progressing from a rough boulder-like appearance in the lowest courses to a nearly smooth surface at the apex of the arch.

Multiple features of the Propylon further dramatized the experience of crossing the ravine and torrent. Its foundations projected into the torrent valley so that the western façade rose high above the terrain, and the descent into the sunken orchestra of the Theatral Circle became much steeper. The marble edifice above consisted of two hexastyle prostyle porches—the one facing the city Ionic, and the one facing the sanctuary Corinthian—divided by a door wall with a single narrow door that funneled visitors in and out of the sanctuary. Traditionally, the door and door wall of a propylon signifies the boundary between sacred and secular space. In the instance of the Propylon of Ptolemy II, that transition extended into the western chamber where the worshippers passed over the tunnel and water feature beneath. From this high vantage, the visitor then descended the steep, stepped causeway that crossed over the rest of the eastern ravine to come into the Theatral Circle on the Eastern Hill, the first ritual station fully within the *temenos* (Fig. 5.4).

The entrance complex marshaled both anthropogenic and natural features—a monumental propylon and a redirected watercourse—to mark the liminal space at the edge of the sanctuary. Architects and engineers harnessed their full capabilities to integrate architecture

FIGURE 5.4 Digital model of the monuments of the sanctuary's Eastern Hill, looking south along the eastern ravine (© American Excavations Samothrace)

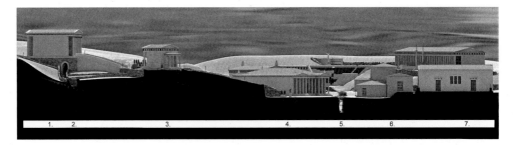

FIGURE 5.5 Cross-section of Sanctuary of the Great Gods, derived from the digital model. 1: Propylon of Ptolemy II; 2: Eastern Ravine; 3: Theatral Circle and Dedication of Philip III and Alexander IV; 4: Central Valley and Hall of Choral Dancers; 5: Central Ravine; 6: Lower Terrace, Western Hill 7: Intermediate Terrace, Western Hill (© American Excavations Samothrace)

and water into one physical and symbolic experience (Fig. 5.5). The boldness of this construction from a hydraulic engineering perspective cannot be underestimated. The arrangement endured for some four centuries before the power of earth and water triumphed in the early 2nd century CE. Following an earthquake that destroyed the Theatral Circle, the torrent found its earlier course, and a new bridge was constructed to replace the causeway (Frazer 1990; Wescoat 2017a).

The Architectural Shape of Water: The Central Valley

Just as the waters of the eastern ravine shaped the architectural elaboration of the Eastern Hill, the central ravine defined the heart of the sanctuary in the valley below. This watercourse ran northwesterly through the southern portion of the sanctuary, carving a deep division between the Altar Court (Fig. 5.2, no. 14) in the valley and the theater (Fig. 5.2, no. 13) that climbed the Western Hill. The channel then turned northward through the remainder of the sanctuary, separating the main valley from the Western Hill. The central ravine reflects and engenders the ritual divide between these two locations as well: to the east, the valley was carpeted with ritual buildings and altars, while to the west rose the edifices for post-initiation gathering, celebration, and honors.

Intensive study of the natural and anthropogenic features of the central ravine has deepened our understanding of the ancient channel (Baillet et al. 2021). Two distinct phases of retaining walls survived: the first phase, made of megalithic boulders, ca. 340–280 BCE; the second, characterized by limestone blocks and small boulders bonded with concrete, is likely from the 1st century CE (McCredie et al. 1992) (Figs. 5.5 and 5.6). New excavations demonstrate that both iterations followed the same slightly curving course. The width of the channel, where preserved, varies from ca. 2.25–3.0 meters (7.4–9.8 feet). While the walls survive to a height of 3.6 meters (11.8 feet) in places today, to meet the ancient ground level around the Rotunda of Arsinoe (where the ravine is at its widest) the retaining walls of the channel would have needed to reach an impressive height of 6 meters (19.6 feet) (Wescoat et al. 2020).

The architectural elaboration of the torrent's course was a manifestation of its long-standing centrality to the sanctuary and its cult. The earliest evidence of cult activity in the sanctuary,

FIGURE 5.6 Ancient retaining walls of the Central Ravine. Left: earlier dry-laid basalt boulder retaining, western bank south of the theater; Right: later concrete and limestone retaining wall, western bank opposite the Rotunda of Arsinoe (© American Excavations Samothrace)

dating from the 7th through 5th centuries BCE is clustered near the banks of the torrent (Lehmann and Spittle 1964; Lehmann and Spittle 1982). As the sacred hub around which the space grew, the central watercourse should be considered the first—and most crucial—monument in the entire sanctuary. The power of water—among other factors—may well have indicated the presence of the divine that spurred the early inhabitants to consecrate the area. From the earliest phases of ritual practice, worshippers would have witnessed the power of this waterway and would have been compelled to find ways to interact with it.

The centrality of this torrent is dual: it gives natural shape to the landscape of the sacred heart of the sanctuary while showing the volatile forces that can be conjured by divine power. Its bridging has several possible interpretations, from an attempt to attenuate its destructive force to a way to harness and direct the power of the gods as made manifest in water. The growing number of buildings that came to cluster along the central sanctuary attest to these variable but inclusive perceptions: the Rotunda of Arsinoe (Fig. 5.2, no. 20), a brilliant benefaction by a Ptolemaic queen and the first edifice one encountered at the bottom of the Sacred Way, moving into the sacred heart of the sanctuary; the Hall of Choral Dancers (Fig. 5.2, no. 17), an enigmatic and impressive two-part building that dominated the central sanctuary and may have served as the focal point of initiation; the Hieron (Fig. 5.2, no. 15), a highly decorated and unusual edifice that backed onto the southern part of the watercourse; the Hall of Votive Gifts (Fig. 5.2, no. 16) where costly dedicatory items may have been displayed and stored; and, the Altar Court (Fig. 5.2, no. 14), which faced and communicated with the theater (Fig. 5.2, no. 13), the two structures both linked and separated by the ravine. The placement and orientation of all these buildings were dictated by the course of the channel (Fig. 5.7). In this way, the sacred water flowing through the space activated its architectural embellishment, implicitly linking the power of water with the initiation rites that occurred within and around the buildings.

FIGURE 5.7 Digital model of the reconstructed Sanctuary, looking north along the central ravine (© American Excavations Samothrace)

Water in, Around, and Through Buildings

The integration of the eastern ravine's watercourse into the structure of the Propylon itself was magnified by the installation of water features near the forecourt of the structure. In many Greek sanctuaries, wells or basins for purificatory waters would be placed at entrances, so that worshipers could cleanse themselves before approaching their gods (Ginouvès 1962; Pimpl 1997). Here, two lines of lead-bound terracotta piping were discovered immediately in front of the Propylon's forecourt, meeting in a T-joint (Frazer 1990) (Fig. 5.8). This pipeline brought water under pressure, most likely to one or more fountains, which would have served

FIGURE 5.8 Propylon of Ptolemy II. Area east of forecourt with extant pipe system, looking south (© American Excavations Samothrace)

a similar purificatory purpose. The east-west incline of the pipes suggests that water then drained away into the ravine. The source of this water system is unknown.

The fusion of water and architecture was not limited to the sanctuary's entrance. In the central valley, terracotta pipes lead from the interior of the Altar Court. The original excavators hypothesized they served to wash away the blood of sacrificial victims (Lehmann and Spittle 1964). Channels formed by a stone-lined basin, have been associated with mid-5th century BCE ritual activity around the so-called Sacred Rock, a natural basalt outcropping that is itself thought to have been washed with libations which would flow off its surface into a nearby drainage channel (Ilieva 2012; Lehmann 1998). Early excavations uncovered evidence of a terracotta pipeline predating the Rotunda of Arsinoe, which could be related to this same early installation (Lehmann 1950). These interpretations reflect the challenges of working with tantalizingly small amounts of evidence. Certainly, piping water from one place to another had purpose; pipes and channels are our best evidence that cleansing and purification must have played a role in these central spaces and cult buildings.

On the western side of the Sanctuary, water was also a critical component, but more in the service of post-initiation activities. The three distinct phases of terracotta water systems on the Stoa plateau (Fig. 5.2, no. 11), which brought water to the west side of the building, must have served for food preparation and perhaps sanitation (McCredie 1965). A large drainage pipe running beneath the diazoma of the Theater likely helped control stormwater from rushing down the theater slope (Bouzek and Ondřejová 1985).

Our research on the role of water in the sanctuary has led to one disappointment. Based on water wear in the building and the discovery of pipes leading from the hillside behind, earlier archaeologists Karl Lehmann and Alec Daykin hypothesized that the famed Nike of Samothrace stood within a monumental fountain (Fig. 5.9), including an upper basin in

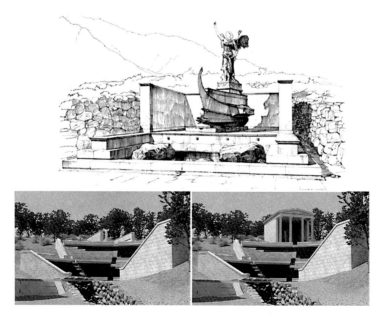

FIGURE 5.9 Nike Monument. Top: reconstruction of monument as fountain (drawing by A. Daykin; © Cindy Allenby); Bottom Left: digital reconstruction of the Nike in an unroofed peribolos; Bottom Right: digital reconstruction of the Nike in a roofed structure (© American Excavations Samothrace)

which the Nike landed upon the prow of a warship, and a lower basin containing large basalt boulders within a natural spring. Set against a backdrop of framing basalt boulder retaining walls and the mountainous interior of the island, such a structure would have created a dramatic environmental sculpture centered on water (Lehmann and Lehmann 1973). The pipes found on the hillside behind the monument, however, are now understood to have directed water to the nearby Stoa, and the subterranean water wear in the purported basin is post-antique. We must now abandon the idea of a fountain in favor of a building, but whether it was open or roofed remains unclear (Clinton et al. 2020; Wescoat et al. 2020). Yet, the monument retains many allusions to water, from the naval associations in the prow to its orientation in line with the central torrent, and its false lion-head waterspouts. The water itself, however, must be conjured in memory.

Water and Sacred Experience in the Sanctuary

Although we will likely never know what happened during initiation, we can establish some of the circumstances that informed the cult in order to explore how the intersection of built fabric and water affected the worshipper's experience. Initiation was a collective experience. Because the *mysteria* could be held multiple times during the sailing season, likely when a sufficient group arrived on the island, the number of participants must have been highly variable (Dimitrova 2008). We know from lists of names that the initiate could undergo both levels of initiation, the *myesis* and *epopteia*, during a single trip to the island; thus, the architecture would need to be responsive to both rites (Clinton 2017; Dimitrova 2008; Lehmann 1998). Initiation was open to all who did not bear unresolved blood guilt, regardless of gender, class, free or enslaved status, or ethnicity (Cole 1984; Dimitrova 2008; Lehmann 1998). The rites took place mostly at night. Dining facilities and sympotic pottery shapes underscored the centrality of feasting as a part of the experience, even if not one of the transformative rites. Bearing these factors in mind, we look to how architecture and water intersect and play off one another to shape the initiates' kinesthetic experience at the height of the sanctuary's operation in the Hellenistic period.

Most Greek sanctuaries exploit upward trajectories, but entrance into the Sanctuary of the Great Gods was one of staged and circuitous descents; the movement of worshippers mirrored the flow of the water torrents through the sacred landscape itself. In our reconstruction, prospective initiates gathered before, entered, and then passed through the Propylon of Ptolemy II (Frazer 1990). Its narrow doorway slowed and funneled the visitors through the building curating a visitor's passage much as the architects managed the passage of water running beneath their feet. The initiates could then spread out and regain a steady flow once through, much as water naturally spreads across a horizontal plane when no longer confined. In this way, the prospective initiates' descent of the steep, stepped causeway to the Theatral Circle further mimics the way water trips down a mountain path. From there, the descent of the Sacred Way pushed around an enormous bedrock outcrop before it cut as a deep paved pathway into the steep hillside, twisting and reconfiguring as it encountered features on the slope, just as the torrents cut their own channels into the earth. A narrow opening between buildings gave on to the valley of the central sanctuary, where the prospective initiates could finally slow, spread, and regroup their energy as they began the main rites of initiation.

This procession took place at night (Lewis 1959: 67–68, 73, 169, 200, 229e), and likely involved ablutions and admonitions in the courtyard before the Propylon and blindfolded and disorienting preliminary rites such as *thronosis* in the Theatral Circle.[1] While not a chasm, when lit by torch, lamp, or moonlight, the magnitude of the eastern ravine over which worshippers passed and skirted around would have been frighteningly exaggerated. It marked a profound demarcation between the space of the polis and the place of the gods. Such constructed resonances would have been even more pronounced when the torrent flowed with cascading water. Even if unseen during the nighttime events, its auditory resonances would have enhanced the beginning of the initiation rites (Rogers 2021).

Once in the narrow central valley, the path of the initiate opened to a small triangular *plateia* bounded to the south by the Hall of Choral Dancers, which surely played a central role in the rites of initiation (Clinton 2017; Wescoat 2017a). To the northeast stood the Rotunda of Arsinoe II, with its unparalleled architectural design but whose function remains obscure (McCredie et al. 1992). To the west lay a long stretch of the monumentalized central ravine (Fig. 5.2). Excavations in the 1990s demonstrated that the Hall of Choral Dancers, which faced northwestward and consisted of two chambers connected by a winged porch, spanned the entire width of the valley. Its northwest corner touches the boulder wall of the central channel and its southeast corner cuts deeply into the hillside (Fig. 5.2, no. 17).

The Hall of Choral Dancers was surely a primary destination, but to reach any other part of the sanctuary, including the sacred buildings to the south and the performance, feasting, and dedicatory structures to the west, worshippers had to cross back and forth over the massive central channel. We once considered but rejected the idea that the entire ravine was covered from the theater to the Rotunda of Arsinoe. The centrality of this water feature to the cult, as well as the impracticality of creating a continuous covering over significant drops in elevation and across a channel of varying width, favor a more restricted system of bridges. Only one bridge survives in the archaeological record, but several more are needed to reach key cult buildings in the sanctuary such as the Hieron and the Altar Court. We propose that the act of crossing back and forth over this watercourse kinesthetically anchored the centrality of the torrent—with its actual and remembered bursts of energy during and after storms—to the sacredness of the place and the power of its gods.

The surviving crossing is located just west of the Rotunda of Arsinoe and over the stretch of channel that frames the triangular *plateia* described above. Sited at the broadest point of the channel, the surviving segment of the Roman era retaining wall measures as much as 3 meters thick (more than 9 feet), which was substantially greater than the surviving retaining wall elsewhere in the channel. Created by a mass of concrete and rubble behind the limestone facing, this reinforced section of wall very likely served as the abutment for a bridge. A series of projecting headers with cuttings for fasteners on the face of the wall would have supported the bridging elements. As there are no surviving elements suggestive of vaulting, a timber beam bridge is the most likely reconstruction. It aligns with the path and staircase leading to the intermediate and lower terraces on the Western Hill and may have been constructed with this region in mind. Only after crossing this major bridge, however, or a smaller one near the northwest corner of the Hall of Choral Dancers, could worshippers progress southwards along a narrow path on the western bank of the channel. Once they had passed the northwest corner of the Hall of Choral Dancers, the magnificent but sequestered hexastyle prostyle Doric façade of the Hieron would come into view on the opposite side. The procession would need to cross back over the channel to reach the northern entrance of the Hieron.

Once again, a tight triangular area, with its longest leg being the water channel, served as a gathering space that funneled the worshippers toward the façade of the building and the remains of what might have been an altar (Lehmann 1969). Unfortunately, the ancient retaining walls are most destroyed in this section of the central ravine, so the location of this crossing remains hypothetical. Modeling visitor's movements using Unity 3D software suggests optimal positions for crossings, in addition to the one west of the Rotunda, that would have provided access to this secondary sacred zone to the south of the Hall of Choral Dancers (Wescoat et al. 2020).

After participating in whatever rites of worship or revelations that took place within the Hieron,[2] the initiates could depart the way they entered or through side doors on the flanks of the building. From the latter, they could go south to a corridor behind the Hieron, which led westward to a short flight of stairs up to a terrace that dramatically opened into the space between the Altar Court and the theater on the opposite side of the monumentalized water channel. The two buildings were situated at nearly identical elevations and faced one another. Their spatial communication demands some means of direct access, either by culvert or bridge (Fig. 5.10). Given the close proximity of the theater's orchestra to the channel and the effectiveness of the Altar Court's colonnaded and inscribed façade to serve as a backdrop, we imagine this southern-most crossing over the water channel also served as a potential performance space.

The architectural and kinesthetic fulcrum defined by the crossing at this place in the terrain also happens to be a crucial point in the path of the torrent. Uphill, the path of the channel is hidden from view because of its strong eastward bend. To the visitor approaching from downstream or the Hieron, the water would have seemed to have sprung directly from the landscape, the scattered basalt boulders coalescing into the rustic boulder retaining walls. Here, bridging was facilitated not only by the channel's narrow width but also by a sudden drop in elevation that sent the water below the ground level between the Altar

FIGURE 5.10 Digital model of the reconstructed Sanctuary, looking southeast with the theater in foreground and Altar Court in background (© American Excavations Samothrace)

Court and the theater, where, after another elevation drop, the channel turned northwards. These cascades served a practical function in slowing the speed of the water at the vulnerable places where the channel changed course. Water falling over these cascades could also generate an auditory backdrop for those in the theater or partaking in rituals within the Altar Court—babbling or roaring depending on how engorged the torrent was. The sound of water played an important role in the Greek imagination as expressed in Greek poetry; a torrent's crashing sound evokes emotive outbursts (Lather 2019). Mystery cults made careful use of manmade and natural sounds (Petridou 2018). On Samothrace, water would play on more than just an initiate's sight.

From this southernmost area of the sanctuary, the visitors had a choice of direction. They could proceed northward along the west bank of the central channel to the many dining facilities that hugged this side of the valley (Fig. 5.2, nos. 6, 7, 8, 10, 32). Or they could ascend the theater to the plateau above, where the 104-meter-long Stoa provided a shelter, a place of display, and a magnificent vista over the central sanctuary and northward to the Aegean. At the top of the theater, they would come upon the greatest naval sculpture of antiquity: the Winged Victory alighting on the prow of a warship. They surely would notice the strong disjunction between the orientation of the statue and the enframing building, for the building faces onto the terrace, but the statue is turned obliquely to bisect the theater and follow the course of the central channel northward to the sea. In either trajectory, initiates could all progress further north to admire the Neorion, which housed an entire warship, again emphasizing the links between seafaring, victory, and the power of the Great Gods (Fig. 5.2, no. 29).

The central watercourse bisected and controlled the sanctuary throughout its entire length. For the most part, the ritual hub of the sanctuary lay on the eastern side of the valley, but sacred structures such as the Hieron could only be reached from the western side. Most of the performative and feasting facilities were on the western side, but they opened onto the waterway. The need for crossings compelled initiates to move through the sacred landscape along relatively fixed passages as each crossing mediated access to an otherwise sequestered part of the space. The channel was thus both a barrier and a liminal entity, for in those seconds in which one hovered on the bridge, suspended over the abyss-like channel, not only one's place but one's existence hung in the balance. Moving back and forth over the channel thus generated a sequence of discrete encounters that coalesced into the experience of initiation.

Conclusion

On Samothrace, water—wild, changeable, and dangerous, but also life-giving, cleansing, and energetic—lay at the heart of the Sanctuary of the Great Gods. Our multidisciplinary approach combining archaeological investigation, architectural study, and digital reconstruction demonstrates that the Samothracians valued water as a principal force shaping the tangible space of the sanctuary and thus the human experience of the cult of the Great Gods. They augmented the physical and symbolic presence of water by manipulating the surrounding land, channeling the water passages, and constructing buildings that relied on the torrents for their form, orientation, and meaning. Massive construction shaped the eastern and central watercourses into architectural monuments in their own right. Equal in agency and intervention to the more traditional buildings within the sanctuary, these channels are, in fact, the longest-lived monuments within the sanctuary. Using 3D modeling to reconstruct the path of prospective initiates and visitors moving through the sanctuary emphasizes how encounters with water repeatedly shaped the experience at key moments of passage. Together, water and built environment functioned in symbiosis to shape the sacred landscape, making it, experientially, at once vast and intimate, constrained and open, rustic and refined. In this environment, the Samothracian mysteries flourished.

Notes

1. For ablutions, see Frazer 1990; admonitions, see Wescoat 2017; *thronosis*, see Clinton 2003.
2. The function of the Hieron is under investigation, now that we identify the Hall of Choral Dancers as the primary place for initiation. For original identification as the hall for the second level of initiation, the *epopteia*: Lehmann 1969; Lehmann 1998. For the Hall of Choral Dancers: Wescoat 2015; Clinton 2017. For a recent proposal that the Hieron functioned as a hestiatorion temple: Clinton 2017.

References

Baillet, Vincent, Ioannis Poularakis, and Andrew Farinholt Ward. "Photogrammetric Modeling and the Central Ravine of the Sanctuary of the Great Gods, Samothrace." *Digital Applications in Archaeology and Cultural Heritage* 20 (2021).

Blakely, Sandra. "Maritime Risk and Ritual Responses: Sailing with the Gods in the Ancient Mediterranean." In *The Sea in History – The Ancient World*, edited by C. Buchet and P. de Souza, 362–379. Paris: Association Oceanides, 2016.

Bouzek, Jan, and Iva Ondřejová. *Samothrace: 1923/1927/1978. The Results of the Czechoslovak Excavation in 1927 Conducted by A. Salač and J. Nepomucký and the Unpublished Results of the 1923 Franco-Czechoslovak Excavations Conducted by A. Salač and F. Chapouthier*. Prague: Univerzita Karlova, 1985.

Bowden, Hugh. *Mystery Cults of the Ancient World*. Princeton, N.J.: Princeton University Press, 2010.

Bremmer, Jan N. *Initiation into the mysteries of the ancient world*. Berlin: De Gruyter, 2014.

Burkert, Walter. "Concordia Discours: The Literary and the Archaeological Evidence on the Sanctuary of Samothrace." In *Greek Sanctuaries, New Approaches*, edited by N. Marinatos and R. Hägg, 178–91. London and New York: Routledge, 1993.

Clinton, Kevin. "Stages of Initiation in the Eleusinian and Samothracian Mysteries." In *Greek Mysteries: The Archaeology and Ritual of Ancient Greek Secret Cults*, edited by M. Cosmopoulos, 50–78. New York: Routledge, 2003.

———. "Two Buildings in the Samothracian Sanctuary of the Great Gods." *Journal of Ancient History* 5, no. 2 (2017): 323–356.

Clinton, Kevin, Ludovic Laugier, Andrew Stewart, and Bonna D. Wescoat. "The Nike of Samothrace: Setting the Record Straight." *American Journal of Archaeology* 124, no. 4 (2020): 551–573.

Cole, Susan Guettal. *Theoi Megaloi: The Cult of the Great Gods at Samothrace*. Leiden: Brill, 1984.

Dimitrova, Nora M. "Theoroi and Initiates in Samothrace." *Hesperia* 77, no. 2 (2008): 363–363.

Frazer, Alfred K. *Samothrace: The Propylon of Ptolemy II*. Vol. 10. Princeton, N.J.: Princeton University Press, 1990.

Ginouvès, R. *Balaneutikè: recherches sur le bain dans l'antiquité grecque*. Paris: Boccard, 1962.

Ilieva, Petya. "Altar or Perirrhanterion: Were There Water Purification Rites in the Sanctuary of the Great Gods on Samothrace?" In *Art and Ideology*, edited by K. Rabadjiev, T. Shalganova, V. Marazova, and Stoychev, 487–502. Sofia: Sofia University Press, 2012.

Lather, Amy. "Pindar's water music: The acoustics and dynamics of the kelados." *Classical Philology* 114, no. 3 (2019): 468–481.

Lehmann, Karl. "Samothrace: Third Preliminary Report." *Hesperia* 19, no. 1 (1950): 1–20.

———. *Samothrace: A Guide to the Excavations and the Museum*. Rev. by J. R. McCredie. Thessaloniki: A.A. Altintzis, 1998.

Lehmann, Karl, and Denis Spittle. *Samothrace: The Altar Court*. Vol. 4, II. New York: Pantheon Books, 1964.

Lehmann, Phyllis Williams. *Samothrace: The Hieron*. Vol. 3. Princeton, N.J.: Princeton University Press, 1969.

Lehmann, Phyllis Williams, and Denis Spittle. *Samothrace: The Temenos*. Vol. 5. Princeton, N.J.: Princeton University Press, 1982.

Lehmann, Phyllis Williams, and Karl Lehmann. *Samothracian Reflections: Aspects of the Revival of the Antique*. Princeton, N.J.: Princeton University Press, 1973.

Lewis, Naphtali. *Samothrace: The Ancient Literary Sources*. Vol. 1. New York: Pantheon Books, 1959.

McCredie, James R. "Samothrace: Preliminary Report on the Campaigns of 1962-1964." *Hesperia* 34, no. 2 (1965): 100–124.

McCredie, James R., George Roux, Stuart M. Shaw, and John Kurtich. *Samothrace: The Rotunda of Arsinoe*. Vol. 7. Princeton, N.J.: Princeton University Press, 1992.

Petridou, Georgia. "Resounding Mysteries: Sound and Silence in the Eleusinian Soundscape." *Body and Religion* 2, no 1. (2018): 69–87.

Pimpl, Heidrun. *Perirrhanteria und Louteria: Entwicklung und Verwendung Grosser Marmor- und Kalksteinbecken auf Figürlichem und Säulenartigem Untersatz in Griechenland*. Berlin: Verlag Köster, 1997.

Rogers, Dylan. "Sensing Water in Roman Greece: The Villa of Herodes Atticus at Eva-Loukou and the Sanctuary of Demeter and Kore at Eleusis." *American Journal of Archaeology* 125, no. 1 (2021): 91–122.

Wescoat, Bonna D. "Coming and Going in the Sanctuary of the Great Gods, Samothrace." In *Architecture of the Sacred: Ritual, Space, and Experience from Classical Greece to Byzantium*, edited by Bonna D. Wescoat and R.G. Ousterhout, 66–113. New York: Cambridge University Press, 2012.

Wescoat, Bonna D. "Recalibrating Samothracian Architecture." In *L'architecture monumentale grecque au IIIe s. a.C.*, edited by Jacques des Courtils, 117–146. Bordeaux: Ausonius Éditions, 2015.

———. "Samothrace: Excavations Conducted by the Institute of Fine Arts, New York University." Vol. 9. *The Monuments of the Eastern Hill*. Princeton, N.J.: Princeton University Press, 2017a.

———. "The Pilgrim's Passage through the Sanctuary of the Great Gods, Samothrace." In *Excavating Pilgrimage: Archaeological Approaches to Sacred Travel and Movement from Classical Greece to Late Antiquity*, edited by T. M. Christensen and V. Friese, 67–86. New York: Routledge, 2017b.

———. "Architectural Documentation and Visual Evocation: Choices, Iterations, and Virtual Representation in the Sanctuary of the Great Gods on Samothrake." In *New Directions and Paradigms for the Study of Greek Architecture: Interdisciplinary Dialogues in the Field*, edited by Philip Sapirstein and David Scahill, 305–21. Monumenta Graeca et Romana 25, Leiden: Brill, 2020.

Wescoat, Bonna D., Susan Ludi Blevins, Maggie L. Popkin, Jessica Paga, Andrew Farinholt Ward, Michael C. Page, and William Size. "Interstitial Space in the Sanctuary of the Great Gods on Samothrace." In *Hellenistic Architecture and Human Action: A Case of Reciprocal Influence*, edited by Annette Haug and Asja Müller, 41–62. Scales of Transformation in Prehistoric and Archaic Societies 10. Leiden: Sidestone Press, 2020.

6

ROMAN WATERSCAPES, ARCHITECTURE, AND RELIGION

Notions of Sacrality and Sensory Experience

Dylan K. Rogers

In the second century CE, the author Pliny the Younger wrote a letter to his friend, Voconius Romanus (*Letter* 8.8). In this epistle, Pliny inquires as to whether or not Romanus had ever visited the source of the Clitumnus River, which is located today between Spello and Spoleto in the Italian region of Umbria. Pliny describes in detail the landscape of the river and its tributaries, along with the built environment that had grown over time to celebrate the sacred character of the waters flowing there.[1] Pliny's evocation of the area around the Clitumnus River demonstrates the rich sensorial assemblage of this religiously charged landscape. He shows how the sensory experience of the water impacts religious behavior, including the ritual of throwing coins into the water, especially through the reflections of the coins through the water. The purity of the water is stressed through its clarity ("clear as glass") and the way in which trees reflect on its surface (Fig. 6.1). Then, the sacred nature of the water provides an opportunity for the construction of a religious landscape that includes small shrines along the banks of the river (dedicated to the spirits of the waters) and a temple for Clitumnus, the eponymous divinity of the main river. Other nearby structures, like baths and a hostel, indicate that the area is heavily frequented by pilgrims, as the area is famous for the oracular powers of these waters.

The landscape and built environment of the Clitumnus River provide a unique example of a Roman waterscape. Defined as "culturally meaningful, sensorially active places, in which humans interact with water and each other," waterscapes were important spaces in the Roman world (Ray 2020: 19). In this example, the environment is arguably overflowing with water—almost as if it was oversaturated. But the notion of a waterscape extends to other spaces in the Roman world. Fountains or water-displays were employed to add artificially flowing water to the built environment and bore the potential to drastically alter the visitor's experience. In order to better understand these waterscapes, especially in terms of religious thought, the religious nature of water in the Roman world is explored here from the perspective of lived ancient religion. This is a scholarly approach that attempts to repopulate spaces with actual people performing religious practices (Gasparini et al. 2020). This repopulation of spaces recalls notions of actual sensory experiences related to flowing water. The sacrality of water, as perceived by the Romans, helped drive fountain construction that grew more audacious over the course of the Roman Empire, fueled by the desire for larger and more

DOI: 10.4324/9781003358824-9

FIGURE 6.1   Reflections off of the Clitumnus River. © *Antonio Dazzetti, Wikimedia Commons, CC BY-3.0*

sensorially pleasing structures. Thus, it will be demonstrated that these buildings had the power to harness the sacrality of water in the artificial material form.

Water, Roman Religion, and Sensory Experience

The role of water in Roman religious practice is multivalent and complicated, especially when considering how religious behaviors have the potential to change over time. Indeed, in the fourth century CE, the writer Servius, in his marginal notes on a copy of Vergil's *Aeneid*, made a gloss for the word *fons*, or spring, to explain *nullus enim fons non sacer*, "for there is no spring that is not sacred" (Servius, *Commentary on the Aeneid of Vergil* 7.84).[2] Evidently, over time, questions were raised as to the sacred nature of water, which can complicate modern discussions of Roman conceptions of water. It can be argued that water was inherently sacred to the Romans, as they practiced hydrolatry in various forms (Ray 2020: 2). But there might be gradations in that sacrality, as the water collected by the Vestal Virgins from Porta Capena in Rome for their rites must have been considered more sacred than the waters of the Clitumnus River where people were allowed to swim (Rogers 2018b: 78). Thus, a few salient points are made in this chapter about water's impact on Roman religious behaviors that will allow us to better understand how architecture could capitalize on water's inherent meanings in sacred contexts.

Water is symbolic, and across cultures and time many of its properties have been interpreted through a religious lens. Water sources, for instance, are often considered to be liminal spaces between the earthly and divine, imbuing a place with a numinous quality (Oestigaard

2011: 39–40; Ray 2020: 8–12). Water is also widely held to be transformative. Sometimes called a "universal solvent," because of its ability to visibly dissolve substances, water can then be used to purify people, especially in religious settings (Oestigaard 2011: 39; De Cazanove 2015: 183–185; Ray 2020: 3; Tvedt 2016: 70).

Indeed, most Greco-Roman sanctuaries provided water for purification as a pilgrim entered the space (Rogers 2021b: 108). Water can also be considered "holy" or "sacred," in which holiness is connected to a specific divinity (e.g., the Ganges River that is thought to be divine), and sacrality to consecrated elements (e.g., water in Christian baptism) (Oestigaard 2013: 39; Tvedt 2016: 72). As such, the holy nature of water sources connected to divinities allows them to act as a mediator between divine beings and mortals (Oestigaard 2013: 39). Water, then, can become a manifestation of the divine, or a hierophany, within a landscape, especially those with special types of water (e.g., those with special mineral compositions) (Ray 2020: 2). Thus, water is a multivalent element that can, in turn, be associated with a multitude of meanings and experiences for people in different cultures and contexts, especially in religious settings.

The Romans assigned certain discernible qualities to waters that were used in connection with religious practice. First, so-called "good" waters (i.e., waters that were venerated) were generally moving and flowing (and thus free from impurities), like those of the Clitumnus (Edlund-Berry 2006: 166; Rogers 2018b: 8). These waters, often associated with spring sources, were sweet to the taste (unlike the bitter salty taste of seawater) and provided a pleasant sensorial experience when consumed. Second, holy or sacred water could be found in a number of naturally occurring places, including rivers, lakes, streams, and springs (Edlund-Berry 2006: 163). These sources could sometimes be tied directly to a deity and thus "holy," while others were tied to the *numen*, or spirit, of a deity (Edlund-Berry 2006: 173). It was the location of these water sources that then determined the location of sacred spaces—thus providing areas for religious activities and rituals (Edlund-Berry 2006: 180; Erdman 2018: 246–248). Finally, it is generally believed that water-related rites were completed by individuals and groups, and not by priests or the traditional Roman state cult (Edlund-Berry 2006: 167, 180). As a result, rituals related to water veneration have the power to unlock the everyday experience of Romans of all social classes.

In this vein, in the study of Roman religion, the approach of "lived ancient religion" has recently developed in order to reconstruct past religious experiences.[3] This approach has the ability to make accessible past actions that have been lost, allowing scholars today to better understand how religious acts were conducted. While there are numerous facets to lived ancient religion, there are some salient points that are important for the discussion here. First, communication between humans and the divine drives religious practice, especially in terms of reciprocity (McDonough 2020: 38). Second, while there is a shared experience within a group related to religion, traces of the individual can be found within lived ancient religion (Kyriakidis 2007: 295). Since attention is paid to individuals, the "religious agency" of a wide swath of society—not just the elite—can be demonstrated (Gasparini et al. 2020: 2). As such, a picture begins to emerge of all levels of Roman society coming together to practice similar religious acts (Edlund-Berry 2006: 180; Gasparini et al. 2020: 3). One important element of lived ancient religion that helps to tie all of these different points together is the embodied experience of religious practice. These religious experiences are "the product of a wide range of sensory stimuli, effects, and inner feelings that are articulated by subjects or interpreted by observers" (Gasparini et al. 2020: 4). Thus, the relationship between the human body and its surroundings, which are understood through sensorial experiences, is an important avenue of inquiry into religious practice. Especially considering the actual element of water itself, which can be experienced through all five canonical western senses.

The recent "sensory turn" in the field of humanities provides a strong foundation for the unpacking of past experiences of individuals.[4] A sensory approach takes into account how the senses impact the ways in which humans perceive the world and give meaning to their surroundings. Sensory archaeology then supplies a theoretical framework to bridge the gap between material culture (including the built environment) and ephemeral episodes tied to the senses.[5] Recent scholarship on the multi-sensory experience of Roman culture has blossomed, due to the convergence of a rich textual tradition, material culture, and landscape (Betts 2017).

The study of Roman fountains through the lens of the senses benefits especially from the ancient literary sources, as seen in the beginning of this chapter with the thoughts of Pliny on the Clitumnus. He elaborates even further in other letters, such as when he describes the fountains in his villa in the Tuscan hills as "a pleasure to hear to and to see" (*Letter* 5.6.23). The robust description of water by the Romans provides a privileged insight into their own experiences with the element (Rogers 2018b: 4–10).

Recent scholarship on the role of the senses in archaeological assemblages has also provided exciting new ways to understand past sensory experiences. The archaeologist Yannis Hamilakis has helped to develop the notion of the "sensorial assemblage," stemming in part from anthropological and philosophical discourses on the relationship between objects and humans. Moving beyond traditional archaeological assemblages, the sensorial assemblage replaces the body, object, and place into the past, in addition to "things, substances, affects, memories, information, and ideas," and provides for affective interactions between humans and their surroundings (Hamilakis 2013: 126). In such a conception, buildings and objects could become active participants in the sensorial assemblage, acting as "sensorial artifacts," impacting the sensorial experience of an ancient viewer. Senses and the memory of sensory perceptions also have the power to blur time for humans, and the senses can trigger past and present sensations and experiences. Thus, the material and immaterial are brought together—which then vitalizes archaeological remains through senses, sensory artifacts, affects, and memories. And it is the vibrant multisensory qualities of water itself that allow for the fruitful examination of water-displays through sensory archaeology.

Examining Roman Water-Displays and the Sacred

In order to understand the sacrality, architecture, and sensory nature of Roman fountains, two water-displays in Roman Greece are analyzed. Both displays are located in the Roman province of Achaia, at Olympia and Argos, respectively. The province of Achaia, which spanned Attica (the region around Athens), the Peloponnese, and as far north as Thebes in Boeotia, was an important area in the Roman world (Fig. 6.2). With its ancient Greek past, especially the famous monuments of Classical Athens, this region had a special place in the minds of the Romans after they fully conquered Achaia by the first century BCE (Rogers 2021a). Thus, during the Roman period, while the presence of the Romans gave rise to new building forms and construction techniques, such as aqueducts made with concrete, those living in the region would have a unique sense of identity that straddled the Greek past and the Roman present (Grigoropoulos et al. 2017; Rogers 2021b). Easily identifiable Roman fountains began to be constructed in the Late Republican period (first century BCE), and they reached their apex in the second century CE with the construction of numerous aqueducts by the emperor Hadrian throughout the region (Longfellow 2011: 107–139).[6]

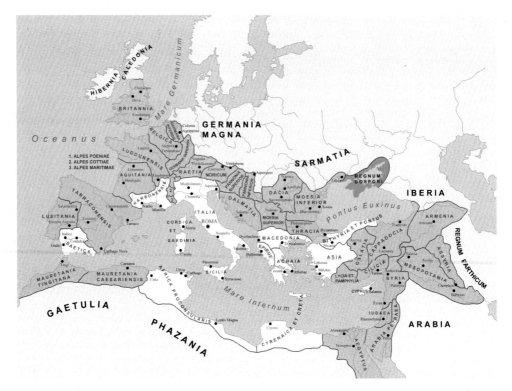

FIGURE 6.2 Map of the Roman Empire in 117 CE. *Map by Andrei Nacu, in the Public Domain*

One important example of a monumental fountain constructed in Roman Greece is the Nymphaeum of Herodes Atticus and Regilla at the Sanctuary of Zeus at Olympia.[7] The sanctuary was renowned for the ancient Olympic Games that hosted international visitors. There was a pre-existing and arguably congested sacred landscape filled with numerous religious structures (including the famous Temple of Zeus, with its chryselephantine statue of Zeus by the sculptor Phidias) and athletic complexes (Fig. 6.3).[8] The Nymphaeum is a complex monument in the topography of both Olympia and Roman Greece. The fountain was dedicated in 153 CE by the famous and wealthy Greek sophist, Herodes Atticus.[9] Herodes was a unique figure in Roman Greece, as he straddled traditional aspects of Greek life, while also rising in the ranks of the imperial regime in Rome, having served as the private tutor to the future emperor Marcus Aurelius (Rogers 2021b, 98–100).[10] The dedicatory inscription at Olympia indicates that the fountain was given by Regilla, Herodes's wife, although it is generally believed that Herodes gave the funds (Longfellow 2012: 142) (Fig. 6.4). Thus, Herodes (and arguably his wife) were able to subscribe to what is termed a "bicultural identity" that manifested itself in different ways in the public and private built spaces he commissioned throughout Greece (Rogers 2021b: 107–108).

The fountain was built from brick, and faced polychrome marble, as a semi-circular exedra-style structure (Fig. 6.5).[11] The two-story façade contains 11 sculptural niches on each level (Fig. 6.6). On the bottom were members of the imperial family, from Hadrian to Lucius Verus, while the family of Herodes Atticus was placed on the second level. Herodes' family wears Greek and Roman dress that illustrates their complex identity in the Greco-Roman landscape of the sanctuary, while also being physically elevated over the imperial family. The

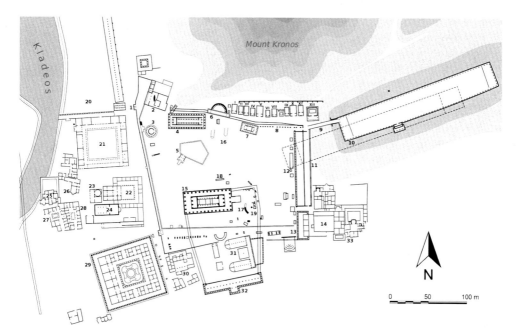

FIGURE 6.3 Plan of the Sanctuary of Zeus at Olympia, Greece: northwest entrance (1); Temple of Hera (4); Nymphaeum of Herodes Atticus and Regilla (6); Metroon (7); Temple of Zeus (15). *Map by Bibi Saint-Pol, in the Public Domain*

FIGURE 6.4 Marble bull on upper basin, with dedicatory inscription of the Nymphaeum of Herodes Atticus and Regilla, Olympia. Greek inscription reads: "Regilla, Priestess of Demeter, [dedicated] the water and the things around the water to Zeus." © *Dylan K. Rogers*

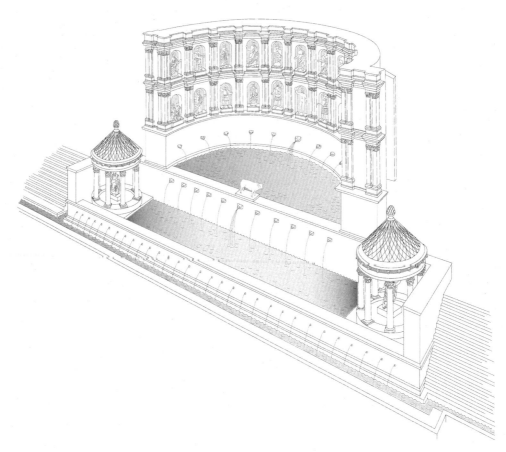

FIGURE 6.5 Reconstruction of the Nymphaeum of Herodes Atticus and Regilla, Olympia. *Adapted from Yegül and Favro 2019: Fig. 9.1*

FIGURE 6.6 Reconstruction of the sculptural niches of the Nymphaeum of Herodes Atticus and Regilla, Olympia. © *Davide Mauro, Wikimedia Commons, CC BY-SA 4.0*

center niche on each level contained a statue of Zeus, the fountain's dedicatee, depicted in the nude. The fountain's water was supplied from a 1-kilometer-long aqueduct, which very importantly was the first time water was known to have been supplied to the sanctuary in excess (Longfellow 2012: 142). The water entered from the back of the structure through a series of 11 lion-head spouts into the upper apsidal basin, which then flowed to a lower intermediate rectangular basin that then emptied through numerous spouts into a long rectangular, pedestrian-accessible trough at ground level (Longfellow 2012: 141). Finally, there were two *monopteroi*, or circular structures, placed on the ends of the intermediate basin in the early third century, with statues of Herodes and Marcus Aurelius (Longfellow 2012: 142).

In terms of the sensorial assemblage of this monument, there are a number of points to consider. Buttressed against Mount Kronos, the water-display was situated in one of the most conspicuous areas of the sanctuary (Fig. 6.3). The monumental height of the façade of the Nymphaeum was something not seen in the sanctuary for centuries—and would have even been equal to that of the Zeus Temple—a bold statement on the part of Herodes. The fountain acted as an important sensorial artifact for the sanctuary's pilgrims during hot summer months, with its plenitude of water cascading down from two upper basins into an accessible drinking trough at the bottom. One can only imagine the sights and sounds of the crashing water, along with the coolness of the air that the movement of water provided. Even today, during the tourist season, with the site packed with visitors from cruise ships, the lack of water is easily discernible—and it is easy to imagine how not only water access but also the sensorial alterations of the space had the ability to drastically change the experience of being a pilgrim.

As patrons, Herodes and Regilla, in addition to creating a new aesthetic backdrop for the northern edge of the sanctuary, provided a magnificent way station for pedestrians.[12] In particular, it should be stressed that this fountain was located in close proximity to one of the main entrances of the sanctuary, which often occurred at religious sanctuaries in the Roman period. This location speaks to the inherent quality and meaning of water for the Romans to act as a purifying agent when crossing through a liminal space into a sacred one (Rogers 2021b: 108–109). Further, in the Roman East, the Romans grafted themselves into pre-existing religious landscapes—often using water as a means to drastically alter the actual experience of those spaces, such as at Eleusis or Xanthos (Longfellow 2012; Rogers 2021b: 108–115).

In terms of other practicalities that formed part of the sensorial assemblage, the accessibility of the lower trough implies that the fountain was used to provide drinking water. The ability to drink water from fountains in religious spaces can be seen in other examples in the Roman world, such as a third-century inscription from Algeria that documents the supplies of a fountain in a religious sanctuary that included drinking cups and towels.[13] Clearly, the fountain at Olympia was meant to be used, not just admired. In fact, in a famous passage of Lucian, the philosopher Peregrinus, noting that in the past there was no water access there, decries that by the year 157 pilgrims had become effeminate because they enjoyed the access to the abundant flowing water of the fountain (*On the Death of Peregrinus* 19-20). The subsequent public outcry against Peregrinus, who incidentally later committed suicide in 165 by self-immolation because of this very episode, only stresses the importance of the Nymphaeum in this space, with not only its plentiful water supply that was clearly valued by the locals, but also its monumental (perhaps even audacious) construction of Herodes, who appears to physically equal himself to Zeus.

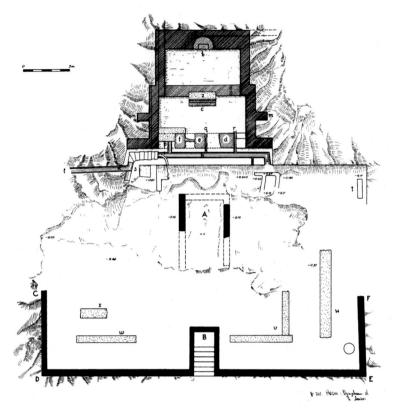

FIGURE 6.7 Plan of Larissa Nymphaeum, Argos. *After Longfellow 2011: Fig. 39*

Moving to the northeast of the Peloponnese, in 124 CE, Hadrian constructed an aqueduct in the city of Argos. The terminus of the aqueduct was on the slopes of Larissa hill, which looms over the city. There, the so-called Larissa Nymphaeum was constructed (Fig. 6.7).[14] Situated above a flat terrace, a barrel-vaulted structure, reminiscent of Italian forms, was built with a temple-like façade, complete with a Syrian arch (Fig. 6.8). Nestled in the bedrock of the Larissa hill, the whole structure was constructed of Roman brick, and the barrel vault included small windows to allow for diffuse light to illuminate the space (Longfellow 2011: 116). Water from the aqueduct entered the back of the room, where it poured from underneath the feet of a large statue of a nude male figure (Fig. 6.9). The water then continued to flow into an upper, then lower basin, via a water stair; after which, water was channeled into a conduit that then conducted the water down into Argos. The water inevitably benefitted the city greatly, which was known in antiquity for its lack of water—as it was often called "thirsty" Argos in ancient literary sources (Homer, *Iliad* 4.171).

The Larissa Nymphaeum, one of the first imperial fountains built in Greece, combines architectural forms that allude to Greek and Roman religious behaviors. The grotto-like appearance of the main structure evoked the shrines seen in the Greek world dedicated to the nymphs (Longfellow 2011: 117). But the structure itself is easily recognizable as Roman, from the use of brick to the barrel-vault superstructure. Even more to the point, however, is how the focal point of nymphaeum is the back niche, where the water pours forth. Immediately above the water is the male statue, which has been interpreted as a heroic nude figure of

Roman Waterscapes, Architecture, and Religion 93

FIGURE 6.8 Hypothetical 3-D reconstruction of the Larissa Nymphaeum, Argos. Courtesy: *Paolo Vitti*

FIGURE 6.9 Hypothetical side-elevation reconstruction of the Larissa Nymphaeum, Argos. Courtesy: *Paolo Vitti*

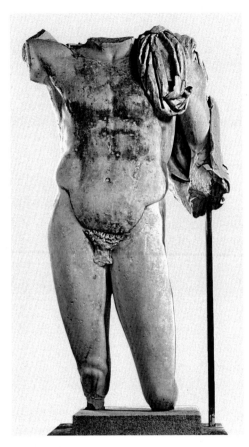

FIGURE 6.10 Hadrian statue from the Larissa Nymphaeum, Argos. *After Aristodemou 2018: Fig. 2*

the emperor Hadrian himself (Longfellow 2011: 117–118) (Fig. 6.10). This makes sense, as Hadrian commissioned the aqueduct and the nymphaeum—and emperors are often featured on the monuments they built, especially if they brought important resources to their people.[15] Further, given the often divinely inspired nature of the emperor, it can be argued that here Hadrian demonstrates his own power (Aristodemou 2018: 354), while also illustrating his divine nature, especially being shown as a heroic nude, with bare feet (Longfellow 2011: 118). Instead of a personification of the local water source (which would have been more appropriate in Greece until this point in history), there is an epiphany of the emperor, who takes on a new status in the meaning of the flowing water: his own hierophany, like the figure of Zeus on the nymphaeum at Olympia. Thus, both cultures blend the sacred nature of water and the emperor's munificence. Further, though, it shows how a structure's previous religious form was appropriated for imperial gain. It capitalizes on the sacred nature of water in order to create a secular monument in the name of the emperor with arguably sacred undertones.

One final element to consider with the Larissa Nymphaeum is its sensorial assemblage. The structure itself, with its barrel vault, along with the cascading water in the interior, would have provided quite a sensorial show, as the waters flowed and their sounds echoed off the walls (Longfellow 2011: 116). In a new architectural study of the fountain, the architectural historian Paolo Vitti has demonstrated the impact of the sensorial artifacts here (namely the structure, the water, and the landscape)—which would have been seen and heard below in the city center of Argos (Vitti 2018). Not only does the structure allude to the sacred nature of water, but its location and construction also provide a sensorial *tour de force* for all in Argos. It reminded them of the power of the waters coming into their city and hydrating it more than ever had been known. The success of the Larissa Nymphaeum, whether in its inherent meaning or sensorial experience, evidently was also noticed in antiquity, as Hadrian would complete another similar fountain complex a few years later on the slopes of the Lykabettos hill in Athens. In a sense, spreading the sacred connotations of the flowing waters through these blended architectural forms (Longfellow 2011: 120–122).

While water appears in a number of traditionally sacred contexts in the Roman world, the blurred lines of the sacred nature of water allowed for the element to be harnessed in secular contexts with potentially new meanings. In the Greek world, naturally occurring springs (often tied to the nymphs) could receive cult that provided spaces for pilgrims to offer votives and use the waters for various purposes (Longfellow 2011: 9–10). Springs or source sanctuaries were also popular throughout the Roman world, highlighting the divine nature of these waters. In addition, they provided, in some instances, opportunities for healing (De Cazanove 2015: 184–188). A famous Roman source sanctuary is located at Zaghoan near Carthage, Tunisia, where an Italian-style barrel-vaulted shrine is surrounded by a monumental semi-circular colonnade. The complex also highlights the aqueduct that Hadrian completed there in 128 CE (Longfellow 2011: 146–147). In Greece, a long tradition of Greek religious practices at springs met the monumental forms of the Romans (in the construction of aqueducts and architectural forms from the Italian peninsula) to create new spaces that straddled the sacred and secular worlds.

Conclusion

This brief discussion of two fountains in Roman Greece shows the perceived nature of water in the Roman world. It could express the sacrality within the element itself or provide sacred meanings to a secular structure. Each demonstrates, in some form or another, hydrolatry in their respective waterscapes. At Olympia, the purifying nature of water at a sanctuary's entrance illustrates its role as a "universal solvent," while at the same time providing pilgrims with important drinking water along with new sensorial experiences. At Argos, architectural forms formerly found in religious contexts were adapted to create new meanings tied to the sacred nature of water, especially in the hierophany of the emperor Hadrian. In addition, sensorially audacious architecture, fueled by flowing water, was created.

Further, by thinking about the lived ancient religion of the spaces, especially at Olympia, when paired with an exploration of the past sensorial experience, a better understanding of the original context of these fountains can be discerned by the modern scholar. Despite the fact that these two examples were found in either religiously or civically important landscapes (especially in terms of identity construction in the Roman period), the water that flowed through these two structures connected these fountains to other parts of the Roman Empire. The fountains and their water allude to wider notions of Roman identity tied to a broader water culture of the Romans. Thus, in terms of sacrality and sensory experiences, fountains were able to harness the sacred nature of water by means of architecture in novel ways that made them uniquely Roman.

Notes

1. On this letter see: Scheid 1996; Rogers Forthcoming.
2. For a discussion of this passage, see Rogers 2018b: 76–78.
3. For overviews of the approach of "lived ancient religion" see most recently Gasparini et al. 2020, especially for previous bibliography.
4. Due to the space constraints of the present chapter, one can consult Rogers (2021b: 91–95) for more on methodologies tied sensory archaeology, along with previous bibliography. See also Skeates and Day 2019.
5. Ibid.
6. For other recent discussions of fountains in Roman Greece, see Rogers 2018a.
7. The original Greek term, *nymphaion*, has ties to places associated with the nymphs, giving it a religious connotation. On the etymology of the Latin term, *nymphaeum*, and potential problems with its usage in modern scholarship (especially with its accepted use in the Renaissance period to describe large-scale fountains), see Rogers 2018b: 46–47.
8. On the history of the sanctuary, see most recently Barringer 2021.
9. The bibliography on the fountain is expansive; but see: Bol 1984; Longfellow 2012: 142–146; Richard 2012, cat. no. 51.
10. Herodes is famous for his *euergetism*, or public benefaction, throughout Greece, especially in Athens, where he constructed his Odeion, or covered theater, on the south slopes of the Acropolis, and reconstructed the Panathenaic Stadium on the eastern side of the city. See Rogers 2021a: 431–432.
11. While the remains today *in situ* are fragmentary, the archaeologist Renate Bol reconstructed the original fountain in 1984, using sculptural remains and architectural elements.
12. On the concept of way stations in Roman architecture, which prompt passers-by to stop, see MacDonald 1986: 99–106.
13. *Corpus Inscriptionum Latinarum* 8.6982; Rogers 2021b: 108.
14. On the Larissa Nymphaeum, see, especially for previous bibliography: Longfellow 2011: 113–120; Richard 2012: cat. no. 8; Aristodemou 2018: 352–354; Vitti 2018.
15. On the inscription naming Hadrian as the benefactor, see Longfellow 2011: 114.

References

Aristodemou, Georgia A. "Fountain Sculptures and Personal Propaganda in Roman Greece." In *Γλυπτική και κοινωνία στη ρωμαϊκή Ελλάδα: καλλιτεχνικά προϊόντα, κοινωνικές προβολές*, edited by Pavlina Karanastasi et al., 351–366. Thessaloniki: University Studio Press, 2018.

Barringer, Judith. *Olympia: A Cultural History*. Princeton: Princeton University Press, 2021.

Betts, Eleanor, ed. *Senses of the Empire: Multisensory Approaches to Roman Culture*. London: Routledge, 2017.

Bol, Renate. *Das Statuenprogramm des Herodes-Atticus-Nymphäums*. Berlin: Walter De Gruyter, 1984.

De Cazanove, Olivier. "Water." In *A Companion to the Archaeology of Religion in the Ancient World*, edited by Rubina Raja and Jörg Rüpke, 181–193. Chichester: Wiley Blackwell, 2015.

Edlund-Berry, Ingrid. "Hot, Cold, or Smelly: The Power of Sacred Water in Roman Religion, 400-100 BCE." In *Religion in Republican Italy*, edited by Celia E. Schultz and Paul B. Harvey, 162–180. Cambridge: Cambridge University Press, 2006.

Erdman, Katherine M. "Small Finds from Springs and Baths: Similar or Different?" In *Thermae in Context: The Roman Bath in Town and in Life*, edited by Heike Pösche, Andrea Binsfield, and Stefanie Hoss, 245–265. Luxembourg: Centre National de Recherche Archéologique, 2018.

Gasparini, Valentino, Maik Patzelt, Rubina Raja, Anna-Katharina Rieger, Jörg Rüpke, and Emiliano Urciuoli. "Pursuing Lived Ancient Religion." In *Lived Religion in the Ancient Mediterranean World: Approaching Transformations from Archaeology, History, and Classics*, edited by Valentino Gasparini et al., 1–8. Berlin: De Gruyter, 2020.

Grigoropoulos, Dimitris, Valentina Di Napoli, Vasilis Evangelidis, Francesco Camia, Dylan Rogers, and Stavros Vlizos. "Roman Greece and the 'Mnemonic Turn.' Some Critical Remarks." In *Strategies of Remember in Greece under Rome (100 BC-100 AD)*, edited by Tama M Dijkstra et al., 21–36. Leiden: Sidestone Press, 2017.

Hamilakis, Yannis. *Archaeology and the Senses: Human Experience, Memory, and Affect*. Cambridge: Cambridge University Press, 2013.

Kyriakidis, Evangelos. "Archaeologies of Ritual." In *The Archaeology of Ritual*, edited by Evangelos Kyriakidis, 289–308. Los Angeles: Cotsen Institute of Archaeology, 2007.

Longfellow, Brenda. *Roman Imperialism and Civic Patronage: Form, Meaning, and Ideology in Monumental Fountain Complexes*. Cambridge: Cambridge University Press, 2011.

———. "Roman Fountains in Greek Sanctuaries." *American Journal of Archaeology* 116, no. 1 (January 2012) 133–155.

MacDonald, William L. *Architecture of the Roman Empire: Volume II, An Urban Appraisal*. New Haven: Yale University Press, 1986.

McDonough, Christopher M. "*Fons et origo*: Observations on Sacred Springs in Classical Antiquity and Tradition." In *Sacred Waters: A Cross-Cultural Compendium of Hallowed Springs and Holy Wells*, edited by Celeste Ray, 35–40. London: Routledge, 2020.

Oestigaard, Terje. "Water." In *The Oxford Handbook of the Archaeology of Ritual and Religion*, edited by Timothy Insoll, 38–50. Oxford: Oxford University Press, 2011.

Ray, Celeste. "Holy Wells and Sacred Springs." In *Sacred Waters: A Cross-Cultural Compendium of Hallowed Springs and Holy Wells*, edited by Celeste Ray, 1–32. London: Routledge, 2020.

Richard, Julian. *Water for the City, Fountains for the People: Monumental Fountains in the Roman East*. Turnhout: Brepols, 2012.

Rogers, Dylan K. "Shifting Tides: Approaches to the Public Water-Displays of Roman Greece." In *Great Waterworks in Roman Greece: Aqueducts and Monumental Fountains, Function in Context*, edited by Georgia A. Aristodemou and Theodosios P. Tassios, 173–192. Oxford: Archaeopress, 2018a.

———. *Water Culture in Roman Society*. Leiden: Brill, 2018b.

———. "Roman Athens." In *The Cambridge Companion to Ancient Athens*, edited by Jenifer Neils and Dylan K. Rogers, 421–436. Cambridge: Cambridge University Press, 2021a.

———. "Sensing Water in Roman Greece: The Villa of Herodes Atticus at Eva-Loukou and the Sanctuary of Demeter and Kore at Eleusis." *American Journal of Archaeology* 125, no. 1 (January 2021b) 91–122.

———. "Sensory Experience and Ritual: The Lived Ancient Religion of Water in the Roman World." In *Archaeology of Ritual in the Ancient Mediterranean: Recent Finds & Innovative Approaches*, edited by Erica Angliker and Michael A. Fowler. Paris: De Boccard, Forthcoming.

Scheid, John. "Pline le jeune et les sanctuaires d'Italie. Observations sur les lettres IV, 1, VIII, 8 et IX, 39." In *Splendidissima civitas: Études d'histoire romaine en hommage à François Jacques*, edited by André Chastagnol et al., 241–258. Paris: Publications de la Sorbonne, 1996.

Skeates, Robin, and Jo Day, eds. *Routledge Handbook of Sensory Archaeology*. London: Routledge, 2019.

Tvedt, Terje. *Water and Society: Changing Perceptions of Societal and Historical Development*. London: I.B. Tauris, 2016.

Vitti, Paolo. "Il ninfeo adrianeo di Argo." *Annuario della Scuola Archeologica di Atene* 96 (2018) 275–299.

Yegül, Fikret, and Diane Favro. *Roman Architecture and Urbanism: From the Origins to Late Antiquity*. Cambridge: Cambridge University Press, 2019.

7

PURIFYING THE STUPA

Symbolism of the Lotus in Buddhist Architecture

Di Luo and Gerald Kozicz

The stupa is the paramount architectural symbol in Buddhism (Snodgrass 1985). Originally serving to enshrine the relics of the Buddha, the stupa was venerated as the ultimate representation of the Enlightened One during the aniconic phase of Buddhist art.[1] While early stupa forms had expressed a strong link to the earth, the growing impact of the cosmology of Mahayana (Greater Vehicle) Buddhism transformed the stupa into a symbol associated with the element of water: the stupa became more elongate, and groups of cosmic Buddhas or Buddhas of previous eons appeared along a base of an increasing number of steps (Fogelin 2012; Behrendt 2004: 7–9, 165, 265–67). Most strikingly, the entire stupa emerged visually from a large lotus flower depicted as a ring of petals detached from the ground (Snodgrass 1985: 97–100).

The lotus is a widely recognized symbol of water and purity since ancient times (Goodyear 1891; Sivaramamurti 1980; Ward 1952). Its introduction to Buddhist iconography affirms the importance of the notion of purity and proper purification rites in Buddhist practice. During the first millennium when Mahayana Buddhism spread across North India, East Afghanistan, Central Asia, East Asia, and the Western Himalayas, the lotus-water imagery permeated every Buddhist sacred site, monument, and ritual artifact. Its appearance on bases, domes, ceilings, and floor tiles suggested the multifaceted connotations of the lotus as emphasized by different Buddhist communities. In this chapter, we provide a glimpse of the complexity of the lotus symbolism in Buddhist architecture through archaeological case studies. The reoccurrence, and at times preponderance, of the lotus motif in Buddhist spaces evidenced a largely shared Buddhist architectural language and a strong, continued interest in water and purification.

Tapa Sardar: Lotus Pedestals and Purification Rites

One of the earliest examples of the lotus pedestal can be found in Tapa Sardar, an archaeological site 2.5 miles (4 kilometers) northeast of the city of Ghazni in East Afghanistan (Fig. 7.1). The architectural remains date from the late 7th to early 8th century, while the foundation of the monastery, once a flourishing Buddhist center, took place in the time of King Kanishka (2nd/3rd century CE) of the Kushan Empire.[2]

Built on a small hill overlooking an open field, the monastery was dominated by a great stupa in the courtyard. Of interest here is a row of small votive stupas made of unbaked clay and lined

DOI: 10.4324/9781003358824-10

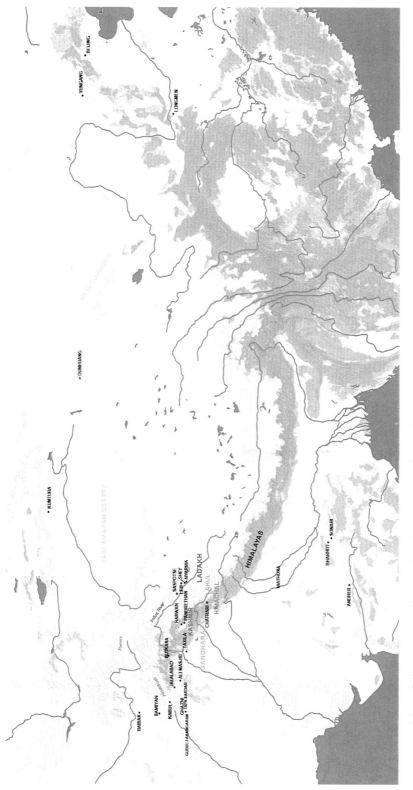

FIGURE 7.1 Map of the major sites discussed in this essay. Map by Stefan Zedlacher, Gerald Kozicz, and Di Luo

 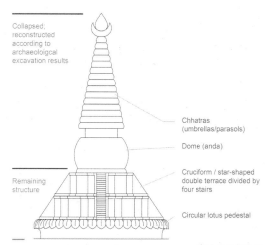

FIGURE 7.2 Left: Row of stupas and thrones of Upper Terrace, Tapa Sardar, showing Stupa 7 in the front. Dia. 6–7 feet (c. 2 meters) at the bottom. Neg 7402-7. Image courtesy of Italian Archaeological Mission in Afghanistan (https://ghazni.bdus.cloud/buddhist/the-buddhist-site-of-tapa-sardar#buddhist_site_2-16). Right: Reconstruction drawing of a votive stupa at Tapa Sardar. Drawing by Gerald Kozicz

up at the rear of the main stupa. Stupa 7, one of the best-preserved of the group, sits on a circular lotus pedestal (Fig. 7.2). The lotus pedestal supports a double-layered terrace, which is divided by four staircases in the cardinal directions. The staircases lead to the bottom of the now-lost hemispherical dome, where a band of eight-petal floral medallions has partially survived.

In Buddhist iconography, a lotus pedestal typically supports a Buddhist deity or stupa (Zimmer 1955: 168–81). The lotus, rooted in the riverbed and blooming on the water without a trace of mud attached to the flower or stem, is easily evocative of a divine, immaculate birth (Goodyear 1891; Ward 1952). Here at Tapa Sardar, the lotus pedestals give birth, both visually and semantically, to the votive stupas. Interestingly, the downward-pointing petals do not touch the ground but appear to "float on the water" (Taddei and Verardi 1978: 134, n. 82). Such conscious separation of the architecture from the surroundings can be traced back to earlier times when a circular fence (*vedika*) was set up to demarcate a sacred area and define a (sometimes raised) path of circumambulation (*pradakshinapatha*) (Harvey 1984: 70; Snodgrass 1985: 153–60). Similarly, the Tapa Sardar "floating lotuses" were probably built to consecrate the ground of the stupa court and delineate a "path of purification." As Buddhist practitioners circumambulated the main stupa, they would receive spiritual cleansing on their journey from the profane to the sacred.[3]

The importance of the "lotus-purified ground" in Buddhist architecture is attested by abundant material evidence. Ceramic tiles from a 5th-century Buddhist temple at Harwan, Kashmir, were impressed with patterns of lotuses, water pots, and aquatic birds (Fisher 1989: 1–16; Kak 1933: 105–11). Some of these tiles were used to pave the courtyard, forming a concentric, radial layout (Kak 1933: 109; pls. XIX–XLII). Such an architectural allusion to a watery environment also characterized early monumental stupas of the 2nd to 1st century BCE at Butkara in the Swat Valley and Mathura, North India (Irwin 1979: 828–32). In one rare case, azure-blue glass tiles paved the circumambulation path of King Asoka's Great Dharmarajika Stupa in Taxila (Fisher 1989: 8).

Many of these early stupas were built adjacent to rivers. In King Asoka's time, the rite of irrigating the sacred tree—which John Irwin terms the "rite of lustration" (Irwin 1979: 840)—was performed at tree shrines and enjoyed equal importance as circumambulation. In particular, the Bodhi Tree under which Buddha Shakyamuni sat in meditation and attained enlightenment was to be lustrated by "no less than 4,000 bowls of water" by the king himself on a usual visit (Irwin 1979: 840–42). The *yasti* (vertical pole of the stupa) is imagined as the World Tree and the *axis mundi* (axis of the world) in Buddhist cosmology.[4] With the gradual conflation of the tree shrine and the stupa, the lotus motif absorbed from the lustration rites additional layers of religious meanings (Irwin 1990; Kozicz 2021; Kim 2018).

From Ghazni to Ladakh and Beijing

To the southwest of Tapa Sardar, the site of Gudul-i Ahangaran has yielded a group of miniature clay stupas. They show stepped cruciform "mounds" seated on red-painted lotus petals, a scheme highly congruent with the Tapa Sardar votive stupas (Taddei 1970). The ubiquity of this blueprint outside Ghazni is demonstrated by, for instance, a miniature clay stupa from the Buddhist site of Nyarma (established c. 1000 CE) in Ladakh, Western Himalayas (Fig. 7.3). Small enough to be placed in the palm of the hand, the Nyarma stupa is made of a central dome and eight "half-domes" enclosed by a lotus flower.

Ghazni is a strategic town that controls the northward traffic to Kabul (see map, Fig. 7.1). It was integrated into the Kushan Empire (1st century BCE–4th century CE) whose vast territories, encompassing parts of modern-day Afghanistan and Pakistan, controlled the gateways to both East Asia and South Asia (Behrendt 2004: 1–2). Ancient caravans marching east from Kabul would cross the Khyber Pass to enter Pakistan, from where they could follow the Indus River up into the mountains and highlands of Kashmir and Ladakh (Klimburg-Salter 1982: 25–37).

In Ladakh, Bengal, and more broadly the entire North India, *tsatsas* were votive objects made of a mixture of water, clay, and sometimes the cremated ashes of local Buddhist monks. *Tsatsas* were often molded into miniature stupas and deposited in large quantities inside a built stupa, while some also became "souvenirs" carried outside their places of origin (Tucci 1988: 53–56). These objects served as containers of "dharma relics" embodied by short, formulaic

FIGURE 7.3 Miniature clay stupa from Nyarma (founded c. 1000 CE), Ladakh. Photo by Gerald Kozicz

FIGURE 7.4 *Tsatsas* from the Wutasi in Beijing. Dia. 2 inches (5 centimeters); h. 2–3 inches (5–7 centimeters). Ming dynasty, 15th century and after. Photo by Di Luo

phrases derived from Buddhist scriptures and liturgical practices. The incantations, distilling the essence of the doctrine into a single line of text, were powerful evocations of the divine presence that turned the *tsatsa* into a *dharmakaya* (body of law) of the Buddha (Skilling 2021; Tucci 1988: 53–56).

The Nyarma *tsatsa* carries a line of inscription between the lotus pedestal and the domes. According to the Italian Tibetologist Giuseppe Tucci, mantras, especially the *ye dharma* prayer, were generally added to animate a votive object and multiply it into millions (Skilling 2021: 83–84; Tucci 1988: 33). The making of *tsatsas* necessitated a ritual carried out in ten meticulous steps, from the mixing of the ingredients, molding, impression, and consecration to the invitation and final dismissal of the gods (Tucci 1988: 57–59). Each step invoked a special verbal "formula," hence the process of making was a distinct vocal performance. As a result, we see Water and Word—the twin generative powers of Creation—here visualized and activated in architectural form.

Via Tibet and the Taklamakan Desert, past the Hexi Corridor, the *tsatsas* found their way into a 15th-century Buddhist temple in Beijing (Fig. 7.4). The multiple domes on top of the lotus pedestal recall their Western Tibetan prototypes. Chinese emperors of the Ming dynasty (1368–1644) emulated their Mongol-Yuan (1279–1368) predecessors in patronizing Tibetan Buddhism, importing Indo-Himalayan art and material culture to the Chinese capital. For centuries, architectural blueprints and Buddhist iconography from the trans-Himalayan region continued to inspire artistic creations at the imperial court.[5]

Shey: Whitewashed Stupas

A living lotus plant is perhaps the last thing one would anticipate encountering in the harsh landscapes of the Western Himalayas. While the lotus motif in religious painting and sculpture was well-established in this region, it is remarkable how the same motif obtained an equal level of architectural significance. After all, mandalas and statues incorporated the flower for internal experience and could be easily hosted under the roof, but stupas had to be built in response to topography and climate. The adoption of the lotus motif at such high altitudes, therefore, implies a conscious embrace of this "exotic" plant and its multilayered religious meaning.

The village of Shey, located approximately 10 miles (15 kilometers) up the Indus River from Leh (modern capital of Ladakh), lies deep beyond a series of turbulent rivers and mountain passes. Shey occupies a pivotal point where it absorbs from and transmits to all surrounding regions. It was the capital of ancient Maryul by the 10th century when it came under the rule of the kings of the Western Tibetan kingdom of Guge and Purang who were dedicated patrons of Buddhism. Earlier, the region had been known to the ancient Greeks as home to the "Dardic people" and the "land of the gold-digging ants" (Francke 1999: 12). There, a multi-directional cultural crossroad bridged East Afghanistan via Kashmir and the Hindukush-Pamir Chains to the Indian Subcontinent and the oasis towns of the Taklamakan (Klimburg-Salter 1982).

Large groups of whitewashed stupas dot the open fields around Shey, overlooked by the ruins of a fortified center of ancient Maryul from a nearby hilltop. Many of the stupas were presumably built between the 10th and 11th centuries, during the Second Diffusion of the Faith, when Buddhism thrived under King Yeshe Od (c. 959–1040) in Western Tibet (Howard 1995; Petech 1997: 233–34). Overall, the Shey stupas are poorly preserved, and most have either eroded or collapsed (Fig. 7.5). The remains typically have a broad square plinth, a stepped terrace in the middle, and a round dome on top. Though they apparently lack Buddhist statues and a planned layout compared to Tapa Sardar, the lotus motif has persisted and become an outstanding feature of these structures.

The lotus petals, molded directly onto the plaster layer of the stupa plinth underneath the whitewash, are flatter and more geometrically fashioned in contrast to the naturalistic petals at Tapa Sardar. In this case, the geometry of the cubic plinth is superimposed with the circular shape of the flower, and the organic form of the aquatic plant had to be geometricized to unite

FIGURE 7.5 Shey whitewashed stupas. H. 10–30 feet (3–10 meters). Photo by Gerald Kozicz

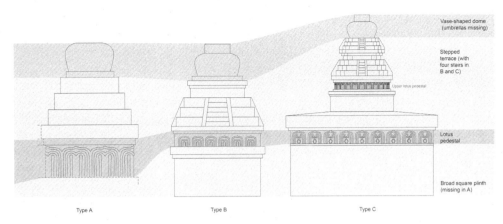

FIGURE 7.6   Elevations of the three main types of stupas at Shey, Ladakh (different scales). 10th–11th century. Drawing by Gerald Kozicz

the square and the circle. The result lacks the elegance of Tapa Sardar stupas, but one ought not to forget the special climatic and technical conditions under which these stupas had to be built.

According to the number and spatial organization of the petals, we categorize the Shey stupas into three subtypes (Fig. 7.6). Type A, the simplest, contains a 12-petal lotus pedestal. Types B and C have 24 and 36 petals (which are smaller in size) respectively and the terrace is divided by four staircases in the four cardinal directions, again alluding to the East Afghan prototype. The number of petals does not seem to have a particular meaning. Still, they do not fail to convey a sense of "levitation" and "detachment" against our normal perception of the massiveness of these heavy, immobile structures.

When Tucci traveled in the area in the 1920s, he classified the stupas into eight types which corresponded to the "Eight Great Events of the Life of the Buddha (*Ashtamahapratiharya*)" according to the Tibetan Buddhist Canon (Tucci 1988: 21–23). Each type had a specific name and was associated with an actual location where a crucial moment in the Shakyamuni Buddha's life took place. The "Lotus-shaped Stupa" or "Stupa of Accumulated Lotuses," for example, stood for Shakyamuni's birth at Lumbini (Tucci 1988: 21–23, 51–52). This clear-cut categorization premised on text is constantly challenged by archaeological evidence and architectural analysis, as stupas with lotus pedestals had been built centuries before the compilation of the Tibetan Canon.[6] On the other hand, the text provides a theological base for scholars to dig into the historical strata of the lotus symbolism and excavate its variations across time and space.[7]

In Upper Ladakh, whitewashed stupas on lotus pedestals are further spotted at Shera, Nyarma, Sabu, Taru, and Gya (Howard 1995; Kozicz 2016). It has to be noted that at Shey, the lotus petals are found in less than 5% of the remaining stupas today. Some of these stupas carry the motif on only one or two sides where it was perhaps least exposed to wind and sandstorms, but what remains of the original moldings has also become largely indistinguishable through "whitewashing." Whitewashing is a local custom of pouring buckets of white paint over the stupas in winter. In a practical sense, it helps to protect the exterior of the structure from weathering; while it is also evocative of the tradition of showering Buddhist and Hindu statues with fragrant water or milk, perhaps even echoing King Asoka's lustration of the sacred trees.

Gandhara: Water Vessels as Reliquaries

The stupa form at Shey is captured by a rare piece of wooden model found in an 11th-century Buddhist sanctuary in Saspotse near Alchi (Fig. 7.7). A row of pilasters supports a lotus pedestal and an elongate stepped terrace divided by four stairs. Above, a secondary lotus pedestal is inserted between the terrace and the vase-shaped dome on top. The shape of the dome (*anda*) resembles a *kundika*—a water jug used for rituals of ablution in pre-Islamic Iran and Central Asia. The Indian equivalent is the "vase of abundance" (*purnakalasha, purnaghata*), an architectural component used as column plinths and capitals in early Buddhist temples in North India (Gairola 1954: 219–22; pls. A–F). The pictorial representation of the vase often shows sprigs of lotus flowers emerging from the container, sometimes supporting a voluptuous goddess figure showered by two elephants squirting water. By the 2nd century BCE, the vase, with its semantics of birth and fertility, had been absorbed into Buddhist iconography and given new theological significance.[8]

The architectural scheme of the Saspotse stupa harks back to Tapa Sardar and further to Gandharan reliquaries. Figure 7.8 shows a stupa-shaped reliquary with a large lotus flower spread over the hemispherical dome (2nd–3rd century CE). The four parasols (*chhatra*) are covered by stylized petals or valances that reinforce the image of the lotus dome. The other example in Figure 7.8, also from Gandhara, shows lotus petals wrapping around both the upper and the lower halves of the globular reliquary.

Indeed, the lotus dome did not always appear with the stupa form but was applied more generally to utensils. Several Buddhist reliquaries (c. 200 BCE) excavated from Sonari and Andher, Central India, are vase-shaped urns carved with lotus petals, medallions, tri-pronged lotus buds (alternatively termed as "palmettes"), elephants, and aquatic birds (Cunningham 1854: pls. XXIX, XXIV). Clearly, the lush water imagery indicates that they are not ordinary

FIGURE 7.7 Wooden stupa model from Saspotse, Ladakh, c. 11th century. Photo by Gerald Kozicz

FIGURE 7.8 Left: Stupa-shaped reliquary. Schist. Pakistan (Gandhara), 2nd–3rd century. Samuel Eilenberg Collection, Metropolitan Museum of Art (1987.142.43a-c). https://www.metmuseum.org/art/collection/search/38105. Photo by Di Luo. Right: Reliquary. Schist with traces of gold leaf. Pakistan (Gandhara), c. 1st century. Metropolitan Museum of Art (1987.258.2a-q). https://www.metmuseum.org/art/collection/search/38115. Photo by Di Luo

vessels but "water vessels" that bestow the power of purification upon the containers. Reliquaries, in tune with stupas, are holders and keepsakes of holy relics and had to be buried underground or deposited in sealed chambers. In these sacralized forms of "preservation" of the dead, the addition of the lotus enabled the cleansing of the burial ground/mound, as if to prevent the sacred content from falling into defilement or eternal darkness. Like a lotus bud waiting to emerge out of the riverbed and bloom under the sky, the proliferation of the lotus on these receptacles destined for concealment indeed confers earnest blessings for rebirth.

Yungang and Himachal: Lotus Ceilings

Peering into the interiors of Buddhist cave temples along the Silk Road, one often finds lotus flowers "suspended" from the center of the ceiling, around which the iconographical program of the entire room is pivoted. Mogao Cave 285 (c. 5th century) in Dunhuang, China, is one of the earliest examples. Its ceiling is framed by a square-and-diamond structure mimicking a wooden lantern.[9] Moving eastward into the heartlands of China, similar lotus ceilings proliferated in the Yungang rock-cut temples of the Northern Wei dynasty (386–535). Here, blue lotus flowers multiply on the ceiling beams and panels in a paradisal scene filled with Atlantean figures and flying deities (Fig. 7.9).

FIGURE 7.9 Lotuses carved in the ceiling of Yungang Cave 9, Shanxi Province, China, c. 484–497 CE, Northern Wei period. Photo by Di Luo

When imperial constructions started at Yungang, the nomadic-born Northern Wei rulers invited eminent monks from Dunhuang to serve as master architects and overseers of the projects. As the court moved the capital in 494 to the east, new excavations commenced in Longmen, where cave ceilings were dominated by a large multilayered lotus flower carved in high relief without an architectural frame. Unlike Yungang and Mogao, this new form of lotus ceiling displays more visual similarity with the Kumtura Caves (5th–6th century) in the Taklamakan and the Haibak Caves (4–5th century) in North Afghanistan, suggesting Northern Wei's awareness of the varied sources of Buddhist architecture west of Dunhuang.[10]

The lotus in the dome was echoed by the lotus on the ground. Two of the imperial caves at Longmen have four and twenty-four lotuses, respectively, carved on the stone floor. As the Indologist Ananda K. Coomaraswamy has analyzed in detail, the upper lotus is a water-sun dual symbol (Coomaraswamy 1935; Snodgrass 1985: 97–100). The twin lotuses symbolize the chthonic water and the heavenly water, which converge in the middle and cleanse the space in between. In Irwin's exhaustive survey of the archaeological evidence of early Indian stupas, the manifold semantics of the twin lotuses take on a temporal dimension: the cyclic creation of the universe is visualized as a primal egg (*anda*, dome) being born out of the cosmic water (earthly lotus) and growing into a World Tree. The Tree (evoked by the central post of every stupa) separates the earth from the sky, while the sun (heavenly lotus) rests at the zenith (Irwin 1979: 843).

Lotus ceilings found outside Buddhist architecture imply the multi-cultural roots of the "heavenly lotus" motif. The Shaktidevi Temple at Chatrari (Himachal Pradesh, India, c. 8th century) has one of the oldest existing wooden lanterns that adopted a range of foliate patterns. The eight-petal central lotus is surrounded by layers of floral roundels and vine scrolls set within a diamond-and-square lantern structure (Fig. 7.10). As much as the lantern ceiling had originated from the opening in the roof that invited natural light into the room, in later developments, the lotus replaced sunlight and became the source of (metaphysical) illumination with its eight radiating petals. The Triloknath Temple in Lahul (c. 9th–10th century) and the Shiva Temple in Pandrethan in Kashmir (c. 10th century) both attest to the reception of the "heavenly lotus" in a broader religious context (Kozicz 2011; 2020). Tracing the

FIGURE 7.10 Wooden ceiling with lotus carvings from the Shaktidevi Temple at Chatrari, Himachal Pradesh, India, c. 8th century. Photo by Gerald Kozicz

symbolism to pre-Buddhist times, Coomaraswamy explains that fire altars dedicated to the Vedic fire god, Agni the "Lotus-born," had to be covered with a lotus leaf to simulate Agni's birthplace and evoke the cycle of cosmogony (Coomaraswamy 1935: 20). Water and fire, two seemingly opposing forces of nature, are harmonized within the lotus.

Prior to the introduction of Buddhism to China, ceilings of Chinese palaces and burial chambers were filled with depictions of the celestial realm, especially the red sun (the ultimate *yang,* or male energy) and the dark-blue moon (the ultimate *yin,* or female energy) (Tseng 2011). Toward the 3rd century, in the late Eastern Han dynasty (25–220 CE), the two celestial orbs started to be replaced by eight-petal (and occasionally four-petal) lotus flowers in tombs (Luo 2022). The eightfold design referred to the four cardinal and four intercardinal directions on the compass, which in Chinese tradition was denoted by the eight trigrams (*bagua*) derived from the dynamics of the *yin* and *yang.* It also corresponded to the Buddhist Eightfold Path represented through the eight-spoked dharma wheel. The lotus, then, assumed the dual identity of the sun and moon, water and fire (light), *yin* and *yang.* Interestingly, the Chinese term for the ceiling coffer (a recessed center in the ceiling structure) was "*zaojing*" (literally, "waterweed well" or "algae well"). Such "wells," where water imagery abounded, were said to be indispensable talismans protecting the wooden building against fire. This practical thread in the semantics of Han ceilings surely facilitated the absorption of the Buddhist lotus into systems of Chinese architectural symbolism (Luo 2020).

Wooden ceilings of Tibetan Buddhist stupas further amplified the importance of the lotus in iconography, turning the aquatic plant into the central field of the cosmogram in every mandala. Additional theological and ritual significance specific to the Vajrayana doctrine was added to the lotus symbolism inherited from the Mahayana tradition, enlarging its purifying, generative, and salvific potentials. To give but a glimpse of the big picture, certain passageway stupas in Ladakh include mantras written on the wooden ceiling panel, encircling the central lotus in a way similar to the inscription on the Nyarma *tsatsa* (see Fig. 7.3). Here, the lotus and the spell are interwoven into a highly formulaic mandala presided over by a Tantric Buddhist pantheon. Placed in the geometric center of such a mandala, the lotus is meanwhile the apex of the vertical axis—the *axis mundi*—whereby a *dharmachaitya* (shrine of the Buddhist law) is sprung.

Conclusion

The investigation into the symbolism of the lotus in Buddhist architecture has taken us on an extensive journey (see map, Fig. 7.1): from the clay stupas in Tapa Sardar, Afghanistan where the earliest existing instances of the lotus pedestal are found to the whitewashed stupas in Shey; from the *tsatsas* in Ladakh, Western Himalayas and Beijing, China to the reliquaries in Gandhara, India; from the ceilings in Chinese Buddhist caves to those of the Hindu temples at the foothills of the Western Himalayas. In all locations, the lotus motif remained central to the creation of a highly distinctive architectural program. During the millennium following the pan-Asian diffusion of the Mahayana doctrine and iconography in the 1st century CE through the Second Diffusion of Buddhism in Tibet in the 10th century CE, the lotus and various water-related motifs continued to fascinate followers of the Faith and channel their imagination of the sacred.

The fields of Shey where these stupas lie were safe havens amidst largely uninviting gorges and glaciers. They constituted a wilderness as formidable as the desolate Taklamakan and the barren highlands of the Pamirs and the Hindukush, where the importance of water cannot be over-emphasized. Even in plains where rains and rivers were abundant, the wish for timely rainfall and the correct use of irrigation water, clean water, and water that douses fire and protects wooden buildings played a dominant role in sacred rituals as well as in mundane aspects of life.

The "earthly" and the "heavenly" water were symbolized by the lower and the upper lotuses that mirrored each other. A lotus pedestal purified the site and elevated the stupa structure from the ground to make it appear floating on water, elevated aboveground, or levitated in the air. From the center of the lotus is engendered, in addition to the stupa proper, a full assembly of the Buddhist deities and their heavenly abodes. A lotus dome again invoked the generative and consecrating power of water and turned Buddhist receptacles into watery vessels of abundance and rebirth. A lotus ceiling can be said to have reversed the lotus pedestal and internalized the lotus dome. Emblematic of water and sun, it cleansed and meanwhile illuminated the interior.

The symbolism of the lotus motif examined in this essay is largely derived from Buddhist purification rites. These included the consecration of land and material before proper constructions commence, the circumambulation of the stupa, the lustration of the Sacred Tree, and the animation and proliferation of votive objects. The multifaceted semantics of the lotus, however, was rooted in and enriched by pre-Buddhist and non-Buddhist traditions. That water is the spring of life and the birthplace of the universe is constantly evoked in Hindu and Vedic imagery, transcending its foundation in primitive fertility cults and becoming a theological conceptualization of cosmogony and spiritual liberation. The Chinese *yin-yang* theories and the imagination of the domed ceiling as a skywell that rendered wooden halls invulnerable to fire, among others, have ensured the Buddhist lotus to be transplanted in lands farther away from home. This symbol of a water flower sanctified the architecture it became a part of.

Acknowledgments

We thank Dr. Anat Geva for her helpful comments on this essay and Dr. Anna Filigenzi for allowing us to publish a photograph from the archives of the Italian Archaeology Mission in Afghanistan.

Notes

1. For a summary of the debate over the theories about "aniconic" versus "no-aniconic" art in early Buddhist sites, including the role stupas and stupa images played, see Linrothe 1993.
2. Taddei 1968; Taddei and Verardi 1978, 1985; Verardi and Paparatti 2005. See also Italian Archaeological Mission in Afghanistan, "The Buddhist Site of Tapa Sardar," https://ghazni.bdus.cloud/buddhist/the-buddhist-site-of-tapa-sardar (accessed on May 7, 2022).
3. Behrendt has noted how the exact nature of these small stupas remains unclear despite their prevalence in the Greater Gandharan region. See Behrendt 2004: 29.
4. *Axis Mundi* or sacred verticality was a concept embodied by religious architecture and shared across world religions (Mann 1993; Geva 2011).
5. Leidy 2010. See Yury Khokhlov, "The Xi Xia Legacy in Sino-Tibetan Art of the Yuan Dynasty," *Asian Art* 2016, https://asianart.com/articles/xi-xia/index.html (accessed May 16, 2022), for the impact of Tangut Buddhist art on the Yuan and Ming periods.
6. The authors will elaborate on this problem in a collaborative book manuscript currently under preparation.
7. Suffice it to mention here that the Eight Pagodas in the Pulesi Temple in the city of Chengde (Jehol), north of Beijing, appear to have resulted from the systemization of the Eight Stupas typology. The stupa types became standardized probably as Vajrayana Buddhism started to take roots in Tibet in the 10th–11th century. Later, such standardization was transplanted into the Chinese capital in the 18th century under the Manchu rulers of the Qing dynasty (1644–1911), when the Pulesi was built.

8. Gairola 1954. See also Zimmer 1955: 158–66, on water goddesses and the evolution of the lotus imagery in Indian iconography; Harvey 1984: 71–72, and Snodgrass 1985: 343–44, 350–51, on the relationship between the vase and the stupa.
9. For lantern ceilings, see Kozicz 2011 and Luo 2020.
10. For plates, drawings, and a preliminary survey of the lotus domed ceiling in Haibak and its possible relation with Northern Wei lotus domes, see Mizuno 1962: 92. Other lotus domes in Chinese cave temples include the Northern Xiangtangshan, the Xiaonanhai, and the Tianlongshan Caves, all dated to the Northern Qi period in the 6th century; see Steinhardt 2014: 215–24.

References

Behrendt, Kurt A. *The Buddhist Architecture of Gandhara*. Leiden: Brill, 2004.

Coomaraswamy, Ananda K. *Elements of Buddhist Iconography*. Cambridge, Mass.: Harvard University Press, 1935.

Cunningham, Alexander. *The Bhilsa Topes or Buddhist Monuments of Central India*. London: Smith, Elder and Co., 1854.

Fisher, Robert. "The Enigma of Harwan." In *Art and Architecture of Ancient Kashmir*, edited by Pal, Pratapaditya. 1–16. Bombay: Marg Publications, 1989.

Fogelin, Lars. "Material Practice and the Metamorphosis of a Sign: Early Buddhist Stupas and the Origin of Mahayana Buddhism." *Asian Perspectives* 51, no. 2 (Fall 2012): 278–310.

Francke, A.H. *A History of Western Tibet*. Delhi: Pilgrims Book House, 1999.

Gairola, C. Krishna. "Évolution du pūrṇa ghaṭa (vase d'abondance) dans l'Inde et l'Inde extérieure." *Arts Asiatiques* 1, no. 3 (1954): 209–26.

Geva, Anat. *Frank Lloyd Wright's Sacred Architecture: Faith, Form and Building Technology*. New York: Routledge, 2011.

Goodyear, W.H. *The Grammar of the Lotus*. London: Sampson Low, Marston and Co, 1891.

Harvey, Peter. "The Symbolism of the Early Stupa." *The Journal of the International Association of Buddhist Studies* 7, no. 2 (1984): 67–93.

Howard, Kath. "Archaeological Notes on Chorten (mChod-rten) Types in Ladakh and Zanskar from the 11th – 15th Centuries." In *Recent Research on Ladakh 4 & 5: Proceedings of the Fourth and Fifth International Colloquia on Ladakh*, edited by Henry Osmaston and Philip Denwood, 61–78. London: School of Oriental & African Studies, University of London, 1995.

Irwin, John. "The Stupa and the Cosmic Axis: The Archaeological Evidence." In *South Asian Archaeology 1977*, edited by Maurizio Taddei, vol. 2, 799–845. Naples: Istituto universitario orientale, 1979.

Irwin, John. "The 'Tree-of-Life' in Indian Sculpture." *South Asian Studies* 6, no. 1 (1990): 27–37.

Kak, Ram Chandra. *Ancient Monuments of Kashmir*. London: The India Society, 1933.

Kim, Sunkyung. "Tree Motifs in Seventh-century Silla Steles." *Acta Koreana* 21, no. 2 (December 2018): 461–80.

Klimburg-Salter, Deborah E. *The Silk Route and the Diamond Path: Esoteric Buddhist Art on the Trans-Himalayan Trade Routes*. Los Angeles: UCLA Art Council, 1982.

Kozicz, Gerald. "Die Laternendecke: Von den Höhlentempeln Bamizans zu den Stupas von Alchi." In *Wakhan: Talschaft zwischen Pamir und Hindukusch*, edited by Robert Kostka, 48–56. Graz: Verlag der Technischen Universität Graz, 2011.

Kozicz, Gerald. "The Buddha, the Temple and the Tree: Observations and Notes on the 'Rammala Stele'." *Journal of Bengal Art* 26 (2021): 43–56.

Kozicz, Gerald. "The Old Stupa of Matho." In *Visible Heritage: Essays on the Art and Architecture of Greater Ladakh*, edited by Rob Linrothe and Heinrich Poll, 114–30. New Delhi: Studio Orientalia, 2016.

Kozicz, Gerald. "Triloknath Revisited: Recent Results from Field Research." *Études mongoles et sibériennes, centrasiatiques et tibétaines* 51 (2020): 1–29.

Leidy, Denise Patry. "Buddhism and Other 'Foreign' Practices in Yuan China." In James C.Y. Watt and Maxwell K. Hearn, *The World of Khubilai Khan: Chinese Art in the Yuan Dynasty*, 87–128. New York: The Metropolitan Museum of Art, 2010.

Linrothe, Rob. "Inquiries into the Origin of the Buddha Image: A Review." *East and West* 43, no. 1/4 (1993): 241–256.

Luo, Di. "Dome of Heaven: From the Lantern Ceiling to the Chinese Wooden Dome." In *Silk Roads: From Local Realities to Global Narratives*, edited by Jeffrey Lerner and Yaohua Shi, 131–59. Oxford & Philadelphia: Oxbow Books, 2020.

Luo, Di. "Yinan and Mylasa: Sino-Hellenic Exchanges in Tomb Architecture." *Scientific Culture* 8 (2022), no. 3: 35–48.

Mann, A.T. *Sacred Architecture.* Shaftesbury, Dorset; Rocksport, Mass.: Element, 1993.

Mizuno, Seiichi, ed. *Haibak and Kashmir-Smast: Buddhist Cave-temples in Afghanistan and Pakistan surveyed in 1960.* Kyoto University, 1962.

Petech, Luciano. "Western Tibet: Historical Introduction." In *Tabo: A Lamp for the Kingdom: Early Indo-Tibetan Buddhist Art in the Western Himalaya*, edited by Deborah Klimburg-Salter, 229–55. Milan, Italy: Skira, 1997.

Sivaramamurti, C. *Approach to Nature in Indian Art and Thought.* New Delhi: Kanak Publications, 1980.

Skilling, Peter. "Buddhist Sealings and the ye dharma Stanza." In *Precious Treasures from the Diamond Throne: Finds from the Site of the Buddha's Enlightenment*, edited by Sam van Schaik, Daniela De Simone, Gergely Hidas and Michael Willis, 76–86. London: The British Museum, 2021.

Snodgrass, Adrian. *The Symbolism of the Stupa.* Ithaca, N.Y.: Cornell University Press, 1985.

Steinhardt, Nancy. *Chinese Architecture in an Age of Turmoil, 200–600.* Honolulu: University of Hawaii Press, 2014.

Taddei, Maurizio. "Inscribed Clay Tablets and Miniature Stupas from Ghazni." *East and West* 20, no. 1/2 (March – June 1970): 70–86.

Taddei, Maurizio. "Tapa Sardar: First Preliminary Report." *East and West* 18, no. 1/2 (March–June 1968): 109–124.

Taddei, Maurizio, and Giovanni Verardi. "Clay Stupas and Thrones at Tapa Sardar, Ghazni (Afghanistan)." In *Zinbun: Memoirs of the Research Institute for Humanistic Studies.* Zinbun Kagaku Kenkyusyo, Kyoto University, 1985.

Taddei, Maurizio, and Giovanni Verardi. "Tapa Sardar Second Preliminary Report." *East and West* 28, no. 1/4 (December 1978): 33–135.

Tseng, Lillian Lan-ying. *Picturing Heaven in Early China.* Cambridge, Mass: Harvard University Asia Center for the Harvard-Yenching Institute, 2011.

Tucci, Giuseppe. *Indo-Tibetica*, translated and edited by Lokesh Chandra. Volume 1. New Delhi: Aditya Prakashan, 1988.

Verardi, Giovanni, and Elio Paparatti. "From Early to Late Tapa Sardar: A Tentative Chronology." *East and West* 55, no. 1/4 (December 2005): 405–444.

Ward, William E. "The Lotus Symbol: Its Meaning in Buddhist Art and Philosophy." *The Journal of Aesthetics and Art Criticism* 11, no. 2 (1952): 135–146.

Zimmer, Heinrich. *The Art of Indian Asia, Its Mythology and Transformations.* 2 volumes. New York: Pantheon Books, 1955.

8
THE SACREDNESS OF WATER AND PLACE

African and Diasporic Religious Cultural Encounters

Peter F. Adebayo, Christopher S. Hunter, and Oluwafunminiyi Raheem

Water is said to pre-date the creation of the earth and the sun (Cleeves et al. 2014) and formed one of the first materials or elements in space long before any known human existence. Water antedates not only the creation of mankind but also any other inanimate or non-human objects which combined eventually to make up the earth itself (Cleeves et al. 2014). Imbued with enormous powers, water has been put to all kinds of uses throughout history (Blount 2017; Hong 2013). Indeed, the exploitation of water's inherent powers has given rise to complex forms of shared processes that have transformed earthly existence and the way civilization evolved from the Stone Age to the present time (Juuti et al. 2007). Water conjures meanings in different socio-cultural spaces which suggest that there exists a historically potent dialogue between water and its adaptation of its utilization by human beings. Societies regard water located in both enclosed and open spaces—dams, rivers, springs, seas, oceans—as a material power that sustains everyday life (Bartholomew 2010); as a result, these watery spaces take on a heritage of place. They similarly become potential agencies for local inflexion, where cultural traditions and environmental practices are facilitated (Ray 2012: 141).

The focus in this chapter provides an explanatory discourse on water's utilitarian and intrinsic value within the context of African traditional beliefs and interrogates both water's transformative component and its functionality in African culture and myths. To illustrate this concept, this chapter examines water's influence on African and Diasporic religious and cultural encounters. Specifically, we examine the relationship of water with West African sacred places such as the Olokun Temple (Nigeria), as well as the Diasporic influence on the development of sacred places of praise and worship during American enslavement.

Although water is a tangible element with the capacity for utilitarian benefits in African belief, it also holds extraordinary spiritual value (Olajubu 2002: 109). With this in mind, over time, many African societies have come up with several aphorisms to explain the value or worth of water. In this respect, water's utilitarian and intrinsic worth is beyond its tangible attributes. The Yoruba proverb, *Omi, baale alejo* (Water, the lord, and master of the visitor), for instance, places water, by its very nature, in the position of a maximal power which a visitor cannot refuse or discard. Yoruba studies scholar, Oyekan Owomoyela demonstrates the connection between desire and nature, which only water could satisfy, as an element of nature

DOI: 10.4324/9781003358824-11

itself (2005: 496). The denotative meaning of the proverb is, thus, captured by Owomoyela: "Water is the ultimate thing with which one welcomes a visitor."

Beyond its idealization in proverbs, water is perceived in several other ways and, in this case, is very much central to the cultural worldview of many African societies, for example, the Yoruba of Nigeria.[1] In illustrating the utilitarian value of water, its potential as a spiritual and physical force also becomes clearer in this excerpt of a popular song rendered in praise of the Osun deity by Yoruba folk music artist, Asabioje Afenapa, in the song titled, *Osun*.[2] The song's deep meanings call for a brief explanation. The utilitarian conception of water among the Yoruba, in this case, is marked by its manifestation as a powerful force. By this, we mean that water evinces the presence of a deity and through such water, humankind can benefit from the "power of place" that a sacred body unconditionally provides. Professor of Environmental Arts and Humanities and Anthropology, Celeste Ray corroborates this view by suggesting that "Sacred sites remained numinous places; only the presiding spirit of the place became an intercessor with the ultimate divine rather than being divine" (2010: 8). The Osun River in Osogbo, Nigeria, for instance, is not only numinous but devotees believe that the Osun deity presides over it and has retained the role of an intercessor up to the present day (Murphy and Sanford 2001: 1). Osun is referred to as "*Ajeje* the mother of the day" and "a mother who has herb in the river, her given child would have longevity" (Fakayode and Origunwa 2012). These poetic citations appear to attribute the powers of creation and life sustainment to Osun, powers exclusive to Olodumare (the Yoruba Supreme Being).

Scholar on the theological studies of the Yoruba, Bolaji Idowu (1970), regards Olodumare as not only the creator of the day but also the one who grants both children and longevity. Possibly, Osun devotees who recite this poetry do so with very little or no concern for the boundaries that exist between the powers of the Osun deity and Olodumare. For her devotees, Osun exists beyond her reductive identity (as river goddess of fertility) and is strongly imagined in multidimensional forms embedded in the "political, economic, divinatory, maternal, natural, [and] therapeutic" (Murphy and Mei-Mei 2001). By referring to Osun in these forms through this specific poetry, her multidimensional powers may indicate that she is equated with the attributes associated with Olodumare, which is not usually the case. Osun, by her proximity to Olodumare, holds the dual role (among others) of intercessor and messenger, and although she is the last of the seventeen *orisa* (deities) and from whom all Yoruba *Odu* (sacred text) are derived, she is considered an indispensable deity (Probst 2004: 33–54). A writer notes that "Without Osun's sanction, no healing can take place, no rain can fall, no plants can bear fruit, and no children can come into the world" (Abiodun 2001: 18). This may explain why Osun's devotees often equate her powers with Olodumare's, although this is not necessitated by any conscious notion of hierarchical boundaries.

Incidentally, the song does not reveal whether this water, to which the artist attributes powerful human strength, refers to Osun, but it is clear that the Osun River's water is regarded with reverence. Water becomes the principal curative agent, which manifests powers without human intervention. Hence, the power inherent in water is such that it can resolve human adversities in the same way that it transforms itself into a destructive power capable of lifting or uprooting a tree, never mind a human being, without the use or need of an arm, leg, or machine. The personal relationship between humans and water fits well with the belief, whether secular or religious, that water is endowed with supernatural qualities or powers that are transformative. In itself, water exists as a sacred body and holds universal affinity, which explains why it appears in many myths, legends, songs, and spirits as a connective agency between the natural world and the *otherworld* imagined by humankind.

Water Songs and Spirits

Early African American religious culture developed as a blend of African heritage with the experiences of the enslaved (Jackson 1997: 31–35). The invention of field songs, created by enslaved persons and which came to be called "spirituals," and the act of spirit possession, are two of the ways enslaved as well as free persons expressed their experiences in America.[3] This expression was achieved through songs, water spirits, and placemaking.

Song

Water's spiritual meaning was presented not only in traditional Christian religious practices such as baptism but also in the context of African American songs, originally known as the "Negro Spirituals."[4] African American spirituals are considered the first distinctive music genre of African people in the American diaspora.[5] Spirituals were inspired by black preachers' messages, or in individual contemplation of the Bible stories heard at home and work. But the spirituals are virtually all anonymous, as the actual composers and lyricists have never been identified. Thus, in a profound sense, the community "wrote" them. For spirituals, water is a frequent subject.

While some spirituals have clear heroes—Moses and Daniel, for example—many songs use water, as well as important symbols such as the River Jordan, which holds significant meaning in Christianity as the place where the Israelites crossed into the "Promised Land." The River Jordan is prominently referred to in spirituals as an allegorical reference for everything from freedom through death, to an expression of current hardships. James H. Cone (1938–2018), an American theologian best known for his advocacy of black theology and black liberation theology, believed the River Jordan had two fundamental meanings in African American spirituals. First, the River Jordan represented the death that was typically seen as liberation from the harsh realities of slave life (Smith-Christopher undated). Thus, "crossing Jordan" was a theme directly linked to "going home," to restore a community lost in oppression and slavery. Second, the Jordan could also represent both the mental and actual physical border between slavery and freedom—the "other side of the Jordan" could just as often suggest the Northern states, or even Canada, and thus, freedom.[6] In the biblical story of Moses leading the Children of Israel out of slavery and across the Red Sea, water becomes an instrument of revenge, drowning the pursuing soldiers.[7] For the enslaved, there was sacredness in the song about a river as a place where the promise of peace and comfort was assured.

Usually led by a pastor, now more often by a choir, spirituals were at the heart of a praise service; they served as a unifying resource for those who sang and experienced sorrow. Spirituals would play a significant role as vehicles for protest during the twentieth and early twenty-first centuries. During the Civil Rights Movement of the 1950s and 1960s, the singing of spirituals supported the efforts of civil rights activists.

In Christianity, baptism is perceived as a personal experience, where one is sprinkled with, or even immersed in, water as a sign of being accepted into the body of the Church. The song, "Take Me to the Water," written by Nina Simore, is a fine example of Afrocentric music intersecting with the spiritual experience of baptism.[8] As Christianity flourished in the African American community, this action became expressive through song as well as action (Staten and Roach 1996). In the Louisiana Delta region, African American Baptists occasionally perform their sacred ritual of outdoor baptisms in rivers, bayous and lakes. In the late 1950s, outdoor baptism was common in both black and white Protestant churches in rural

North Louisiana (Staten and Roach 1996). Although the majority of urban and modernized rural churches have indoor baptismal pools, some African American urban congregations, along with older churches without indoor facilities, have chosen to maintain the earlier, natural setting for this important rite of passage, which is both symbolic ritual purification and initiation. Participants in the act of immersion are typically clothed in white, with family and the "church family" in attendance, while the pastor performs the baptism. As each candidate is brought out of the water, the congregation applauds and sings refrains from favorite baptismal songs. These services are generally spirit-filled and overwhelmed with the congregation singing, shouting praises, and shedding tears, as they watch their children being baptized.[9]

Water Spirits

Nature worship was a major component of West African spiritual practices, which later became part of the African American religious experience. Evidence exists of water spirits being part of enslaved people's belief system, especially those residing in the Lowcountry region of coastal South Carolina. These spirits, called "cymbee," or "simbi," often helped to define, and sometimes protect, physical areas where enslaved people worked and lived.[10] These physical places, where it was believed that water spirits existed, would be claimed by the spirits themselves; in extreme cases, the spirits were even feared. Professor and editor, Darrell J. Pursiful defines the cymbee as water spirits that hail from Western and Central Africa.[11] The "spirits" live in unusual rocks, gullies, streams, springs, waterfalls, sinkholes, and pools—areas which the cymbee effectively "adopts" acting as territorial guardians.

Cymbee are said to be able to influence the fertility and well-being of the people living in their territory.[12] At the same time, they can and will cause trouble if they are not treated with respect. The word "cymbee" is a phonetic spelling of the Kikongo word *"simbi,"* heard among enslaved Africans in the American South in the 1800s.[13] The same sort of being is called a *kilundu* or *kalundu* in the Kimbundu language of Angola. Their existence in South Carolina's Lowcountry reveals how enslaved people were concerned about maintaining their community, as well as their spiritual and material survival. As such, cymbee were vital features of enslaved people's cultural landscape.

Ras Michael Brown, an Associate Professor of History and Africana Studies at Southern Illinois University, describes the simbi in their various manifestations playing evolving roles in the spiritual culture of African-descended people throughout the Lowcountry. Brown notes that their stronghold remains the (water) springs. While the simbi could occupy many features and spaces, the limestone region's springs were specially marked as both natural landmarks and spiritual sites, and served as the home of the simbi (Brown 2012: 4–12). Though the cymbee's presence was often desired, the general belief among enslaved people of the Lowcountry was that cymbees were to be feared (Adams 2007). The "claiming" of a place by the cymbee, however, substantiates the act of placemaking, albeit through fear, by the enslaved living within these coastal regions (Brown 2012).

Mami Wata, a water spirit originating from the West, Central, and Southern African regions, is also present within the African diaspora.[14] Knowledge of this spirit spread throughout enslaved people's communities on southern plantations and was worshipped through dance and possession. The deity is believed to be a woman (though elsewhere a man), with a human upper body and the lower half being either a fish (with a tail) or a snake (Kwekudee 2012). The deity possesses the ability to transform wholly into any form of her choice. Mami Wata provides spiritual and material healing to her worshippers, while also protecting their emotional and mental health and growth. She is also the protector of the water bodies (Kwekudee 2012). Many traditional groups in Africa today do not go to the beach or go fishing on certain days, out of respect for the water deity's home. During the African diaspora, Mami Wata is believed to have traveled across the Atlantic with enslaved Africans, protecting them and relieving them of their pain. She is said to have capsized many slave ships that did not make it to their western destinations. She often appears as a human to enslaved people, as a way of protecting them when they did not have access to bodies of water. Over the course of decades, by appearing in human form, she reminded enslaved people that she had not forsaken them.[15]

There has always been a spiritual connection between water and Christianity, a connection that has never been lost on African Americans (Hughes et al. 1994). As enslaved Africans and their descendants were introduced to Christianity, blending this new religion with their rooted West African worship practice presented the opportunity for a new understanding of water's significance. As Africans and African Americans syncretized their cultural-religious practices with Christianity, a new form of appreciation and understanding emerged of water's influence and value.[16] Whether this value was embodied in song as a form of worship, within the context of a poem, or in the creation of a sacred place, water took on and established a presence in all these creative forms, attaining a measure of reverence and respect from both enslaved and free people: an application of sacredness.

Water as Sacred Placemaking

Olokun Temple, Nigeria

One of the most important sacred agencies within the Olokun Temple is the holy well, Olokun (Fig. 8.1). At the Olokun Temple, visitors are confronted with an unconventional and unusual round ring, made from red faded bricks. Enclosed within the ring is what traditions say is the remnant of the ocean after human habitation was established on Earth (Ile-Ife), and the site where the Olokun deity resides.[17] Local accounts point to the fact that the water of the Olokun well originally flowed along a wide area, crossing beyond the Temple's boundaries, but receded gradually until it rested at its current spot.[18] Even while the water receded, there were periods when it also overflowed, particularly in the wet season, which initiated the quest for gated structures symbolized by the layers of red bricks built around the well. As previously observed, these gated structures are in most cases human-made, not natural, features and constructed for reasons ranging from controlling the water flow to maintaining the well's taboo, protection from unnecessary intrusion, and establishing separate areas for specific ritual tasks, among others. Furthermore, the gated structures are unique markers for ritual practices by devotees, the chief priest, palace chiefs, or the traditional ruler of the place where a holy well is situated (Raheem 2021).

The Olokun Temple's sacred landscape incorporates a small iron emblem, which is strategically placed close to the shrine and represents Ogun, the Yoruba deity of iron, whose presence in the Temple is indicative of Olokun cult's recognition of the deity's vital force. Taboos are strictly observed at the Temple, initiation rites are held, and prayers, invocations and folk songs are also part of this devotion to Olokun. The Olokun well is the highest point of spiritual devotion within the Temple's landscape. Those in search of wealth and fertility can derive well-being from the remedial qualities present in the holy well's water. Here, devotees pray to Olokun, making a votive deposition at the well to conclude the ritual.

FIGURE 8.1 Olokun holy well in the Walode Compound, Ilode Quarters, Ile-Ife, Nigeria.
Photo: Author

Hush Harbor, United States

A "hush harbor" was necessarily a secluded place, typically located in a heavily wooded area, near ravines, swamps, or other bodies of water. The invention of field songs, created by enslaved persons and which came to be called "spirituals," and the act of spirit possession, are two of the ways enslaved as well as free persons expressed their experiences in America.[19] This expression was achieved through songs, water spirits, and placemaking.

Risking their lives, enslaved people would gather for secret religious meetings held under the cover of darkness (Nelson 2019) The hush harbor (also called "brush arbor," or "bush arbor") can be considered an early African American example of a riparian, as well as religious, form of placemaking Early African American religious culture developed as a blend of African heritage with the experiences of the enslaved (Nelson 2019). The invention of field songs, created by enslaved persons and which came to be called "spirituals," and the act of spirit possession, are two of the ways enslaved as well as free persons expressed their experiences in America.[20] This expression was achieved through songs, water spirits, and placemaking. Spaces defined by the activities of the enslaved became places often involving the presence of water. The roots of what is today known as the institution of the Black Church in America reside in the hush harbor's creation.[21]

Reverend Angela Ford Nelson comments on the existence and impact of the hush harbor on the enslaved:

> hush harbor[s] … enabled slaves to worship in spirit and in truth in thickly forested areas which were hidden from their masters … [and they] were free to combine both

African and Christian worship practices. It was in the hush harbor, buried deep within the untended woods on the plantation that slaves remembered the forests of their homeland.[22]

Nelson offers another explanation regarding the activities which took place in hush harbors:

> it was there that [enslaved peoples] were able to practice African rituals and to rest in knowing that the spirits of their ancestors [had] followed them—even into slavery. The hush harbor would eventually serve as not only a place for worship, but also as a place where unrelated slaves would become a sustaining family of faith.
>
> *(Nelson 2019)*

The natural setting of the hush harbors' woods and thickets harkened back to nature's presence and influence in West African spirit worship. In addition, waterways may well have provided the means for enslaved people to reach the predetermined place of worship undetected; traveling through or near a body of water would conceal their scent and throw off their pursuers:

> [They] were primarily located in places like the dismal swamp or ravines, ditches, and thickets. Because of the fear of being caught and brutally punished they never held clandestine church services in the same place ... The first people to arrive at the meeting used a broken tree bough to point towards the hush harbor... to suppress the sounds, the slaves ... filled a kettle with water.[23]

With the creation of hush harbors and specifically their locations in swamps or near bodies of water, African Americans placemaking could be correlated to the Yoruba places identified as temples and shrines, the gathering places for people to worship.

Black Sacred Spaces

Ancestral Shrines (Olokun Temple)

The Yoruba people created temples and shrines as expressions of sacred architecture, with the use of water features as part of their spiritual practices to honor their deities, and thus these structures are examples of West African placemaking. A sacred landscape is a "constructed sacrality," that exists as both a physical structure, such as temples and shrines, and non-physical ones, that are motivated by meanings that could either be by chance or deliberate.[24] The site becomes sacred when a connection is formed with a divinity that demarcates the newly acquired sacred construct from the profane: "something sacred [that] shows itself to us" (Eliade 1958: 7). Hence, sacred landscapes are structures that

> find expression in ... architecture and mythology and exist as part of a dialogue between the individual, society, and the natural world. The sacred is sensed or proclaimed by people, and without them, the space reverts to an undifferentiated medium, and any meaning is lost.
>
> *(Burns 2020)*

While this description identifies some features found within a sacred landscape, others are missing. Here, we discuss the Olokun Temple in the Yoruba town of Ile-Ifẹ, Nigeria, and

FIGURE 8.2 Members of Olokun Cult
Photo: Author

"hush harbors" in America—hidden places where enslaved people would practice their form of religion. Hush harbors were generally located in the southeastern region of the United States (Virginia, North and South Carolina, Georgia, Alabama, Tennessee, Mississippi, Louisiana, Arkansas, and Texas). We analyze how these two types of sacred spaces for Africans are configured through (re)negotiated religious devotion and ritual practices.

The Olokun Temple covers a very extensive land area, as shown in Figure 8.2, and has been greatly impacted over a lengthy period by both human and natural causes, for instance, a Christian church at the back of the Temple was built by a local church group. Though the Temple's main entrance does not have a gate, the Temple itself is secured on both sides with a welded wire-mesh fence which is joined to a fairly high block wall that covers the residual part of the Temple. Why these constructed forms were made is not clear, but they were likely built to safeguard the once extensive landmass of the Temple from further encroachment. This may also have been spurred to prevent the further expansion of the church building.

Sacred temples (or shrines/groves) of this nature usually included spacious courtyards that, in several instances, were carved out from surrounding farmland (Wolff and Warren 1998: 39). These lands, linked with human survival and habitation, attract a large population who migrate there and eventually settle into one or several families within a compound(s). Each group's migration to this particular spot usually introduces new cultures, attitudes, and religious practices. These bring new deities, who are adopted into the family compound's religious life, where they become objects of devout worship. If the deity's power is highly regarded, the family compound receives a greater advantage in the socio-political scheme of things. It also garners for itself a large following and/or a close relationship with many important and renowned people or agencies (Stevens-Arroyo and Mena 1995: 85). The above statement is significant in that it shows that temples in the past

FIGURE 8.3 A part of the extensive land area of the Olokun Temple
Photo: Author

were constructed, as Burns affirms, as open and "ungated" areas, except for those places selected within the Temple for the attendance of key devotees or the Temple's chief priest (*Walode*) and certain rituals.

The Olokun Temple retains a small building or structure known as the Olokun Shrine, shown in Figure 8.3. The shrine's interior comprises a small cubicle chamber accessible only to the chief priest and others that he allows to join him.[25] The shrine is surrounded by a compact area for Olokun devotees[26] to perform designated religious and non-religious activities. There is a difference between the Temple and the shrine. While the former is a vast expanse of land where all kinds of worship or activities associated with Olokun are performed, the shrine is a small building within the Temple where the crucial aspects of rituals are performed to Olokun. Both are usually open to the public which suggests that both devotees and non-devotees are free to enter and make supplications, or express appreciation to the Olokun deity. The cubicle chamber's entrance, however, is covered with flowing white cloth for privacy and serves especially as a form of boundary for women, who are prohibited from entering the cubicle, as indicated by the cult's taboos.[27] The shrine hosts a 17-day meeting (*Itadogun*) where many issues affecting members of the Olokun cult are discussed and ultimately acted upon.

For Olokun shrines elsewhere, several physical images or ritual objects which symbolize the iconography and cosmography of Olokun dot their landscapes (Ben-Amos 1973). Ironically, these objects were discovered to be missing from the Olokun Temple. This stems from the historic and cultural relationship between Ile-Ifẹ and several Yoruba communities in Nigeria, West Africa, and in the diaspora where diffusion of the Olokun deity or Olokun cult had occurred in the past (Mason 1996). In this Olokun Temple, the only available image to be seen which complements the Olokun deity was a white painted wall and the cult members' white clothing. Both sides of the entrance leading into the shrine and the cubicle chamber show evidence of mural drawings of fish, cowries and gourds which appeared minimal and inconspicuous. There is a suggestion that the Olokun Temple holds an ancestral image, possibly a terracotta head, which represents the Olokun deity. This image is believed to be in a secret location and only appears at the shrine for appeasement during the annual Olokun festival (Ogunsola 2013). However, we did not see this image during the Olokun festivals we witnessed in 2019 and 2021.

From close observation, the Olokun Temple was discovered to be empty while the shrine lacks the necessary traditional objects or ancient materials (artifacts, mud or wooden images, cowries among others) that are found in several Yoruba and Afrocentric shrines or sacred landscapes. Several decades of deliberate stripping and decay mean that no remnants of these objects or recent materials that symbolize the Olokun deity exist within the Temple today. This is supported by the fact that most sacred shrines in Yorubaland and, indeed, the larger sacred temples or groves, even as they are in decline, still retain sacred symbols or artifacts, either placed on the floor or hung on the walls (Luzzatto 2009). The *Oluorogbo* shrine in Ile-Ife is a good example of a sacred site retaining very old wall paintings.[28] As in many Yoruba towns, the art of shrine painting is not lost in Ile-Ife but is a tradition well preserved by the *Orisa Ikire* painting school (Okediji 1989). These religious murals, found on the entrance walls of Yoruba shrines are not mere decoration; rather they express a deeply distinct spirituality, representing devotees' and priests' responses to a deity's power. Images of animals and, in many other cases, general abstract figures symbolize the shrine's deity. It is possible that in the past the Olokun shrine would have been covered with beautiful mural paintings, mud images, and other elaborate iconographies representing Olokun, with beads being an important insignia. Interestingly, the gate leading out of the Temple shrine contains eight medium-sized gourds, a few of which are also lined up at various distances from the shrine itself. From the way they are roughly placed, they appear to serve an aesthetic purpose rather than symbolize any ritual quality. It is important to note that the present shrine in the Olokun Temple may not have been the original shrine known in earlier times: it could have either been washed away (since this structure was made of mud) or demolished to make way for the current one. This may likely explain why the Olokun shrine appears to be "drained" of the requisite sacred objects, images, or materials that many ancient or modern Yoruba and Afrocentric shrines are identified with.

As well as wall art paintings, Yoruba and Afrocentric shrines also contain wooden sculptures which usually represent the deity of the shrine's chief priest (Probst 2015: 247). The cult of Olokun is ancient, and as one of the foremost sacred water deities in Yorubaland and the Black Atlantic, the Olokun Temple likely housed at some point many important sacred objects. From both earlier and more recent archeological excavations, for instance, evidence indicates that Igbo-Olokun (a sister grove) contained several categories of ritual and non-ritual sacred objects, many of which were found buried deep inside the grounds (Frobenius 1913). How these objects were used in the past is still unknown, but they were usually disinterred during annual sacrifices or for ritual offerings after which they were re-buried. If this was the case with Igbo-Olokun, the same could also be said of the Olokun Temple. Earlier known as the Grove of Olokun Walode, this particular sacred landscape was excavated by renowned British archeologist, Bernard Fagg, in 1953. On the site, he found a "few inches below the surface ... a fragmentary face ... in a remarkably unweathered condition ... [and] a small head with enormous ears found with it ... noticeably eroded" (Willet 1967: 25). Close to the excavated site, Fagg discovered "Individual fragments from a variety of terracotta sculptures: the leg of a bush cow, the left thighs of two different kneeling figures, two hands holding a bowl, a right hand holding a matchet, a fragment of a right foot of about two-thirds of Ife-size, and a dozen other pieces, apparently all from different sculptures" (Willet 1967: 25).

These items, as Willett points out, were excavated by Fagg from different parts of the Grove of Olokun Walode. Also found was a fragment and complete set of glass-making crucibles, the latter held in the safe custody of the Walode family. Artifacts also included a terracotta head, used in the worship of the deity in the Grove of Olokun Walode. This terracotta head seems to be the ancestral stone earlier alluded to. Although there is no mention by Fagg of the presence of beads in the items found in the Grove of Olokun Walode, it may be assumed that these were present but in minimal quantities. There are reasons to believe that artifacts from the Grove of Olokun Walode are in many respects similar to those excavated by Frobenius four decades earlier, as Willett suggested that both Igbo-Olokun and Olokun Walode were closely connected (Willet 1967). What is, however, important is that these artifacts acted as mediating materials in the relationship between the institution of kingship and what art critic for the *Washington Post*, Sebastian Smee, calls the "collective power of the Ife people."[29]

The African American Church House

As African Americans began to construct church buildings, such as the First African Baptist Church of Savannah, Georgia, founded in the late 1700s (Fig. 8.4), a rural church house would find it easier to conduct baptism immersions if sited near a body of water. However,

FIGURE 8.4 The First African Baptist Church, Savannah, Georgia
Photo: Author

beginning in the twentieth century, more African American churches were built in urban settings and the newly constructed building would probably have a baptismal pool included in its structure. Today, as in most churches based on Christian belief, a baptism pool is likely designed and located prominently within the church's sanctuary, for all worshippers to witness and experience. How the baptismal pool is designed within the church house is a contemporary example of placemaking rooted in the creation of the hush harbor.

Praise houses in Lowcountry South Carolina and Georgia were constructed examples of placemaking. The construction of late nineteenth- and early twentieth-century wood-and-brick buildings housing water sources or "holy wells" within their walls were the next evolutionary step in the architectural design of these places. Today, the current and contemporary architecture of churches designed to highlight the religious experience of water immersion represents twenty-first-century worship practices in now clearly defined black placemaking.

It has been argued in academic and mainstream circles as to whether any aspect of Afrocentric culture and spiritual practice survived the Middle Passage and the institution of slavery. One of the most well-known of these intellectual debates occurred between E. Franklin Frazier, an African American sociologist who argued that African Americans were culturally American without any traces of their African past, and Melville J. Herskovits, a German American anthropologist, known for his exploration of African cultural retention. This debate is relevant to the question of whether there is cultural evidence of the sacred nature of placemaking informed by the presence of water.

The Franklin–Herskovits debate[30] asks: to what degree of success did the institutions that upheld slavery have in eradicating the humanity of the enslaved? More succinctly, spiritual beliefs have historically provided the greatest level of personhood. For the enslaved, the ability to develop an interpretive meaning for water in their physical, psychological, and spiritual lives established a substantial level of personhood, to the point that an enslaved person would risk their lives to "steal away" to a hush harbor for spiritual and social sustenance.[31] This perspective would suggest that enslaved people's personhood survived the Middle Passage, creating a newly blended worldview of Eurocentric religion with Afrocentric culture, motivated by the desire to survive. The horrors of chattel slavery established the foundational experience for the creation of "Negro" spirituals and worship practices as a reinvention of water's influence in song, to reflect African Americans' living conditions.[32] The process of blending different African cultures with their American experiences did not start from a void. It is our position that enslaved people's elements of personhood had certainly already existed and were not completely eradicated from black consciousness, and though severed from its origins, were redefined by Africans living in America based on the context in which they resided. This position would contradict the argument that Franklin (1894-1962) makes about African culture's complete elimination in favor of an American belief system, while not entirely endorsing the point of view of Herskovits (1895–1963).

In his effort to argue for Afrocentric culture's survival, Melville Herskovits posits that the influence of the Baptist denomination of Christianity and its evocation of water confirms a cultural connection to certain West African religious practices.[33] Albert J. Raboteau, an American scholar of African and African-American religions, cites:

> "The strong appeal of the Baptist denomination for Negroes was due partially to the West African religious background, where water cults are extremely important. The Baptists' insistence on immersion was an attractive rite to Africans familiar with

water cults because the concept of baptism is one "that any African would find readily understandable".

(2004: 57)

This observation attempts to link cultural practices centered around water cults with the Eurocentric religious practice of water immersion as part of the baptism exercise of accepting Christ as a spiritual savior. This immersion exercise was embraced by enslaved Africans and later free African Americans (Staten and Roach 1996). With remarkable regularity across human cultures, water has been used to communicate the sacred value of life, the spiritual dimension of purification, protection and healing, and the profound symbol of suffering and redemption in human life.[34] The nineteenth-century practice of baptism by immersion was for many African Americans typically performed in a river which likely was near a church building. Henry H. Mitchell (1919–2002), a religious leader, professor of religion as well as Pan-African Studies writes about the baptism exercise:

> Among African Americans, the immense and immediate popularity of the new Baptist faith, with its baptism by immersion, was a clear throwback to the powerful importance of water rituals in African traditional religion. And the same might be said of communion services, as kin to the ever-present African rite of pouring libation.
>
> *(2004: 14)*

Hush harbor activities did not take place indoors but were held in a natural, outdoor setting, consistent with many African religious practices which were physically centered in nature, as W.E.B. DuBois, an American sociologist, socialist, historian, and Pan-Africanist civil rights activist (1868–1963) researched and documented (DuBois 2011). There was no need for a building, nor was it relevant to the religious practices in either Africa or the antebellum South. Further, it is unknown if baptism by immersion occurred in gatherings at hush harbors.

When they had the opportunity, and increasingly so after the American Civil War, African Americans built structures such as praise houses on or near their old plantations during the years after Reconstruction, from the 1870s to the 1900s.[35] The praise house's function had persisted since before Emancipation and its basic architectural form has been retained.[36] The activities held in the praise house, as well as the building itself, can be considered a precursor to today's African American worship experience. As such, the African American church house became a space that was controlled, owned, and protected by its users. These worshippers did not need a Eurocentric yardstick to define the value or quality of their churches' religious beauty, nor did the buildings need to refer to venerated architectural styles to achieve relevance and substance.

Enslaved people experienced conflict between the spirituality they had created and developed in their brush arbors, and the efforts to resist the controlling efforts of plantation owners and clergy to Christianize them (Raboteau 2004). This conflict encouraged the enslaved population to attempt to define for themselves how they would interpret Christianity. This interpretation would honor African traditions without yielding their culture to the plantation owners' controlling efforts. Our conclusion is that enslaved Africans attempted to understand and determine which parts of the Gospel to syncretize with their own culture, and how far to emulate white Christian denominations. Protestant and Catholic faiths embrace the church building's symbolism, using design and material applications such as cruciform-shaped building plans and stained-glass windows, to tell

FIGURE 8.5 The Contemplation Court in the National Museum of African American History and Culture, Washington, D.C.
Photo: Author

biblical as well as ethnic stories to a congregation. The belief, however, that people of color may need to emulate white denominations to integrate into American society was probably one reason why African Americans believed it necessary to consider holding their spiritual services inside a building of their own (Hunter 2018). As a result, baptismal immersion practices would eventually move from a natural setting to one where a pool would be constructed in the church house, maintaining the continued connection of water to African American religious practice.

The "Contemplative Court," shown in Figure 8.5, is a secular and contemporary example of water's influence on African Americans and their worship patterns. It is located in the National Museum of African American History and Culture in Washington, DC, which opened in 2016, designed by the architectural collaboration of The Freelon Group, Sir David Adjaye, and the Bond Smith Group. The Contemplative Court has a water feature oriented in a circular pattern, and rains downs from the ceiling to the floor. The circle reminds visitors of the Olokun Temple's circled well, while the space provides seating that offers visitors the opportunity for personal thought and reflection, especially for those who have visited the museum's exhibits, many of which can generate strong emotions. In a contemporary context, this water feature provides the opportunity to think about the meaning and struggles of the African American experience, defining a place that for many is now sacred and hallowed ground, and potentially evoking an almost spiritual experience.

Conclusion

African people have always had a fundamental connection to water, celebrating its spiritual sacredness, its ability to make and define a place, and its continued influence on African and African American culture. From temples to hush harbors and black churches, the element of water has had a historically profound influence on African people both from the homeland and the diaspora. On both sides of the Atlantic, spiritual deities emerged in each Afrocentric society, reflecting the need for a presence in daily life, the feeling of protection, and the creation of a place that can identify with the communal needs of its people. In the Yoruba culture, water's spiritual meaning has created an unbroken path of worship and acceptance where practices and rituals continue to be conducted around the source of water. For enslaved Africans and their descendants in America, the water took on a different interpretive form. Water reflects survival—from the journey through the Middle Passage to water's symbolic representation of freedom in song and literature—and its ability to define and defend placemaking within a syncretized belief system. Places like the Ohio River literally embodied freedom for the enslaved, while the Mississippi River was the reinforced place of continued bondage.

It is necessary to understand the historic and cultural and spiritual connection water has had for Africans and those living in the diaspora. Water symbolizing freedom, sorrow, protection, spiritual healing, and collective experiences influenced the community's placemaking and their sacred structures. This relationship is worthy of continued examination but also needs to be celebrated more by African people as one more link which spans the Atlantic and ties both sides of the Afrocentric world together.

Notes

1. The Yoruba are one of the three major ethnic groups found mainly in southwest Nigeria.
2. Asabioje Afenapa and Traditional Ifá/Òrìṣà Bata Musical Band, *Isese Lagba* (Tradition and Culture is the Best) (CD Track 3: "Osun"). Okanran-Onile Productions, Nigeria, 2007.
3. African American Spirituals. *Library of Congress* [undated]. https://www.loc.gov/item/ihas.2001197495/. Accessed September 24, 2021.
4. Ibid.
5. Costen, Melva. "Wade in the Water." *First Church UCC* [undated]. http://phoenixucc.org/caffeinated-rablings/wade-in-the-water. Accessed September 14, 2021.
6. Smith-Christopher, Daniel L. "Places: The River Jordan in Early African American Spirituals." *Bible Odyssey* [undated]. https://www.bibleodyssey.org:443/en/places/related-articles/river-jordan-in-early-african-american-spirituals. Accessed August 31, 2021.
7. Freeman, Linda. "Undercurrents in a Deep River: The Hidden Meanings of Spirituals." *Choir of the Sound*, February 6, 2016. https://www.choirofthesound.org/undercurrents-in-a-deep-river-the-hidden-meanings-of-spirituals/. Accessed August 5, 2021.
8. Lyrics.com, STANDS4 LLC, 2022. "Take Me to the Water Lyrics." Accessed March 29, 2022. https://www.lyrics.com/lyric/6300171/Nina+Simone
9. Staten, Annie and Roach, Susan. "Take Me to the Water: African American River Baptism." *Louisiana Folklife* [1996]. https://www.louisianafolklife.org/LT/Articles_Essays/creole_art_river_baptism.html. Accessed September 24, 2021.
10. Natalie. "The 'Cymbee' Water Spirits."
11. Pursiful, Darrell J. "Cymbees: African Water Spirits." *Into the Wonder*. November 8, 2013. http://intothewonder.wordpress.com/2013/11/08/cymbees-african-water-spirits/. August 5, 2021.
12. Natalie. "The 'Cymbee' Water Spirits."
13. Ibid.

14. Johnson, E. Ofosuah. "Mama Wata, the Most Celebrated Mermaid-like Deity from Africa who Crossed Over to the West." *Face to Face Africa*. July 20, 2018. https://face2faceafrica.com/article/mami-wata-the-most-celebrated-mermaid-like-deity-from-africa-who-crossed-over-to-the-west. Accessed September 14, 2021.
15. Ibid.
16. Parry, Tyler. "The Role of Water in African American History." *Black Perspectives. African American Intellectual History Society*, May 4, 2018. https://www.aaihs.org/the-role-of-water-in-african-american-history/. Accessed May 30, 2022.
17. Adisa, Omotayo Kolawole, Chief Priest of Olokun worldwide, at Olokun Temple, Ile-Ifẹ, Interview. December 15, 2019.
18. Ofori, Ato, Yeyemokun Olokun, at the Olokun Temple, Interview. April 23, 2019.
19. African American Spirituals.
20. Ibid.
21. Raboteau, Albert J. "The Secret Religion of the Slaves." *Christian History Magazine*, 1992. http://christianhistoryinstitute.org/magazine/article/secret-religion-of-the-slaves. Accessed May 30, 2022.
22. Nelson, The Reverend Angela Ford. "The Message of the Hush Harbor: History, Theology of African Descent Traditions." *South Carolina United Methodist Advocate*, March, 2019. https://advocatesc.org/2019/03/the-message-of-the-hush-harbor-history-and-theology-of-african-descent-traditions/. Accessed July 28, 2021.
23. Attawell Summer. "Hush Harbors." *Attawell Summer*. November 21, 2016. https://www.attawellsummer.com/forthosebefore/during-antebellum-america-a-hush-harbor-or-hush. Accessed July 28, 2021.
24. Burns, Luke. "What makes a Place Sacred." *The Online Centre for Religious Studies*. April 13, 2020. http://www.ocrs.online/2020/04/13/what-makes-a-place-sacred/?fbclid=IwAR3gaGafC2wYnXiF5TwOczYe3rlA5VZes_juXyzMyjndiyrOzPDIOwJDdlc. Accessed April 13, 2020.
25. Raheem, Oluwafunminiyi. Personal observation made during fieldwork at the Walode Compound Quarters, Ile-Ifẹ. April 9, 2019.
26. Supporting pictures are unfortunately not available for public viewing.
27. Adisa, Omotayo Kolawole, Chief Priest of Olokun worldwide.
28. Raheem, Oluwafunminiyi. Personal observation made during fieldwork at the Ilode Quarters, Ile-Ifẹ. December 22, 2019.
29. Smee, Sebastian. "A Thing of Beauty." *Washington Post*, July 22, 2020.
30. The 'debates' was not a debate in the traditional sense. The sociological contrast occurred when Herskovits' study 'the Myth of the Negro Past' was published in 1941. This study took an opposing view to the prevailing belief at the time established by Franklin that nothing of the African culture could have survived the experience of slavery.
31. Tyler. "The Role of Water."
32. African American Spirituals.
33. Albert. "The Secret Religion."
34. *Healing Earth*. "Water and Spirituality." *Healing Earth* [undated]. http://healingearth.ijep.net/print/water/water-and-spirituality. Accessed June 24, 2021.
35. In most instances formerly enslaved persons called their community by the name of their former plantation or plantation owner. See Poole, W. Scott. "Praise Houses." *South Carolina Encyclopaedia*, June 20, 2016. https://www.scencyclopedia.org/sce/entries/praise-houses. Access May 30, 2022.
36. National Register. "Gullah Saint Helena Island, South Carolina." *National Register of Historic Places Nomination* [undated]. http://www.gullahcommunity.org. Accessed June 15, 2018.

References

Abiodun, Rowland. "Hidden Power: Ọ̀ṣun, the Seventeenth Odù." In *Ọ̀ṣun across the Waters: A Yorùbá Goddess in Africa and the Americas*, edited by Joseph M. Murphy and Mei-Mei Sanford, 1. Indiana: Indiana University Press, 2001.

Adams, Natalie P. "The 'Cymbee' Water Spirits of St. John's Berkeley." *The African Diaspora Archaeology Network*, June 2007. http://www.diaspora.illinois.edu/news0607/news0607.html. Accessed May 30, 2022.

Bartholomew, Alick. *The Story of Water: Source of Life*. Edinburgh: Floris Books, 2010.

Ben-Amos, Paula. "Symbolism in Olokun Mud Art." *African Arts* 6, no. 4 (1973): 28–31+95.

Blount, Jerry. *Noah and the Great Flood: Proof and Effects.* Ohio: Gatekeeper Press, 2017.

Brown, Michael R. *African-Atlantic Cultures and the South Carolina Lowcountry.* Cambridge: Cambridge University Press, 2012.

Cleeves, Ilsedore L., Edwin A. Bergin, Conel M.O'D. Alexander, Fujun Du, Dawn Graninger, Karin I. Oberg and Tim J. Harries. "The Ancient Heritage of Water Ice in the Solar System." *Science* 345, no. 6204 (2014): 1590–1593.

DuBois, W.E.B. *The Negro Church.* Oregon: Cascade Books, 2011.

Eliade, Mircea. *Patterns in Comparative Religion.* New York: Sheed Ward, 1958.

Fakayode, Fayemi A. and Origunwa, Obafemi. *Oríkì Àwọn Òrìṣà: A Practitioner's Guide to Daily Devotion.* lulu.com, 2012.

Frobenius, Leo. *Voice of Africa: Being an Account of the Travels of the German Inner Africa Exploration Expedition in the Years 1910-1912.* Vol. 1 (translated by Rudolf Blind). London: Hutchinson & Co., 1913.

Hong, Zhao. "The South China Sea Dispute and China-ASEAN Relations." *Asian Affairs* 44, no. 1 (2013): 27–43.

Hughes, Langston, Arnold Rampersad and David Roessel, *The Collected Poems of Langston Hughes.* New York: Alfred A. Knopf, Inc. 1994.

Hunter, Christopher S. 'Influences of African American Religious Practices on the Architecture of Early African American Church Buildings 1842-1917.' PhD diss., Texas A&M University, 2018.

Idowu, Bolaju. *Olódùmarè: God in Yoruba Belief.* London: Longmans, 1970.

Jackson, Joyce Marie. "'Like A River Flowing with Living Water': Worshiping in the Mississippi Delta." In *The Smithsonian Institution's 1997 Festival of American Folklife.* Washington, D.C.: Smithsonian Institution Press, 1997.

Juuti, Petri, Tapio S. Katko and Heikki S. Vuorinen. *Environmental History of Water: Global Views on Community Water Supply and Sanitation*, edited by Petri S. Juuti, Tapio S. Katko and Heikki S. Vuorinen. London: IWA Publishing, 2007.

Kwekudee. 'Mami Wata: The Sacred Female African Water Deity.' Blogger.com (blog).

Luzzatto, Paola C. *Sussane Wenger: Artist and Priestess.* Florence: Firenze Atheneum, 2009.

Mason, John. *Olookun: Owner of Rivers and Seas.* New York: Yoruba Theological Archminstry, 1996.

Mitchell, Henry H. *Black Church Beginnings: The Long-Hidden Realities of the First Years.* Michigan: Wm. B. Eerdmans Publishing Company, 2004.

Murphy, Joseph M. and Mei-Mei, Sanford. "Introduction." In *Oṣun across the Waters: A Yorùbá Goddess in Africa and the Americas*, edited by Joseph M. Murphy and Mei-Mei Sanford, 1. Indiana: Indiana University Press, 2001.

Ogunsola, Yemi. "A Near-Encounter with Olokun, Yoruba Deity of the Ocean." *The Guardian*, 20 July 2013.

Okediji, Moyo. "Orisa Ikire Painting School." *Kurio Africana: Journal of Art and Criticism* 1, no. 1 (1989): 116–129.

Olajubu, Oyeronke. "Reconnecting with the Waters: John 9.1-11." In *The Earth Story in the New Testament*, edited by Norman C. Habel and Vicky Balabansky, 109. London: Sheffield Academic Press, 2002.

Oyekan, Owomoyela, *Yoruba Proverbs.* Lincoln: University of Nebraska Press, 2005.

Probst, Peter. "Celebrating Indigeneity in the Shadow of Heritage: Another Version of the Osun Osogbo Festival in Nigeria." In *African Indigenous Religious Traditions in Local and Global Contexts: Perspectives on Nigeria*, edited by David O. Ogungbile. Lagos Mainland: Malthouse Press, 2015.

———. "Keeping the Goddess Alive: Performing Culture and Remembering the Past in Osogbo, Nigeria." *Social Analysis: The International Journal of Anthropology* 48, no. 1 (2004): 33–54.

Raboteau, Albert J. *Slave Religion: The Invisible Institution in the Antebellum South.* New York: Oxford University Press. 2004.

Raheem, Oluwafunminiyi. Folk Liturgies and Narratives of Holy Wells among the Yoruba (Southwest Nigeria). *ETNOLOŠKA TRIBINA: Journal of Croatian Ethnological Society* 44, no. 51 (2021): 109–122.

Ray, Celeste, Ireland's Holy Wells: Healing Waters and Contested Liturgies, *Anthropology News*, February 2010.

Ray, Celeste. "Beholding the Speckled Salmon: Folk Liturgies and Narratives at Irish Holy Wells." In *Landscapes Beyond Land: Routes, Aesthetics, Narratives*, edited by Arnar Arnason, Nicolas Ellison, Jo Vergunst and Andrew Whitehouse, 141. New York: Berghahn, 2012.

Staten, Annie and Roach, Susan. "Take Me to the Water: African American River Baptism." *Louisiana Folklife* [1996]. https://www.louisianafolklife.org/LT/Articles_Essays/creole_art_river_baptism.html. Accessed September 24, 2021.

Stevens-Arroyo, Anthony M. and Andres I. Perez Mena. *Enigmatic Powers: Syncretism with African and Indigenous Peoples' Religions among Latinos*. edited by Anthony M. Stevens-Arroyo and Andres I. Pérez. New York: Bildner Centre for Western Hemisphere Studies, 1995.

Willet, Frank. *Ife in the History of West African Sculpture*. London: Thames and Hudson, 1967.

Wolff, Norma H. and Michael D. Warren. "The Agbeni Shango Shrine in Ibadan: A Century of Continuity." *African Arts* 31, no. 3 (1998): 39.

PART III
Environmental Impact

9
THE "SACRED" ARCHITECTURE OF ANUPAM MISHRA'S WATER-CULTURE

Ricki Levi

This chapter examines and analyzes the varied ways by which water and architecture sanctify each other as postulated in Mishra's study of water culture. Anupam Mishra (1948–2016) was a Gandhian environmental researcher and activist and is considered a prominent reviver of traditional Indian water-harvesting systems (Anand 2017; Guha 2017; Levi & Mishori 2015, 2017; Thakkar 2017). Water-harvesting refers to an assortment of methods for collecting, storing, and conserving rainwater. In-depth, ecological knowledge is required to tailor these methods to fit specific situations so that during the rainy season, maximum rainwater can be harvested and stored in ponds, lakes, wells, etc. The objectives of water-harvesting are to provide water and food security, rejuvenate rivers and creeks, recharge groundwater, revive local flora and fauna, and prevent populations from becoming environmental refugees (Agarwal & Narain 1997; Mishra 1993, 2001;). Due to these comprehensive benefits, water-harvesting has gained widespread attention from governmental agencies and policymakers,[1] academic scholars (Levi & Mishori 2015, 2017; Montaut 2001), and numerous social Non-Governmental Organizations[2] (Gupta 2017a) in the last two decades.

The prominent Indian environmentalists, Anil Agarwal and Sunita Narain argue "that Indians have historically been the world's greatest water harvesters" because their inhabitants learned the patterns of their rain (Agarwal & Narain 1997, 25). As such, the Indian culture differs from other societies in the scale and sophistication of its water-harvesting methods (Agarwal & Narain 1997; Mishra 1993, 2001, 2011).

The monsoon – the Indian rainy season lasts from July to October rejuvenating Nature and bringing prosperity and life to both humans and non-humans. The monsoon is preceded by a long dry, hot summer and is followed by a cold, dry winter, usually without precipitation. To extend the brief period of abundance during the monsoon season, Indians developed sophisticated water-harvesting Traditional Ecological Knowledge (TEK), resulting in water security and an abundant water environment lasting for the whole year (Agarwal & Narain 1997). Mishra argues that from the dawn of Indian civilization till the time of British Colonial rule, water-harvesting systems were an inherent characteristic of the Indian culture; hence he named it a *"water culture"* (Mishra 1993, 2001). As such, Mishra shares Agarwal and Narain's views.

Traditional Ecological Knowledge (TEK) is defined as "knowledge about species, ecosystems or practices held by people whose lives are closely linked to their natural environment"

(Rist et al. 2010:1). It correlates with the knowledge and science system accumulated and embedded in the Indian traditional harvesting systems TEK (Levi & Mishori 2017). Furthermore, TEK reflects a non-anthropocentric holistic perspective, whereby humans and Nature are integrated and interdependent, viewed as a "family" or "community" (Pierotti & Wildcat 2000) – an insight demonstrated throughout Mishra's work – enabling these systems to sustain and thrive. Mishra's role in reviving the traditional water systems can be summarized in two stages. First, he published his findings in two books written in Hindi (1993, 1995 [English edition 2001]) that were distributed without copyrights and financed mainly by the *Gandhi Peace Foundation* in Delhi. Soon his books were translated into local vernaculars like Marathi, Urdu, Gujrati, Punjabi, Tamil, etc. This led to a wide phenomenon of "cultural remembrance," as many people began to research their local water harvest methods and started to harvest water again (Anand 2017; Gupta 2017).

Mishra argues that the water-harvesting systems found exemplary expression in India's driest state, Rajasthan (Mishra 2001). Located in northwest India,[3] Rajasthan's receives an average annual precipitation of 60 millimeter (almost 2.5 inches), slightly lower than the yearly national average of 110 millimeter (4 inches) (Mishra 2001: 22). However, in the deepest areas of the Thar desert, in Jaisalmer and Bikaner districts for example, precipitation is marginal, varying between 15 and 25 millimeter (0.6–1 inch) per year (Mishra 2001: 22). Nevertheless, Rajasthan is one of the most populated deserts in the world (Mishra 2011: 22; Singh 2007: 11–14). What is even more surprising, if we look at the history of Rajasthan, is the fact that it was for generations one of the most important centers of governance, architecture, and art in India. Mishra argues that its people were able to create a vibrant life even in a harsh desert climate because the importance of water was embedded into their culture (Mishra 2001: 22). In this sense, the Rajasthani desert is very far from the modern stereotype of a desert "as being arid, sparsely populated and on the fringe of civilization" (Montaut 2001: 6).

Authors Levi and Mishori argue that Mishra's description of the Indian water culture comprises three significant aspects (Levi & Mishori 2015, 2017). The first is the rich TEK experiences accumulated for generations, making the Rajasthani people experts in recognizing different types of rain, clouds, and raindrops. The second is *commons*. Defined broadly as "a general term that refers to a resource shared by a group of people" (Hess & Ostrom 2007, 4). Water TEK was managed collectively in many cases by well-defined, organized mechanisms. These reflected sustainable water management, enhancing the participation and responsibility of commoners toward their precious shared resource of water. The third aspect is the broad cultural foundations of water culture embedded in religious practices and social and moral virtues (Levi & Mishori 2015, 2017).

Talaab, literally in Hindi, is a pond or a pool. However, it is also a symbol of Mishra's water culture. He notes that certain communities tattooed a symbol of *talaab* onto their bodies, usually on the inner part of the calves (Fig. 9.1). Mishra argues that it is plausible to assume that tattooing the symbol of *talaab* on their bodies might indicate the care they must have felt toward their ponds and lakes (Mishra 1993). The *talaab* motif symbolizes the interconnectedness of humans with Nature.

In the center of the pond there is a single drop of water, symbolizing life itself, as, without water, life cannot exist. As soon as one drop is added to the others, they become waves that touch the edges of the pond, enabling the growth of flowers and trees. Hence, according to the *talaabic* symbolism, water allows humans to fulfill and exhaust the sensory and sensual experiences of life. It indicates a continuous movement, starting with the existential aspect (the single sacred drop) manifested in the recognition of human dependence on water for

FIGURE 9.1 *Talaab*
Source: Anupam Mishra, cover of the book *The Ponds are Still Relevant, 1993*.

sustenance and extending to the spiritual and aesthetic aspects of life – the human need for beauty and a sense of meaning (Mishra in an interview Levi 2014). For Mishra, the aesthetic aspect of the water culture is a testimony that despite its location, Rajasthan is perceived as a land of abundant inhabitation.

The aesthetic dimension is a dominant aspect of Mishra's study of water culture. As will be presented later in the chapter, doorways leading into man-made water tanks in Rajasthan, built by the *gazdhars* or architects of these reservoirs, are breathtaking in their beauty. Mishra posits architecture as a cardinal element of water culture.

Following Mishra's relation to architecture and water, this chapter explores in four parts the significance of the architectural dimension in water sanctification and also the ways in which water blesses the architectural structure. The first describes the dominant and essential architectural features that characterize many of the water bodies such as the *agor* (catchment area), *pal* (dike), and *nestha* and *afra* (spillways). I discuss each structure or the specific process by which it sanctifies the water or both. The second part focuses on the multilayered functions of decorative elements (nonessential in terms of function) such as statues, canopies and gates, and the ways by which they sanctify water and the architectural structure. The third part studies the status of the *gazdhars* – the water architects in Mishra's water culture. Their social and cultural role extended far beyond a view of the architect being a person who merely bears functional professional engineering skills and knowledge. The *gazdhars* were seen as the ones who not only held the physical yardstick for measuring the ponds but were also perceived as being a reflection of the resilience and morality of the society (Mishra 1993, 2001). The fourth and last part presents the *baori* or stepwell, a unique Indian architectural typology. *Baori* exemplifies the peak of the architectural knowledge, skills, and craftsmanship of the *gazdhars* (Mishra 1999, 2001). Often viewed as temples, *baoris* offer a complex integration of water and architecture, and the multiple ways in which one sanctifies the other. The conclusions elaborate on the relevance of Mishra's work in discussions on sacred architecture and water sanctification processes by presenting a unique Indian example, expanding the scope of discussion far beyond that of a "professional" debate on architecture. It illustrates how architecture can create and reflect resilience and social cohesion.

Essential Elements of the Sanctification Processes of Water Bodies

Mishra's work is full of vivid descriptions of the architectural know-how applied in the construction of the different types of water bodies and their multiple aspects – structural, social, cultural, and religious. He delineates three essential generic structural parts inherent to the water body's design, predominantly in that of ponds and lakes (Mishra 1993, 2001).

The first is the *agor*, the catchment area of the water body. The *agor* can vary from less than a meter (~3.0 feet) of wells or small ponds to tens of kilometers (~6.0 miles) of big ponds or lakes, depending on the water body's type and size (Fig. 9.2). Since the *agor* is the area where the water is first collected, to maintain the purity of the water, the place had to be kept spotlessly clean throughout the year and also cleaned meticulously before the start of the rainy season. Often, stone pillars were carved with religious texts and symbols and were positioned at the entrance to the *agor*, indicating the transition of the space into a "sacred" one. As soon as a person crossed the pillar and entered the *agor*, he/she had to change their behavior. He/she had to remove the shoes, not to curse, shout or spit, and to adhere to the typical standard normative code of behavior followed in temples in India (Mishra 2001). Thus, in this sense, the pillar sanctified both the water and the *agor*, transforming the *agor* to a "sacred space" and water into a "sacred matter."

FIGURE 9.2 Pillar at the entrance to the agor of Gharsisar lake, Jaisalmer
Source: Author

The second architectural feature is the *pal* – the dike or the wall which surrounds the water body. The *pal* could either encircle the water body completely or could be located at one or more of its sides (Mishra 1993: 22).

To strengthen the foundations of the *pal*, different structures such as *ghats* (steps descending to a water body), *baradaris* (pavilions designed to offer a free flow of air), and minarets were built (Fig. 9.3). Multiple niches were constructed in the *pal*, and inside them were placed idols of gods, goddesses or mythological figures such as *jal apsaras* or water nymphs (Doniger 2015). In this way, Mishra says, the gods guarded the *pal*, keeping it safe and sound (Mishra 1993, 2001). In the *pal* of lake Amarsagar, built in the 16th century, the image of the elephant-headed God, Ganesh, validates the sacredness of the *pal* (Fig. 9.4). Hence, in this case, the sanctification of the lake is done by an additional architectural element. The presence of the images of the god's inset into the *pal* of the water body reinforces the argument that it

The "Sacred" Architecture of Anupam Mishra's Water-Culture 137

FIGURE 9.3 The *pal* of Amarsagar lake in Jaisalmer district
Source: Author

FIGURE 9.4 Image of the god Ganesh installed on the pal of Amarsagar lake, providing the pal "divine" protection
Source: Author

was perceived as a temple, where the *pal* is protected by "divine" forces that guarded the most precious element of life – water.

The third architectural features are the *nestha* and *apra*, the spillways of the water body, i.e. the parts responsible for exiting the excess water, diverting them to a different water body and preventing overpressure on the *pal*, which could cause it to collapse. *Nestha* is a larger spillway than the *apra* and is capable of diverting a large quantum of water rapidly, for instance, in case of heavy rain (Mishra 2001). Mishra is most impressed by the *nestha* of Gharsisar Lake in Jaisalmer built during the 12th century. He writes:

> A society which knows how to fill Gharsisar drop by drop, does not consider its excess water just as plain water but rather as blessed water (*jal rashi*). The water exiting from the *nestha* is then stored in another lake further down. Then if the *nestha* still does not stop, then one of the second lakes is opened and another lake is likewise filled [...], this process can carry on filling up to nine lakes.
>
> (Mishra 2001: 78)

Hence, explains Mishra, the series of *nesthas* are the architectural features responsible for the proper functioning of Gharsisar, providing water security to the city located in the heart of the Thar desert in Rajasthan. It is worth noting that Mishra differentiates between plain water – *pani* in Hindi, a word commonly used to describe water in everyday usage, to the Sanskrit word *jal*, which confers cultural-religious connotations to water (Jones & Ryan 2007). Thus, it can be deduced that the *nestha*, an essential architectural element, transforms the water from *pani* to *jal* or sanctified water.

The *apra* was a spillway commonly used to protect the *ghats*. As noted, the purpose of situating idols of deities within the niches was to guard the *ghats*. The idols were installed at the height of the *apra* (Mishra 1993). In case of heavy rain and an increase in the water level, the moment the water rose high enough to touch the feet of the deity, the *apra* would start flowing and excess water would be diverted to an outer pond. "Thus," Mishra says, "the water level will cease to rise. Thus, the *ghat* is protected jointly by both human and divine force" (Mishra 1993: 26).

A similar example of joint forces protecting the water body can be seen at *Shyam Sagar*, a pond in the Alwar district in Rajasthan, dating to the 15th century. However, in this case, Mishra draws a connection between Vedic literature dating to the second millennium BCE (Doniger 2015) and the traditional Indian water-harvesting systems. At *Shyam Sagar*, the deity protecting the *ghat* is Varuna: "The moment the water level touches the feet of Varuna, the *apra* starts flowing and the water doesn't cross that level in the pond and Varuna never drowns" (Mishra 2001: 29). According to the Vedas, Varuna is the lord of water, associated with every form of water, residing in oceans and seas, rivers and rain (Doniger 2015; James 1969). Hence, the divine presence of Varuna is integrated into the architecture of the water-harvesting traditions. It is interesting to note that the *apra* prevents the drowning of Lord Varuna. This indicates the perception of the architects that the relationship between the divine and the human is one of interdependence (James 1969). I argue, that Mishra's cultural account suggests that the architects are familiar with the cultural perception (of human-divine interdependence) and that this belief finds expression in an architectural feature, such as the installation of statues of idols. Through a joint effort, Mishra says, humans and gods create water security enabling a vibrant society in the desert (Mishra 1993).

The Sanctifying Role of Decorative Architectural Elements

This part focuses on two main categories of decorative elements used in many of the water bodies described in Mishra's work. Both categories fulfill two primary purposes – that of *informing* and *remembering*. Here I examine both water and architectural sanctification aspects in the context of these complex psychological processes.

The Usage of Decorative Elements as Tools of Informing

Authors Levi & Mishori recognize the "commons" as a cardinal aspect of Mishra's water culture. Even though Mishra does not explicitly use this term, he describes certain traits of the water culture that are characteristic of the discourse on commons. For example, since water TEK is founded on a shared commitment of communities to preserve their common resource, its description is inherently sustainable as referring to what is understood to be commons.[4] Another quintessential trait of the commons discourse is a long-term intergenerational obligation that the community bears concerning its shared resource (Barnes 2006; Weston & Bollier 2013). In numerous places, Mishra writes that the water culture is intergenerational in principle. For example, regarding the maintenance of water bodies, he says: "…such precautions are taken at the *agor* […] that it is only the next generation needs descend inside to clean it" (Mishra 2001: 56).

Water is widely regarded as sacred in India; hence it involves various rules of purity and impurity, generally coded as an exclusion of lower castes and menstruating women (Doniger 2015). Discussing Mishra's views on these complex social issues is beyond the scope of this chapter. However, following the discourse of TEK and commons, which ensures access to water for all sections of society (human and non-human), it does not necessarily imply an equal distribution of the resource, both in terms of quantity and quality.

On the *pal* of Amarsagar lake, alongside the minarets, canopies, *baradaris*, and *ghats*, every few meters along with the *pal* are statues of elephants and horses (Fig. 9.5). These did not carry a solely aesthetic value. The statues indicated the water level in the lake – if the water reached the elephants' legs, everyone in town knew that there was sufficient water for six or seven months. However, if the water reached up to the horses' legs, water was guaranteed for the entire year. Hence the statues were a vital tool for informing the public about their water status (Mishra 1993; 2001), a practice that evolved as part of the management and maintenance of water as commons. As indicators of the quantum of water available, the statues helped instill a greater sense of care and responsibility in the community towards their shared water resource.

Serving the same purpose of informing the community about their water status and thereby leading to responsible usage of water, in many cases pillars of stone or of wood which does not rot in water, were erected at different depths in the water bodies. Many of these pillars were not marked with numbers but with religious-cultural symbols, "charging" them with sanctity and cultural significance. Mishra says:

> Pillars are made in the middle of the pond, in the place from where irrigation is made, and in the *agor*. Rather than making marks of feet, yards etc. on them, signs of *padam* (lotus), *shankh* (conch), *naag* (snake), *chakra* (wheel) etc. are made to indicate a specific depth of the pond.
>
> *(Mishra 1993: 27)*

The symbols that Mishra refers to are commonly seen in Hindu iconography. The *padam* (lotus) is a symbol of purity, enlightenment, beauty, and perfection (Jones & Ryan 2007; Doniger 2016). Various gods and goddesses such as Lakshmi or Ganesh, are depicted seated on a lotus flower or holding one in their hands. The *shankh* (conch) is associated chiefly with Lord Vishnu and symbolizes qualities of purity and prosperity. The conch also represents water and is often associated with women's fertility (Jones & Ryan 2007). The *naag* (snake) commonly represents death and rebirth (Jones & Ryan 2007; Doniger 2015). Two familiar images in Hindu iconography are of *Lord* Vishnu, the great Preserver of the world reclining on the multi-headed Shesh Naag, the Cosmic Serpent (Jones & Ryan 2007). The other is of Lord Shiva wearing a cobra, representing *ahamkara* (literally, "ego") around his neck (Jones & Ryan 2007). The *Naga* sadhus are also considered ascetic warriors. The *chakra* (wheel or discus) is a weapon of Lord Vishnu and symbolizes protection. Additionally, in several Hindu

FIGURE 9.5 Statues of a horse and an elephant in Amarsagar lake serve as indicators of the water level in the lake
Source: Author

schools of thought, the *chakra* is viewed as an energy center in the body, connected with higher states of consciousness (Jones & Ryan 2007). Hence, even though the pillars could have been marked with "objective" and "indifferent" numbers, marking them with highly "loaded" religious-cultural symbols indicates an intentional act of sanctifying the pillars and in turn the water, in addition to informing about water levels.

Decorative Elements as a Means of Remembering

Memory and remembrance echo throughout Mishra's work. It seems as if he recognizes that the act of "memorizing" is most fundamental to maintaining a sustainable water system. The mental faculties of memory, remembrance, and memorizing link the ponds to the psyche of the society, immersing water consciousness inseparably into its culture. Mishra says:

> The ways of collecting the drops of *palar* i.e., of rainfall, are as unending as the names of clouds and drops. The pot, like the ocean, is filled up drop by drop. These beautiful lessons are not to be found in any textbook but are actually couched in the memory of our society. It is from this memory that the *shrutis* [oral revelation] of our oral traditions have come. What the people of Rajasthan consigned to their memory, they also shared and consolidated, and no one knows exactly when this water work became a monumental, organized structure binding the whole society.
>
> *(Mishra 2001: 39)*

Architecture is an important field where memorizing is manifested as an active, living action. This can be illustrated by two examples. The first relates to the *agor* of the *Amarsagar* lake. Due to its relatively small size, parts of the lake would dry up in the blazing summer heat, exposing its bed. To keep the memory of the lake alive, and to continue drawing people to the lake so they will not forget it "when it is most needed" (Mishra 1993: 57), the architects constructed seven *beris* (wells) in the bed of the lake, enabling a seepage of water from the underground aquifer that reached up to the steps of the *beri* (Fig. 9.6). By assimilating the act of remembering, a mental faculty translated into practical architectural knowledge, Mishra views the invention of the *beri* as a high point in the evolution of the architect's craftsmanship, knowledge and skills. He writes, "the architects of Amarsagar executed some work which went down in the annals of the history of architecture."[5] As trees often grow close to the *beris*, people could dangle their feet in the cool water of the *beris*, enjoying the beauty of the lake throughout the year.

The second example relates to Gharsisar lake in Jaisalmer. According to Mishra, it is considered to be the most beautiful artificial lake in Rajasthan (Mishra 2001). Linked to the Silk Route, Jaisalmer was a vibrant urban center with a population of about 35,000 residents during the 18th century (Mishra 2001). Mishra argues that Gharsisar's *pal* was known for its exquisite beauty (Mishra 1993; 2001). It was adorned with temples, schools, and verandahs. There were large canopies located in various parts of the lake which could be reached by boat and offered different views of the lake and the city (Mishra 1993: 53).

Mishra says that the lake resided in everyone's heart, as in the case of the wealthy courtesan Tilon who wished to build a beautiful gateway, enhancing Gharsisar's beauty (Fig. 9.7). But when news of the construction of the gateway reached the king's ears, he decided to demolish it, viewing it as being inappropriate for him to enter the lake by way of a gate financed by a courtesan; while Tilon had a temple built overnight at the gate (Mishra 1993, 2001). The king, says Mishra: "revised his decision. Ever since that day, the people of the city have been

FIGURE 9.6 *Beri* in the bed of Amarsagar lake. Intended to draw people to the lake even when it is dry in an attempt to keep it alive as a "memory" throughout the year
Source: Author

FIGURE 9.7 The gateway of Gharsisar lake was built by the courtesan Tilon. One of the many canopies set in the lake is directly in the line of sight as one passes the gate
Source: Author

entering the pond premises through this very gateway, and they remember it in the name of Tilon only" (Mishra 1993: 55). Hence the temple, in this case, adds to the lake's sanctity, contravening social restrictions and obligating even kings.

The *Gazdhars* – Architects and Sanctifiers of water, ponds, and society

The meaning of the word "*gazdhar*" is "the one who wields the 'gaz' i.e., yardstick" (Mishra 1993: 12). The architects belonged to diverse religions - they "were Hindus and later Muslims also" (Mishra 1993: 12). It was entirely their responsibility to provide water to all human habitation as well as oversee building and maintenance work. Their work ranged "from town-planning to the meanest construction works" (Mishra 1993: 12). Seldom was the educational institution of the *gazdhars* associated with "the alma mater of caste and somewhere else it formed a line of such artisans beyond the barricades of caste" (Mishra 1993: 12). Some were located in a particular area, while others traveled from one place to the other (Mishra 1993: 13) (Fig. 9.8).

Gazdhars were usually trained under the mentor-disciple tradition (Mishra 1993: 12). A good *gazdhar* was "defined as one who did not touch the tools. He decided simply by just checking the site and deciding what had to be done" (Mishra 1993: 13). These abilities accorded them high prestige. Often, they were viewed as being gifted with a mystical intuition (Mishra 1993: 14).

Due to their skills and expertise and because of the significance of water to society, the *gazdhars* were considered as role models. They were regarded as "*Mahatmas*" or great souls. Mishra says: "Whosoever made a pond was revered by the people as *Maharaj* or *Mahatma*, i.e. a pious soul. A grateful society immortalized its pond-makers" (Mishra 1993: 5). Therefore, according to Mishra, the title *gazdhar* not only echoed the importance of the actual ponds (manifested by the act of measuring the pond) but was also the index of social cohesion and morality. "Society did not treat him (*gazdhar*) as someone just wandering here and there with a three-feet long iron stick. He was conferred the status of someone capable enough to fathom the depth of society" (Mishra 1993: 12). Hence fulfilling a much more significant role than

FIGURE 9.8 The *Gazdhars* of Taron Bharat Sangh – a prominent NGO that built thousands of ponds in the last few decades
Source: Anupam Mishra, courtesy of Mishra's family.

just being a professional architect. After completing the water body, in addition to receiving remuneration, the *gazdhar* would also be honored. He would be dressed in a *siropa* – a robe of honor, and a *pugri*, a decorated turban. Gifts such as gold, silver, and even in some cases, a piece of land were bestowed upon him (Mishra 1993: 12-13). More importantly, since the pond could not be used until the *gazdhar* conducted its consecration ceremony, his role could even be viewed as being equivalent to that of a priest. Mishra defines this process whereby the pond is infused with life as a "wedding." He says:

> The pond cannot be used before the wedding. Neither can anybody draw water from the pond nor will they cross it. [...] Soil from the nearby temples is brought. Water of Ganges i.e. *Gangajal* is also brought and mixing it with water from another 5-7 wells or ponds, the wedding is solemnized.
>
> (Mishra 1993: 61)

The *gazdhars* would sanctify the pond, hence becoming "water priests," on par with the status of temple priests. *Gangajal* – sanctified water brought from the holy *Ganga*, water from active waterbodies and soil taken from a temple, were mixed together to sanctify the architectural structure and the water in the pond (Mishra 1993). Thus, the "pond wedding" can be viewed as the climax of the integrated sanctification process – the inherent sacredness of water, architecture, and architects resolving in a holistic vision of water culture.

Stepwells, Sacred Typology of Indian Water Architecture

The connection between architecture and water expressed the interconnected affinity between the "mundane" and the "sublime," the "secular," and the "sacred" (Gupta 2017).[6] Some scholars argue that of all the architectural structures invented in the rich and diverse water traditions, stepwells are considered the most sublime and refined. They represent a unique Indian architectural typology and serve as a testimony to the exemplary Indian water culture and the architects' refined building and artistic skills (Gupta 2017; Lautman 2017; Mishra, 1993, 2001).[7]

Stepwells are called by various names – *baoris*, *vavs* or *bawadis*. Jutta Jain-Neubauer, among the first to research the Indian stepwells, defines it as a unique underground well perceived as a temple.[8] Stepwells started to evolve in the 7th century AD and were built predominantly in northwest India, in Rajasthan, Gujarat, and Madhya Pradesh.[9] Stepwells were temples and places of worship, but at the same time, were secular, social, and functional spaces. They were built in various shapes and sizes. Whereas small ones were built by communities, the grand and highly sophisticated ones were financed mainly through the state or by wealthy patrons (Figs. 9.9 and 9.10). The art of stepwells reached its peak between the 11th and the 13th centuries AD, as significant architectural developments occurred under Islamic dynasties as well (Gupta 2017). Starting from the 18th century, water-harvesting traditions began to dissolve and decline. As a result, stepwells, like many other water bodies, were neglected and forgotten. Some of them were utterly destroyed, while others turned into landfills (Gupta, 2017).[10]

Interestingly, researchers argue that stepwells received marginal scholarly attention in comparison to Indian temple architecture, which was researched thoroughly (Gupta 2017; Lautman 2017). As a result, they are rarely mentioned in architectural books or included in any curriculum (Gupta 2017). In *The Vanishing Stepwells of India* (2017),

FIGURE 9.9 *Abaneri Chand Baori*, 9th century AD. Located between Jaipur and Agra.
Source: Author

Victoria Lautman reinforces the lack of scholarly interest and wishes to change this tendency. She says:

> How does an entire category of architecture slip off the grid of history? Few people have heard of these ingenious and beautiful subterranean marvels, let alone seen one. […] In a tradition that stretches back thousands of years, stepwells were among India's most efficient water-harvesting systems.
>
> *(Lautman 2017: 13)*

FIGURE 9.10 *Rani Ki Vav* in Patan, Gujarat, was built as a subterranean temple, having seven stories underground. Considered to be the largest, most sophisticated stepwell in India
Source: Author

Stepwells provide an outstanding unique experience as they force a perspective change. While temples are elevated and lifted from the ground, they are spotted at first glance and from a long distance, stepwells on the other hand, are dug deep into the ground, thus barely noticeable from the surface. The moment one enters the stepwell, its beauty unfolds gradually, constantly changing as you descend into the structures (Lautman 2017).

Conclusion

As viewed in the chapter, the architectural dimension served the cardinal purpose of "translating" the ethos of water culture into a concrete water manageable design. The sanctification of water and structures, and the priestly status of architects are a prevailing thread throughout Mishra's architectural account, emphasizing the immense importance of water to society from the ecological to the social and aesthetic points of view. As water shortage is one of the most crucial factors in the current environmental crisis, the revival of traditional Indian water-harvesting systems can perhaps be seen as a valuable contribution toward conserving this precious resource. Architecture can serve as an important tool for achieving this goal.

The holistic approach to water and its unique sacredness, embedded thoroughly in Mishra's account is gaining popularity, predominantly in the Indian rural habitats. His approach can and should be led by architects and architecture shifting toward a sustainable water design. Water Sensitive Urban Design (WSUD) is an excellent example of a holistic view of water as the entire water cycle is integrated into urban design. Hence, water-harvesting methods are a prominent tool combined in various design scales (building, neighborhood, city) (Wong 2006). In this manner, architecture (alongside urban planners, engineers, and other related disciplines) has an important role in "shifting the paradigm" toward comprehensive water management, embodying a sustainable "multi-dimensional" ecological-social-ethical perspective of the built environment. Most importantly, Mishra's account predominantly viewed architecture as the medium that reflects the sacred stewardship between humans, water, and the divine. A reciprocal-interconnected phenomenon results in ecological resilience and social cohesion.

Notes

1. Ministry of Water Resources, River Development & Ganga Rejuvenation. *'Repair Renovation and Restoration (RRR) of Water Bodies'*. Government of India, 2017. Accessed September 20.21 https://www.indiastat.com/agriculture-data/2/water-resources/355600/repair-renovation-and-restoration-rrr-programme-for-water-bodies/1227587/stats.aspx
2. For a comprehensive explanation of the benefits of the Indian water-harvesting systems initiated by NGOs, view "India's Water-Revolution," by Andrew Millison, April 2020. Accessed September 2021. https://www.youtube.com/watch?v=jDMnbeW3F8A&ab_channel=AndrewMillis
3. A map of the state of Rajasthan, North-West India. Source: Encyclopedia Britannica Inc. Accessed February 2022. https://www.britannica.com/place/Rajasthan
4. https://www2.hu-berlin.de/transcience/Vol6_No2_1_25.pdf
5. https://www.arvindguptatoys.com/arvindgupta/anupam.pdf
6. Jain-Neubauer, Jutta. 'Stepwell'. Oxford Art online com, 2003. Accessed September 2021. https://www.oxfordartonline.com/groveart/view/10.1093/gao/9781884446054.001.0001/oao-9781884446054-e-7000081320
7. Ibid.
8. Ibid.
9. Ibid.
10. Ibid.

References

Agrawal, Anil. & Narain, Sunita (eds.). *Dying Wisdom: Rise, fall and Potential of India's Traditional Water-Harvesting Systems.* New Delhi: Centre for Science and Environment, 1997.

Anand, Umesh. 'Why Anupam Mishra was our Water Guru', *Gandhi Marg*, 38, no. 3–4 (Combined Issue October-December 2016 & January- March 2017): 429–433.

Barnes, Peter. *Capitalism 3.0: A Guide to Reclaiming the Commons.* San Francisco: Berrett-Koehler, 2006.

Doniger, Wendy. *The Hindus- An Alternative History.* New Delhi: Speaking Tiger Publishing PVT. LTD, 2015.

Guha, Ramachandra. 'The Quiet Fighter', *Gandhi Marg*, 38, no. 3–4 (Combined Issue October-December 2016 & January–March 2017): 422–424.

Gupta, Divay. 'Foreward'. In *The Vanishing Stepwells of India*, edited by V. Lautman. London and New York: Merrell Publishers, 2017.

Gupta, Joydeep. 'The Man who Slaked India's Thirst', *Gandhi Marg*, 38, no. 3–4 (Combined Issue October-December 2016 & January–March 2017a): 433–435.

Hess, Charlotte & Ostrom, Elinor (eds.). *Understanding Knowledge as a Commons: From Theory to Practice Cambridge.* MA: MIT Press, 2007.

James, Edwin Oliver. *Creation and Cosmology: A Historical and Comparative Inquiry.* Leiden: E. J. Brill, 1969.

Jones, Constance & Ryan, James. *Encyclopedia of Hinduism.* New York: Facts on File-An Imprint Infobase Publishing, 2007.

Lautman, Victoria. *The Vanishing Stepwells of India.* London and New York: Merrell Publishers, 2017.

Levi, Ricki & Mishori, Daniel. 'Water, Virtue Ethics and TEK in Rajasthan: Anupam Mishra and the Rediscovery of Water Traditions'. In *Global Water Ethics: Towards a Water Ethics Charter*, edited by Rafael Ziegler & David Groenfeldt, 197–214, London: Routledge, 2017.

_____. 'Water, the Sacred and the Commons of Rajasthan: A Review of Anupam Mishra's Philosophy of Water', *Transcience: A Journal of Global Studies*, 6, no. 2 (2015): 1–25.

Levi, Ricki. Personal Interview with Anupam Mishra, Delhi, India, 03.10.2014.

Mishra, Anupam. 'The Radiant Raindrops of Rajasthan'. In *Touched by Water- The 2011 Hannsgrohe Water Symposium*, edited by Lanz Klaus, Anke Messerschmidt, & Carsten Tessmer, 26–46. Germany: Hansgrohe SE, 2011.

_____. *The Radiant Raindrops of Rajasthan.* New Delhi, India: Published by Research Foundation for Science, Technology and Ecology, 2001. https://www.arvindguptatoys.com/arvindgupta/anupam.pdf

_____. *Aaj Bhi Khare Hain Talab* [The Lakes Are Still Alive] (in Hindi). New Delhi: Published by Gandhi Shanti Pratishthan (Special English edition, 2012; translated by Parvesh Sharma), 1993.

Montaut, Annie. 'Anupam Mishra's Rajasthan: Desert or Water Culture?'. In *The Radiant Raindrops of Rajasthan*, edited by Anupam Mishra, 3–20. New Delhi, India: Published by Research Foundation for science, Technology and Ecology, 2001.

Pierotti, Raymond & Wildcat, Daniel. 'Traditional Ecological Knowledge: The Third Alternative'. *Ecological Applications*, 10, no. 5 (October 2000): 1333–1340.

Rist, Lucy, Shanker, Uma, Milner-Gulland, Eleanor, & Ghazoul, Jaboury. '*The Use of Traditional Ecological Knowledge in Forest Management: An Example from India*', *Ecology and Society*, 15, no.1 (2010): 1–20. https://www.ecologyandsociety.org/vol15/iss1/art3/

Singh, P. Report of the Task Force on Grasslands and Deserts. Government of India, 2007. Accessed April 2022. https://web.archive.org/web/20111210071534/http://planningcommission.nic.in/aboutus/committee/wrkgrp11/tf11_grass.pdf

Thakkar, Himanshy. 'India Will Be Hard-Pressed to Find Another Anupam Mishra', *Gandhi Marg*, 38, no. 3–4 (Combined Issue October–December 2016 & January–March 2017): 436–438.

Weston, Burnes & Bollier, David. *Green Governance: Ecological Survival, Human Rights, and the Law of the Commons.* New York, NY: Cambridge University Press, 2013.

Wong, Tony. 'Water Sensitive Urban Design – The Journey Thus Far. Australian' *Journal of Water Resources Water Resource*, 10, no. 3 (2006): 213–222. Accessed March 2022. https://doi.org/10.1080/13241583.2006.11465296

10
SACREDNESS IN THE PRESENCE AND ABSENCE OF WATER

The Case of Stepwells in Ahmedabad, India

Priyanka Sheth

Multitudes of Sacrality of Water in the Indian Subcontinent

In the book *India: A Sacred Geography* (2013), Diana Eck, a scholar of comparative religion and Indian studies observes that in India, sacrality extends to the landscape and environment. It manifests at different scales, often nested across regions through myths and stories such that regional or local landscapes are linked to a broader sacred geography. Ganga, the holy river, is one of the seven sacred rivers of India and is referred to as *Maata* (Mother goddess) or *Devi* (goddess). Across the subcontinent, rivers are considered to be manifestations of the holy Ganga, representing the vital feminine energy *(shakti)* that nourishes and sustains life (Eck 2013).[1] In myths and in many languages of the Indian subcontinent, bodies of water are female, especially the rivers. The notional femininity connecting fertility to water is ancient, predating Hinduism, Buddhism, and Jainism in the Indian subcontinent. This relationship was prevalent in various ancient cultures through myths where the goddesses were associated with water, such as the Egyptian goddess Isis who divided the river Phaedrus; Acuecucyoticihuati, the Aztec goddess of the ocean; and Tiamat, the Sumero-Babylonian goddess of the sea (Neimanis 2017).[2]

In the semi-arid landscape of western India, such as the region and present-day state of Gujarat (Fig. 10.1), the rivers are not perennial like the mighty Ganga. These rivers are seasonal, with large swathes drying up in the summers. The region receives almost all its fresh water from the southwest monsoon between June and September. The regional topography is largely flat, with gently undulating alluvial plains, and the wrinkled terrain lets water flow to create seasonal streams and rivers during and post-monsoon. Natural depressions in the terrain are filled with rainfall and runoff during the monsoons. Underneath the alluvial tracts there are shallow, unconfined aquifers that hold groundwater (Jain, Sheth, and Sheth 2020).[3]

Across the subcontinent, different traditions of harvesting water evolved in response to regional climatic, geographical, and cultural specificities (Agarwal & Narain 1997). Such traditional water systems need to be examined and revisited in light of the present-day water crisis. Water harvesting practices have a particularly enduring legacy in the region of north and central Gujarat. There, structures built for tapping into the aquifer, such as wells and stepwells sustained life in the region for centuries (Jain-Neubauer 1981). The inscription in

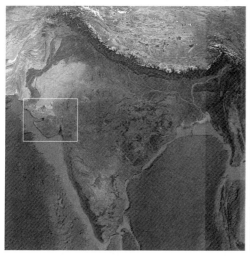 

FIGURE 10.1 The city of Ahmedabad marked in the present-day state of Gujarat in western India
Source: Author

Rudabai vaav, a stepwell at Adalaj outside the city of Ahmedabad states, "Good Queen Rudabai caused this well to be made, which is like the heavenly river Ganges" (Jain-Neubauer 1981: Appendix 3). In this semi-arid landscape, in addition to rivers, the aquifer or the well water was also perceived to be a manifestation of the sacred Ganga, and by extension, structures such as stepwells that tap into the aquifer embodied that sacrality. Likening well water to the holy waters of the Ganga is a theme in the folklore and poetry of the region and the comparison between the stepwells water and the Ganga is depicted in folk songs. (Mehta Bhatt 2014)

The Functionality of the Stepwell

A typical stepwell in the region of Gujarat locally known as *vaav* consists of an open well shaft that is accessed by a long linear flight of steps sandwiched between strong retaining walls. The well shaft grants access to groundwater, whereas the subterranean linear stepped corridor doubles as a cistern that stores rainwater directly from the sky (Fig. 10.2). As the water level recedes and expands seasonally, steps are gradually revealed or submerged. Stepwells from the seventh century to the mid-nineteenth century have been identified in Gujarat. Many such stepwells were built in and around the city of Ahmedabad and were deeply intertwined with the ritualistic routines of women, who frequented the stepwells to fetch water usually in pots for their households. A large volume of water for irrigation purposes was extracted from the well using draft animals that pulled large leather sacks (*kos*) over a pulley (Hardiman 1998). The stepwell also served as a meeting and resting space for the local community and travelers. Many stepwells were located along historic trade routes to provide water and shelter for trading caravans, pilgrims, armies, and pastoralists (Momin 1998). However, it is important to remember that stepwells were part of a longstanding tradition where access to water was deeply entrenched in social inequality (Morrison 2010).[4]

Stepwells ranged widely in size and form based on geographic factors, such as the depth of the aquifer, soil profile, and immediate site conditions, as well as socio-economic factors, such as the availability of funds and labor (Jain, Sheth, and Sheth 2020). Some stepwells were organized and maintained at the community level. These simple, utilitarian structures were

FIGURE 10.2 The stepped corridor leading to the well shaft at the eleventh-century Queen's stepwell in Patan
Source: Author

often found within or at the edge of small villages. Alternatively, kings, queens, nobles, courtiers, and merchants philanthropically commissioned other stepwells. These structures typically featured intricate architectural designs and ornamentation, and niches of the retaining walls were adorned with stone inscriptions that documented the names of patrons.

The Sacrality of the Stepwell

Water has been associated with fertile abundance by virtue of its role in agriculture. In the semi-arid landscape of western India, this literal and symbolic association between water, femininity, and fertility is even more pronounced (Jain, Sheth, and Sheth 2020). Apart from stepwells, the region is also home to other water structures like tanks and stepped ponds *(kund)*. A *kund* is a square or rectangular funnel-shaped basin that stores rainwater (Fig. 10.3). The sides of *kunds* are usually set at a steep angle, much greater than the natural slope of the ground. A large number of steps, often laid out in complex triangular or pyramidal forms, are required to buttress the terraced walls (Hegewald 2001).

In the book *Steps to Water: The Ancient Stepwells of India* (2002), Morna Livingston, an architectural photographer and scholar of ancient and medieval water systems distinguishes between the specific function of the typical linear stepwell *(vaav)* from the stepped pond *(kund)*, which is also found in the Gujarat region. Unlike the stepwell or *vaav*, the *kund* was always associated with the institution of the Hindu temple, usually adjoining one, and was

FIGURE 10.3 The eleventh-century *Suryakund,* an example of a stepped pond or *kund* at the Sun Temple complex in Modhera
Source: Author

used for temple rituals. The eleventh-century *Suryakund* at the Modhera Sun Temple complex (Mehsana) and the twelfth-century *Kundvav* at Kapadwanj are noteworthy examples of this type. However, the stepwell, though not always associated with the institution of the temple, still had sacred or cosmic associations of its own. Niches resembling little shrines are often carved into the retaining parallel walls of the stepped corridor. While stepwells had ornamentation, it was not as elaborate as the temple (Livingston 2002).[5]

It was at water buildings like stepwells that local deities and goddesses were honored through rituals while also serving the utilitarian purposes of providing water for drinking or irrigation. Thus, the stepwell was associated with rituals pertaining to healing, fertility, motherhood, and abundance, performed in the honor of the goddess. In her book *The Stepwells of Gujarat: In Art-historical Perspective,* art historian Jutta Jain-Neubauer (1981), an expert on the stepwells in Gujarat, suggests that the deities of popular Hinduism were different from those of Brahmanical Hinduism. The goddesses that inhabited the stepwell and its waters were fluid and ever-changing with their localized avatars specific to the village or settlement.

The sculpture and embellishment in early stepwells were scaled down and sparse compared to temples. Livingston attributes the sparseness of figurative sculpture in stepwells as a reason for the continuation of stepwells even in the Muslim period because "the well's iconic sculpture was too small, obscure or archaic, or even too personal to carry an indelible Hindu imprint" (Livingston 2002: 29). Even in modest stepwells, a noteworthy architectural feature that one finds is the shrine or the niche, an element that continued to be part of stepwells built under Muslim patronage (Livingston 2002).

The exception to the aforementioned sparseness of figurative sculpture is the eleventh-century stepwell at Patan. Here, the sculpture is comparable to the excesses of a temple.[6] Rani Udayamati, the Hindu queen of the Solanki dynasty,[7] commissioned this elaborate—and the region's largest known—stepwell (Mankodi 1991). Generally referred to as the Queen's stepwell, this structure is an exquisite repository of sculpture featuring mythological and secular imagery. Figures depicting mighty female goddesses conquering demons, alongside women engaging in activities like drawing water, adorning themselves, or dancing lends a feminine character to the embellishment (Fig. 10.4). This stepwell was flooded by the Sarasvati River, was buried under mud and silt, and was practically unknown for centuries until it was excavated by the Archaeological Survey of India (ASI) in the late 1980s.

Muslim Sultans established power in Gujarat starting in the twelfth century. This was consolidated with the founding of Ahmedabad as the capital city in 1411 CE by Sultan Ahmad Shah, the ruler of the Gujarat Sultanate (Gillion 1969). He built a citadel on the eastern bank of the seasonal Sabarmati River, marking the formal establishment of the city. The basic need for water led to the continued building of stepwells under Muslim rule in Gujarat. The architecture of some of the stepwells in and around Ahmedabad illustrates the unique amalgamation of Hindu and Islamic water buildings, which Livingston refers to as "fusion wells."[8] She also points out that with the arrival of Islam, the hegemony of Brahmin tradition and its synonymity with political power was already breaking down, leading to a resurgence of the more vernacular forms of Hinduism that worshipped local deities. This transition of political power is observed in the stepwells with the change in the representation of symbols and motifs. (Fig. 10.5). This led to the borrowing of new details from Islamic architectural styles where Livingston (2002) comments:

> "In response to Islam's distaste for the human figure, Hindu masons created a lingua franca of ornament for stepwells composed of symbols intelligible to both Hindus and Muslims. The Muslim curb on figurative art redirected carving into leafy form:

FIGURE 10.4 Secular and sacred figurative sculpture at the Queen's stepwell in Patan
Source: Author

FIGURE 10.5 Non-figurative, vegetal motifs at the fifteenth-century *Rudabai vaav* near Ahmedabad
Source: Author

sun symbols became sunflowers and Hindu wishing vines were reconfigured with one stem like a Muslim tree of life. The stucco animals chiseled into the well cylinders were sufficiently neutral so that a Hindu and a Muslim could experience them in separate ways. The transformation of stepwells was a rare and historically unusual synthesis in the spread of Islam. The ambiguity in sculpture was not acceptable everywhere; temples and mosques were too loaded with religious import for it, and palaces too central to Muslim power to participate. But the common need for wells encouraged a give and take."

(81).

Women and Stepwells

Many stepwells in Gujarat were commissioned by women for women, and recent scholarship has shed light on the historical and contemporary agency of women with respect to water. The scholar and historian Purnima Mehta Bhatt (2014) has beautifully elaborated the historic relationship of women with stepwells. Many stepwells of Gujarat, she notes, were commissioned by queens or the wives of rich merchants. Women also emerged as the central characters or muses, or as mistresses and courtesans, in the romanticized historical tales of some stepwells. Many other structures commissioned by men were often built to honor a wife, mother, mistress, or local goddess. Mehta Bhatt emphatically challenges the historical stereotype of women as passive by shedding light on their agency as patrons of, and frequently, the sole donors to, stepwells.[9] The economic and political influences of women in the merchant and pastoralist societies, whether Hindu or Muslim, that dominated the Gujarat region were significant (Sheikh, 2010).

Closer to Ahmedabad, adjacent to the village of Adalaj, *Rudabai vaav* was built in 1499 under the patronage of a noblewoman named Rudabai. An inscription on the stepwell states that the patroness provided funds from her personal treasury for the construction of this intricately carved structure (Jain-Neubauer 1981).[10] Likewise, the *Bai Harir vaav,* located in the former suburb of Harirpur, now the Asarva locale of Ahmedabad, was also commissioned by a woman in the late fifteenth or early sixteenth century, adjoining the mosque and tomb of Bai Harir (Jain-Neubauer 1981). The structure has minimal figurative sculpture, but the stepwell's proximity to the mosque and tomb is noteworthy. While Bai Harir's identity is contested, most historical accounts suggest that she was the superintendent of the sultan's harem, and her philanthropy is evident from an inscription found in the stepwell (Jain-Neubauer 1981)[11] (Fig. 10.6).

Apart from the philanthropy of elite women, many ordinary women's lives and routines were intricately connected with these structures. As the women performed the daily chore of collecting water for their families—labor that women in many parts of India are still responsible for, even today—they found companionship with other women at the stepwells. The structures became the settings where their social and recreational lives played out as they formed friendships, shared sorrows and joys, and discussed daily life and village politics. The region's folklore is often set in stepwells with songs depicting prayers offered by women in the hope of becoming a mother. These songs are representative of fertility rituals that were frequently performed at the stepwells by women (Mehta Bhatt 2014).

FIGURE 10.6 Inscription in a niche in the fifteen-century *Bai Harir vaav* in Ahmedabad
Source: Author

Decline of Stepwells as Sources of Water

Stepwells faced decline or substantial degradation during the early nineteenth century, which was reinforced by a result of a range of colonial actions, such as the imposition of ruinous land tax rates, land commodification, and the dismantling of community control over natural resources (Hardiman 1998). These rendered a series of traditional water harvesting structures, including stepwells, obsolete. The arid regions of India were not on the radar of the East India Company until the nineteenth century, and India's northwest frontier was incorporated into the British domain by the middle of the nineteenth century. It was then that British engineers and surveyors used extensive empirical documentation techniques to understand water in India (Amrith 2018).[12]

With the establishment of institutions like the Archaeological Survey of India (ASI) in 1861 the colonial apparatus was at work when such empirical documentation was produced for historic structures, which were methodically documented as antiquated artifacts or monuments (Guha 2002). However, the original objective of the Survey was not to get involved in the preservation, but to conduct systematic documentation of Indian monuments, much of which was undertaken during the tenure of the director generals, Alexander Cunningham and James Burgess, in the nineteenth century (Guha 2002).[13] Some of the stepwells in and around the city of Ahmedabad were also documented during that period, primarily in the form of architectural drawings and photographs.[14] Thus, the ornate and architecturally complex stepwells that were identified as monuments worthy of such documentation were confined to being relics, things of the past rather than living sources of water.

In the early twentieth century, the use of mechanized pumps was encouraged by the colonial state to expand irrigation in Gujarat (Hardiman 1998). Gradually, these new technologies rendered wells and stepwells obsolete. In the 1960s and 1970s, Gujarat suffered multiple droughts (Bhatia 1992). At this time, the post-colonial government upheld centralized, technological solutions for water security as a matter of great urgency (Morrison 2010). Large dam projects were built and tube wells became ubiquitous, resulting in drained water tables and dry wells (Acciavatti 2017). The decline of stepwells was further accelerated by waterborne diseases, with the Indian government sealing off stepwells in the 1980s and 1990s to check the spread of Guinea worm disease (Livingston 2002).

An extensive list of stepwells sealed off by the colonial or local authorities in Gujarat in the colonial and post-colonial periods is difficult to obtain. It is impossible to ascertain which stepwells dried out due to depleting water tables. Nevertheless, many stepwells without water have continued to survive today, albeit with a change of function. As mentioned before, the historical role of stepwells as designated places of worship was not in the same vein as temples. With the outmoding of the stepwell as a source of water, and through firsthand field visits, it was observed that many of the structures have been converted into temples and are now explicitly designated as places of worship. As a result, they continue to function as public places for community use at a grassroots level. Across the region of Gujarat, this phenomenon is prevalent in villages where innumerable stepwells now host shrines dedicated to the goddess, *Maata* or *Devi* (Livingston 2002).[15]

Sacred Inhabitation in Stepwells of Ahmedabad

Ahmedabad is now a growing metropolis of 5.5 million people. In 2016, *Stepwells of Ahmedabad*, an independent, collaborative research initiative was launched by a group of architects in the city, where I was involved as one of the lead researchers along with my colleagues. Our group documented seventeen stepwells in the city producing architectural drawings, photography, and a short film.[16] During this process, it was easier to come across significant written and visual documentation of the well-known and architecturally intricate stepwells in and around the city. The extensive fieldwork led us to many obscure stepwells within the metropolitan limits of present-day Ahmedabad. The process of locating extant stepwells involved direct engagement with communities residing around stepwells, consulting with local experts, and referencing archival material such as historical travel accounts and old maps. Satellite imagery helped identify former historic settlements and their adjoining reservoirs, which often indicated the presence of stepwells. Out of the seventeen stepwells documented by our group, only three still access groundwater seasonally (Fig. 10.7). The current conditions of Ahmedabad's stepwells vary greatly and can be broadly divided into three categories: those preserved by governmental agencies; stepwells that have been socially integrated into neighborhoods as places of worship enshrining local goddesses *(Maata)*; and neglected, physically degraded stepwells.

Invariably, stepwells that have been given the protected heritage status in Ahmedabad are the ones that had already been documented in the nineteenth century under the auspices of the former colonial institution of the ASI. This institution is now part of the post-colonial government of India and manages many historic sites, including undertaking preservation work for some of the stepwells in Ahmedabad. Such stepwells are currently maintained through

FIGURE 10.7 The pool of water at the lowest levels of the fifteenth-century *Rudabai vaav* near Ahmedabad was observed in 2014. Visitor access to the water has been cut off by the ASI
Source: Author

institutionalized processes that restore and preserve only their physical structures but do not acknowledge them as sources of water. For example, *Rudabai vaav* at Adalaj has been declared a protected heritage site by the ASI, and its surroundings have been altered to accommodate manicured gardens, parking facilities, and visitor amenities. Similarly, *Bai Harir vaav* is part of a larger ASI complex that includes the mosque and tomb of its patroness. However, these institutionalized efforts have also contributed to the decontextualized musealization of stepwells much like the attitudes adopted by the colonial ASI in the nineteenth century, instead of reviving their ecological and social dimensions. Such stepwells are not used for worship or rituals anymore, even if that may have been the case in the past. The ASI actively prevents worship at protected stepwells because of fears of potential damage to the structures.

A vast majority of stepwells that were documented by our research group have been repurposed by local communities for religious purposes and are identified by the names of the local goddesses *(Maata)* they enshrine. These stepwell-shrines were observed in greater numbers in parts of the city that had seen significant migration from villages in Gujarat with the onset of industrialization. The mercantile enterprises that led to the establishment of various industrial textile mills marked the eastward expansion of the city in the twentieth century beyond the fortified historic core (Gillion 1969). It almost seems that this migration has also brought the village goddesses and deities to the city. This is evident in the names of such stepwell-shrines which bear the names of the goddesses. These stepwells located in such neighborhoods have been altered to varying degrees to accommodate their new functions.

For example, the oldest known stepwell of Ahmedabad, *Maata Bhawani vaav* at Asarva, is dry, but now houses various small shrines, mostly created by area residents (Fig. 10.8). Built in the eleventh century, the stepwell still invites regular contact with neighborhood families, particularly through the addition of a shrine to the local presiding goddess in the rear wall of its circular well shaft. Those who reside along the edge of the stepwell have continued to add numerous small shrines and figurative images throughout the years, reflecting worshippers' present-day sensibilities and aesthetics (Jain, Sheth, and Sheth 2020)[17] (Fig. 10.9).

In the Bapunagar area of eastern Ahmedabad, *Ashapura maata vaav* is a combination of old and new. Its first pavilion is now covered by bright red tiles, converting it to a temple, while the rest of the structure below remains untouched. The stepwell's other pavilions have been repurposed to support new activities for inhabitants of the informal settlement that has grown around the structure. A concrete bird feeder painted in bright blue adjoins the stepwell and displays the name of the goddess, *Ashapura maata* (the Mother goddess that fulfills wishes). Ceremonial clay pots and other paraphernalia used by women to perform rituals in honor of the goddess lie in the stepwell's upper pavilions, although it is unknown when this structure came to be associated with the goddess (Fig. 10.10). Folklore and stories of the divine feminine energy still intrigue the community even today. For example, the original stepwell's lower levels create an inviting play space for neighborhood children, who during our documentation process, recounted dramatic stories of how they still hear the goddess's anklets jingle from the depths of the stepwell.

The stepwells *Khodiyar maata vaav* and *Ambe maata vaav* have undergone major spatial transformations, rendering them nearly unrecognizable, compared to their original state. These temple conversions are further amplified by their settings in dense urban neighborhoods of Ahmedabad. In 2016, our research group observed that brightly painted walls decorated with mirror tiles stand alongside figurines and images of the presiding goddesses. The structures have been altered with new staircases and concrete slabs, which block access to their lower stories. However, their original well shafts, though neglected, provide evidence of their former structures.

Sacredness in the Presence and Absence of Water **159**

FIGURE 10.8 Additions of shrines and potted plants at *Maata Bhawani vaav* in Ahmedabad
Source: Author

FIGURE 10.9 Images and figurines honoring the female deity at *Maata Bhawani vaav* in Ahmedabad
Source: Author

FIGURE 10.10 Pots used for temple rituals in the upper pavilion of *Ashapura Maata vaav*
Source: Author

On the outskirts of Ahmedabad is an unnamed, partially excavated stepwell, covered with dense vegetation. On special occasions, priests from an adjoining temple dedicated to *Kaali maata*—yet another incarnation of the Mother goddess—light lamps to decorate the stepwell's ruins, suggesting that even a dilapidated stepwell can be honored and venerated.

Though originally built for water, stepwells are still considered sacred even in the absence of water. Amid the urbanity of the twenty-first century, women continue to visit them to perform ancient rituals honoring the mother goddess, and communities still utilize them for the cadence of daily life. The dynamic relationship between communities and stepwells enables the structures to thrive as exuberant, vivacious, and celebratory spaces that revere, through shrines, the feminine goddess.

Future of Stepwells in the Urban Realm

The current state of stepwells in Ahmedabad echoes the environmental and ecological degradation that is symptomatic of Indian cities brought on by rapid urbanization where stepwells are at risk of being forgotten as providers of the fundamental need for water in urban areas. These structures were historically deeply embedded in social, ritualistic, and ecological rhythms of life in the semi-arid regions of western India. However, in recent decades, droughts, and mega infrastructure initiatives in Ahmedabad further led to the neglect of many of the region's stepwells. (Jain 2021).[18]

Jawaharlal Nehru, India's first prime minister, referred to dams as "modern temples" in a famous speech in 1954 (D'Souza 2008). In this speech, post-colonial Indian modernity was tied to science and technology. Nonetheless, he did not refrain from invoking the "cosmic" in his emphatic argument for embracing modernity. When the Bhakra dam project opened in 1954, he referred to technological accomplishment as the most exalted form of sacrality and simultaneously attempted to appeal to various religious groups that form the tapestry of belief systems in India:

> When I walked around the site, I thought that these days, the biggest temple and mosque and gurdwara is the place where man works for the good of mankind. What place can be greater than Bhakra Nangal, where thousands of men have worked or shed their blood and sweat and laid down their lives as well? Where can be holier than this; which can we regard as higher?
>
> *(Singh 1997: 55)*

The water infrastructure paradigm in post-colonial India has adopted this direction with a preference for large river dam projects.

With current attitudes to water and the challenges posed by the climate crisis, how does one read the phenomenon of these community stepwell shrines dedicated to goddesses? Toward the end of *The Great Derangement,* acclaimed writer Amitav Ghosh (2016) claims that religious regroupings have the potential to mobilize action against climate change and they possess the power to move people in far greater numbers than any others. This claim is due to the fact that religious worldviews transcend nation-state boundaries and acknowledge intergenerational thinking and are not subservient to economic ways of thinking.[19] Historian Prasenjit Duara (2015) has examined the concept of transcendence as a framework to suggest that certain traditional forms of knowledge or belief systems from Asia might provide clues for embracing "sustainable modernity," "sacral modernity," or "ecological modernity" and how transcendence can potentially tie into the discourse on environmental sustainability.[20] Interestingly, Duara also writes about the idea of secular transcendence in *The Crisis of Global Modernity: Asian Traditions and a Sustainable Future.* Cultural theorist Astrida Neimanis emphasizes in *Bodies of Water: Posthuman Feminist Phenomenology* (2017) that the myths of "feminine waters" in conversations surrounding the contemporary water crisis where "ocean acidification, the draining of aquifers, the rising sea levels, and the traces of climate change in all of this- are *reinstalling* the imaginary of feminine, aqueous origins at every turn" (117).[21] These contemporary arguments, varied as they are, reiterate the importance of the "sacred," "spiritual," "reverential," or "transcendent" in relation to the environment and water.

The ecological decline of stepwells, especially in urban areas, was a result of colonial attitudes to water that continued in the post-colonial period—one that privileges extractive modernity (Jain 2021). Revisiting attitudes that reveal a sacred reverence for water might be needed to imagine the future of water infrastructure in light of the current climate crisis. When contemplating the future of stepwells amid shifting notions of function and identity, it is important to remember their past where that sacrality was not divorced from functionality.

My research colleagues and I often discuss that the fact that many of these stepwells have sustained community engagement because of their conversion to shrines and temples perhaps offers a silver lining.[22] It is precisely this kind of community mobilization that is necessary for conserving these stepwells—not just as religious shrines, but also for the potential of reviving them mindfully for water harvesting through collective action. Tanvi Jain, one of the co-researchers from the *Stepwells of Ahmedabad* initiative, presents a provocative argument where she proposes that the aquifer deserves to be recognized as a "living, breathing entity" and needs to be accounted for in urban design and policy-making (Jain 2021).[23] My understanding of this provocation is that not only are legal protections for the aquifer necessary, but a collective reverence for water sources that goes beyond the worldly authority of legislation is absolutely critical. Stepwells and traditional water structures have the potential to address the water challenges of the twenty-first century because of their sacred and functional relevance through mindful restoration and revival. However, it is also equally important to not replicate the models of inequality that formerly prevented certain castes from accessing the water commons because of pre-ordained unequal social structures (Morrison 2010). The other question that looms is how can this idea of "secular sacrality" be deployed to mobilize community-based water conservation against the backdrop of increasingly divisive political rhetoric with religious connotations, where reclaiming sites for Hindu temples and the idea of origins are increasingly contrived in a polarized society in India today? Perhaps the social history of the stepwells, where fluid and variegated notions of sacrality were enmeshed with the elementality of water, might offer some clues.

Notes

1. Eck has expanded upon the concept or *tirthas* or "fords" by highlighting *tirthas* and their holy association with rivers and the Ganga in particular.
2. Neimanis also refers to water in Judeo-Christian creation stories.
3. The terrain, surface water, and groundwater are ecologically linked to one another. Water that percolated through the various layers of the earth was considered pure for drinking.
4. Communities were internally differentiated by caste and showcased a complex interplay of power relations involving unequal access to water sources.
5. Livingston elaborates how the temple was strongly associated with Brahminical hegemony and power. The Brahmins, considered to be the highest caste within Hinduism, incorporated the Mother goddess as a wife, but not an equal, of the Gods.
6. "Rani-ki-Vav (the Queen's Stepwell) at Patan, Gujarat." UNESCO, 2021. https://whc.unesco.org/en/list/922/. Accessed September, 2021. This stepwell is now a UNESCO World Heritage Site. The description suggests that the stepwell was designed as an "inverted temple."
7. The Solanki dynasty, which ruled the Gujarat region from 950–1300, preceded the Gujarat Sultanate.
8. See Chapter 4, "Fusion Wells," of Livingston, *Steps to Water: The Ancient Stepwells of India*.
9. Patron itself is male-centric, stemming from the root word *pater*, which means "father."
10. See Appendix 3 for the translation of the inscription found in *Rudabai vaav*. The inscription states that the patroness built this stepwell in the memory of her deceased husband.
11. See Appendix 2 for the translation of the inscription found in *Bai Harir vaav*.
12. The British were assisted by innumerable Indian assistants, observers, draftsmen, and recorders, whose names for the most part have been obscured from historical record.
13. Nineteenth-century archaeological photography used in the documentation of the Archaeological Survey of India presented romanticized photos contributing to the antiquated imagination of these structures.
14. "Ahmadabad: Dada Harir's well, west half," British Library Online Gallery. http://www.bl.uk/onlinegallery/onlineex/apac/other/019wdz000002222u00008000.html. Accessed September, 2021. This drawing along with many other measured drawings are attributed to James Burgess in the British Library Online Gallery, while the names of the Indian surveyors and draftsmen are not listed in the records, as pointed out by Amrith (see note 12).
15. Livingston refers to the mother goddess as "Devi, the diva of vernacular preservation."

16. This research has been part of the traveling exhibition *Stepwells of Ahmedabad* with various iterations in Ahmedabad at the Kanoria Centre for Arts and Gandhi Memorial Museum (2016), Yale Architecture Gallery (2018), and at the Cooper Union for the Advancement of Science and Art (2020).
17. The stepwell is so deeply enmeshed in the life of its neighborhood that it has become an embodiment of a living well.
18. This is exemplified by the eleven-kilometer-long Sabarmati Riverfront Development Project, where two large barrages hold a perennial water supply for aesthetic purposes as a spectacle for the city.
19. Ghosh refers to the Pope's letter, *Laudato Si*, and the Paris Climate Agreement, both of which were published in 2015 in response to climate change. By pointing out these differences in the choice of language between the two, he comes to the conclusion that religion has the potential to move people to act in a way that nation states cannot.
20. Duara elaborates upon how he employs the concept of transcendence as "not about how we know but a *way* of knowing." See page 5 of *The Crisis of Global Modernity* for further reading.
21. Neimanis argues that new imaginaries of "biogenetic kinship" work to "unsex" the idea of the Mother Sea, yet do not fully eliminate the life-giving, gestational notions of water.
22. I would like to acknowledge my colleagues Tanvi Jain, Aashini Sheth, and Riyaz Tayyibji, who have been an integral part of the *Stepwells of Ahmedabad* research initiative and have been involved in the curation of related exhibitions. Their insights have been invaluable, and the collective work on stepwells continues to evolve.
23. Jain presents a compelling argument about shifting to design practices that acknowledge the aquifer. Jain does not suggest that the stepwell needs to be replicated in form, but rather, she identifies how contemporary practices can adopt some of the lessons that the stepwells have to offer, such as prioritizing decentralized water infrastructure for a resilient future and visibility of the source of water.

References

Acciavatti, Anthony. "Re-imagining the Indian Underground: A Biography of the Tubewell." In *Places of Nature in Ecologies of Urbanism*, edited by Anne Rademacher and Kalyankrishnan Sivaramakrishnan, 206–237. Hong Kong: Hong Kong University Press, 2017.

Agarwal, Anil, and Sunita Narain. *Dying Wisdom: Rise, Fall and Potential of India's Traditional Water Harvesting Systems*. New Delhi: Centre for Science and Environment, 1997.

Amrith, Sunil. *Unruly Waters: How Rains, Rivers, Coasts and Seas Have Shaped Asia's History*. New York: Basic Books, 2018.

Bhatia, Bela. "Lush Fields and Parched Throats: Political Economy of Groundwater in Gujarat." *Economic and Political Weekly* 27, no. 51/52 (December 1992): A142–A170.

D'Souza, Rohan. "Framing India's Hydraulic Crisis: The Politics of the Modern Large Dam." *Monthly Review* 60 (July 2008): 112–122.

Duara, Prasenjit. *The Crisis of Global Modernity*. Cambridge: Cambridge University Press, 2015.

Eck, Diana L. *India: A Sacred Geography*. New York: Three Rivers Press, 2013.

Ghosh, Amitav. *The Great Derangement: Climate Change and the Unthinkable*. Chicago, London: The University of Chicago Press, 2016.

Gillion, Kenneth L. *Ahmedabad, a Study in Indian Urban History*. Canberra: Australian National University Press, 1969.

Guha, Sudeshna. "The Visual in Archaeology: Photographic Representation of Archaeological Practice in British India." *Antiquity* 76, no. 291 (March 2002): 93–100.

Hardiman, David. "Well Irrigation in Gujarat: Systems of Use, Hierarchies of Control." *Economic and Political Weekly* 33, no. 25 (June 1998): 1533–1544.

Hegewald, Julia A. *Water Architecture in South Asia: A Study of Types, Development, and Meanings*. Leiden: Brill, 2001.

Jain, Tanvi. "Stepwells of Ahmedabad: Water-harvesting in Semi-arid India." *The Architectural Review: Underground* (April 2021): 50–55.

Jain, Tanvi, Priyanka Sheth, and Aashini Sheth. *Stepwells of Ahmedabad: Water, Gender, Heritage*. Madrid: Calmo, 2020.

Jain-Neubauer, Jutta. *The Stepwells of Gujarat: In Art-historical Perspective*. New Delhi: Abhinav Publications, 1981.

Livingston, Morna. *Steps to Water: The Ancient Stepwells of India*. New York: Princeton Architectural Press, 2002.

Mankodi, Kirit. *The Queen's Stepwell at Patan*. Bombay Project for Indian Cultural Studies, 1991.

Mehta Bhatt, Purnima. *Her Space, Her Story: Exploring the Stepwells of Gujarat*. New Delhi: Zubaan, 2014.

Momin, K. "Route Indicators of the Sultanate Period in Gujarat." *Journal of the Maharaja Sayajirao University of Baroda* XXXI–XXXII, no. 1 (1998): 121–130.

Morrison, Kathleen D. "Dharmic Projects, Imperial Reservoirs, and New Temples of India: An Historical Perspective on Dams in India." *Conservation and Society* 8, no. 3 (January 2010) 182–195.

Neimanis, Astrida. *Bodies of Water: Posthuman Feminist Phenomenology*. London: Bloomsbury Academic, 2017.

Sheikh, Samira. *Forging a Region: Sultans, Traders, and Pilgrims in Gujarat, 1200-1500*. New Delhi: Oxford University Press, 2010.

Singh, Satyajit. *Taming the Waters: The Political Ecology of Large Dams*. New Delhi: Oxford University Press, 1997.

11

TETHERING BUDDHISM TO CLIMATE CHANGE

Lessons from the Ladakhi Ice Stupa

Carey Clouse

In the desert landscapes of Ladakh, north India, water is not only a scarce and valuable commodity, but it is also a resource imbued with sacred meaning (Wadham 2021). Buddhists from this region have historically highlighted the presence of deities in the water commons at river crossings, ponds, and potable springs—with an assortment of symbolic devices and associated devotional practices. Religious markers have thus become inscribed into the landscapes of Ladakh, and these signifiers include ancient stone *mani* walls, masonry *stupas*, intricate prayer wheels, and colorful strands of prayer flags (Dollfus 1996, 1999; Dollfus & Labbal 2009; Wangchok, 2009; Bray & Lo Bue, 2014). According to anthropologist Karine Gagné, "water as the materiality of ethics is a process mediated by deities, as people interact with a sacred geography" (Gagné 2020: 9). Indeed, in Ladakh, water and sacred space appear to be inextricably linked (Figs. 11.1 and 11.2).

In recent years, this reverence for water has infused a new kind of sacred architecture, in the creation of the ice stupa (Figs. 11.3 and 11.4). The design of the ice stupa tethers Buddhist symbolism to broader climate change advocacy goals, in clear and compelling ways. As an environmental management strategy or water cache, the design intervention could effectively

FIGURE 11.1 Chortens, or stupas, and mani walls stand out against the desert landscapes of Ladakh
Image: Author

DOI: 10.4324/9781003358824-15

FIGURE 11.2 Religious meaning can be found in freestanding structures, denoting sacred landscape features, in Ladakh and Zanskar
Image: Author

FIGURE 11.3 An ice stupa in Ladakh shows the immense scale of some of these structures
Image: Nishant Tiku

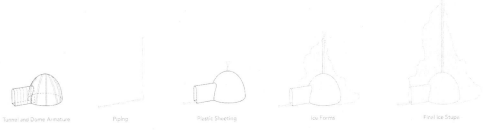

FIGURE 11.4 This diagram shows how ice stupas are formed, with pipes, armature, and time
Image: Author

be shaped as or housed in any number of different vessels (Clouse 2021). However, the intentional pairing of the venerated stupa (also known as a *chorten*) with this new climate-adaptive project enables the ice stupa to seamlessly fit into the existing social, cultural, and religious context of Ladakh.

The ice stupas of Ladakh highlight a local, grounded form of climate-adaptive design thinking, with both benefits and drawbacks that stem from its appropriation of the sacred symbolism. However, the intentional laminating of traditional Buddhist landscape imagery across an otherwise unproven sustainability project provides a new approach to climate-adaptive land management, in which community buy-in and religious context hold significant shaping power. For design practitioners, the ice stupa offers a model to learn from, in which unconventional and even radical climate-adaptive design projects can be made to resonate with local communities through social, cultural, or religious connections. This chapter identifies several of the adaptive techniques employed by the designers of the Ladakhi ice stupa and offers insight into how the intentional pairing of sacred architecture with environmental interests could inform climate-adaptive projects in other parts of the world.

Background

Compared to the rest of the subcontinent, Ladakh, north India, is a rural, remote, and mountainous place (Demenge 2013) (Fig. 11.5). The region hosts dozens of subsistence agricultural villages nestled between high-altitude glaciers and the headwaters of the Indus River. These communities rely upon meltwater captured from glaciers and snowfields to wash and irrigate crops (Dollfus & Labbal 2009). Because so much of the meltwater available to Ladakhi farming enclaves arrives via gravity-fed streams and channels, it must be caught as it courses down the mountain. The resulting socio-hydrological system for water allocation is both sophisticated and well-established. Moreover, the communal management of water resources draws upon shared religious values, social codes, and legal agreements, with practices that have become codified over many centuries (Crook & Osmaston 1994, Nüsser et al. 2012).[1]

Climate change, which has caused many glaciers in the area to shrink, as well as new precipitation regimes which diminish snowfields, threatens the age-old practice of capturing meltwater for use throughout the year (Mingle 2015, Sharma 2019, Wadham 2021).[2] Although mountain water access has always been susceptible to fluctuations in weather, and

FIGURE 11.5 Map of India showing Phyang Village in Ladakh
Image:: Author

this vulnerability is well documented in Ladakh (Rivzi 1998, Field & Kelman 2018), exposure to this risk only deepens under a changing climate (Gutschow 1997, Mingle 2015). In recent years, water stress has become a reoccurring concern for Ladakhi farmers and households, while regional climate instability is only projected to grow (Wilson et al. 2017, Gagné 2020).[3] Climate-adaptive design interventions have been explored in this region, often built by farmers, NGOs, and engineers in an effort to expand sustainable, reliable, and energy-efficient methods of water management (Nüsser et al. 2012, Gladfelter 2018, Clouse 2021). The design of the ice stupa was born out of this context, as a means of stockpiling meltwater collected in the fall and winter, as ice, for use during the following spring.

Building the Ice Stupa

Ladakhi inventor and educator Sonam Wangchuk created the Ice Stupa Project in the winter of 2013–2014, working with a team of volunteers and students to pilot the first version of this design, downstream from the village of Phyang.[4] Since then, the group has worked to develop the concept through a variety of prototypes, and then marketed the project for popular adoption in each successive winter season (Field & Kelman 2018).[5] The Ice Stupa Project has garnered widespread national and international attention for its groundbreaking work linking Ladakhi climate change to an iconic design, which not only helps to raise awareness about the water crisis in north India, but also has captivated the attention of potential donors and allies abroad (Kolbert 2019, Kumar-Rao 2020).[6]

The design of the ice stupa works by spraying meltwater onto an armature such that layers of ice become built up over the course of the winter, creating an enormous pyramidal tower that can then slowly melt through the spring and early summer, when water is most needed for irrigation (Fig. 11.6). This temporal structure has been intentionally tied to social, religious, and cultural interests through programming, imagery, and language. Without these frames, the ice stupa might otherwise be viewed as a simple water feature in the landscape. In this respect, the ice stupa builds upon the design thinking of the region's popular artificial glacier and could be considered an outgrowth of this more established climate-adaptive design solution (Norphel & Tashi 2014, Nüsser & Baghel 2016, Nüsser et al. 2018) (Fig. 11.7). Artificial glaciers trap meltwater throughout the winter months in long, low-slung basins that have been built into hillsides, similar to frozen dams. In the winter the pools fill with ice, held in place by stone walls, and in the spring and summer, outflow gates are opened to release the stored water via gravity-fed channels. The ice stupa borrows the engineering principles from the artificial glacier model in practice, but intentionally incorporates a different design language that more explicitly resonates with collective conceptions of the sacred.

Because ice stupas are built up over the course of the winter, and then melt in the spring, they have no fixed form. This ephemeral condition evokes the impermanence of Buddhist theoretical frames. They exist either in a state of accumulation or dissolution and may be produced and erased from one year to the next. As an agricultural intervention, ice stupas depict agrarian concerns: the cycles of the season, fluctuations in weather, and shifting use of the land.

When they take shape, ice stupas are built up into mounded pyramids made of ice. The thickened walls of ice eventually become white, or blue-white as they reflect the sky. Buddhist prayer flags may be draped across the surface, along with other decorations or signage. Ice stupas consist of a cavity in the center, which allows builders to enter to place the water pipes that enable it to grow; a low-lying tunnel, to allow this access to the cavity; pipes and armature to build up the ice mass; and the conical exterior ice walls. The designers of the Ice Stupa

Tethering Buddhism to Climate Change 169

FIGURE 11.6 The ice stupa is formed from spraying water above the crown of the structure so that it freezes upon contact with the exterior walls. These walls grow up incrementally, with pipes moving upwards over time, throughout the winter months
Image: Nishant Tiku

FIGURE 11.7 An artificial glacier in Ladakh holds ice in flat sheets as a dam
Image: Nishant Tiku

FIGURE 11.8 An "Ice Café" is noted with signage at the entrance tunnel to this ice stupa
Image. Nishant Tiku

Project replicated these components in their first five years of prototyping, but as community members have built their own versions, central features have shifted to represent new values. One example of this shift in use beyond water retention can be seen in the demarcation of an ice café at the entrance of one ice stupa, moving the construct beyond water storage to engage new notions of architectural space (Fig. 11.8).

Buddhist Connection: Sacred Architecture

Since the beginning of the Ice Stupa Project, Buddhist monks have held a central and formative role in the project's conception and branding.[7] In various events, blessings and ceremonies, the leadership of Phyang monastery, and His Holiness Drikung Kyabgon Chetsang Rinpoche, have formally shepherded these adaptation structures into broader Buddhist consciousness. The monastery provided the project's initial pilot site below the village of Phyang, and then promoted the sacred architectural qualities of the ice stupa by working with project team members to overlay markers of religious symbolism (Sharma 2019). Perhaps most importantly, the monks have actively participated in public celebrations and ceremonies, offering their blessings and effectively sanctioning this new practice. By ushering an otherwise unglamorous technical intervention into religious dialog, the Ice Stupa Team harnessed new forms of stakeholder support within Buddhist groups.

The sacred or spiritual qualities of the ice stupa are thus both physically applied to the exterior of the ice formation and also designated by local religious authorities. However, it is also worth noting that the Ice Stupa Project achieves religious significance primarily due to its resemblance to the white masonry stupas that dot contemporary Ladakhi landscapes. These freestanding structures are "spiritual monuments" (Dorjey 2016: 27) and typically have embedded religious messages or materials, mark significant sites, and throughout time undergo both religious rituals and regular maintenance (Myer 1961, Goepper 1993) (Fig. 11.9).

As ubiquitous and revered landscape features, stupas have become embedded into the backdrop of public space in Ladakh. It is not uncommon to see stupas carrying out multiple functions, marking graves, entrances, or other sites of importance. The remarkable chorten described by Bruneu, Devers & Vernier (2012) in Markha Village is not only a religious monument, but also serves as a retaining wall. The Queen's chorten in Cucikzhal, Zanskar is described by Rob Linrothe (2015) as an overlooked and undervalued marker, used primarily

FIGURE 11.9 Village women mix paint to apply to stupas in Zanskar
Image: Author

as a windbreak and animal pen. Some stupas, like the one described by Goepper (1993) at Alchi, are large enough to be entered by humans, replete with second stories, interior rooms, murals, and utilitarians storage spaces. Other stupas may exist in a field of chortens, standing among a mass of structures that comprise a landscape rather than a single object.

Despite these differences, stupas can be read as a legible genre of religious monuments forming Ladakhi public space. They vary according to their relative age, use, and location. However, the construction of a stupa indicates meritorious work—an act of aligning with Buddhist devotional practice and supporting the "spiritual well-being of the builder and of his relations" (Tucci 1988: 24). Across the region, white stupas stand out against brown desert hues, producing the visible, ubiquitous backdrop of sacred architecture that this project emulates. The Ice Stupa Project borrows this iconic color and shape, making clear references to Buddhist sacred architecture.

However, beyond these explicit references to Buddhism, the physical ice tower made by the stupa is a practical shape, drawn as much from the gravity-informed construction process as any desire to explicitly connect it to a hand-built masonry structure (Fig. 11.10). In calling this project a stupa, rather than a mound or mountain or fountain, for instance, designers help people to see ice cultivation with fresh eyes, and almost unequivocally re-branded as a sacred object. In so doing, and despite the relatively unconventional appearance of the ice stupa, the application of Buddhist imagery, symbols, and ritual helps to ground it more directly into the religious language of Ladakh.

Ontological Frameworks

In addition to its conical shape, the surface application of Buddhist symbolism, and the rites and rituals applied by monastic leadership, the ice stupa embodies a number of specific Buddhist principles and values. Its seasonal nature, which mandates its own impermanence, fits squarely into Buddhist conceptions of natural processes. Water production is something that might be tethered to human effort and manipulation, a resource that anthropologist Karine Gagné (2020: 5) notes "is seen as intricately linked to human actions." Gagné continues, "In the Buddhist Himalayas, where the ontology of water is not always premised on the creations of boundaries between nature and culture, water is part of a network of reciprocity and produced through ethical actions." This conception of water resources as a broader part of

FIGURE 11.10 A series of ice stupas in the context of the desert Ladakhi landscape
Image: Nishant Tiku

a socio-hydrological landscape, and as one tied to religious values, enables the ice stupa design to adopt broader significance as a form of sacred architecture.

In the pairing of science and religion, the ice stupa grounds a technocratic design intervention within the ritual and chthonic elements of Buddhist practice in Ladakh. Just as tree planting rituals in the region, described by scholar Andrea Butcher, enable an environmental remediation act to address "the negative pressures of modern lifestyles on the environment in an era of climate insecurity, while also becoming a contemporary form of merit-generation" (Butcher 2017b: 27), the ice stupa overlays irrigation with meritorious performance. According to Butcher, the weaving together of religious and environmental goals is common in Ladakh, where:

> "Practical solutions and adaptations developed by local actors combine externally designed sustainability policies and technologies with ritual ceremonies and architectural schemes aimed at subduing malevolent forces and establishing a 'moral climate' conducive to the flourishing of the Buddhist teachings. The result is an assemblage of climate management that connects scientific evidence, sustainable development, moral exegesis, supernatural actors, and practices of 'everyday religion'—defined here as performances of household and monastic ritual and ceremony aimed at removing pollution, restoring blessing, and arresting the decline into an era of demerit".
>
> *(Butcher 2017b: 6)*

The very act of making an ice stupa may conjure up the same merit generation originally assigned to masonry stupas (Tucci 1988), but with a new overlay of environmental improvement, and associated merit, as well.

Much like other Buddhist landforms in the area, durability and longevity are expressed and attended to through management practices. Ancient stone *mani* walls may be incrementally built up over time, while stupas and prayer wheels require regular painting and upkeep, and the application of prayer flags is meant to weather and degrade over time. According to scholar Sophie Day, environmental processes in Ladakh might be construed as inextricably linked to religion, specifically Buddhism, where "nature is controlled through ritual."[8] Meanwhile, "The flow and condition of water is indicative of the success or failure of monastic ritual activity and human behavior; activities that have undergone significant transformations in recent years" (Butcher 2013: 110).

Thus, the cultivation of ice, in stupas or in any other shape, might then be considered to have sacred qualities. While the ice stupa makes an immediate and obvious connection to sacred architecture through its reference to the stone chortens in the region, the underlying message and processes might also carry Buddhist symbolism, meaning, and reverence. In this sense, the branding adopted by the Ice Stupa Team helps to seat this type of environmental project within local religious frameworks, allowing for comfort in adoption. In a context where religion might be routinely intertwined with other domains and processes, such as the development of infrastructure and buildings (Butcher 2017a), medicine (Pordié 2007), or conceptions of color (Dollfus 2015), the blending of water production and sacred placemaking is not problematic. Moreover, the act of building a stupa, of either ice or stone, marks an effort by stakeholders to tame environmental forces (Gagné 2018). Anthropologists working in Ladakh have shown that religion and environmental management are not only knitted together but that even the new approaches to ice cultivation might benefit from being brought under the umbrella of local, place-based knowledge rather than merely technical innovation (Gagné 2020).

Discussion

The Ice Stupa Project stands out for its enterprising and adept appropriation of religious symbolism in pursuit of environmental management objectives. This approach, which is not new, nevertheless powerfully demonstrates the gains that can be made when environmental advocacy projects become tethered to religious ideals. One widely recognized example of an intertwined religious and environmental campaign is seen in the ordination of trees by Thai monks, which can protect the trees from being cut down (Darlington 2013). Meanwhile, in Ladakh specifically, "the ways that religious ceremony and development practice together have creatively sought solutions to environmental conservation and climate change adaptation" (Butcher 2017a: 30) suggest that there is a broad precedent for a hybrid religious-environment design approach. The ice stupa could be considered one of these projects, in which agricultural needs and social interests have become intertwined in mutualistic terms.

Moreover, a purely utilitarian reading of the ice stupa discounts its broader design implications and potential. It is precise because the ice stupa has been co-opted as a Buddhist structure that it has become visible, accessible, and even celebrated as a landscape feature. The literal and metaphorical connections to spirituality fortify the project with an intrinsic responsibility for stewardship and promotion among practicing Buddhists in the area. Butcher suggests that Ladakhi landscapes are bound up in both attention to environmental processes and religious ritual, as village inhabitants actively maintain "good relations with the chthonic inhabitants of skies, mountains, soil and water" (Butcher 2017a: 27). Her research draws upon a 2003 study of village life by Martin Mills, in which he suggests that "villagers' lives and goals were formed amidst a perceived world of threats and opportunities from capricious local gods, easily angered water spirits, and wandering gods and demons whose influence on health, fertility, the weather, and many other fulcra of human happiness and misery, demanded constant care and propitiation" (Mills 2003: 149). While religion may be infused into Ladakhi landscapes, it is made visual through architecture and ornament rather than naming. Against this social and religious backdrop, and when cast as an affiliated program, the Ice Stupa Project can almost count on affiliated Buddhists to support the work. In this way, the design of the stupa gains additional endorsement through an alliance with the Buddhist community- connections to allies and supporters who might not have otherwise chosen to become involved with what is, at the end of the day, just an irrigation project.

Beyond capitalizing on this essential stakeholder support, the Ice Stupa Project amplifies the common theoretical ground that already exists between Buddhist environmental goals and climate change adaptation measures in the region. This is perhaps most pronounced in the "Go Green, Go Organic" campaign launched by Chetsang Rimpoche below the village of Phyang, and affiliated tree planting programs in the area.[9] In this sense, there are co-benefits for Buddhist leaders, religious devotees, and proponents of the ice stupa as an irrigation device.

The Indian State perceives water as a resource, in which it "is framed as capital with transient value that can only be captured via the construction of dams, which allow for its accumulation" (Wilson et al. 2017: 13). Ice stupa sites become these points of accumulation, which may allow people to plan for their future based on known caches of water, and while small in scale, contribute to economic well-being. In most state-sponsored irrigation initiatives, it "… is through this process of controlling water via the development of megaprojects (dams, canals, irrigation infrastructure, etc.) that its value is captured and translated" (Wilson et al. 2017: 13). However, there is an additional value in the ice stupa that transcends a straightforward reading of water held in a cache. The sacred architecture of the ice stupa reflects the overlay of additional values, interests, and politics, embodying the social, religious, and environmental hybridity that perhaps reflects the region more accurately (Nüsser et al. 2012, Gagné 2020).

Ice stupas have literally become sacred objects in Ladakh, venerated, protected, and reproduced, as much for their religious value as for their drought mitigation. The alignment of Buddhist symbolism has linked religious values with environmental interests, in compelling and productive ways. The lesson, for politicians, architects, landscape architects, and urban designers, is that innovative climate-adaptive design projects might gain a foothold in local contexts if they also carry social, cultural, or religious meaning. In the ice stupa, this framing is in no way superficial and it becomes a critical feature of the project's success.

Ice Stupa Project designers may have simply intuited the value, gains, and power that would result from this connection. However, in offering recommendations for future practice, several discernable principles can be inferred. This project helps to illuminate the following suggestions or lessons, developed by the author:

1. *Even Utilitarian Projects May Benefit from Expansive Design Thinking*
    Design thinking can help to frame new concepts within acceptable norms. This attention to charismatic qualities or branding may make a difference between whether a project is successful or ultimately fails, and whether it is, ultimately, human-centered.

2. *Sacred Concepts May Elevate Infrastructure to More Meaningful Levels*

   The ice stupa elevates irrigation infrastructure to the realm of sacred architecture. Built objects carry meaning in Ladakhi landscapes, and this design builds upon a long history of the territorial display of religious symbolism. Likewise, architects, landscape architects, and urban designers work in spaces that are already steeped in meaning. Connecting to this existing context in profound ways through design enables a built project to transcend functional value to become objects of interest, affection, or even veneration.

3. *Stakeholder Connections to Projects Lay the Groundwork for Acceptance*

   The Ice Stupa Project doesn't merely engage Buddhist symbolism and approval; it also brings people together through events and rituals. These events include singing, dancing, prayer, and other cultural offerings; they are places to meet up and socialize. Indeed, functional infrastructure, buildings, and landscapes may lack public acceptance unless they are adopted by local stakeholder groups. In this sense, the idea of the ice stupa adroitly makes this connection, tapping into established social, cultural, and religious frameworks.

4. *Sustainability Efforts Can Serve Multiple Purposes*

   Layering dual uses and interests onto one environmental feature is an effective way of amplifying co-benefits. Ice stupa projects in Ladakh may address religious values, but they also harness social, cultural, political, and economic opportunities. This multifunctionality enables the project to grow a strong, varied base of supporters, and to satisfy multiple objectives at once.

Limitations

Although the Ice Stupa Project relies on local monastic leadership to frame and validate their work in religious terms, individual Buddhist stakeholders also have an expanded role to play in ongoing stewardship. According to Butcher, the entire Buddhist population might feel compelled to participate in environmental adaptations, because:

> the reproduction of material and religious life is managed by the laity (in their roles as both farmers or waged earners, and religious patrons), the local development administration, enlightened rulers, transcendental protector deities, sacred technology, and the supernatural guardians of weather, soil and water that dwell within the landscape.
>
> *(2017b: 9)*

This view makes explicit the need for community buy-in, particularly among Ladakhi stakeholders on the ground, that can be brokered by monastic leadership. In the case of the Ice Stupa Project, the Ladakhi Buddhist community[10] has largely absorbed and appropriated the work, to the exclusion of other religious groups in the region. Ladakh hosts a significant Muslim population, as well as Sikhs, Christians, Hindis, and other sects (Srinivas, 1998)[11]. Thus, other religious groups and their supporters may have been inadvertently left out by this project's framing and discourse. Religion may be a uniquely polarizing affiliation; in claiming one religion, a project necessarily neglects another. Unlike more inclusive affiliations, such as cultural or social interests that might transcend identity groups, religion stands out as a particularly divisive marker.

While non-affiliated religious groups still may access traditional methods of water harvesting in the region through networks of canals and reservoirs, and *could* participate in ice stupa building, they lack representation. This lack of religious inclusivity is particularly problematic in Ladakh, a region that is not only broadly represented in terms of religion but also has historically experienced periods of religious strife and animosity (Srinivas 1998, Deboos 2013).[12] At a time when the problem of climate change might be considered a universal concern that can bring people together, the ice stupa invokes more polarizing affiliations. A central question for designers is whether the support gained among a Buddhist following is enough to outweigh the loss of potential support from underrepresented groups. Ultimately, it raises the question: might the project have been more successful, and more universal, with different branding? Could alternative ice formations speak to other religious groups in the region? Or even better, is there some common ground for framing that might be invoked instead?

Conclusion

Buddhist values of environmental stewardship, as well as the sacred quality of water, have become both conceptually imbued and literally expressed in the design language of the ice stupa. The ice stupa form, as a freestanding tower in an open landscape, stands out as a symbolic reminder that Buddhist groups are actively grappling with the topic of climate change in their own ritualistic terms. The ice stupa is more than just an expression of sacred architecture in the landscape: it is evidence of stakeholder action and engagement with climate activism. In this sense the stupa structures in Ladakh connect to other Buddhist environmental action projects, such as tree ordination (Darlington 2013), to depict an organized environmental defense effort. This work is bound up in the spiritual relationship that people have with the environment, where "water is produced as people interact with a sacred geography, because the Himalayan landscape is a place of potential encounters with the divine in its various forms" (Gagné 2020: 6). In addition to highlighting yet another sacred source of water in the high mountain landscapes of Ladakh, the ice stupa functions as a valuable irrigation device, particularly as a means of adapting to climate change-induced water scarcity.

Climate change adaptation projects in Ladakh primarily target the problem of water scarcity. This project, at the intersection of water management, sacred architecture, and climate change adaptation, highlights the value that comes from linking multiple narratives. The pairing of Buddhism and meltwater storage in the shape of an ice stupa highlight the intersection of religious values such as stewardship, and environmental adaptation in practice. This work illuminates the latent potential that comes from bundling design thinking, spirituality, and water husbandry and the common terrain that might be forged in the face of environmental change.

While the intertwining of religious rhetoric with environmental conservation may not be an entirely new strategy, its use in Ladakh suggests an emerging model for climate change actions. Climate change adaptation projects such as the ice stupa in Ladakh could represent a desire to "tam[e] the environment," that reinforces colonial approaches to hazards in the region (Field & Kelman 2018: 652). It moves beyond technocratic engineering, however, to embody the hybridity of religion and culture that reflects the attitudes of local people (Butcher 2017a). In the case of the Ice Stupa Project, Buddhist spiritual concepts have been intentionally applied to an otherwise secular adaptation intervention in an effort to help the project gain traction among local residents. Not surprisingly, this pairing has also led to broader opportunities such as increased tourism and funding from donors, who are drawn to a project with religious significance.

Designers will need to overlay a variety of interests and agendas if they want to effectively attract people to climate change adaptation projects. This work requires addressing stakeholder interests, practices, and values in order to harness broad civic support (Wagle et al. 2021). The prospect of incorporating sacred conceptual frameworks into environmental adaptation and mitigation projects provides a powerful source of connection for humans, but it also risks leaving some groups out. In the meantime, climate change, as a ubiquitous challenge in and of itself, might be viewed as a more universal common ground.

Notes

1. Sharma, Arjun., & Kunel Bharat. (2017). One's waste, another's right: Translating history and making the Ladakhi commons, *IACS Conference Proceedings*. https://www.iasc2017.org/wp-content/uploads/2017/06/11N_Arjun-Sharma.pdf Accessed 29 September, 2021.
2. Grossman, Daniel. "As Himalayan Glaciers Melt, Two Towns Face the Fallout." *Yale Environment 360*, March 24, 2015. https://e360.yale.edu/features/as_himalayan_glaciers_melt_two_towns_face_the_fallout Accessed 29 September 2021.
3. Gladfelter, Sierra., & Yonetti, Eben. "Ladakh's Artificial Glaciers, Ice Stupas, and Other Attempts to Survive a Warming Planet." *Tibet Himalaya Initiative*, March 11, 2018, Boulder, CO: University of Colorado Boulder. https://www.colorado.edu/tibethimalayainitiative/2018/03/11/ladakhs-artificial-glaciers-ice-stupas-and-other-attempts-survive-warming-planet Accessed 29 September 2021.
4. Sharma, Arjun., & Kunel Bharat. (2017). One's waste, another's right: Translating history and making the Ladakhi commons, *IACS Conference Proceedings*. https://www.iasc2017.org/wp-content/uploads/2017/06/11N_Arjun-Sharma.pdf Accessed 29 September, 2021
5. Ice Stupa Project. (2021). About the Project. http://icestupa.org/about Accessed September 29, 2021.
6. Rolex Awards. Ice Towers in the Desert. *Rolex Awards Online*. https://www.rolexawards.com/40/laureate/sonam-wangchuk Accessed September 29, 2021.
7. See promotional material on the project's website: About the Project. http://icestupa.org/about Accessed September 29, 2021.
8. Day, Sophie. (1989). "Embodying Spirits: Village Oracles and Possession Ritual in Ladakh, North India." Doctoral Dissertation, *London School of Economics and Political Science*. Page 57.
9. See more about these initiatives on the project's website: https://www.gogreengoorganic.net Accessed February 16, 2022.
10. The most recent available census reports that 66.4% of Leh District in Ladakh is Buddhist (Census, 2011). Census of India. "Leh District Population Census 2011–2020, Jammu and Kashmir literacy sex ratio and density." *www.census2011.co.in*. Accessed February 16, 2022.
11. According to the most recent available census reports, 17.14% of Leh District in Ladakh is Hindu, 14.28% is Muslim, .49% is Christian, .82% is Sikh, .08% is Jain, .04% is Other, and .75% is Not Stated (Census, 2011). Census of India. "Leh District Population Census 2011-2020, Jammu and Kashmir literacy sex ratio and density." *www.census2011.co.in*. Accessed February 16, 2022.
12. Pandit, Saleem M. "Ladakh Tense over Muslim-Buddhist 'love-jihad' marriage." *The Times of India*. September 12, 2017. https://timesofindia.indiatimes.com/india/ladakh-tense-over-muslim-buddhist-love-jihad-marriage/articleshow/60471076.cms Accessed February 16, 2022.

References

Bray, John, & Lo Bue, Erberto F. *Art and Architecture in Ladakh: Cross-Cultural Transmissions in the Himalayas and Karakoram*. Boston: Brill, 2014.

Bruneau, Laurianne, Devers, Quentin, & Vernier, Martin. "An Archaeological Account of Ten Ancient Painted Chortens in Ladakh and Zanskar," in *Art and Architecture in Ladakh: Cross-Cultural Transmissions in the Himalayas and Karakoram*, edited by Erberto Lo Bue & John Bray, 100–140. Boston: Brill, 2014.

Butcher, Andrea. "Keeping the Faith: Divine Protection and Flood Prevention in Modern Buddhist Ladakh." *Worldviews: Global Religions, Culture, and Ecology*, 17:4 (2013): 103–14. DOI 10.1163/15685357-01702002.

———. "Development, Well-being, and Perceptions of the 'Expert' in Ladakh, North-West India." *Anthropology in Action*, 24:3 (2017a): 22–31.

———. "Networks and Practices of Weather and Climate in the Western Himalaya," in *European Bulletin of Himalayan Research*, 4, edited by William Sax, 5–35. Kathmandu: Social Science Baha: Spring, 2017b.

Clouse, Carey. *Climate-Adaptive Design in High Mountain Villages: Ladakh in Transition*. London: Routledge, 2021.

Crook, John, & Osmaston, Henry. *Himalayan Buddhist Villages: Environment, Resources, Society and Religious Life in Zangskar, Ladakh*. Bristol: University of Bristol Press, 1994.

Darlington, Susan. *The Ordination of a Tree: The Thai Buddhist Environmental Movement*. Albany: State University of New York Press, 2013.

Deboos, Salomé. "Religious Fundamentalism in Zanskar, Indian Himalaya." *Himalaya*, 32:1 (2013): 35–42.

Demenge, Jonathan. "The Road to Lingshed: Manufactured Isolation and Experienced Mobility in Ladakh." *Himalaya*, 32:1 (2013): 51–60.

Dollfus, Pascale. "No Sacred Mountains in Central Ladakh? In reflections of the mountain: Essays on the history and social meaning of the mountain cult in Tibet and the Himalaya," in *Reflections of the Mountain Essays on the History and Social Meaning of the Mountain Cult in Tibet and the Himalaya*, edited by A. M. Blondeau & E. Steinkellner, 3–22. Vienna, Austria: Verlag der Österreichischen Akademie der Wissenschaften, 1996.

———. "Mountain Deities among the Nomadic Community of Kharnak (Eastern Ladakh), Ladakh: Culture, History, and Development between Himalaya and Karakoram," in *Recent research on Ladakh 8, 8th Colloquium of the International Association for Ladakh Studies, Moesgaard*, edited by Martijn van Beek, Kristoffer Brix Bertelsen, & Poul Pedersen, 92–118. Aarhus, Denmark: Aarhus University Press, 1999.

———. "Perceiving, Naming and Using Colours in Ladakh." *Tibet Journal*, 40:2 (2015): 261–280.

Dollfus, Pascale, & Labbal, Valérie. "Ladakhi Landscape Units," in *Reading Himalayan Landscapes Over Time: Environmental Perception, Knowledge and Practice in Nepal and Ladakh*, edited by Joëlle Smadja, 85–106. Paris: Institut Français de Pondichéry, 2009.

Dorjey, Skalzang. "Ladakh Monastic Art and Architecture: A Case Study of Its Developmental Perspective in Relation with Tibet." *The Tibet Journal*, 41: 2 (Autumn/Winter 2016): 21–28.

Field, Jessica, & Kelman, Ilan. "The Impact on Disaster Governance of the Intersection of Environmental Hazards, Border Conflict and Disaster Responses in Ladakh, India." *International Journal of Disaster Risk Reduction*, 31 (2018): 650–658. DOI 10.1016/j.ijdrr.2018.07.001.

Gagné, Karine. *Caring for Glaciers: Land, Animals, and Humanity in the Himalayas*. Seattle: University of Washington Press, 2018.

———. "The materiality of Ethics: Perspectives on Water and Reciprocity in a Himalayan Anthropocene." *WIREs Water*, 7:4 (July/August 2020): e1444. DOI 10.1002/wat2.1444

Gladfelter, Sierra. "Ladakh's Artificial Glaciers, Ice Stupas, and Other Human-Made Ice Reserves." *Fulbright-Nehru Student Research Fellowship Final Report*, Delhi: United States-India Educational Foundation, 2018.

Goepper, Roger. "The 'Great Stūpa' at Alchi." *Artibus Asiae*, 53:1 (1993): 111–143.

Gutschow, Kim. "Lords of the Fort, Lords of the Earth, and No Lords at All: The Politics of Irrigation in Three Tibetan Societies," in *Recent research on Ladakh 6: Proceedings of the Sixth International Colloquium on Ladakh, Leh 1993*, edited by Henry Osmaston & T. Tsering, 105–115. New Delhi: Motilal Banarsidass Publishers, 1997.

Kolbert, Elizabeth. "The Ice Stupas." *The New Yorker*, 20 May 2019. 54.

Kumar-Rao, Arati. "One Way to Fight Climate Change: Make Your Own Glaciers." *National Geographic*, 238:1 (2020): 98.

Linrothe, Rob. "Site Unseen: Approaching a Royal Buddhist Monument of Zangskar (Western Himalayas)." *The Tibet Journal*, 40:2 (Autumn 2015): 29–95.

Mills, Martin. *Identity, Ritual and State in Tibetan Buddhism: The Foundations of Authority in Gelukpa Monasticism*. Abingdon: Routledge Curzon, 2003.

Mingle, Jonathan. *Fire and Ice: Soot, Solidarity and Survival on the Roof of the World*. New York: St. Martin's Press, 2015.

Myer, Prudence R. "Stupas and Stupa-Shrines," *Artibus Asiae*, 24:1 (1961): 25–34.

Norphel, Chewang, & Tashi, Padma. Snow Water Harvesting in the Cold Desert in Ladakh: An Introduction to Artificial Glacier," in *Mountain Hazards and Disaster Risk Reduction*, edited by H.K Nibhanupudi & R. Shaw, 199–210. Tokyo: Springer, 2014.

Nüsser, Marcus, & Baghel, Ravi. "Local Knowledge and Global Concerns: Artificial Glaciers as a Focus of Environmental Knowledge and Development Interventions," in *Ethnic and Cultural Dimensions of Knowledge*, edited by P. Meusburger, T. Freytag & L. Suarsana, 191–209. Heidelberg: Springer, 2016. DOI: 10.1007/978-3-319-21900-4_9

Nüsser, Marcus, Dame, Juliane, Kraus, Benjamin, Baghel, Ravi, & Schmidt, Susanne. "Socio-hydrology of 'Artificial Glaciers' in Ladakh, India: Assessing Adaptive Strategies in a Changing Cryosphere." *Regional Environmental Change*, 19:5 (2018): 1327–1337. DOI: 10.1007/s10113-018-1372-0

Nüsser, Marcus, Schmidt, Susanne, & Dame, Juliane. "Irrigation and Development in the Upper Indus Basin." *Mountain Research and Development*, 32:1 (2012): 51–61. DOI: 10.1659/MRD-JOURNAL-D-11-00091.1

Pordié, Laurent. "Buddhism in the Everyday Medical Practice of the Ladakhi Amchi." *Indian Anthropologist*, 37:1 (2007): 93–116. https://shs.hal.science/halshs-00516414v2/document

Rivzi, Janet. *Ladakh: Crossroads of High Asia*. Delhi: Oxford University Press, 1998.

Sharma, Arjun. "Giving Water Its Place: Artificial Glaciers and the Politics of Place in a High-Altitude Himalayan Village." *Water Alternatives,* 12:3 (2019): 993–1016.

Srinivas, Smriti. *The Mouths of People, the Voice of God: Buddhists and Muslims in a Frontier Community of Ladakh*. Calcutta, India: Oxford University Press, 1998.

Tucci, Giuseppe. *INDO-TIBETICA 1*, trans. Uma Marina Vesci. New Delhi: Aditya Prakashan, 1988.

Wadham, Jemma. *Ice Rivers: A Story of Glaciers, Wilderness, and Humanity*. Princeton: Princeton University Press, 2021.

Wagle, Nisha, Dhakal, Madhav P., Shrestha, Arun B. "Adaptation Strategies to Address Challenges to Traditional Agricultural Water Management in the Upper Indus Basin." *Mountain Research and Development*, 41:3 (August 2021): R24–R31. DOI: 10.1659/MRD-JOURNAL-D-20-00059.1

Wangchok, Sonam. "Sacred Landscapes in the Nubra Valley," in *Mountains, Monasteries and Mosques: Recent Research on Ladakh and the Western Himalaya: Proceedings of the 13th colloquium of the International Association for Ladakh Studies*, edited by John Bray & E. Elena de Rossi. Filibeck, 271–283. Pisa, Italy: Fabrizio Serra Editore, 2009.

Wilson, Alāna, Gladfelter, Sierra, Williams, Mark W., Shahi, Sonika, Baral, Prashant, Armstrong, Richard & Racoviteanu, Adina. "High Asia: The International Dynamics of Climate Change and Water Security." *The Journal of Asian Studies*, 76:2 (May 2017): 457–480. DOI: 10.1017/S0021911817000092

PART IV
Water Systems

12

HYMN TO THE WATERS

Anāhitā in Ancient Persian Architecture

Stephen Caffey

Even before the rise of Zoroastrianism, the peoples who traversed the arid regions of ancient Persia worshiped the water goddess *Arəduuī Sūrā Anāhitā*, known today as the Achaemenid deity *Anāhitā* (Fig. 12.1). This chapter explores the role of water as a divine substance for bodily and spiritual sustenance in the pre-Zoroastrian and Zoroastrian belief systems. The first section contextualizes water within a framework of current and emerging scholarly

FIGURE 12.1 Iran Regions Map. After Peter Fitzgerald (2012)
 Source: Wikimedia Commons

DOI: 10.4324/9781003358824-17

assessments of *Anāhitā* and her attributes. The second considers the Persian *qanat* as a system that transcended the practicalities of hydraulic infrastructure to transmit *Anāhitā's* divine presence into private domestic and imperial spaces, as well as public sacrificial and ritual spaces. The concluding section samples shrines and temples associated with *Anāhitā* and ponders the current and prospective status of water in 21st-century Iran.

Naming Sacred Water

The river goddess *Arəduuī Sūrā Anāhitā* originated with the nomadic Indo-Aryans who migrated across the Iranian plateau in the second millennium BCE. "The oldest Iranian water deity ... was gradually superseded by a female deity of presumably Mesopotamian origin, Anahita, goddess of rivers."[1] The complex polytheistic belief system also included supreme ruler Ohrmazd, his consort Spəntā Ārmaiti (earth), and Miθra.[2] With the emergence of the Mazdayasnian religion, ancient Iranians' belief systems slowly and sporadically shifted. Following a personal encounter with Ohrmazd Zaraθuštra (Zarathustra), a Spitamid *zaotar* (priest) and *mąθrān* (poet-seer-sacrificer) established the Mazdayasnian religion. Zaraθuštra "elevated Ohrmazd to a position of supremacy that approaches monotheism."[3] Tradition holds that Zaraθuštra composed the *Gathas*, a collection of sacred songs constituting the core of the Zoroastrian liturgy.[4] The *Gathas* emphasized the existential conflict between Truth and Falsehood played out between humans and between deities: the *ahuras*, following Ohrmazd, favored cosmic order and Truth, while the *daēvas* aligned themselves with Aŋra Mainiiu, a force of supernatural affliction[5] (Malandra 1983). Those born into the religion that would later become Zoroastrianism preserved the *Gathas* through oral tradition for centuries before they were committed to text, possibly as early as the Arsacid era (c. 250 BCE–240 CE). Once transcribed, the *Gathas* combined with other songs, poems, and narratives to form the collection of scriptural texts known as the *Avesta*.

Anāhitā rituals and traditions predated Zaraθuštra by as many as 1,000 years. Though Zaraθuštra's doctrinal reorganization of the divine realms relegated *Anāhitā* to the status of *yazata*, an angelic entity worthy of prayer and adoration, the river goddess retained ritual prominence (Azarnoush 1987). In the *Ābān Yašt*, the third-longest of the 21 hymns addressed to the *yazatas*, Ohrmazd sacrifices to *Anāhitā* and entreats Zaraθuštra to do the same. Historian Jenny Rose translates *Anāhitā's* identity as "*sūrā* ('strong') and *anāhitā* ('undefiled'), asserting her identity as both powerful and chaste" (Rose 2015: 275). Other scholars translate *Anāhitā* as unbounded, boundless, or unrestrained.[6] The third epithet, *Arəduuī* (moist), ensured abundance in harvest and herd, purified semen and womb, eased childbirth, and facilitated mothers' milk production. Most importantly, "the beneficence of Anahita is linked with the flow of life-sustaining water from the earth" and on the earth's surface, whether placid pool or raging river[7]. The *Ābān Yašt*'s length, complexity, and specificity testify to *Anāhitā's* status as a water goddess and thus to the spiritually integral nature of water in pre-Zoroastrian and Zoroastrian notions of the sacred (Brosius 1998)[8].

Transmitting Sacred Water

Water's symbolic significance and practical importance inform the Zoroastrian "vision of the world as a harmony of elements ... interrupted and unbalanced by an invasion of something intrinsically disharmonious. The maintenance of purity is the symbolic and performative restitution of order in a disorderly world."[9] Water purifies and thus must remain pure.[10] At the cosmological scale, "water was the second of the seven 'creations.' ... Since the creation

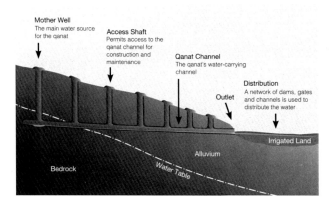

FIGURE 12.2 Cross-section of a Qanat. After Samuel Bailey (2009), Wikimedia Commons

was essential to their life, the ancient Iranians evidently made offerings to it, to keep it pure and vivifying."[11] Rather than sit passively and await *Anāhitā's* beneficence, inhabitants of the Iranian plateau deployed a system of "gravity-flow tunnel-wells" called *qanats*, dating to at least the 13th century BCE (Fig. 12.2). In the 2nd century BCE, the Greek historian Polybius observed, "these people at infinite toil and expense constructed these underground channels through a long tract of country, in such a way, that the very people who now use the water are ignorant of the sources from which the channels were originally supplied." The source was, of course, *Anāhitā*, whose temple at the ancient Median capital city of Ekbātān (present-day Hamedan) Polybius described in a passage immediately preceding his account of the *qanat* system (Shuckburgh 1889, 26–27).

Qanats are "artificial underground water channels up to 305 m (about .19 miles) deep beneath the surface of the earth ... relying solely on gravity to move the water from its source to its point of use."[12] Up to 37,000 Iranian *qanats* supply water today, the longest of which runs some 75 kilometers (46.6 miles) from Farhaj village in eastern Yazd province to Zārch, near the city of Yazd. Most operate at a depth of 30 to 45 meters (about 98 to 148 feet). The cities Ekbātān and Persepolis relied on the *qanat* system for drinking, bathing, irrigation, and ritual. The technology expanded beyond the Iranian plateau during the reign of the Achaemenids (550–331 BC), who incentivized construction "by allowing *qanat* builders [known as *muqannis*] and their heirs to retain profits from newly-built *qanats* for five generations" (Ahmadi et al. 2010; Shuckburgh 1889: 27).[13]

Muqannis ensure continuous access to sacred waters (English 1968; Taghavi-Jeloudar et al. 2013). In the preface to *The Extraction of Hidden Waters*, Persian mathematician and engineer Abū Bakr Karaji (953–1029 CE) observes, "I do not know any other profession more beneficial than extraction of hidden water, as it flourishes and cultivates lands, improves people's welfare, and grants ample profits"[14] (Bensi 2017: 50). Though not explicitly acknowledged by non-Zoroastrians, the ever-present threat of *daēvas'* malevolent meddling persists. Muslim *Muqannis* avoid working on "unlucky" days; a sneeze will keep a *muqanni* home on a workday, as well. Locals consider *muqannis* who survive into old age fortunate, if not specially blessed. Iranian villagers say a special prayer for a *muqanni* before each descent (Afkhami 1998).[15]

Qanat systems drove Persian settlement patterns.[16] Rural residences aligned with the single *qanat* watercourse (*shahjub*). Larger towns expanded along "a spatial skeleton of parallel pathways" serving as "trunk lines of human activity."[17] Urban centers instituted a system of *payabs*

FIGURE 12.3 Persian Qanat: aerial view, Joupar (2014). S. H. Rashedi. The UNESCO.

(staircases leading to the subsurface water) and cisterns of various scales. Homes in wealthier neighborhoods retain the ancient private *payabs* that descend to subgrade rooms with direct access to the flowing *qanat* stream. These rooms open upward into *badgirs* (windcatcher towers) that channel summer winds across the chilled, sacred water, providing relief from the intense heat (Honari 1989).[18]

The tradition of locating first shrines and later mosques at *qanat* exit points demonstrates the "enduring influence that Iran's ancient culture exerts ... between water and sacred places" (Khaneiki 2020, 15). The pre-Zoroastrian Gohar-riz *qanat* of Joupar in Kerman province, south-central Iran, exemplifies the practice (Arbarghoei Fard, 16; Pourahmad 1990).[19] Comprising 6 chains and 129 wells, the Gohar-riz *qanat* extends to 3,556 meters (2.2 miles) with a central tunnel depth of 20 meters (65.6 feet) (Fig. 12.3). Writing about a species of fish occupying this *qanat*, ichthyologist Anthony Smith recounts a local *muqanni* story: "on one day a year the largest fish wore a golden crown which it borrows from the treasure that lies at the head of every qanat" (Smith 1953, 78.) One can easily link the lore of the crowned *qanat* fish to *Anāhitā*'s gold diadem (mentioned in the *Ābān Yašt*) and her role in granting "ample profits" to the treasure hidden in each *qanat* mother well (Sala 2008).

Through residual bonds to *Anāhitā*, the Persian *qanat* system in Iran evolved and today retains a distinctive sacred identity. Villagers sing songs and recount myths and legends about the *qanat*, assigning each a gender and a name (Sala 2008). In an annual ritual known as a "*qanat* wedding," villagers stage a marriage ceremony, complete with "music and a banquet." In another ritual, a young boy "marries" two *qanat* sources by carrying water from one *shahjub* to another[20] (Foltz 2002, 360).

Materializing Sacred Water—Inscribing *Anāhitā*

Linking *Anāhitā* with one or more sites, structures, spaces, materials, relief sculptures, and inscriptions provokes reactions ranging from mildly skeptical to vigorously contentious (Kia 2016, 23–24).[21] Ancient sources such as the *Histories of Herodotus of Halicarnassus* (c. 480–425 BCE) report that the earliest Zoroastrians preferred open-air sacrifice to enclosed altars. More recent translations and interpretations disagree as to whether Persians crafted cult statues of the gods of fire and water prior to the reign of Artaxerxes II Mnemon (404–359 BCE), whose devotion to *Anāhitā* survives in epigraphic, sculptural, and architectural evidence

(Rose 2010; Schmidt 2011). Fragmentary texts from the writings of the Babylonian priest Berossus (c. 350–281 BCE) identify Artaxerxes II Memnon as "the first to set up the statues of [*Anāhitā*] in Babylon, Susa, and Ecbatana, and to enjoin this worship upon Persians and Bactrians, upon Damascus and Sardis" (Clement of Alexandria [ca. 150–215 CE] 1919, 149).

Epigraphic evidence for the worship of *Anāhitā* also traces to the reign of Artaxerxes II Mnemon. In trilingual text inscribed on the ruins of a many-columned hall in Susa, Artaxerxes II proclaims,

> Darius my ancestor built this Apadana; afterwards, in the time of my grandfather Artaxerxes, it then burnt down, then by the grace of Ahuramazda, Anahita and Mithra, I had the Apadana rebuilt. May Ahuramazda, Anahita, and Mithra protect me from all evil, and that which I have built may they not shatter nor harm![22]

The Susa inscription elevated *Anāhitā* to the realm of Ohrmazd and Miθra, rendered permanent the ruler's request for protection of the restored apadana, and reiterated his claim to Achaemenid heritage. Artaxerxes II and his successors commissioned inscriptions, sculptural representations, and temples or sanctuaries dedicated to the goddess in Pasargadae, Ekbātān, Eṣṭakr, Kangavar, and Bišapur.

Anāhitā's popularity survived Alexander the Great's conquest of Persia, ensuing Seleucid (312–64 BCE) rule, and the assertion of Parthian power with the rise of the Arsacids (250 BCE–226 CE). The Sasanians (224–650 CE) adopted *Anāhitā* as their "patron divinity," adding royal investiture to her list of sacred functions. Monumental relief sculptures projecting from the rock face at Naqš-e Rostam (northwest of Persepolis) and Ṭāq-e Bostān (northeast of Kermānšāh) depict Anāhitā in this role, as do a collection of carved stone capitals also located at Ṭāq-e Bostān.[23] *Anāhitā*'s prominence in the *Avesta*, in the Achaemenid-era inscriptions, and in her role as goddess of the waters (associated with Aməša Spənta *Haurvatat* or "wholeness") signaled "spiritual and physical legitimation" for the Sasanians (Herrmann 1989, 46).[24]

Part of a much larger complex of royal tombs and relief sculptures, the Naqš-e Rostam investiture scene comprises five anthropomorphic figures (Fig. 12.4). Reading from the viewer's right to left, *Anāhitā* stands in full-length, body frontal with mural-crowned head in profile. Based on a comparison with the flames arising from the king's and child's legs, her clinging beribboned garment terminates in a series of diagonal waves that spill out over the bottom edge of the relief panel, suggesting flowing water. A billowing scarf and train echo these waving lines. *Anāhitā* grasps in her right hand a diadem, beneath which a child faces her.

Receiving the diadem from *Anāhitā*, the sculpture of Persian king Narseh (293–302 CE) shows that he wears a large crown with korymbos, necklace, and an earring in his right ear. Two adult male courtiers stand behind him. Like his Achaemenid predecessor Artaxerxes II Mnemon, Narseh cast *Anāhitā* in a central role to validate his political and spiritual authority. One additional detail bears consideration: the Achaemenid king Darius I (550–486 BCE) chose Naqš-e Rostam for his tomb, a large cruciform structure carved from the rock face above a natural spring flowing from the ground directly below (Canepa 2018, 213).

Three centuries after Narseh's reign, Kosrow II (r. 590–628 CE) commissioned a monumental investiture scene in a large, deep *ayvān* (rock-cut barrel vault) in the royal funerary complex at Ṭāq-e Bostān (Fig. 12.5). The scene constitutes one of several bas reliefs towering over the spring-fed reflecting pool at the base of the rock face. Kosrow II stands between Anāhitā and Ohrmazd, each of whom presents a diadem fastened to a large, deeply pleated

FIGURE 12.4 Shallow rock relief carving of full-length, standing figures. Narseh Investiture Scene from Naqsh-e Rostam. After Diego Delso, delso.photo, License CC-BY-SA. (2016). Wikimedia Commons.ter Diego Delso, delso.photo, Narseh Investiture Scene from Naqsh-e Rostam. License CC-BY-SA. (2016), Wikimedia Commons

FIGURE 12.5 High-relief of Anahita, Khosro II, Ahura Mazda.jpg (2006). After Philippe Chavin. Taq-e Bostan, Wikimedia Commons

ribbon. As Anāhitā waits to bestow upon the king her blessing, water empties from the ewer in her left hand, "suggesting the increase and benefit that Anāhitā bestows" in divine sanction (Rose 2010, 123).

Monumentalizing Sacred Water—Repurposed *Anāhitā* Pilgrimage Shrines

Prior to the construction of sacred *qanats* that fed both cities and shrines, the earliest nomadic Persians most likely "worshipped at many natural sanctuaries throughout the land, created by lake or mountain stream."[25] Porphyry (c. 232–305 CE) noted Zoroastrians' ritual devotion to "water which trickles, or is diffused" in caves, caverns, and grottos (Taylor 1823, 175). The 2001–2004 excavations at Čale Ğar 1, an ancient copper mine in western Iran's Vešnave district, revealed an especially intriguing example of water devotion. Jewelry, coins, personal objects, and small ceramic vessels appear in and near water that flows within Čale Ğar 1's cave-like setting. Archeologists identify the site as a "long-lived holy area" where women began making offerings to the waters as early as the second half of the first millennium BCE (Stöllner 2012, 10, 22). As Islam took hold in Persia, such "places of goddess worship that once belonged to Anahita slowly converted into Muslim shrines of worship of 'real' women from legends that spread after the Arab invasion."[26]

Natural settings reimagined for Islamic contexts and later re-territorialized through architecture include two shrines dedicated to real women saints (*pīr*) near the Iranian city of Yazd. Pīr-e Bānū Pars (Lady of Pars) and Pīr-e Sabz (Green Shrine, also known as Čakčak), originated as early as the 7th century BCE as shrines to *Arəduuī Sūrā Anāhitā* and retain their importance to Zoroastrians (Watson 1866).[27] A third site, Bībī Shahrbānū at Mount Ṭabarak, overlooks the ancient city of Ray, south of the capital city of Tehran. In these Zoroastrian shrines, the arrival of Islam necessitated a shift from explicit *Anāhitā* worship to devotion to Sasanid saints, muting (without erasing) any deterministic associations that might present as pagan idolatry.[28]

The natural spring and sacred rock at Pīr-e Bānū Pars memorialize a daughter of the last Sasanian king, Yazdegerd III (r. 632–651 CE), who was invested at the Esṭakr Adūr Anāhitā fire temple in Fars[29] (Shavarebi 2018, 183). While fleeing invading Muslim soldiers, the daughter cried out to Ohrmazd for help.[30] The mountain opened and swallowed the princess alive. The rock face rises above a natural stone platform abutting a spring-fed pool. Beneath, a dry riverbed joins three other river courses. During the rainy season, runoff floods the riverbed, roaring past boulders and crashing against the mountain ridge. Prior to the arrival of Islam, the shrine was likely open to its surroundings. In 1962 a small brick masonry enclosure with a domed sanctuary replaced the "tiny, mud-brick cell" earlier erected by the local Muslim community.[31] Vertical courses of polychrome glazed tiles adorned with *ziyārat-nāme* ("visitation supplications") in white Persian calligraphy frame the shrine entrance (Fig. 12.6). Above the door, a lintel emblazoned with additional text surmounts a winged *fravashi* symbol on a field of blue glazed tile (Farridnejad 2021).

Before conversion from Zoroastrian sanctuary to Sasanid shrine, Pīr-e Bānū Pars likely served as a place for ritual offerings to the goddess of the waters "like those mentioned in the Avestan texts" (Gropp 1998, 33). Through the Sasanid period and beyond, Iranian Zoroastrians and Parsis from around the world have made a pilgrimage to the site.[32] The exhilarating rush of water during the rainy season, the presence of the natural spring, and the proximity to riverbeds and flowing rivers evoke *Anāhitā's* presence, but Bānū Pars is not explicitly mourned in the pilgrims' prayers, rituals, and songs. Zoroastrians never venerate the dead, so the princess's

FIGURE 12.6 Entrance to the pilgrimage site Pir-e Bānu-Pārs © Rashid Shohrat (2021).

FIGURE 12.7 Interior of Pir-e Sabz Shrine. After Arteen Arakel Lalabekyan (2017), Wikimedia Commons

enfoldment into the mountain while still alive eased the transition from the worship of the waters to devotion to the emperor's daughter.

Pīr-e Sabz (Green Shrine), also known as Čakčak ("drip drip"), marks the mountain rescue of Nikbanu, whose tale resembles that of her elder sister Bānū Pars[33] (Afšār 1975, I:63–65, II:855–58; Langer 2008, 328–351). In a desert location east of Ardakān-e Yazd, Pīr-e Sabz draws Zoroastrian and non-Zoroastrian visitors year-round (Fig. 12.7). Zoroastrians pray in a permanent structure adjacent to the rock face and in the grotto from which the sacred water drips. Pilgrims use an outdoor platform for ẖeyrāt (distribution of free food), singing and chanting, and other rites and rituals. Shelters constructed near the shrine serve as sleeping quarters during the pilgrimage (Farridnejad 2021). The annual journey to Pīr-e Sabz "has become a kind of national event for Iranian Zoroastrians," and photographs of the shrine adorn the walls of many Zoroastrians' private residences.[34]

The ziyārat-nāme, supplication, site appropriation, and syncretism common to Pīr-e Bānū Pars and Čakčak apply to another Iranian locale: the Bībī Shahrbānū shrine in the ancient city of Ray[35] (Savant 2013). Dedicated to another sister of the women venerated at Bānū Pars and Pīr-e Sabz/Čakčak, the Bībī Shahrbānū shrine's history intersects with that of Shī'a Islam. An oral tradition dating to the 9th century CE held that Muslim forces captured and transported Shahrbānū to Medina, where she married Imam al-Ḥosayn and gave birth to ʿAlī Zayn al-ʿĀbedīn, the 4th of the 12 Imams (Farridnejad 2021). Fleeing Imam al-Ḥosayn's Umayyad assassins, Shahrbānū traveled to Ray and, facing death at the hands of her pursuers, she beseeched Mount Ṭabarak for help.[36] The Umayyads arrived, only to find a small piece of her clothing protruding from within the rock.

FIGURE 12.8 Bībī Shahrbānū Shrine, Ray. (n.d.), Wikimedia Commons

Like the sites at Pīr-e Bānū Pars and Čakčak, the Bībī Shahrbānū pilgrimage site originated as a shrine dedicated to *Arəduuī Sūrā Anāhitā*, whose presence appeared in the spring-fed pool below the shrine enclosure (Fig. 12.8). The current structure rose in phases between the 10th and 18th centuries (Farridnejad 2021, 135–138).[37] Today, only women and male descendants of Muhammad may enter the inner shrine. Many women who visit do so with the hope of conceiving a child. The protective mountains at Pīr-e Bānū Pars, Čakčak, and Bībī Shahrbānū "seem to be animate individuals who helped humans in danger" and today promise good fortune to those who make the pilgrimage (Gropp 1998, 33).

Monumentalizing Sacred Water—*Anāhitā* Temples

Whether naturally occurring, constructed in the form of sacred qanats such as that at Joupar, or in dedicated temples, architectural forms have not superseded the importance of the pilgrimage, the performance of ritual, or the presence—or later, absence—of water in Iran. The subgrade *Anāhitā* temple, situated within the ruins of the palace complex of Šāpūr I (r. 239–270 CE) at Bīšāpūr, and the Nahid Temple, Kangavar, provide key examples. Whether implicitly or explicitly, each set of ruins echoes the *Abān Yašt* description of *Anāhitā*'s architectural expression. In the case of the Bīšāpūr temple, engagement with proximate water courses evokes "at every stream," while the Nahid Temple acknowledges the "supporting pillars" in the form of its many columns (quoting *Abān Yašt*, Kuz'mina 2007, 57).

Anāhitā devotees entered the "purpose-built aniconic shrine to the waters" at Bīšāpūr via a long stairway, similar to the *payabs* used to access *qanats*, leading to a square enclosure open to the sky (Rose 2010, 124). Cut stone revetment conceals the temple's rubble masonry construction. A door in each of the four thick walls opens into a vaulted ambulatory surrounding

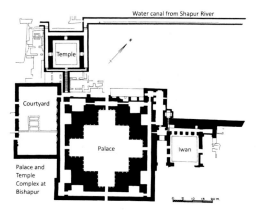

FIGURE 12.9 Plan of Bishapur Palace and Temple Complex (2018), Wikimedia Commons

the central ritual space (Fig. 12.9). A series of small conduits connect a deep well to the nearby Shāpūr River. The site's elaborate hydraulic infrastructure regulates the flow and direction of the water such that it enters from the river, floods the temple floor, and exits in the opposite direction (Rose 2010, 124).

Like other temples dedicated to *Anāhitā*, the Bīšāpūr complex cella housed a fire for *Pāw mahal*, liturgical rituals performed within the temple space.[38] A separate pavilion, open on all four sides with four arches supported by columns and surmounted by a cupola housed another fire. Stylistic analyses, archeological evidence, interpretations of rock reliefs, and inscriptions such as those at Naqš-e Rostam suggest that Roman prisoners of war built the Bīšāpūr Anāhitā temple, accounting for the distinctively dressed stones in the shrine walls and the vaulted ambulatory corridors (Ball 2000, 117–119).

A second exemplar, the Nahid Temple, abuts a hill in the center of the city of Kangavar, on the Khorasan road in western Iran (Fig. 12.10). Resembling its Achaemenid antecedents,

FIGURE 12.10 Nahid Temple, Kangavar (1991), Wikimedia Commons

the temple's two lateral stairways led to a stone platform measuring 209 × 224 meters, with outer walls up to 18 meters thick. Peaking at 32 meters above the surrounding field, visibility of and from the platform creates a vivid sense of monumentality (Barnoos et al. 2020, 2–3). A triple colonnade in a modified Doric order surrounds but does not enclose the platform, with columns reaching 3.54 meters in height (Kleiss et al. 1973, 196). Within the colonnade, "a vast amount of space surrounds the sanctuary building," which could have accommodated pilgrims and locals during *Ābānāgan*, the annual feast-day celebration of the birthday of the waters (Ball 2000, 331). The absence of architraves and connecting beams suggests that the platform had no roof, but springing found on at least one of the ruined columns indicates the possibility of arcading over the entrances (Ball 2000, 330–331).

The Nahid Temple's lack of a roof structure preserves the Zoroastrian preference for open-air prayer. *Avestan* tradition dictates that the faithful perform the Yasna to the waters in the presence of sunlight. Nighttime prayers could reach *daevas*, inviting calamity (Meherjirana 1982, 68). Scholars disagree on the site's chronology and whether the complex is indeed the one mentioned by 1st-century CE Greco-Roman geographer Isidorus of Charax in *Parthian Stations*. Artifacts suggest continuous use during the Achaemenid, Parthian, and Sasanian eras and provide evidence that Muslims used the site for various purposes during the early Islamic period (Barnoos et al. 2020, 3).[39] Whether monumental inscriptions, converted shrines, or purpose-built temples, these architectural reminders telegraph *Anāhitā*'s spiritual and religious legacies.

Conclusion

In ancient Persia, as in present-day Iran, water was and remains "at once a physical entity and a divine reality...never a neutral, objective substance, but rather substance and divinity in one" (Malandra 1983: 117). Sacred water's cleansing, purifying, sustaining, and symbolic functions continue to resonate across the geographical and historical realms of Zaraθuštra. "Because of water['s] sacredness, it has been [a] most fundamental aspect of locating and shaping the spaces in architecture."[40] The *qanat* system, individual and collective rituals, community festivals, and pilgrimage acknowledge, perform, and celebrate water's physiological, psychological, and spiritual importance. And despite abundant evidence connecting that importance to the goddess *Anāhitā*, scholars disagree on how best to interpret the associated architectural sites. Such disagreements deter neither pilgrims nor tourists: sites connected to *Anāhitā* attract both, regardless of religion. *Anāhitā* is a central character in the creation narrative of pre-Zoroastrian Persia. Her presence permeates all bodies of water natural and manmade. She is one of three Zoroastrian deities worthy of shrines and temples, and the only female figure whose approval legitimized Sasanian political power. *Anāhitā* played and continues to play an important role in the lives of many Iranians today.

In the first quarter of the 21st century, water assumes additional dimensions in the collective narrative of the Iranian people. Global climate change, rapid urban development, and resource mismanagement have severely curtailed the water supply in some parts of Iran, leading to sporadic, sometimes large-scale public protests. As was the case with imperial investiture, this politicization complicates and enriches—without overshadowing—water's sacred, spiritual, and religious aspects in both built and natural environments. Since 1980, over 14,000 of Iran's 50,000 active *qanats* have dried up because of water table depletion by pump wells (Alemohammad and Ghariri, n.p.). Though many of the *qanats* have been replaced with modern plumbing infrastructure, thousands of them continue to provide water to neighborhoods, villages, and towns across Iran. From among those thousands, many, such as the Joupar *qanat*, retain explicit associations with *Anāhitā*; for others, the association is implicit. In many ways, the fate of water as a secular necessity and as a sacred substance reflects ongoing changes in Iranian society and prophesies painful changes to come. As this chapter has demonstrated, water continues to sanctify architectural sites, structures, systems, and spaces in Iran. Whether those sites, structures, and spaces withstand the ravages of climate change and whether the ever-dwindling supplies of sacred water spark social, environmental, and political change in Iran remain to be seen.

Notes

1. Foltz, Richard and Manya Saadi-nejad. "Is Zoroastrianism an Ecological Religion?" *Journal for the Study of Religion, Nature and Culture* 1, no. 4 (2007): 421. Accessed 30 September 2021. https:/doi.org/10.1558/jsrnc.v1i4.413/.
2. Schmidt, Hanns-Peter. "Mithra i: Mithra in Old Indian and Mithra in Old Iranian." Encyclopædia Iranica. 2006. Accessed 30 September 2021. https://iranicaonline.org/articles/mithra-i/.
3. Malandra "Zoroastrianism i: Historical Review Up to the Arab Conquest." Encyclopædia Iranica. 2012. Accessed 30 September 2021. https://iranicaonline.org/articles/zoroastrianism-i-historical-review/.
4. Stausberg, Michael, Yuhan Sohrab-Dinshaw Vevaina, and Anna Tessmann, editors. *The Wiley-Blackwell Companion to Zoroastrianism*. Malden: John Wiley & Sons. 2015, 321–327. https://doi.org/10.1002/9781118785539/.
5. Humbach, Helmut. "Gathas." Encyclopædia Iranica. 2012. Accessed 30 September 2021. https://iranicaonline.org/articles/gathas-i-texts/.
6. Saadi-nejad, Manya. "*Anāhitā*: Transformations of an Iranian Goddess." PhD dissertation, University of Berlin. 2019, 47–49. Accessed 30 September 2021. https://doi.org/10.17169/refubium-2373/.
7. Munn, Mark. "Earth and Water: The Foundations of Sovereignty in Ancient Thought." In *The Nature and Function of Water, Baths, Bathing and Hygiene from Antiquity Through the Renaissance*, edited by Cynthia Kosso and Anne Scott, (2009): 208 (quoting from the *Yašt*). Leiden: Brill. Accessed 30 September 2021. https://doi.org/10.1163/ej.9789004173576.i-538.42/.
8. For a complete description of *Anāhitā* in English translation from the *Abān Yašt*, see Saadi-nejad 2019, 67–70.
9. Stausberg, Michael, Yuhan Sohrab-Dinshaw Vevaina, and Anna Tessmann, editors. *The Wiley-Blackwell Companion to Zoroastrianism*. Malden: John Wiley & Sons. 2015, 346. https://doi.org/10.1002/9781118785539/.
10. McIntyre-Tamwoy, Susan. "18 April 2011 – International Day for Monuments and Sites: The Cultural Heritage of Water." ICOMOS. 2011. Accessed 30 September 2021. https://www.icomos.org/18thapril/2011/18April_2011_STamwoy_essay_EN_final_20110329.pdf/.
11. Boyce Mary, quotes from from Iranicaonline, 1982.
12. Taghavi-Jeloudar, Mohsen, Mooyoung Han, Mohammad Davoudi, and Mikyeong Kim. "Review of Ancient Wisdom of Qanat, and Suggestions for Future Water Management." *Environmental Engineering Research* 18, no. 2 (2013): 57–58. https://doi.org/10.4491/eer.2013.18.2.057/.
13. English, Paul Ward. "The Origin and Spread of Qanats in the Old World." *Proceedings of the American Philosophical Society* 112, no. 3 (1968): 170–81. https://www.jstor.org/stable/986162
14. Ataie-Ashtiani, Behzad, and Craig. T. Simmons. 2020. "The Millennium-Old Hydrogeology Textbook 'The Extraction of Hidden Waters' by the Persian Mathematician and Engineer Abubakr Mohammad Karaji (c. 953 – c. 1029)." *Hydrology and Earth System Sciences* 24, no. 2: 761–69. https://doi.org/10.5194/hess-2019-407/.
15. English, Paul Ward. "The Origin and Spread of Qanats in the Old World." *Proceedings of the American Philosophical Society* 112, no. 3 (1968): 170–81. https://www.jstor.org/stable/986162
16. Ibid.
17. Ibid, 178
    Salek, Arash. "Rediscovering Community Participation in Persian Qanats: An Actor-Network Framework." *European Journal of Creative Practices in Cities and Landscapes* 2, no. 1 (2019): 155. https://doi.org/10.6092/issn.2612-0496/8674/.
18. English, Paul Ward. "The Origin and Spread of Qanats in the Old World." *Proceedings of the American Philosophical Society* 112, no. 3 (1968): 170–81.

19. Qanat Irrigated Agricultural Heritage Systems. *Proposal for a Globally Important Agricultural Heritage System (GIAHS).* 2014. Food and Agriculture Organization of the United Nations. Accessed 30 September 2021. https://www.fao.org/3/bp794e/bp794e.pdf/.
20. Foltz, Richard and Manya Saadi-nejad. "Is Zoroastrianism an Ecological Religion?" *Journal for the Study of Religion, Nature and Culture* 1, no. 4 (2007): 422. Accessed 30 September 2021. https:/doi.org/10.1558/jsrnc.v1i4.413/.
    Sala, Renato. "Underground Water Galleries in Middle East and Central Asia: Survey of Historical Documents and Archaeological Studies." Laboratory of Geo-archeology, Institute of Geology, Academy of Sciences of Kazakhstan. 2008. Accessed 30 September 2021. http://www.lgakz.org/Texts/LiveTexts/8-KarezTextEng.pdf/.
    Yazdi, Ali Asghar Semsar, and Majid Labbaf Khaneiki. *Qanat Knowledge: Construction and Maintenance.* Dordrecht: Springer Science+Business Media. 2017, 3. https://doi.org/10.1007/978-94-024-0957-4/
21. Boyce, Mary, L. Chaumont, and C. Bier. "ANĀHĪD." Encyclopædia Iranica. 1989. Accessed 30 September 2021. https://www.iranicaonline.org/articles/anahid/.
    Herrmann, Georgina and V. S. Curtis. "Sasanian Rock Reliefs." Encyclopædia Iranica. 2002. Accessed 30 September 2021. https://www.iranicaonline.org/articles/sasanian-rock-reliefs/.
22. Hanaway, William L., Jr. "Anāhitā and Alexander." *Journal of the American Oriental Society* 102, no. 2 (1982): 290–291. Accessed 30 September 2021. https://doi.org/10.2307/602528/.
    Vallat, François. "The Main Achaemenid Inscriptions of Susa." In *The Palace of Darius at Susa,* translated by Jean Perrot, edited by J. Perrot, 2013, 281–95. London: I.B. Tauris.
23. Boyce, Mary, L. Chaumont, and C. Bier. "ANĀHĪD." Encyclopædia Iranica. 1989. Accessed 30 September 2021. https://www.iranicaonline.org/articles/anahid/.
24. Rose, Jenny. "Investiture." Encyclopedia Iranica. 2012. Accessed 30 September 2021. https://iranicaonline.org/articles/investiture#prettyPhoto.
25. Boyce, Mary, L. Chaumont, and C. Bier. "ANĀHĪD." Encyclopædia Iranica. 1989. Accessed 30 September 2021. https://www.iranicaonline.org/articles/anahid/.
26. Mirjalili, Faranak. "Goddess of the Orient: Exploring the Relationship Between the Persian Goddess Anahita and the Sufi Journey to Mount Qaf." *Religions* 12, no. 9 (2021): 704. https://doi.org/10.3390/rel12090704/.
27. Boyce, Mary. "Bībī Shahrbānū and the Lady of Pārs." *Bulletin of the School of Oriental and African Studies* 30, no. 1 (1967): 30–44. Accessed 30 September 2021. https://doi.org/10.1017/S0041977X00099080/.
28. Ibid.
29. Boyce, Mary, L. Chaumont, and C. Bier. "ANĀHĪD." Encyclopædia Iranica. 1989. Accessed 30 September 2021. https://www.iranicaonline.org/articles/anahid/.
    Daryaee, Touraj. "Yazdegerd III." In *The Oxford Dictionary of Late Antiquity.* Oxford: Oxford University Press. 2018. Accessed 30 September 2021. https://www.oxfordreference.com/view/10.1093/acref/9780198662778.001.0001/acref-9780198662778-e-5108/.
30. Boyce, Mary. "Bībī Shahrbānū and the Lady of Pārs." *Bulletin of the School of Oriental and African Studies* 30, no. 1 (1967): 30–44. Accessed 30 September 2021. https://doi.org/10.1017/S0041977X00099080
31. Boyce, Mary. "BĀNŪ PARS." Encyclopædia Iranica. 1988. Accessed 30 September 2021. https://iranicaonline.org/articles/banu-pars-lady-of-pars-the-name-of-a-zoroastrian-shrine-in-the-mountains-at-the-northern-end-of-the-yazd-plain
32. Choksy, Jamsheed K. "Ancient Religions." *Iranian Studies* 31, no. 3-4 (1998): 661–79. https://doi.org/10.1080/00210869808701939/.
33. Boyce, Mary. "Bībī Shahrbānū and the Lady of Pārs." *Bulletin of the School of Oriental and African Studies* 30, no. 1 (1967): 30–44. Accessed 30 September 2021. https://doi.org/10.1017/S0041977X00099080
34. Stausberg, Michael. "Zoroastrian Rituals." Encyclopaedia Iranica. 2014. Accessed 30 September 2021. https://iranicaonline.org/articles/zoroastrian-rituals/.
35. Boyce, Mary. "Bībī Shahrbānū and the Lady of Pārs." *Bulletin of the School of Oriental and African Studies* 30, no. 1 (1967): 30–44. Accessed 30 September 2021. https://doi.org/10.1017/S0041977X00099080
    Mills, Margaret A. "Refuge in the Rock: Chthonic Rescue and Other Narrations of Women in Peril." *Narrative Culture* 8, no. 1 (2021): 82–105. Accessed 30 September 2021. https://doi.org/10.13110/narrcult.8.1.0082/
36. Amir-Moezzi, Mohammad Ali. n.d. "Šahrbānū." Encyclopædia Iranica. Accessed 30 September 2021. https://doi.org/10.1163/2330-4804_EIRO_COM_1364/.
37. Boyce, Mary. "Bībī Shahrbānū and the Lady of Pārs." *Bulletin of the School of Oriental and African Studies* 30, no. 1 (1967): 30–44. Accessed 30 September 2021. https://doi.org/10.1017/S0041977X00099080
38. Choksy, Jamsheed K."Altars, Precincts, and Temples: Medieval and Modern Zoroastrian Praxis." *Iran* 44 (2006): 327-346. https://doi.org/10.1080/05786967.2006.11834693.

Stausberg, Michael. "Zoroastrian Rituals." Encyclopaedia Iranica. 2014. Accessed 30 September 2021. https://iranicaonline.org/articles/zoroastrian-rituals/.
39. Kleiss, Wolfram, A. A. Sarfaraz, P. P. Delougaz, Helene J. Kantor, G. Dollfus, Dietrich Huff, A. D. H. Bivar, G. Fehérvári, Robert H. Dyson Jr., M. Y. Kiyani, Kambakhsh Fard, Karl Kromer, W. M. Sumner, Akbar Tadjvidi, Ali Hakemi, Raffaele Biscione, Grazia Maria Bulgarelli, Marcello Piperno, Maurizio Tosi, David Whitehouse, Grazia Maria Bulgarelli, Hans J. Nissen, L. Vanden Berghe, and Eugenio Galdieri. "Survey of Excavations in Iran 1971–1972." *Iran: Journal of the British Institute of Persian Studies* 11, no. 1 (1973): 196–197. https://doi.org/10.1080/05786967.1973.11834177/.
Shekofteh, Atefeh, Omid Oudbashi, Giuseppe Cultrone, and Masoud Ansari. "Geochemical and Petrographic Identification of Stone Quarries Used for the Construction of the Anahita Temple of Kangavar (West Iran)." *Heritage Science* 8, no. 1 (2020): article 14. https://doi.org/10.1186/s40494-020-0361-z/.
40. Vahdat, A. K. Hosseini. "Management, Design, and Development of Irrigation System in Desert Regions Case Study: Bagh-E-Shazdeh (Prince Garden)." In *Proceedings of Low Impact Development 2010: Redefining Water in the City*, edited by Scott Struck and Keith Lichten, (2010): 335. Reston: American Society of Civil Engineers. https://doi.org/10.1061/41099(367)30/.

References

Afkhami, Amir A. "Disease and Water Supply: The Case of Cholera in 19th Century Iran." In *Transformations of Middle Eastern Natural Environments: Legacies and Lessons*, edited by Jeff Albert, Magnus Bernhardsson, and Roger Kenna, 206–20. New Haven, CT: Yale University. 1998.
Afšār, Iraj. *Yādgārhā-ye Yazd*. 3 vols. Tehran: Anjuman-i āthār-i millī. 1975.
Ahmadi, Hassan, Aliakbar Nazari Samani, and Arash Malekian. "The Qanat: A Living History in Iran." In *Water and Sustainability in Arid Regions: Bridging the Gap Between Physical and Social Sciences*, edited by Graciela Schneier-Madanes and Marie-Françoise Courel, 125–38. Dordrecht, Netherland: Springer. 2010.
Abarghoei Fard, H. "A Contemplation on Ritual Landscape Representations in Kerman Province." *Journal of Art & Civilization of the Orient* 7, no. 24 (2019): 13–20. doi:10.22034/JACO.2019.89248.
Azarnoush, Massoud. "Fire Temple and Anahita Temple: A Discussion on Some Iranian Places of Worship." *Mesopotamia* 22 (1987): 391–401.
Ball, Warwick. *Rome in the East: The Transformation of an Empire*. London: Routledge. 2000.
Barnoos, Vahid, Omid Oudbashi, and Atefeh Shekofteh. "The Deterioration Process of Limestone in the Anahita Temple of Kangavar (West Iran)." *Heritage Science* 8, no. 1 (2020): 1–19. doi:10.1186/s40494-020-00411-1.
Bensi, Negar Sanaan. "The Qanat System: A Reflection on the Heritage of the Extraction of Hidden Waters." In *Adaptive Strategies for Water Heritage*, edited by Carola Hein, 41–56. Cham, Switzerland: Springer. 2017.
Brosius, Maria. "Artemis Persike and Artemis Anaitis." In *Studies in Persian History: Essays in Memory of David M. Lewis*, edited by Maria Brosius and Amélie Kuhrt, 227–38. Leiden, Netherland: Nederlands Instituut voor het Nabije Oosten. 1998.
Canepa, Matthew P. *The Iranian Expanse: Transforming Royal Identity Through Architecture, Landscape, and the Built Environment, 550 BCE–642 CE*. Oakland, CA: University of California Press. 2018.
Clement of Alexandria. *Protrepticus*. Translated by G. W. Butterworth. London: W. Heinemann. (ca. 150–215 CE) 1919.
English, Paul W. "The Origin and Spread of Qanats in the Old World." *Proceedings of the American Philosophical Society* 112, no. 3 (1968): 170–81.
Farridnejad, Shervin. "Zoroastrian Pilgrimage Songs and Ziyārat-nāmes." In *Zaraθustrōtəma: Zoroastrian and Iranian Studies in Honour of Philip G. Kreyenbroek*, edited by Shervin Farridnejad, 115–92. Leiden, Netherland: Brill. 2021.
Foltz, Richard. "Iran's Water Crisis: Cultural, Political, and Ethical Dimensions." *Journal of Agricultural and Environmental Ethics* 15 (2002): 357–380.
Gropp, Gerd. "The Zoroastrian Endeavour to Venerate and Care for the Earth." In *Mehregan in Sydney: Proceedings of the Seminar in Persian Studies During the Mehregan Persian Cultural Festival Sydney, Australia*, 28 October - 6 November 1994, edited by Garry Trompf and Morteza Honari, 31–4. Sydney, Australia: School of Studies in Religion. 1998.

Herrmann, Georgina. *The Sasanian Rock Reliefs at Naqsh-i Rustam: Naqsh-i Rustam 6, the Triumph of Shapur I*. Berlin: Dietrich Reimer. 1989.

Honari, Morteza. "Qanats and Human Settlement in Iran." In *Qanat, Kariz and Khattara: Traditional Water Systems in the Middle East and North Africa*, edited by Peter Beaumont, Michael Bonine, and Keith McLachlan, 61–85. London: School of Oriental and African Studies. 1989.

Khaneiki, Majid L. *Cultural Dynamics of Water in Iranian Civilization*. Cham: Springer Nature. 2020.

Kia, Mehrdad. *The Persian Empire: A Historical Encyclopedia*. Santa Barbara, CA: ABC-CLIO. 2016.

Kleiss, Wolfram, A. A. Sarfaraz, P. P. Delougaz, Helene J. Kantor, G. Dollfus, Dietrich Huff, A. D. H. Bivar, G. Fehérvári, Robert H. Dyson Jr., M. Y. Kiyani, Kambakhsh Fard, Karl Kromer, W. M. Sumner, Akbar Tadjvidi, Ali Hakemi, Raffaele Biscione, Grazia Maria Bulgarelli, Marcello Piperno, Maurizio Tosi, David Whitehouse, Grazia Maria Bulgarelli, Hans J. Nissen, L. Vanden Berghe, and Eugenio Galdieri. "Survey of Excavations in Iran 1971–1972." *Iran: Journal of the British Institute of Persian Studies* 11, no. 1 (1973): 196–197.

Kuz'mina, Elena. *The Origin of the Indo-Iranians*. Edited by J. Mallory. Leiden: Brill. 2007.

Langer, Robert. 2008. *Pīrān und Zeyāratgāh: Schreine und Wallfahrtsstätten der Zarathustrier im Neuzeitlichen Iran*. Leuven, Belgium: Peeters. 2008.

Malandra, William W., translator and editor. *An Introduction to Ancient Iranian Religion; Readings from the Avesta and Achaemenid Inscriptions*. Minneapolis: University of Minnesota Press. 1983.

Meherjirana, Dastur Earchji Sohrabji. *A Guide to the Zoroastrian Religion: A Nineteenth Century Catechism with Modern Commentary*. Translated and edited by Piroze M. Kotwal and James W. Boyd. Chico, CA: Scholars Press. 1982.

Pourahmad, Ahmad. *Geography and Construction of Kerman City*. Kerman, Iran: Kerman Studies Center Publications. 1990.

Rose, Jenny. *Zoroastrianism: An Introduction*. London: I.B. Tauris & Co. 2010.

Rose, Jenny. "Gender." In *The Wiley-Blackwell Companion to Zoroastrianism*, edited by Michael Stausberg, Yuhan Sohrab-Dinshaw Vevaina, and Anna Tessmann, (2015):273–287. Malden, MA: John Wiley & Sons.

Sala, Renato. *Underground Water Galleries in Middle East and Central Asia: Survey of Historical Documents and Archaeological Studies*. Almaty: Laboratory of Geo-archeology, Institute of Geology, Academy of Sciences of Kazakhstan. 2008.

Savant, Sarah Bowen. *The New Muslims of Post-Conquest Iran: Tradition, Memory, and Conversion*. Cambridge, England: Cambridge University Press. 2013.

Shavarebi, Eshan. "The Temples of Anāhīd at Estakhr (Southern Iran): Historical Documents and Archaeological Evidence." In *Sacralization of Landscape and Sacred Places: Proceedings of the 3rd International Scientific Conference of Mediaeval Archaeology of the Institute of Archaeology, Zagreb, 2nd and 3rd June 2016*, edited by Juraj Belaj, Marijana Belaj, Siniša Krznar, Tajana Sekelj Ivancan, and Tatjana Tkalcec, 179–194. Zagreb, Croatia: Institute of Archaeology. 2018.

Shuckburgh, Evelyn S., translator. *The Histories of Polybius: Translated from the Texas of F. Hultsch*. London: Macmillan & Co. 1889.

Smith, Anthony. *Blind White Fish in Persia*. London: George Allen and Unwin. 1953.

Stöllner, T. "On Holy Waters, Caves, and Women: Introduction of the Results of the Vešnave Project." In *Water and Caves in Ancient Iranian Religion: Aspects of Archaeology, Cultural History and Religion*, edited by Natascha Bagherpour-Kashani and Thomas Stöllner, 5–37. Archäologische Mitteilungen aus Iran und Turan. Berlin: Dietrich Reimer Verlag GmbH. 2012.

Taghavi-Jeloudar, Mohsen, Mooyoung Han, Mohammad Davoudi, and Mikyeong Kim. "Review of Ancient Wisdom of Qanat, and Suggestions for Future Water Management." *Environmental Engineering Research* 18, no. 2 (2013): 57–58.

Taylor, Thomas, translator. *Select Works of Porphyry: Containing His Four Books on Abstinence from Animal Food; His Treatise on the Homeric Cave of the Nymphs; and His Auxiliaries to the Perception of Intelligible Natures; with an Appendix Explaining the Allegory of the Wanderings of Ulysses*. London: Thomas Rodd. 1823.

Watson, Robert Grant. *A History of Persia from the Beginning of the Nineteenth Century to the Year 1858, with a Review of the Principal Events that Led to the Establishment of the Kajar Dynasty*. London: Smith, Elder and Co. 1866.

13
TOWER AND TEMPLE

Re-sacralizing Water Infrastructure at Balkrishna Doshi's GSFC Township

Daniel Williamson

While driving through the northern outskirts of Vadodara in the northwest state of Gujarat, India, a brick cylinder suddenly appears floating among the thick foliage that lines the west side of the highway (Fig. 13.1). The cylinder is the reservoir of a water tower, supported on an elegant, tapered concrete frame of slender twisted columns and shallow vaults and arches, that serves as the central landmark for the Gujarat State Fertilizers Corporation (GSFC) township (Fig. 13.2). The township was designed by architect Balkrishna Doshi between 1964 and 1969 as a new community for white-collar workers drawn from across India to the company's training facilities and corporate headquarters, which were also designed by the architect (Doshi 2019b).

The corporation, founded in 1962 as a joint venture between private and public investments, was emblematic of India's commitment to rapid, heavy industrialization, as envisioned by the country's first prime minister, Jawaharlal Nehru, during the initial decades of independence (Curtis 1988; Steele 1998). Nehru specifically targeted the agriculture sector, where scaled-up manufacture of oil-based fertilizer and the rerouting of India's rivers for irrigation purposes was meant to spark a Green Revolution that could provide basic sustenance for

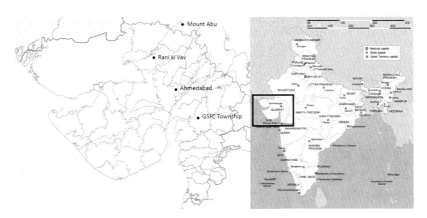

FIGURE 13.1 Map of India and Gujarat showing the location of key sites
Source: Author and Wikimedia Commons

DOI: 10.4324/9781003358824-18

FIGURE 13.2 Balkrishna Doshi, Gujarat State Fertilizer Corporation (GSFC) township water tower. Vadodara, Gujarat, India, 1969. Photographed by the author in December 2019

FIGURE 13.3 Doshi, GSFC Township Temple. Vadodara, India, 1969. Photographed by the author December 2019

India's burgeoning population (Khorakiwala 2017). Balkrishna Doshi's decision to center the GSFC township around a modern piece of water infrastructure, particularly one in the rugged Brutalist aesthetic of brick and raw concrete, symbolically reinforces this commitment to material and economic growth through industrial development.

At the same time, Doshi overlaid the rugged material expression of the industrial water tower with cultural resonances rooted in Hindu water cosmology and in the pivotal role of water in sustaining community in precolonial India. While the water tower dominated the township's central square, on its outskirts, Doshi designed a small temple dedicated to Shiva that echoed the water tower's form and integrated water elements into its sacred design (Fig. 13.3). The visual echoes between the water tower and the township's temple, as well as resonances with preindustrial water infrastructure like Gujarat's historical stepwells, were a means to re-sacralize India's modern industrial water infrastructure. This essay traces how Doshi used the dialectic of water tower and temple to revive traditional connections between water, the sacred and community and to synthesize them with India's post-independence celebration of industrial infrastructure as a means for achieving prosperity.

Tower, Water, and Community

A dedication to affordable, modern housing that fosters a sense of community is one of the major throughlines of Balkrishna Doshi's career as an architect (Kries et al. 2019). GSFC township was Doshi's second manifestation of this commitment, after completing his first housing project for the Ahmedabad Textile Industry Research Association (ATIRA) in 1958. That project was conceived as an ideal village with ATIRA's offices as its heart (Williamson 2016). Both Doshi and ATIRA's director, Vikram Sarabhai, hoped the village concept, which had been central to Gandhi's vision of the collective in India, would foster a sense of community among ATIRA's staff (Williamson 2016). Doshi, however, had been unsatisfied with the results. The housing was clustered according to income group, creating a socio-economically stratified community that reflected lingering caste divisions (Doshi 2019b). When Doshi accepted the GSFC township project, he hoped to learn from ATIRA, though he was still constrained by a brief that divided residents by income and status (Doshi 2019b). Moreover, because many of the residents would be transient, living in the township temporarily while attending the nearby training facilities, a sense of community would be even harder to foster than at ATIRA. Doshi developed several design solutions to these problems, including backing the segregated housing clusters around shared courtyard spaces to increase interaction among the various income groups (Doshi 1979). Most importantly, the entire project was organized around a central town square: an open green flanked by low-rise loggias shading commercial spaces, with recreational facilities, a library, and schools placed nearby. Anchoring this town square was Doshi's water tower (Fig. 13.4).

As Doshi would later explain, the water tower was a practical necessity for the GSFC township that would also act as the symbolic core of its community (Doshi 2019b). In this, Doshi recalled the importance of the "simple village well… which binds the community very strongly." (Doshi 2019b, 83). To reinforce the water tower's role in fostering community at GSFC, he overlaid other functions. He transformed it into a lookout tower and staging ground for festivals and performances, arguing that "all elements must be considered…as multifunctional. That is what Indian culture has grown with and that is how the Indian temperament is built." (Doshi 2019b, 87). Doshi not only envisioned the tower as "a real central place like the temple of old," but as a "landmark" that could be "seen from miles around" and would therefore announce the town's presence on the skyline (Doshi 2019b, 93). It also became a visually striking icon and synecdoche for the township that anchored photo spreads

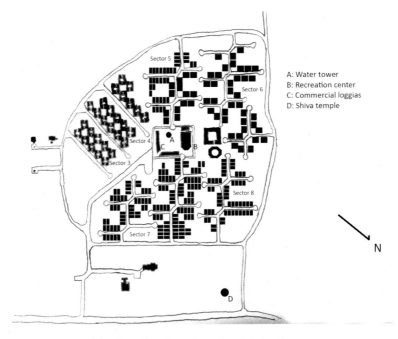

FIGURE 13.4 GSFC Township Plan, showing phase 1 and 2 developments
Source: Adapted by author from plan prepared by Vastu Shilpa Consultants

of the project as it was disseminated through international architectural journals and publications (e.g. Nicolais 1973; Curtis 1988; Kries, et al. 2019).

Doshi's belief that a water tower should serve as the symbolic heart of a modern housing community in India emerged from his first encounter with Louis Kahn, who would become, after Le Corbusier, Doshi's key mentor (Doshi 1992). In 1960, Doshi visited the United States on a Graham Fellowship and was invited to show his work at the University of Pennsylvania in a talk attended by Kahn. Doshi showed images of his ATIRA housing, but Kahn found that the "beautiful works… were still out of context and had no position" (Kahn 2003a, 74). After Doshi's lecture, Kahn was

> moved to go to the blackboard where I drew in the center of the board a towering water tower, wide on top and narrow below. Like the rays of a star, I drew aqueducts radiating from the tower. This implied the coming of the trees and fertile land and a beginning of living. The buildings not yet there which would cluster around the aqueduct would have meaningful position and character.
>
> *(Kahn 2003a, 74)*

Kahn saw this as a fundamental lesson in organizing architecture around a generative beginning that anchors the project in its essential idea, and he returned to the anecdote of his encounter with Doshi more than once in his lectures and writings (Kahn 2003a, 2003b). On one occasion, Kahn explained succinctly that he believed the water tower with radiating aqueducts "would be an appropriate beginning for a town in India… a modern beginning for India" (Kahn 2003b, 77). Kahn's emphasis on fertility and the integration of architecture and landscape was a means of re-sacralizing water infrastructure in the modern Indian context and placing that sacred infrastructure at the heart of a community.

Though Doshi adopted Kahn's idea for the GSFC project, he departed from Kahn's vision in a manner that revealed fundamental differences in their design philosophies. While Kahn's design philosophy focused on discovering a singular essence that captured the nature of an institution or project (Anderson 1995), Doshi sought to layer multivalent resonances onto his buildings (Doshi 1992). While Kahn searched for design solutions that abstracted back to a mythical, universal origin in what he called the "volume zero of history," Doshi searched for design solutions that transformed specific historical building types to preserve older cultural values in modern architectural forms (Anderson 1995; Williamson 2016).

Indeed, when Doshi showed Kahn his GSFC tower, the latter "expressed his puritanical views of water tower to be like a bubble suspended in space. This was against my oriental exuberant solution of the tower becoming an amphitheater below, with a cone like tower above linked by a spiraling staircase outside the tapering body of the tower" (Doshi 1992, 29). As Doshi experimented with variations in how to integrate the tower and staircase in sketches, he expressed doubts that seemed to evoke Kahn's position, writing underneath a series from August 1965 that he was "asking the tank to do too many things. Let them do only what they can do best. Every object must perform its duties" (Bader 2018, 188).

The solution came by clearly separating out the various functional elements of the tower, particularly the water tank and its structural support, and integrating new functions into the interstitial spaces. This allowed Doshi to layer multiple purposes into the building while respecting Kahn's demand for functional clarity. Thus, the swirling staircase both adds to the building's dynamism, and calls attention to the staircase as an independent element. The tower's function as a lookout is announced by a concrete, abstracted *jharokha* that provides controlled views from the northeastern façade.[1] Two additional communal spaces are announced each time that Doshi employs concrete arches. At the apex of the tower, below the arches and dome that directly support the cylindrical water tank, Doshi creates a modernized *chhatri* that serves as a second viewing platform, providing radial views of the countryside.[2] At ground level, arches open the tapered tower support to provide a shaded platform for the festival activities and performances that Doshi hoped would unite the community. In doing so, Doshi evoked the *mandapa*, the pillared halls of Indian temples that were used for public functions like dance performances (Tadgell 1994).

If the various layered functions of the water tower were articulated through abstracted historical reference, the material expression was rooted in the exposed brick and raw concrete that Le Corbusier had pioneered in India in the 1950s (Williamson 2016). Despite the weighty presence and rugged surfaces of these materials, Doshi made them supple and kinetic. The concrete frame supporting the tower is inordinately slender. Its eight piers elegantly twist as they rise over the outdoor stage. To execute this graceful transformation of rugged industrial materials, Doshi turned to the structural engineer Mahendra Raj, with whom he was already collaborating on the Tagore Memorial Theater in Ahmedabad (Williamson 2016). Doshi and Raj also introduced the effect of the twisting, dancing column in that building's foyer, another modern space that Doshi saw as rooted in the temple *mandapa* (Doshi 1979). The twisting form of these columns echoed the sculptures of twisting dancers attached to bracket supports that were common in *mandapas* in Jain and Hindu temples, like the eleventh-century Vimala-Vasahi temple in Mount Abu (Tadgell 1994) (Fig. 13.5).

FIGURE 13.5 Comparison of supports for the GSFC Water Tower, Tagore Memorial Hall, and dancing bracket figure from Vimala-Vasahi Temple, Mount Abu.
Tagore Hall photographed by the author in December 2008; water tower photographed by the author in December 2019. Photograph of dancing figure courtesy of University of Pennsylvania libraries

Yet, it was not just a sense of community that Doshi sought to communicate in his estheticized water tower. The graceful transformation of rugged, industrial materials into exuberant structural forms was also a visual celebration of modern infrastructure that echoed Jawaharlal Nehru's optimistic rhetoric around industrialization (Mehta et al 2016). At the same time, as Louis Kahn had suggested, the water tower was also a potent symbol of fertility and abundance, an idea that not only connected the township and the landscape but also tied to the community's purpose as an industrial source of fertilizer. Through the idea of fertility, Doshi sought to connect modern, industrial water infrastructure to older, sacred concepts of water in the Indian context.

Sacred Wells and Secular Water Towers

The integration of water into sacred architecture is a key component of many of the religions on the Indian subcontinent. Both Islam and Hinduism emphasize rituals of cleansing and purification. As such, water tanks are common components of both mosques and temples. In Hindu cosmology, water holds deeper meanings beyond its role in ritual cleansing. As Ananda K. Coomaraswamy, the pioneering historian of Indian art argued, this cosmology focuses on the interrelated conceptualization of water as a primordial cosmic sea and as the fertile source of life (Coomaraswamy 1993). The waters of the cosmic sea, upon which Vishnu dreams into existence Brahma and our universe, represent the shrouded mystery of our origins. At the same time, water's life-sustaining role caused it to become associated with fertility and the mother goddess. The sacred river goddesses, whose waters sustain life in India represent this association between water, the female, and fertility (Eck 2012; Feldhaus 1995).

Thus, it is no surprise that water imagery is an integral part of the ornamental schema of the Hindu temple. By the medieval period, it was common to flank the entrances of Indian temples in the north with *makaras*, crocodiles representing the sacred waters, from whose mouths flow interlaced garlands of lotuses forming a lobed arch above the visitor (Coomaraswamy 1993). Column capitals depicting water vessels of overflowing vegetation suggest water's fertile power. In India, the sacred was not just confined to temple precincts but suffused the entire landscape (Eck 2012).

Thus, sacred connotations spread to the practical water architecture and infrastructure of precolonial India, including its tanks and wells (Hegewald 2002). In Gujarat, the integration of the sacred, the community and water infrastructure was particularly potent in the stepwells that proliferated throughout the region from the seventh century through the nineteenth century (Jain-Neubauer 1982). These stepwells usually consisted of two parts, a circular tank and a long corridor of steps that led to various platforms that could be used as the water level rose or fell. According to author Jain-Neubauer, they were multifunctional, used for both drawing water, bathing, and as places for cooling retreat during hot months. Thus, in addition to anchoring towns and villages, they were built along with highways to provide rest for pilgrims and travelers. In villages they became communal gathering spaces, the kind architect Doshi sought to emulate in his water tower (Jain-Neubauer 1981).

In addition, the stepwells were also overlaid with multiple references to the sacred. Gujarati stepwells typically included an octagonal pool for *pradikshina* (ritual circumambulation) at the lowest level, as well as spaces for shrines. Rituals associated with water deities were performed at the entrance to the stepwells (Jain-Neubauer 1981). The stepwells symbolically linked the connection of water to fertility and the mother goddess through these elements, as well as in the buildings' sculpture. Perhaps the most spectacular example of the overlay of the sacred

FIGURE 13.6 Rani ka Vav (Queen's Stepwell). Patan, Gujarat, India, ca. 1063-1083.
Photographed by author in December 2008.

onto a stepwell was at the Rani-ki-Vav in Patan, Gujarat which was patronized by the Solanki Queen Udayamati in the eleventh century (Fig. 13.6). Layers of shrines devoted to diverse deities line the walls on the descent. Moreover, the whole stepwell is organized like a temple: the water tank acts as a *garbhagriha*, through which one can gain *darshan* with Vishnu who is depicted in relief on the backside of the tank floating on the cosmic sea.[3] The water in the tank becomes part of the sacred depiction; it is the cosmic sea upon which Vishnu rests. The relief of Vishnu is sculpted multiple times onto the tank so that it can be seen at various levels as the water rises and falls. (Mankodi 1991).

As the British took control of water supply systems throughout much of India during the nineteenth century, water's sacral nature was deemphasized in favor of systems that focused on technocratic solutions to the issues of sanitation and shortage (MacGeorge 1894). The British sought to present their worldview as materialist and rational against an Indian worldview steeped in timeless spirituality as a means to justify colonial rule (Chatterjee 1994). Thus, the British portrayed the sacred conceptualization of water infrastructure as rooted in irrational superstition that impeded sanitary progress (Masani 1918). In Bombay, the construction of the Vihar waterworks became the British Raj's first attempt to centralize a city's water supply to control its quality and curb cholera outbreaks (Dossal 1991; Broich 2007).

Tensions between the colonial government's emphasis on sanitation and traditional sacred conceptions of water flared up in many places. In Bombay, bureaucrats began closing the private tanks and wells that directly were completed with the Vihar waterworks, mostly on sanitary grounds (MacGeorge 1894). These measures were met with protests from the owners and users who argued that the wells had a special sanctity that other sources of water could not provide. Hindus claimed that ancient texts required that water for purification ceremonies come from ground wells, while the Parsi community in Bombay claimed that spirits inhabited many of the wells they frequented (Masani 1918). In Benares, the holy city on the banks of the Ganges, the British attempted to build a pumping station directly adjacent to the Lolark *kund*, a stepped water basin, which served as a key node in pilgrimage routes. The maharaja who owned the land adjacent to the *kund* refused to sell, because of the negative effect the station would have on the sacred landscape (Desai 2017). In Gujarat, the British were able to exert more control over the state's water infrastructure (Jain-Neubauer 1981). Many of the communal stepwells throughout Gujarat were closed because the British authorities considered them breeding grounds for mosquitoes (Jain-Neubauer 1981). Other wells dried up as British infrastructure altered the water table (D'Souza 2006).

The relationship between the sanitary reform and sacred conceptions of water was not always antagonistic. When the municipal corporation reorganized Bombay's markets for sanitary reasons in the 1860s, they organized their new market hall, the Crawford Markets, around a central fountain (Metcalf 2002). This fountain, designed in a Gothic style by the architect Arthur Crawford, included relief sculptures by the sculptor and arts educator John Lockwood Kipling. It features four sacred Indian river goddesses lounging languidly in saris (Metcalf 2002). However, this kind of fusion of sacred Hindu imagery with the new British water infrastructure was fairly rare.

As British systems replaced traditional wells with the modern gravitational system, water towers proliferated on the Indian landscape. Simultaneously, debates emerged regarding their materials and esthetics. Because they were the most visible structures associated with water reform, some British engineers were anxious that these buildings would look impressive (Temple 1929). Implicit in British anxiety about architectural esthetics in India was their role in promoting imperial dominance and communicating Britain's proper place in India's broader history (Metcalf 2002).

In 1929, the engineer F.C. Temple gave a presentation on ten water towers he had designed for various Indian cities at a meeting of the Institution of Engineers of India (Temple 1929). In the paper, he argued that engineers should embellish their water towers with architectural ornament, given their prominence on the Indian landscape and their status as imperial creations (Temple 1929). Most of his designs blended Classical motifs with Indianizing elements like *chajjas* (Fig. 13.7).[4] Temple made sure to note that he consulted on esthetics with architect George Wittet, whose most famous building, the Gateway of India, draped a triumphal arch with ornament derived from Gujarati Mosque architecture (Temple 1929). Thus, Temple sought to elevate the water tower's esthetics to the level of Britain's major public monuments in India, as an extension of the triumphalist narrative of British dominance.

At the same time, water towers were becoming prominent examples of British engineers' mastery of the new structural potentials of reinforced concrete (Tappin 2002). After Temple's presentation in 1929, the engineer G. Bransley Williams countered that water towers should embrace the emerging "engineering architecture" by which he meant that "a structure derived a certain beauty from being entirely suited for the purpose it served, but it could acquire nothing but ugliness from meaningless excretions" (Temple 1929, 112). To demonstrate this radical embrace of modernist principles, he presented his own water tower, which he felt "reached a higher aesthetic standard than most water towers in this country" (Temple 1929, 112). While Williams still saw the water tower as a means of expressing colonial rule, it was through an architectural language that celebrated the colonial engineer's mastery of technology, rather than through the manipulation of historical architectural form.

After India's independence, water towers continued to proliferate in urban settings. These new water towers primarily reflected the esthetic values of Bransley Williams, and they fit the

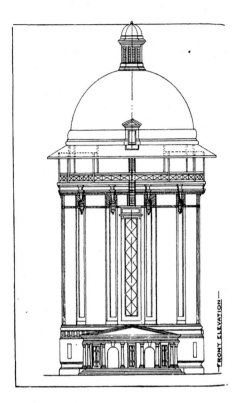

FIGURE 13.7 F.C. Temple, Patna New Capital Water Tower. Patna, Bihar, India, ca. 1920s. Elevation
Source: Journal of the Institution of Engineers (India) 8 (April 1929), 104

Nehruvian era's embrace of rapid modernization as a necessary means of safeguarding independence and alleviating poverty (Nehru 1989a). Photographer Randhir Singh, who documents the diversity of Delhi's water towers, has interpreted their unique sculptural massing on the skyline as symbols of modernization.[5]

As such, they were smaller versions of the large-scale water projects that Prime Minister Nehru sponsored like the Bhakra-Nangal dams in Himachal Pradesh. On July 8, 1954, Nehru visited the site of Bhakra-Nangal dams, then under construction, and declared

> these days the biggest temple and mosque and gurdwara is the place where man works for the good of mankind. Which place can be greater than this, this Bhakra-Nangal, where thousands of men have worked, have shed their blood and sweat. …Where can be a greater holier place than this?
>
> *(Nehru 1989b, 3)*

At this moment, Nehru attempted to re-sacralize India's water infrastructure according to a new set of principles aligned with his socialist political philosophy. For Nehru, "the modern mind… is governed by a practical idealism for social betterment…. Humanity is its god and social service its religion" (Nehru 1989a: 557). Paradoxically, Nehru hoped to shift Indian citizens' conception of the sacred from religious devotion to the secular project of collective action in service of the nation-state (Madan 1997).

The sublation of religious identity as part of the nationalist project was a reaction to British colonial discourse that emphasized communalism as an intractable feature of Indian society that impeded self-rule (Tejani 2016). Nehru's secular vision for a more rational society was echoed in other places in the early years of independence. Mulk Raj Anand, the editor of the influential arts journal *Marg*, argued that while the temple had historically served as the cultural heart of the towns and villages of India, it would need to be replaced by new secular institutions like museums as "reason and accurate judgment succeed in conquering the ancient worlds of magic through the new magic of science" (Anand 1948: 4). From one perspective, the communal heart of the GSFC township conforms to Anand's vision. The open theater beneath the water tower was meant to shelter the social functions, pageants, and dances that typically took place in a temple *mandapa*. The library and athletic facilities pointed to a more secular vision of human improvement. Yet the temple at GSFC, haunting the site's periphery, was a reminder that religion lived on. Moreover, Doshi's architecture was not merely in service of a rationalist, social vision, but he saw spiritual and sacred values as an essential bond to hold communities together.

By the 1980s, scholars like T.N. Madan and Ashis Nandy began to challenge Nehru's emphasis on a secular state (Madan 1997). Against a backdrop of rising Hindu Nationalism, they argued that Nehru's secularism was an elitist imposition on a fundamentally religious nation. Secularism left a religious vacuum in the public sphere, allowing the Hindu nationalists to fill it with their extremist vision (Madan 1997).

As Balkrishna Doshi designed the GSFC Township, he was also beginning to question Nehru's vision of modern India as a secular, highly industrialized state. In 1967, Doshi presented a paper at the Congress on Religion, Architecture, and the Visual Arts in New York entitled "The Proliferating City and Communal Life: India." In the paper, Doshi criticized the "cult of machine civilization where machine has become the God and the creation has become greater than the creator" (Doshi 1968, 67). For him, the cities of India had become "nightmares," because industrialized modernity had severed the bonds of community. In opposition, Doshi, like Gandhi in the early twentieth century, saw a highly idealized vision of village life as a source of Indian renewal (Doshi 1968). Doshi turned to a Gujarati folk song popular during the Navratri dance festival that described village life in terms of the interconnected professions of villagers that sustain a sense of unity and harmony (Doshi 1968). For Doshi, the temple played a key role in maintaining that harmony, not just as a source of religious activity, but as a "place of learning and enjoying all the arts" (Doshi 1968, 68). He ended the talk not by rejecting the machine outright, but calling for the design of new Indian towns that retain a sense of community so that "they can get all the advantages of the emotional qualities of man and the advantages of the service of the machine" (Doshi 1968, 69).

Doshi's willingness to embrace India's religious traditions as part of the modern project reflected a growing spiritual interest in his personal life. In the 1960s, Doshi had begun carefully studying India's sacred texts under the guidance of his uncle-in-law, the religious scholar Rasiklal Parikh (Doshi 2019a). Doshi's growing ambivalence to industrialization, in part, reflected his mentor Le Corbusier's own vision of a second machine age, in which humanity, nature, and the machine would be harmoniously integrated. It opposed the prodigious production and consumption that dominated the post-war West (Prakash 2002). The water tower's dancing form celebrated industrialization, but it was equally important to overlay additional functions that spoke to a spiritual past that invited community integration.

Tower, Temple, and the Resacralization of Water Imagery

Beyond the idea that water is an essential element for bringing together and sustaining a community, Doshi sought to sacralize the water tower by tying it to the Hindu temple that he designed for the township (Fig. 13.3). Unlike the tower, Doshi set the temple on the outskirts of the township in a clearing next to an ancient Banyan tree. In doing so, Doshi sought a balance between respecting the inevitable pluralism of the township's community and his belief that deep cultural resonances, drawn in part from Hindu conceptions of the sacred, were necessary to foster a successful sense of community in the Indian context.

Like the water tower, the temple's *shikhara* takes the form of a conically shaped tower resting on eight supports that converge toward a cylinder, though the temple's cylinder is skeletal, rather than solid brick (Fig. 13.3). These supports are braced by concrete cast arches similar to those that open the base and viewing platform of the water tower. In Hindu temples, the *shikhara* rises above the central image of the deity and represents Mount Meru, the sacred mountain that serves as the cosmic axis of the universe (Michell 1988). A central pole, supported by the skeletal structure reinforces this image of the cosmic axis, while a solid, elongated dome set within the bracing arches of the conical structural frame is a visual echo of the Shiva *linga* that sits below this modernist *shikhara*.[6] A pathway for *pradakshina* (ritual circumambulation) is articulated by a platform suspended over the ground and a parasol roof of shallow poured in place, concrete vaults that cantilever out over the platform from the *shikhara* (Fig. 13.8). The structural armature supporting these vaults extends beyond them and transform into drainage spouts.

The drainage spout was a key feature of Le Corbusier's buildings in Ahmedabad, Gujarat, where he transformed it into a sculptural form deployed rhythmically across the surfaces of

FIGURE 13.8 Doshi, GSFC Temple, detail of parikrama, subsidiary shrines, and cantilevered water-spouts. Photographed by the author in December 2019

FIGURE 13.9 Le Corbusier, Water spout on Sanskar Kendra, interior courtyard, 1954. Photographed by the author in November 2008.

his buildings. Le Corbusier's source for this form appears to be the drainage spouts of the mosque architecture of the Gujarati Sultanate, like the fifteenth-century mosque at Sarkhej Roza (Williamson 2016). At the Sanskar Kala Kendra, the city museum for Ahmedabad, Le Corbusier designed a fountain in its central courtyard by suspending a drainage spout over a pool abstractly bent into the shape of India. Drawing on the generative associations of water, he created a rich symbol of India's past represented in the museum's collections giving sustenance to the new nation-state of India (Williamson 2016) (Fig. 13.9).

At the GSFC temple, Doshi delicately suspended the eight spouts over eight cylinders that contain shrines to subsidiary gods, suggesting their power flows from the central, supreme god Shiva. Spouts attached to these cylinders collect the water from the central shrine and pour it into the ground. During monsoon, water washes down the *linga* embedded in the structural armature of the *shikhara* and flows out through the suspended spouts. The introduction of water as an architectural element in the temple creates multilayered resonances across India's architectural history and deep into Hindu theology. As the monsoon rains wash over the *shikhara*, the filtering of the heavy rains through the interconnected system of spouts also recalls the story of the descent of the river goddess Ganga described by Viswamithra to Rama in the *Ramayana*, as well as in many other texts (Eck 2012).

In that tale, the sage Bhagiratha beckoned Ganga to descend from the heavens and bring his ancestors, the sixty-thousand Sagaras, back to life. Ganga complies, but the full force of her descent threatens to flood the earth. Shiva is called upon to help and uses the locks of his hair to filter Ganga's descent from a deluge to a trickle, as her arrival on earth forms the Ganges and other sacred rivers. In this story, the goddess' waters are associated not just with fertility, but with *soma*, the nectar of immortality locked in the vault of heaven (Eck 2012). It is only through the intermediary role of Shiva that the power of Ganga's waters is transformed from destructive to fertile and sustaining. As anthropologist Anne Feldhaus points out, Ganga falls on Mount Meru before falling on the head of Shiva, though the two are often conflated in temple settings (Feldhaus 1995). In the GSFC temple, the *shikhara* represents Mount Meru, while its arched framework recalls Shiva's crown. Doshi uses the drama of flowing water and cantilevered spouts to reenact their role in distributing the waters of Ganga.

The descent of the Ganga is reenacted in temples with ritual bathing of the *linga* with waters from the Ganges. Many temples suspend a pot of water over the *linga* representing the conjoining of the male power of Shiva and the female power or *shakti* of the goddess (Eck 2012). The cylindrical reservoir of the GSFC water tower, suspended on arches over a tapered form visually echoes this common temple device. Thus, the temple, tower, and sacred connotations are brought together through echoes in form, the rich symbolism of water, and narratives of Shiva and Ganga. Louis Kahn's vision of a water tower at the heart of the village radiating its fertile waters outwards has been overlaid with an image of Shiva distributing the fertile waters of Ganga, anchoring that vision to the Indian context. These connections invert the gendering of the historical stepwells of Gujarat, which were associated with the feminine through their connections to the goddess, patronage, and sunken form. Doshi's towers celebrate the male control of this feminine power, tying the industrial capture of water in the rugged water tower to Shiva's control of the Ganga.

Conclusion

Pritzker Prize-winning architect Balkrishna Doshi (1927) developed modernism as a synthesis that integrated India's cultural past with the industrial world in order to tame industrialization and bring it back into harmony with human and environmental rhythms. At the GSFC Township, the rational, engineered control of the town's water supply was celebrated through the contrast of its water tower's rugged form and delicate and dynamic shape. At the same time, Doshi overlaid additional functions, articulated with references to India's historical forms, that positioned the tower as both a symbol of the township community and its key gathering space. In creating visual connections with the township's temple, he was also able to invoke a sacred reverence for water's fertile power, while simultaneously celebrating its harnessing and control. In this postcolonial project, Doshi sought to reconnect modern India to a past that had been ruptured by colonialism, but not through the rejection of one and the revival of the other. Instead, he re-sacralized the modern industrial water infrastructure that had emerged in the colonial era with India's deep and venerable cosmology of water.

Notes

1. A jharokha is a corbeled balcony common to Rajput palace architecture.
2. A chhatri is a domed pavilion on pillars common to Rajput and Mughal palace architecture.
3. A garbhagriha is the sacred womb chamber or inner sanctum of a Hindu temple where the deity resides. Darshan is the visual connection created between the visitor and the deity.
4. A chajja is a projected overhang that serves as a shading device.
5. Singh, Randhir. "Water Towers." Accessed September 24, 2021. https://www.randhirsingh.net/watertowers remove and move to endnotes
6. The linga of Shiva is an icon that represents his unmanifest form and procreative power (Michell 1986).

References

Anand, Mulk Raj. "Museums: Junk Shops or Culture Centres." *Marg* 2, 4 (1948): 4–8.
Anderson, Stanford. "Public Institutions: Louis I. Kahn's Reading of Volume Zero." *Journal of Architectural Education* 49, 1 (1995): 10–21.
Broich, John. "Engineering the Empire: British Water Supply Systems and Colonial Societies, 1850–1900." *Journal of British Studies* 46, 2 (April 2007): 346–365.

Chatterjee, Partha. *The Nation and Its Fragments: Colonial and Postcolonial Histories*. Princeton, NJ: Princeton University Press, 1994.

Coomaraswamy, Anand. *Yaksas: Essays in the Water Cosmology*. New Edition, edited by Paul Schroeder. Delhi, India: Oxford University Press, 1993.

Curtis, William. *Balkrishna Doshi: An Architecture for India*. New York: Rizzoli, 1988.

Desai, Madhuri. *Banaras Reconstructed: Architecture and Sacred Space in a Hindu Holy City*. Seattle, Washington: University of Washington Press, 2017.

Doshi, Balkrishna V. *Le Corbusier and Louis I Kahn: The Acrobat and the Yogi of Architecture*. Ahmedabad, India: Vastu Shilpa Foundation, 1992.

———. "Architecture and Attitudes, 1979." In *Balkrishna Doshi: Writings on Architecture & Identity*, edited by Vera Simone Bader, 74–99. Berlin, Germany: ArchiTangle, 2019a.

———. *Paths Uncharted*. Ahmedabad, India: Mapin Publishing, 2019b.

———. "The Proliferating City and Communal Life: India." *Eksitics* 25, 147 (February 1968): 67–69.

Dossal, Mariam. *Imperial Designs and Indian Realities: The Planning of Bombay City, 1845-1875*. Bombay, India: Oxford University Press, 1991.

D'Souza, Rohan. "Water in British India: The Making of a 'Colonial Hydrology.'" *History Compass* 4, 4 (2006): 621–628.

Eck, Diana. *India: A Sacred Geography*. New York: Three Rivers Press, 2012.

Feldhaus, Anne. *Water and Womanhood: Religious Meanings of Rivers in Maharashtra*. New Delhi, India: Oxford University Press, 1995.

Hegewald, Julia A.B. *Water Architecture in South Asia: A Study of Types, Development and Meanings*. Boston, MA: Brill, 2002.

Jain-Neubauer, Jutta. *The Stepwells of Gujarat: An Art Historical Perspective*. New Delhi, India: Abinav Publications, 1981.

Kahn, Louis. "Form and Design (1960)." In *Louis Kahn: Essential Texts*, edited by Robert Twombly, 62–74. New York: W.W. Norton, 2003a.

———. "The New Art of Urban Design: Are We Equipped? (1960)." In *Louis Kahn: Essential Texts*, edited by Robert Twombly, 75–80. New York: W.W. Norton, 2003b.

Kries, Mateo, Khushnu Panthaki Hoof, and Jolanthe Kugler. *Balkrishna Doshi: Architecture for the People*. Weil am Rhein, Germany: Vitra, 2019.

Khorakiwala, Ateya A. *The Well-Fed Subject: Modern Architecture in the Quantitative State, India (1943-1984)*. PhD diss, Harvard University, 2017.

MacGeorge, George Waiter. *Ways and Works in India: Being an Account of the Public Works in that Country from the Earliest Times Up to the Present Day*. London: Archibald Constable and Company, 1894.

Madan, T.N. *Modern Myths and Locked Minds: Secularism and Fundamentalism in India*. New Delhi, India: Oxford University Press, 1997.

Mankodi, Kirit. *The Queen's Stepwell at Patan*. Bombay, India: Franco-Indian Research Pvt., Ltd., 1991.

Masani, R.P. *Folklore of Wells: Being a Study of Water-Worship in East and West*. Bombay, India: D.B. Taraporevala Sons & Co., 1918.

Mehta, Vandini, Rohit Raj Mehndiratta, and Ariel Huber. *The Structure: Works of Mahendra Raj*. Zurich, Switzerland: Park Books, 2016.

Metcalf, Thomas R. *An Imperial Vision: Indian Architecture and Britain's Raj*. 2nd edition. Oxford, UK: Oxford University Press, 2002.

Michell, George. *The Hindu Temple: An Introduction to Its Meaning and Forms*. Chicago, IL: The University of Chicago Press, 1988.

Nehru, Jawaharlal. *The Discovery of India*. Centenary Edition. New Delhi: Oxford University Press, 1989a.

———. "Temples of the New Age." In *Jawaharlal Nehru and Water Resources Development (Some of his Speeches: A Compilation)*, 1–5. New Delhi, India: Government of India, Central Water Commission, 1989b.

Nicolais, John. "Balkrishna Doshi: A Socially Conscious Architect Combines the Traditional Forms and Evolving Technologies of India." *Architectural Forum* 138, no. 4 (May 1973): 33–41.

Prakash, Vikramaditya. *Chandigarh's Le Corbusier: The Struggle for Modernity in Postcolonial India*. Seattle, WA: University of Washington Press, 2002.

Steele, James. *Rethinking Modernism for the Developing World: The Complete of Balkrishna Doshi*. New York: Whitney Library of Design, 1998.

Tadgell, Christopher. *The History of Architecture in India*. New York: Phaidon Press, 1994.

Tappin, Stuart. "The Early Use of Reinforced Concrete in India." *Construction History* 18 (2002): 79–98.

Tejani, Shabnum. "Secularism." In *Key Concepts in Modern Indian Studies*, edited by Gita Dharampal-Frick, Monika Kirloskar-Steinbach, Rachel Dwyer and Jahnavi Phalkey. New York: New York University Press, 2016.

Temple, F.C. "Some Water Towers in India." *Journal of the Institution of Engineers (India)* 8 (April 1929): 81–119.

Williamson, Daniel. "Modern Architecture and Capitalist Patronage in Ahmedabad, India." Phd diss, New York University, 2016.

14

GEOTHERMAL SYSTEMS AND RELIGIOUS ETHICS

Frank Lloyd Wright's Unity Temple, and First Unitarian Society of Madison

Joseph M. Siry

The Unitarian Universalist Association, like other religions, sees fostering sustainability as a stewardship offered to God (Greenwood and Harris 2011: 166–68). The last of seven principles adopted by the Association's general assembly in 1985 is "Respect for the interdependent web of all existence of which we are a part."[1] Water stewardship relates directly to this principle because "freshwater links all living things together."[2] This leads to heightened awareness of the use of water in energy management in buildings. In notable cases, this goal involves new additions to or restoration of historic houses of worship using water for geothermal heating and cooling.

This chapter examines such congregational commitments at two church buildings originally designed by Frank Lloyd Wright. One is the comprehensive restoration of Unity Temple in Oak Park, Illinois, a process initiated in 2004 and completed in 2017 under architect Gunny Harboe. Another project is the major addition to Wright's building for the First Unitarian Society of Madison, in Madison, Wisconsin, designed by Kubala Washatko Architects and completed in 2008. Both cases used water-to-water heat pumps (see details later), linked to geothermal wells, as an efficient way to transform their heating and cooling systems. Commitment to and consciousness of geothermal systems have symbolic resonance for these congregations, which are two of the nearly 1100 Unitarian Universalist congregations in North America (Shin and Miller 2014: 5). Water as a geothermal medium signifies these congregations' religious ethics and fosters a sense of environmental stewardship as an ethical practice among parishioners. This denominational culture has a long tradition of environmental consciousness. Its roots go back to Unitarian origins in the eighteenth century when there emerged the conviction that, in the spirit of Newton, religious truths were discoverable in light of rational exploration of Nature (Robinson 1985). Such beliefs were closely related to the Unitarian ideal of the oneness of divinity, from which the denomination derived its name (Robinson 1985: 14–17). Formed in this tradition, Frank Lloyd Wright shared these values, perceiving Nature as the visible manifestation of divinity. As he said late in life, "Nature is all the body of God we mortals will ever see" (Wright 1957: 72). Wright said, "I've always considered myself deeply religious," and spoke of Nature, spelled with a capital N, as his church (Meehan 1984: 292). Using geothermal for heating and cooling would be consistent

DOI: 10.4324/9781003358824-19

with his environmentally conscious approach to church design (Geva 2012). Geothermal or ground-source systems use the stable temperature of the earth to keep water in wells at 50°–60°F (10°–15°C) year-round. This water can be used alternately for heating in winter and cooling in summer without using electricity derived from burning fossil fuels (Grondzik and Kwok 2015: 469–73). The buildings' prominence as Frank Lloyd Wright's architecture helps to amplify this message.

Unity Temple, Oak Park, Illinois

As Wright's first major church building, Unity Temple, designed and built from 1905 to 1909, has served continuously since then as the home of its Unitarian Universalist congregation (Fig. 14.1). This cubic building is a poured-in-placed concrete structure with a high thermal mass that slows heat absorption in summer to decrease the cooling load, while its single-pane art glass windows (retained in the most recent restoration of 2017) do allow solar gain (Geva 2005: 593). Working with contractors, Wright developed what in its time was an innovative system of mechanically powered heating and ventilation. A set of underfloor concrete ducts led from an originally coal-fired boiler in a room near the basement's southeast corner. Ducts supplied warm air through floor registers to Unity House, the social hall on the building's south end, and north into Unity Temple's basement (Fig. 14.2) (Siry 1996: 247).[3] This system preceded Wright's later adoption of hot water pipes in floors to provide radiant heating, as he did in religious structures beginning with the Pfeiffer Chapel at Florida Southern College (1938–41) (Geva 2012: 243). Yet concrete ducts lined with vitreous clay pipe were better at absorbing heat than conveying it.

FIGURE 14.1 Frank Lloyd Wright, Unity Temple, 1905–09, west front, after the restoration of 2015–17 by Harboe Architects; Architectural Consulting Engineers (mechanical, electrical, and plumbing). Photograph: Tom Rossiter

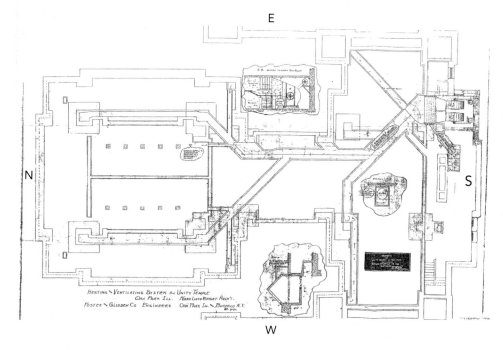

FIGURE 14.2 Unity Temple, heating and ventilating system, basement plan of underground ductwork, revision c. 1908-09 of the original scheme of 1906, showing new steam and condensate piping being routed to Unity Temple building (left) from the boiler room under Unity House (right). Foster and Glidden, Co., Engineers. Courtesy Unity Temple Restoration Foundation

In the first winter after Unity House opened (1907–08), the original heating system failed to keep the building sufficiently warm, and the congregation started incrementally installing upright standing and wall-mounted cast iron radiators (Siry 1996: 247), still seen today inside the outer walls of both temple and house. In about 1921, the air handling unit was shut down and made inoperable, but by then it had been largely replaced with radiators throughout the building.[4] Yet Wright's structure had no air conditioning for summer cooling and humidity control for over a century (Van Hampton 2009: 23). Thermostatically controlled heating and cooling is important because Unity Temple's monolithic concrete shell has a thermal mass effect, whereby it tends to heat up or cool off slowly and retain the heat or coolness which the building absorbs from the outside (Wiss, Janney, Elstner Associates, Inc. 1987: 45–47) (Fig. 14.3). Analysis of climatic discomfort showed that it was too cold inside during over half the annual occupancy hours, and too hot in only 1 percent of those hours, revealing the interior effect of Chicago's cold winters (Geva 2005: 593). The new geothermal heating and cooling system was installed as part of the 2017 restoration, protecting the building's materials from extreme winter and summer weather, and stabilizing temperature and humidity levels year-round.[5]

In June 2004 the Unity Temple Restoration Foundation (UTRF) engaged Architectural Consulting Engineers (ACE) of Oak Park, led by mechanical engineer Mark Nussbaum, to prepare a feasibility study and conceptual design for a new environmental management system.[6] Nussbaum recalled that they wanted a system with "the best environmental footprint."[7] Completed in

FIGURE 14.3 Unity Temple, interior looking south toward pulpit, after the restoration of 2015–17. Photograph: Tom Rossiter.

September 2004, the study recommended a ground source heat pump system to produce chilled and hot water. This would be distributed via piping routed in the existing underground tunnel system to air handling units concealed within the hollow columns of Unity Temple and elsewhere.[8] The new system was to be part of the building's total restoration, which was to be completed by its centennial in 2009.[9] The congregation wanted a system that would reduce operating costs and, true to Unitarian Universalist denominational principles, have relatively few adverse effects on the environment (Bowen 2006: 139). Geothermal systems, designed to be efficient, could by the early 2000s produce on average three to five times the energy that they consume (Van Hampton 2009: 20). In December 2004 the UTRF and the congregation hired ACE to design a geothermal and ventilating system in detail, which would not architecturally alter this national landmark.[10]

While initially perhaps twice as expensive as installing a new furnace and air-conditioning, a geothermal system would cost less to operate, with the return on investment initially estimated at between five and ten years. It was to reduce the restored Unity Temple's heating and cooling costs by up to 50 percent.[11] From the viewpoint of preservation, a geothermal system would be virtually silent and invisible. The system's mechanical equipment, including air handlers, was not to affect acoustics (Bowen 2006: 140). As UTRF's director said in 2005: "Every work of art needs to be maintained and preserved in a stable environment. Geothermal—or ground source energy—is a durable, proven technology. The price of fossil fuels will creep higher and higher, crippling many businesses in the future, especially churches. The bottom line is that this HVAC [heating, ventilating, and cooling] system is compatible with the highest standards in historic preservation. I believe Mr. Wright would approve of this plan."[12]

Wright may have approved, for reasons of his monument's preservation, although he did not favor conventional air conditioning, at least for houses. As he wrote in *The Natural House* (1954): "I think it is far better to go *with* the natural climate than try to fix a special artificial climate of your own. Climate means something to man. It means something in relation to one's life in it" (Wright 1995: 120–21). When Wright designed mechanical heating, ventilating, and air conditioning for larger buildings, such as the SC Johnson Administration Building in Racine, Wisconsin (1936–39), he held to a naturalistic ideal for environmental control, telling his client: "You make a natural climate instead of an artificial condition."[13] Wright did not use geothermal heating and cooling, yet as UTRF's director said, "[Wright] was the father of organic architecture—the whole idea of buildings fitting into the landscape. One of his greatest inspirations was nature. So, he'd favor technology that complemented the environment instead of working against it."[14]

Unity Temple's geothermal system was first proposed in detail in 2005 (Fig. 14.4) and went through modifications in design before it was finally realized in 2017. In winter, heat from the earth would be transferred to the building via an antifreeze-and-water mix through a closed loop of horizontal polyethylene underground pipes from the well field to the mechanical room on Unity House's south end. The loop water would interact with a reversible chiller/heat pump, which uses refrigerant, compressors, and heat exchangers in the summer to produce chilled water for cooling from the relatively cool loop water.[15] In the winter the heat pump draws heat from the relatively warm loop water to produce hot water for heating. The chilled or hot water is circulated to the air handling units, from which the cooling or heating effect is transferred to the ventilation supply air, moving through existing ducts.

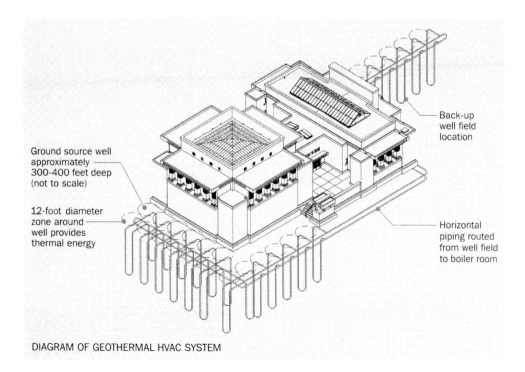

FIGURE 14.4 Diagram of the original design for the geothermal HVAC system for Unity Temple, 2004. Courtesy Unity Temple Restoration Foundation

Pipes carrying loop water to and from the wells, and hot or chilled water around the building, would be mostly in original underground ducts. When Unity Temple's system was first proposed, nearly one million like it had been built nationwide in the previous twenty years.[16]

A master plan of 2006 by preservation architect Gunny Harboe projected Unity Temple's $25 million restoration in three phases, with the first as a $7.5 million effort to stabilize the building envelope. The new $2.5 million geothermal and HVAC systems were part of the second phase. Restoration of interior finishes, the most expensive part, was the final phase. Construction documents for the project were created in December 2014, and actual work on the building's exterior began in the spring of 2015. The congregation held its last service in the structure in June. Work continued over the next two years, with the restored building opened in June 2017, in time for the one-hundred-and-fiftieth anniversary of Wright's birth.[17] As built, the geothermal system included nine 500-foot (152 meters)-deep, six-inch (15 centimeters) diameter wells that supplied a water-to-water heat pump that transfers heat or coolness from the well water to the building's heating and cooling water system, which in turn conveys warmth or coolness to interior air. Wells were set in Unity Temple's north lawn, staggered to maximize each one's field of thermally stable earth unaffected by heat exchange from neighboring wells. Since heat pumps can only supply water up to 120°F. (49°C.), for extreme Chicago winter weather, the new system still had a gas-fired boiler to supply water at up to 180°F. (82°C.) (Van Hampton 2009: 23). Because of the high cost of drilling, Nussbaum and his team reduced the number of wells, but they made wells deeper because more energy can be extracted from deeper wells than shallower ones.[18] As in 2004, horizontal loop piping runs from the well field (north) to the original boiler room (south). There, loop water interacts with a chiller/heat pump to produce chilled water for summer cooling or hot water for winter heating. Chilled or hot water circulates to air-handling units, and the cooled or heated air from these then circulates to interiors mostly in original ducts, including vertical ones inside hollow columns (Fig. 14.5).

As foreseen, the $1.2 million geothermal system had a high cost of $24,000 per ton of refrigeration, which was more than twice the local cost of a typical HVAC system. But with heating and cooling costs reduced by 40 percent to 50 percent, this initial expense was projected to be recovered in five to seven years.[19] And the advent of air conditioning allowed the church to plan for an additional four months of full programming and tourism.[20] The system was to reduce reliance on fossil fuels by sixty to 80 percent, even though a geothermal system with heat pumps required much electricity.[21] Given anticipated shortages and rising costs of fossil fuels, the UTRF and the congregation chose the system "because it was a green solution. It was something that was done with an eye on the long term" (Van Hampton 2009: 24). The choice represented both environmental and financial stewardship. These twin ethical goals were distinguishable but inextricable from each other in the discourse around the project. Unity Temple's inclusion of geothermal heating and cooling exemplified a national trend of restoring landmarks to high standards of sustainability, including H. H. Richardson's Trinity Church in Boston, which framed its decision as an ethical act of environmental stewardship (Bowen 2005; Rosenblum 2006). Yet the case of Unity Temple aligns distinctly with Unitarian Universalist environmentalism. Given the use of a water-to-water heat pump, water was essential to the geothermal heating and cooling system of the sacred place. Its capacity to lessen dependence on fossil fuels embodied the Unitarian Universalist principle of the interdependence of all life, an ideal served by practicing environmental sustainability. This principle was also at the heart of the First Unitarian Society's program for water use in its 2008 addition.

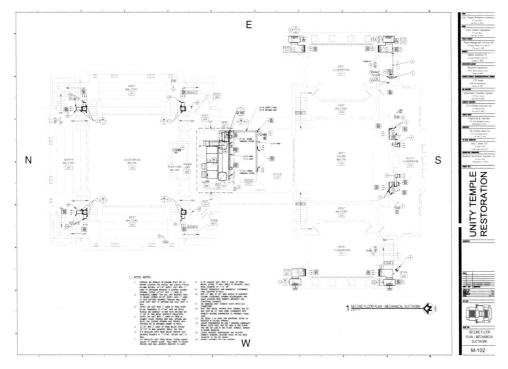

FIGURE 14.5 Unity Temple, restoration of 2015–17, second-floor plan for mechanical ductwork showing air handlers in Unity House (south) and Unity Temple (north).
Architectural Consulting Engineers, Oak Park

First Unitarian Society of Madison, Madison, Wisconsin

The 2005–08 expansion of Frank Lloyd Wright's First Unitarian Society of Madison's Meeting House, originally designed and built 1946–52, included a geothermal system[22] as a central component. But the addition embodied a holistic program that included a green roof and management of the site's rainwater. Together these features modeled its ideal of "participatory environmentalism," rooted in Unitarian Universalist principles (Haglund and Still 2005). Wright's original building centered on a generously lit sanctuary built of limestone and oak and included a radiant floor heating system installed as part of his design in 1947 (Geva 2012: 243). He used pipe coils located under the floor slab for circulating hot water and included an automatic thermostat. His father had been a founder of the society in 1879, and Wright himself valued his own affiliation (Siry 2012: Chapter 6). The building's triangular geometry in both its plan and three dimensions signified Unity, yet as Wright said, "the triangle stands for aspiration. Here is a church where the whole edifice is in an attitude of prayer" (Gaebler et al. 1952: 86). Indeed, the building's soaring roof also symbolizes praying hands (Fig. 14.6) (Geva 2012: 138, 153; Siry 2012: 271). The structure had been designed for a congregation of 150, but by the early 2000s, the society had over 1,400 members, making it the largest Unitarian Universalist congregation in the United States (Kubala 2014: 182). Early in 2005, the growing society commissioned Kubala Washatko Architects to design a major addition. The firm began extensive conversations with the congregation and other constituencies to identify key issues. Among these was the Wright building's designation as a National Historic

FIGURE 14.6 Frank Lloyd Wright, First Unitarian Society of Madison, 900 University Bay Drive, Shorewood Hills, Wisconsin, 1946–52; view from northeast.
Photograph by Balthazar Korab courtesy of the Library of Congress

Landmark in 2004, and concerns for its preservation. Thus, the expansion first occupied in 2008, conformed to strict guidelines to leave the site's historic parts unaltered while adding to Wright's sanctuary a second 500-seat auditorium (the Atrium) and other community spaces (Kubala 2014: 182). Seating 252, the meeting house's original sanctuary would function as a special chapel (Fig. 14.7).

As in Unity Temple, the architects of the First Unitarian Society's addition recalled: "Every decision about the design was then made in the shadow of the building's national significance" (Kubala 2014: 185). The program ultimately led to an addition of 20,000 square feet, which almost doubled the size of the church.[23] Every effort was made to carefully integrate the addition with Wright's building so that the resulting campus would feel like a single entity, to evoke the denominational ideal "Unity." The arc of new construction is southwest of the original Meeting House, using that building's pulpit as the central point from which the curvature of the addition was swung (Fig. 14.8). The addition won many architectural awards, including one from the Frank Lloyd Wright Building Conservancy (Shin and Miller 2014: 24 n2).

The architects emphasized, "The First Unitarian Society has an environmental ethic emanating from its core. It was a given that the new addition would manifest that ethic in as many ways as possible" (Kubala 2014: 194). Dave Weber, the FUSM representative for the addition from 2006 to 2008, recalled that in the planning process, members expressed strong support for the educational role of the First Unitarian Society and desired the addition to be

Geothermal Systems and Religious Ethics **223**

FIGURE 14.7 Frank Lloyd Wright, First Unitarian Society of Madison, interior view looking northwest toward pulpit. Room arranged for Sunday morning services, 1991.
Photograph by Balthazar Korab, courtesy of the Library of Congress

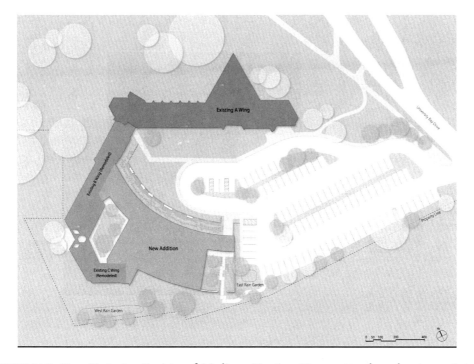

FIGURE 14.8 First Unitarian Society of Madison Meeting House, site plan, showing existing complex and new addition, 2005–8. Kubala Washatko Architects. Drawing 2008; Courtesy Kubala Washatko Architects

a demonstration of sustainability. Spiritual issues were voiced through a long period of congregational input. Rev. Michael Schuler, who served as the society's minister from 1988 to 2018, was a very strong supporter. For a time, the society weighed using only solar panels for photovoltaic power versus comprehensive LEED certification.[24] But Rev. Schuler encouraged the latter as a more visible demonstration of ideals.[25] For him, the Unitarian Universalist principle of respect for the interdependent web of existence meant placing immediate decisions in a global context. As he wrote, "Absent a concerted and sustained global effort to mitigate the underlying sources of climate change, they'll soon be impossible to ignore."[26] This overarching idea, as a shared assumption characteristic of this denominational culture, guided design choices for the addition. The society wrote, "As part of our intent to live our commitment to social justice and the web of life, we chose to be certified by LEED."[27] As a key person through the process, Weber said: "It is a discipline—it forces you to make a LEED compliant choice when you are at a decision point."[28] The addition earned a LEED Gold rating, with a 42 percent reduction in energy use relative to a standard building's consumption (Kubala 2014: 194). As of 2009, the addition was one of the thirty-seven buildings, and one of two religious buildings, that were LEED-certified in Wisconsin.[29] It was one of about thirty religious buildings nationally, among over 63,000 buildings of all types, that were LEED-certified by 2013 (Shin and Miller 2014: 1). The addition attained such a goal with a combination of spatial, material, and mechanical strategies. As the society described it, "the new building, as a whole, … operates as an integrated eco-system."[30] LEED guidelines translated the ideal of environmental stewardship into tangible goals of reducing environmental impact and energy use, so that its green credentials have social significance (Shin, Castellano and Miller 2012; Shin and Miller 2014: 9–10).

The addition's material envelope has poured concrete floors and walls, multilayered insulated roofs, and a textured visible wood frame structure with large glass areas admitting plentiful natural light that reduces the energy needed for artificial illumination. As the lighting consultant said, the lighting for the addition was "dictated by the abundance of daylight and the use of electric light during the day was minimal if at all" (Hall 2011: 28). In addition, and following Wright's style, the exposure of the south glass areas to the winter sun contributes to heat the building by preheating ventilation air, while the roofs' eaves shade them from direct sunlight in summer months to lower cooling loads. The glass is thermally high-performance in its resistance to heat gain or heat loss. In moderate weather, the addition's interiors, arranged along their linear arc, are naturally cooled and ventilated with minimal fan power.[31] As per LEED guidelines, materials, furniture, and finishes were selected for high recycled content and lack of toxic off-gassing into interiors both during construction and afterward (Kubala 2014: 194). Though the process of LEED certification is costly, the society invested the added time and funds since, as Weber put it, "some things we do are difficult, but they are a spiritual practice."[32]

Beyond these important passive and material measures, the addition's use of water, as in Unity Temple, centered on its geothermal system for heating and cooling, with a large field of sixteen wells bored to a depth of 250 feet (76 meters) below the parking lot, set between the addition and Wright's original building.[33] The design team felt fortunate that the property was large enough for such a field, and that the ground was sandy to a depth of about 300 feet, thus facilitating boring.[34] In winter, wells supply stable-temperature water through a closed loop to heat pumps that extract heat from the well water and circulate it to one of three air handlers (one for the lower crossing, one for the classrooms, and one for the auditorium), which take in and filter outside air that is then heated by water from the heat pump. The air handlers are in the north and south mechanical rooms near the juncture of the addition and the original structure. Water warmed with heat transferred via heat pumps from the well water is also piped to the building's in-floor tubing beneath the new Atrium and the adjacent Commons spaces for radiant floor heating. This system is analogous to but differs from the radiant floor heating using boiler-fired hot water that Wright used in the original Meeting House (Shin and Miller 2014: 6).

That building had no cooling beyond natural ventilation, whereas the addition's geothermal system in summer pulls 53°F (12°C) water from the well field. This cool water runs to the heat pumps that then function as chillers, to either cool air in the air handlers or supply cool water to the radiant floor piping for interior cooling.[35] In summer the water, having lost its coolness, returns to the well field below the parking lot, where the heat dissipates into the earth. Water in the pipes is there re-cooled and re-circulated to pull additional heat from interiors via the air handlers or the radiant flooring. Since the geothermal heating and cooling system uses electricity to run the pumps and fans, it consumes no natural gas or fuel oil directly.[36] The system's additional first cost relative to a more conventional design was $150,000, but this was to be recovered in energy savings within twelve years. And each year the system emitted 134 fewer tons of CO_2, or a reduction of 40 percent relative to a conventional system.[37] Thus, as at Unity Temple, the geothermal system signified both financial and environmental stewardship.

A measure of the congregation's commitment to environmental stewardship was the addition's reliance on mechanically assisted natural ventilation rather than full mechanical air. The society offers worship services once on Saturday evenings and twice on Sunday mornings, when regular attendees totaled around 650, split about evenly between the two services (Shin, Castellano and Miller 2012: 250 n3). Fans and vents pull fresh air through the Atrium and the addition as a whole, as well as bringing in the cool night air to chill the Atrium's floor slab in warm weather on Saturday nights before Sunday morning services (Fig. 14.9). As in Wright's Meeting House, the addition's windows include operable sash panels for localized access to fresh air and breezes as needed. Wright had used radiant floor heating with embedded hot water tubes, but the Meeting House had no cooling, whereas cool water flowing beneath the floor slab cools the new Atrium. In the addition's environment, the society's most extraordinary commitment was its agreement to raise the set point for cooling conditions in the new Atrium above the standard of 72°F (22°C) and 52 percent relative humidity.[38] Fan-assisted natural ventilation allows the congregation to accept an engineers' computer model where, on the hottest August day, the addition would start at 65–68°F (18–20°C) at 9 am on Sunday morning, but then, with the heat emitted by the hundreds of persons attending services, the Atrium would gradually be allowed to heat beyond 72°F (22°C) to 78°F (26°C) and 54 percent relative humidity by 12:30 p.m., when people leave. This willingness to accept a higher-than-standard temperature and humidity permitted a 75 percent reduction in the capacity of cooling equipment, and fan and duct sizes, thereby lowering not only the building's first cost but also ongoing operating costs and energy use.[39] The decision was reasonable, because the system would run at capacity only on Sundays.

Church members similarly distinguished themselves by agreeing to a site plan for the addition that reduced the number of proximate paved parking spaces by thirty-nine. Congregants were willing to carpool, walk, bicycle, or park in an adjacent existing hospital parking lot rather than building a new paved lot at the church. Limiting the paved parking area reduced storm water runoff, and enabled the shading of remaining paved areas, reducing the local heat-island effect. Heat islands increase temperatures by removing vegetation and replacing it with asphalt and concrete roads and other structures. The energy required to handle higher

FIGURE 14.9 First Unitarian Society of Madison Meeting House addition, auditorium, and fellowship hall, looking southeast. Kubala Washatko Architects, 2008.
Photograph: Dave Weber, 2022

cooling loads results in more air pollution, greater resource extraction impacts, meaning more fuel consumed to generate electricity for air conditioning, and higher energy costs because of heightened demand for power (Lechner 2015: 352–55). Striving to achieve LEED gold certification guided the congregation to place environmental stewardship above convenience (Kubala 2014: 194–95).

Also reducing the campus's heat island effect was its 7,000-square-foot (650 square meters) green roof, its slope attuned to that of Wright's originally specified copper roof (Fig. 14.10). Most of the addition's roof is planted with ten varieties of sedums selected for their hardiness, disease resistance, and low maintenance in the local environment and that vary seasonally in their flowering and color so that the roof flourishes like a meadow.[40] Its four inches (0.1 meter) of specially engineered, largely inorganic soil protects the vinyl roofing beneath it. Because green roofs hold and evaporate water, plant transpiration acts as a natural cooling system to keep the building cooler in summer, lowering roof temperatures by as much as 70°F (21°C). Although initially more expensive than a conventional roof, the living roof reduced the cooling system's capital cost and was projected to reduce air conditioning operating costs by 25 to 50 percent.[41] On an 85°F (29°C) day, the Meeting House's copper roof heats up to 115°F (46°C), but the green roof remains at 85°F (29°C).[42] Green roofs reduce storm water runoff by absorbing storm water and partly holding it until it evaporates. By decreasing runoff, they reduce the probability of storm water surges and sewage overflows (Weiler 2009). This was of

FIGURE 14.10 First Unitarian Society of Madison Meeting House addition, green roof looking southwest. Kubala Washatko Architects, 2008.
Photograph: Zane Williams

particular concern for the First Unitarian Society's campus, which had only one storm sewer drain on the property, in the southeast corner, causing stormwater runoff from the parking lot onto the neighboring property to its south. The addition's large area, with its immense increase in the building's overall impervious surface, would have made stormwater runoff much worse.[43] The living roof represents an ethical commitment to water resources as well as energy conservation. The roof sloping low to the ground helps the addition to blend visually into the earth. Thus, it not only signifies a green agenda but also embodies Wright's ideal of his organic architecture's continuity with and representation of nature, as at his nearby Taliesin (Levine 1996: Chapter 4).

The roof's design was one part of the addition's plan for "water stewardship" over the campus. Rather than a drainage system that removed surface water from the site, most rainwater runoffs were retained on the society's property, where water either evaporates or soaks into the ground and replenishes underground water reserves. The roof was angled down to drain into the terrace along the addition's inner curvature. After filtering through the terrace's stones and fabric, water passes through pipes to underground infiltration chambers in the property's center, between the addition and the original meeting house. In the chambers, water percolates through 250 feet (76 meters) of sand to the water table.[44] Excess roof runoff is channeled into rain gardens on the southeast and southwest of the addition's outer curvature. Inside the building, low-water-use fixtures (toilets, urinals, faucets, and showers) yield a water savings of 35 percent over conventional fixtures, thus flushing fewer gallons of valued potable water down the drain.[45] Management of storm water along with other sustainable measures demonstrates that an ethos of stewardship practice governed all aspects of the addition's relationship to the environment. From a distance, the green roof stands out as iconic in its own right, complementing Wright's original 40-foot-high roof as a metaphor for prayer, as an alternative symbol of transcendence.

Conclusion

Unity Temple's restoration and the First Unitarian Society of Madison's addition were carried out by Unitarian Universalist congregations that embraced the technology of geothermal heating and cooling for environmental and financial reasons. Similar systems have been installed with the restoration of several of Wright's houses (Hession 2011), but these two churches are his only non-residential buildings to include geothermal systems. Other religious communities have taken similar steps (Reeve 2009). Yet in Unity Temple and the First Unitarian Society, denominational values align closely with Wright's profound concern for a symbiotic relationship between architecture and environment. These sacred buildings' geothermal systems extended his ideals and the congregations' liberal religious culture. The new role of water in geothermal and storm water systems made it a symbol of environmental commitment and took Wright's principles of organic architecture into a new dimension. In both these sites, water, flowing in invisible systems, serves as a touchstone for these religious communities' ethical aspirations. Their values manifested in water's stewardship link its role to the Divine. Congregational consciousness of achieving thermal comfort in environmentally responsible ways reinforces communal awareness of the broader social purposes that emerge from houses of worship.

Notes

1. See the association's website: https://www.uua.org/beliefs/what-we-believe/principles Accessed May, 2022.
2. "Water Stewardship," in First Unitarian Society, "The Unitarian Meeting House: Building a Sustainable Future," 2008. [hereafter FUS-Sustainable] First Unitarian Society Archives, Box: Green Vision 2005–2009, Shelf 5B2.
3. Architectural Consulting Engineers (ACE), HVAC System Feasibility Study for Frank Lloyd Wright's Unity Temple [hereafter ACE, HVAC System], 30 September 2004, 2. I thank Mark Nussbaum for his input.
4. On the building's early heating system, see ACE, HVAC System, 11–13.
5. "Wells to Provide Energy Source," 2005: 8.
6. ACE, HVAC System, 2.
7. Nussbaum, conversation with author, 12 May 2021.
8. ACE, HVAC System, 2.
9. Hal Dardick, "Wright's Temple Gets Help with Renovation," *Chicago Tribune*, 7 October 2004, 2C.1.
10. Nussbaum, conversation with author, 12 May 2021.
11. Tara Burghart, "Group Wants Green Heating Technology in Frank Lloyd Wright's Unity Temple," *Canadian Press*, 20 October 2005.
12. Keith Bringe, quoted in "Wright's Landmark," 2005: 17–18.
13. Wright to Herbert Johnson, 24 August 1936, Frank Lloyd Wright Archives, fiche id. J00A06.
14. Bringe, quoted in Burghart, "Group Wants Green Heating Technology."
15. Nussbaum, e-mailed comments to author, 28 September 2021. The antifreeze-and-water mix was a formula of glycol, ethanol, or another environmentally benign substance.
16. Burghart, "Group Wants Green Heating Technology"; Bowen 2006, 139; and Nussbaum, e-mail to author, 28 September 2021.
17. Caitlin Mullen, "Dust Flies as Unity Temple Restoration Gets Underway," *Chicago Tribune*, 6 August 2015, 7.
18. Nussbaum, conversation with author, 12 May 2021.

19. Steve Johnson, "Big Fix," *Chicago Tribune*, 30 July 2015, 1; and Nussbaum, e-mail to author, 28 September 2021.
20. Johnson, "Big Fix."
21. "Wells to Provide Energy Source," 2005: 8.
22. Architect Vince Micha of Kubala Washatko Architects confirms that geothermal was then the correct term, rather than geoexchange. e-mail to author, 4 May 2022.
23. John Pilmaier, "Green Roof Harmonizes Historic Church Designed by Frank Lloyd Wright," *ForConstructionPros.com*; Fort Atkinson, 30 March 2012.
24. Initiated by the United States Green Building Council in 2000, the Leadership in Energy and Environmental Design (LEED) Rating System was the country's first to assess larger buildings for their effects on energy, water use, municipal infrastructure, transportation energy, resource conservation, land use, and indoor environmental quality. LEED certification levels go from basic to silver, gold, and platinum. Updated information is at: https://www.usgbc.org/
25. Weber, conversation with author, 14 May 2021.
26. Michael Schuler, "We Have the Tools to Fight Climate Change," [Madison] *Capital Times*, 7 August 2019.
27. "Leading Naturally," FUS-Sustainable.
28. Weber, quoted in "Leading Naturally," FUS-Sustainable.
29. "Leading Naturally," FUS-Sustainable; and Shin, Castellano, and Miller 2012: 247.
30. "Harmony by Design," FUS-Sustainable.
31. "Solar Sense," FUS-Sustainable.
32. Weber, quoted in "Leading Naturally," FUS-Sustainable.
33. "Comfort from Below," FUS-Sustainable.
34. Weber, conversation with author, 14 May 2021.
35. "Comfort from Below," FUS-Sustainable; and David Weber, conversation with author, 14 May 2021.
36. "Comfort from Below," FUS-Sustainable.
37. Ibid.
38. "Breathe Easy," FUS-Sustainable.
39. Ibid., and Kubala 2014: 194.
40. "Green and Growing," FUS-Sustainable; and Pilmaier, "Green Roof."
41. Ibid.
42. Pilmaier, "Green Roof"; and "Green and Growing," FUS-Sustainable.
43. "Green and Growing," FUS-Sustainable.
44. Weber, conversation with author, 14 May 2021.
45. "Water Stewardship," FUS-Sustainable.

References

Bowen, Ted S. "H. H. Richardson's Romanesque Revival Masterpiece Prompts Inspired, Green Preservation." *Architectural Record* 193, no. 12 (December 2005): 167–170.

Bowen, Ted Smalley. "Unity Temple Will Use Geothermal Energy after Its First Major Restoration." *Architectural Record* 194, no. 2 (February 2006): 139–140.

Gaebler, Max D. et al. "A Church in the Attitude of Prayer." *Architectural Forum* 97, no. 6 (December 1952): 85–92.

Geva, Anat. "The Use of Computerized Energy Simulations in Assessing Thermal Comfort and Energy Performance of Historic Buildings." In *Structural Studies, Repairs and Maintenance of Heritage Architecture IX*, edited by C.A. Brebbia and A. Torpiano, 587–596. Southampton UK and Boston MA, USA: WIT Press, 2005.

———. *Frank Lloyd Wright's Sacred Architecture: Faith, Form, and Building Technology*. New York: Routledge, 2012.

Greenwood, Andrea, and Mark W. Harris. *An Introduction to the Unitarian and Universalist Traditions*. Cambridge, UK: Cambridge University Press, 2011.

Grondzik, Walter T., and Alison G. Kwok. *Mechanical and Electrical Equipment for Buildings*, 12th ed., Hoboken, NJ: John S. Wiley & Sons, 2015.

Haglund, Brent, with Thomas W. Still, *Hands-On Environmentalism*. San Francisco: Encounter Books, 2005.

Hall, Elizabeth. "First Unitarian Society's Meeting House Addition." *Lighting Design and Application* 41, no. 10 (October 2011): 28.

Hession, Jane King, ed., "The Wright Shade of Green." *Save Wright* 2, no. 2 (Fall 2011): 1–26.

Kubala, Tom. "A Geometry of Respect: Adding to Frank Lloyd Wright's First Unitarian Meeting House." In *Frank Lloyd Wright: Preservation, Design, and Adding to Iconic Buildings*, edited by Richard Longstreth, 180–197. Charlottesville: University of Virginia Press, 2014.

Lechner, Norbert. *Heating, Cooling, Lighting: Sustainable Design Methods for Architects*. Hoboken, NJ: John Wiley & Sons, 2015.

Levine, Neil. *The Architecture of Frank Lloyd Wright*. Princeton, NJ: Princeton University Press, 1996.

Meehan, Patrick J., ed. *The Master Architect: Conversations with Frank Lloyd Wright*. New York: John Wiley and Sons, 1984.

Reeve, Ted. "Greening Sacred Spaces: Beautiful, Abundant, and Sustainable Living." *Anglican Theological Review* 91, no. 4 (fall 2009): 589–99.

Robinson, David. *The Unitarians and Universalists*. Westport, CT: Greenwood Press, 1985.

Rosenblum, Charles. "Going Green." *Preservation* 58, no. 5 (September/October 2006): 36–41.

Shin, Jung-hye, Devan Castellano, and Shadeequa Miller. "Communicating the Mission of Earth Stewardship through Green Buildings: A Cross Case Analysis of LEED Certified Religious Buildings in Madison, WI." *International Journal of the Constructed Environment* 2, no. 2 (2012): 247–268.

Shin, Jung-hye, and Shadeequa Miller. "Audio-Visual Environment and the Religious Experiences in Green Church Buildings: A Cross-Case Study." *Journal of Interior Design* 39, no. 3 (2014): 1–24.

Siry, Joseph M. *Beth Sholom Synagogue: Frank Lloyd Wright and Modern Religious Architecture*. Chicago: University of Chicago Press, 2012.

———. *Unity Temple: Frank Lloyd Wright and Architecture for Liberal Religion*. New York: Cambridge University Press, 1996.

Van Hampton, Tudor. "As More Buildings Go Geothermal, Project Teams Are Thinking Outside the Borehole." *ENR: Engineering News-Record* 263, no. 17 (30 November 2009): 20–25.

Weiler, Susan K. *Green Roof Systems: A Guide to the Planning, Design, and Construction of Landscapes over Structure*. Hoboken, NJ: John Wiley & Sons, 2009.

"Wells to Provide Energy Source: The Earth Will Be Used to Heat and Cool the Nearly Century-Old Unity Temple in West Suburban Oak Park." *Midwest Construction* 9, no. 12 (1 November 2005): 8.

Wiss, Janney, Elstner Associates, Inc. *Unity Temple: Historic Structures Report*. Chicago, 1987.

Wright, Frank Lloyd. "Architecture and Music." *Saturday Review of Literature* 40 (28 September 1957): 72–73.

———. "*The Natural House* (1954)." in *Frank Lloyd Wright: Collected Writings, vol. 5, 1949–1959*, edited by Bruce Brooks Pfeiffer. New York: Rizzoli, 1995.

"Wright's Landmark Utilizes Geothermal Energy." *Environmental Design + Construction* 8, no. 9 (October 2005): 17–18.

PART V
Modern Practice

15
SACREDNESS AND WATER IN CONTEMPORARY JAPANESE ARCHITECTURE: REINTERPRETATION OF ANCIENT TRADITIONS

Galia Dor

> *In Japan…since the temple is made of wood, the divine spirit inside the building is eternal, so the enclosure doesn't have to be.*
>
> Architect Tadao Ando[1]

Contemporary architect Hiroshi Sambuichi once said that he "pursues an architecture that breathes like an indigenous plant by mapping out all moving materials."[2] By "moving materials" (*ugoku sozai*), Sambuichi referred to water, air, and sun—vital for a plant to live and, consequently, vital for contemporary Japanese architecture. I maintain that this articulated veneration of constantly changing natural elements resonates with traditional Japanese concepts of sacredness and is key to any exegesis of Japan's contemporary architecture.

By incorporating age-old values of simplicity, traditional techniques, and natural elements such as water—with modern materials and contemporary *content*—a uniquely Japanese sacredness is evoked. In order to relate to the essence of this sacredness, let us take a brief look at Japanese religiosity—a complex facet of its culture and one that tends to escape strict (Western) definitions. For instance, though the culture thrives with rituals, festivals (*matsuri*), pilgrimages, and visits to Shinto and Buddhist shrines and temples, the Japanese themselves would tend to deny adherence to a "religion" (Kasulis 2004).[3] This is partly because Shinto—literally, "Way of Spirits," Japan's "vernacular religion" (i.e., its folk or popular beliefs and practices)—holds nature as *sacred* due to *kami* (mythic spirits and deities) that dwell in it. Importantly, the influential anthropologist Takutaro Sakurai (1917–2007) remarked that out of all natural manifestations, "mountain and water (watersheds, rivers, rain, etc.) are the most sacred" (2016: 226), and he emphasized that "the Western dichotomy between the sacred and the profane…lead us to misunderstand when we approach *kami* in a dualistic manner" (2016: 262).[4] This adds *context* to Sambuichi's reference to the natural growth of a plant and water as a symbol of motion, change, and impermanence.

Behind Japanese sacredness, however, lies yet another significant and intriguing concept—namely, the tripolar cycle of *ke* (healthy, mundane life, and work), *kegare* (ill and polluted state), and *hare* (purification rites). *Ke* is related to ancient agrarian times and is "the power

DOI: 10.4324/9781003358824-21

of the *sacred* connected to the rice plant" (Sakurai 1968); *kegare* is tiredness or disease that corrupts *ke* and needs to be dispelled; the way to do that is by utilizing *hare*. The cycle thus goes back to the state held as most sacred—that is, *ke*, the mundane! The Japanese vernacular religion rests less on cognizant belief and more on "activity, ritual, and custom" (Reader and Tanabe 1998: 7), which means that sacredness can indeed be pronounced in spaces conventionally defined as secular, as I will attempt to demonstrate.

Water is conceptualized in these *hare* rites as an agent of purification that can clear away the path and a connection to the sacred, and importantly, early mythological texts describe how the creator-deity Izanagi bathed in an *onsen*-river after being polluted in the afterlife world. Contemporary Japan demonstrates a rich array of such rituals, e.g., *harae* (ritual washing at the *chozuya* before entering a shrine; Fig. 15.1), bathing in public baths (*onsen*), *uchimizu* (sprinkling water on pavements), or *misogi* (waterfall purification).[5]

As Japan is predisposed to natural disasters such as *tsunamis* and typhoons, it has learned the hard way of water's dual facets, and with time, it has evolved into a "threshold symbol" between life and death, chaos and order, change and impermanence. Not only surrounded by water, but Japan also encloses rivers, lakes, and inland seas—all intermingled with thick forests, *geysers* (named "mouths of hell"), and hot springs. The Japanese landscape is thus hosted to all possible states of water (vapor, liquid, ice, and snow), which, as architect Kengo Kuma says, "makes our attempts to categorize and separate the world look foolish" (2000: 82). Furthermore, Japan's typical "island landscape" is thought to have inspired its garden design as reproducing "the oceans that surround the country" (Angenp 2013: 47) and ponds as focal points that reflect the universe (Fig. 15.2).

It is thus a challenging task to attempt to define sacred architecture in contemporary Japan, firstly because, as stated, the natural world by itself is held sacred; and secondly, because

FIGURE 15.1 The *harae* ritual—washing at the chozuya just before entering a Shinto shrine
Photo: Author

FIGURE 15.2 Kenrokuen Garden, Kanazawa: the pond as a focal point that "reflects all phenomena"
Photo: Author

water, as a natural element heavily invested with local meanings, serves in contemporary spaces (conventionally) considered secular, as a "gate to the sacred." Consequently, this chapter introduces examples that fall into this elusive liminal space between mundane and sacred rituality, such as *onsens* and museums.[6]

I have previously related Izanagi as the first to dispel his impurity by washing in an *onsen*; after him, as Peter Grilli says, "the gods of the sun, moon and agricultural fertility were all borne out of the bath…" (1992: 24). However, most Japanese would not consider the *onsen* a religious space. It constitutes an intriguing instance of *ke* and *hare* put together: (1) a purification in water coming up from the underground; (2) the bathing is conducted in a highly ritualized way and demands a detailed etiquette; and (3) it constitutes a social gathering which eliminates status differences (as nakedness is mandatory). It is interesting, therefore, to study the design of contemporary *onsens* as reinterpretations of this ancient "sacred-mundane" Japanese institution. Architect Kengo Kuma, for instance, designed Horai *onsen* in 2003, saying that it reflects "the mere expression of the tranquil ritual of bathing, conveying the richness of natural phenomena and a profound sense of liberating lightness within the sublime ephemerality of the surrounding unbounded environment" (2000: 36).[7]

In order to tangibly express this distilled emotion of ritual bathing, his *onsen* touches upon intangibility. It is a completely open structure bounded by a wooden deck and sitting on a narrow edge of a steep hillside (with spectacular views of the sea). Yet another architect, Terunobu Fujimori, gives an interesting take on *onsens*, saying that he only got a sense of his own project (Soda Pop Spa, 2005) when he had realized how "the hot water of the bath is analogous to the water used in tea, both called *yu* in Japanese" (Buntrock 2010: 61).

Indeed, *onsens* and tea-rooms, of different contexts notwithstanding, both facilitate a here-and-now meditative state through a medium that is *essentially water* and is both conducted as a communal gathering for personal revelation. This brings us to "skillful means" (*upaya*) in Zen Buddhism, which emphasizes repeated practice as a path to enlightenment and involves—in the same way as *onsen*—the practice of mundane activities, such as cleaning or cooking. By applying a state of nonduality in the mind with a concrete experience, the practitioner, "moves freely in the realm that is at once both sacred and secular" (Parker 1999: 122). *Chado* ("Way of Tea"), known in the West as the Tea Ceremony, constitutes a conspicuous example of such skillful means that evolved in fourteenth- and fifteenth-century Kyoto. Its accompanying architecture—the tea-room (*chashitsu*)—carries some interesting characteristics. Hidden and modest, it is revealed at the end of a path, traditionally made of stones and choreographed through a sequence of steps. Water is constantly present: sprinkled on the path as an indication that the *chado* and its accordant spaces have been appropriately prepared, in the waiting area containing a stone basin for cleansing, and in the *chado* itself which utilizes water for tea; as Kuma says, "when your progress is defined by the spatial rhythm of the stones, you are naturally led into a separate realm" (2010: 86). Inside, the space is rustic, small, and empty, apart from the *toko-no-ma* (a niche, "gap"), which displays artistic items, such as *ikebana*. It constitutes an instance of *wabi-sabi* aesthetics that finds beauty in simplicity and impoverished rusticity.

One contemporary tea-room gives an exciting and innovative interpretation to the traditional tea-house, namely, the Kou-An Glass Tea House designed by artist Tokujin Yoshioka (Fig. 15.3). It was first exhibited in 2011 at the fifty-fourth La Biennale di Venezia and then moved to its present location at the Shoren-in Temple, Kyoto. It is transparent just like water and entirely made of glass. Coarse slabs of glass constitute the floor, on which functional tea utensils are placed; three additional slabs of glass serve as benches—one inside and two outside. The structure is mesmerizing in its lucidity; it evokes the feeling of staring right into the depths of a bottomless clear lake. I find three overlapping meanings in this transparency: (1) the whole abode hosting tea making (water) becomes the embodiment of water itself; (2) if the tea-house was once, as described above, a hidden, rustic, intimate, and dim space and experience, Kou-An Glass Tea House is just the opposite—it is in fact, an architecture of light and glass as representing water; and (3) isn't this also an attempt by Yoshioka to visually convey a distilled essence of *chado*, Zen, and Japanese culture? As the room is devoid of the traditional *toko-no-ma*, the natural substitute for scrolls, or *ikebana*, are the rays of the sun as they break through the prism of the glass—exactly like a rainbow on the ripples of water! The sacredness evoked in this space is carried out through connectedness with the natural

FIGURE 15.3 The Kou-An Tea-Room in Shoren-in Temple, Kyoto
Photo: Wikipedia permission CC BY-SA 4.0 File: Glass Tea

time in which all is immersed. As there is no separation between inside and outside, and all is one transparent whole, clarity of mind can be achieved. Indeed, Yoshioka himself attests that he aimed to "design Time as it is created along with nature"; in order to achieve that, he continues, "our sensations need to be relieved of superficial designs, to be integrated with nature and to sense light itself."[8]

Swiss architect Mario Botta once said that "the first step of 'making architecture' begins by putting a stone on the ground, and this action in itself has a *sacred* meaning" (Lang 2015: 47). In Japan, such spatial designation utilizes a sacred tree, the *sakaki* 榊, which had been used in early times and consisted of, as architect Fujimori says, "simply a fence…marked as sacred…shrines like this were the only way of worshipping until the sixth century" (Buntrock 2010: 25).[9] When shrines did begin to be built, the spatial choice was linked with a sacred essence of nature or a mythological deity, and they began to acquire an important marker of sacredness— namely, the *torii* gate. These conspicuous gates are positioned on the way 道 (*michi* Japanese, *dao* Chinese) to the shrine, with the last one constituting a "fluid barrier" between the "purified" (inside) and the "polluted" (outside); after passing through them, one arrives at an empty space of white gravel, only to realize that the shrine consists of the same efficacious "empty space" (*ma* 間, "space in-between," or "gap").[10] This is very different from Buddhist temples that host a statue of Buddha at the furthermost section of the temple.

Another form and symbol of water in architecture is the pond in traditional Japanese gardens, especially in the "strolling type" created during the Edo period (1603–1868). Here, one is led along a winding path through a succession of alternating landscapes. With each turn of the path and through the utilization of reveal-and-hide techniques, scene after scene is revealed, aiming at yet higher aesthetic feelings in one's mind/heart. Along this exploratory journey, the pond constitutes a centerpiece, revealed to the eyes as a sudden revelation. A remarkable example that plays a modern variation on the traditional Japanese garden, while fusing the two "sacred contents" of Buddhism and nature, is architect Tadao Ando's Water Temple, on Awaji Island, constructed between 1989–1991 (Fig. 15.4). In reference to this project, Ando recalls: "I once traveled through India during the rainy season, where I saw a scene of a temple standing in obscurity on the opposite side of a broad lotus pond, and I thought it resembled the image of one of the Buddhist paradises. The idea of a hall under a pond covered by the greenery of lotus flowers probably emerged from that memory" (2014a: 192).

It is intriguing to witness the way an ontological vision corresponds with one's cultural background, such as the lotus as a conspicuous Buddhist symbol and the visual image of a Buddhist paradise. The (white-gravel) path to the temple is choreographed so that any information about what's next to come is held back. One ascends from the foot of a hill up to the original site of the (Shingon Buddhism) Honpuku-Ji temple, accompanied on the right side by a traditional cemetery. After a left turn, a series of two white-washed concrete walls appear, blocking the view. Now the atmosphere transforms, becoming contained, dark and intimate. At the end of the wall, one is startled by the revealed scene: a mirror-like pool that reflects (and recreates) the mountains, the sky, and the bamboo canes that surround its edge. Indeed, the belief in Japan, as Kengo Kuma says, is that in order for a garden to be complete, they need to, "tell us that all the mountains, sky, the universe as a whole are an extension of the garden" (2010: 118).

The pond is very still with some water lilies and (at season) lotus flowers floating on its surface; it immediately calms the mind, forming a gate to a sacred experience of the Buddhist "here and now." The most surprising and exceptional phase of this explorative journey is the concrete stairway in the middle of the pool, which cuts it into two symmetrical halves and invites visitors to descend down, into some unknown, mysterious world (Fig. 15.4).

FIGURE 15.4 The *torii* gate of Itsukushima shrine (Miyajima) during low tide
Photo: Author

If the visitor experienced the natural light of the sun and the natural transparency of water before, he/she is now taken aback by the colors of the "mido hall"—a circular space filled with an intense vermilion red. Only then will the visitor arrive at the innermost sacred space in which a statue of *Amida Buddha* is housed (Fig. 15.5). At this point, visitors can pray, bow to the Buddha, or just sit and meditate, taking everything in. A multilevel recreation of Buddhist ideas occurs here: philosophically, respecting the natural cycle of life and "living the moment"; religiously, attaining self-liberation—represented by a white lotus flower rising from a muddy pond; and, importantly, evoking the image of the Buddhist paradise (Sukhavati), in which, as scripts describe, Buddha sits on a lotus flower in the center of a pond. As the newly dead enter the lotus buds, a moment of rebirth occurs when "the aspirant awaken atop a lotus flower as its petals open" (Yiengpruksawan 1995: 649). Tadao Ando emphasizes his wish that the temple would serve as "a place for people to escape from everyday life and to take time for contemplation, and by creating through time and space, a dramatic shift from the profane to the sacred" (2014b: 182). Importantly, referring to museums in general, Ando says, "I take the museum space also as sacred in a sense."[11,12]

Yet another form of fusing a shrine/temple with water constitutes positioning the *torii* gate in the water so that it seems to float. One such place is the ancient Itsukushima Shrine on the sacred island of Miyajima (Fig. 15.6). The ferry that carries people to the island allows for the wonderful scenery of the tangerine-colored *torii* gate to unfold. With the cycle of high and low tides, the gate changes in appearance, and thus, though it is a man-made architecture, it is whole and inseparable from the sea. After a short walk, one reaches the front veranda of the shrine, floating just at the edge of the water. Here, the space is transitional—a threshold between inside and outside, open and closed, nature (water) and man-made construction, the profane and the sacred. Itsukushima Shrine is one in a long line of ancient shrines and temples

Sacredness and Water in Contemporary Japanese Architecture **239**

FIGURE 15.5 The Water Temple, Awaji island: the stairway leading down to underneath the pool
Photo: Author

to be built on the edge of the water as a mutual reinforcement of sacredness. Quite a long line of contemporary architects enter into a dialog with this theme and design a mirror-like body of water adjacent to the building itself. Many of architect Kengo Kuma's projects, for instance, are named Water/Glass, River/Filter, or Sea/Filter, which, as he says, "doubles the presence of his buildings through reflection" (Buntrock 2010: 87).

The following works constitute examples of sacred architecture in which themes of "floating on the edge on the water" or "fused with mirror-like pond" are utilized. The first example is sacred as it is related to death, the fear of which, according to philosopher Arthur Schopenhauer, "is the beginning of philosophy, and the final cause of religion" (Durant 1977: 328). Indeed, this awareness and fear have created numerous visions of the afterlife, with consequential burial rituals and deeply sacred structures surrounding death. A contemporary

FIGURE 15.6 The Water Temple, Awaji island: The Mido Hall of the underwater temple
Photo: Author

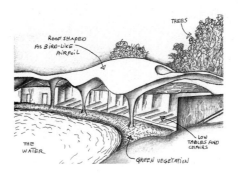

FIGURE 15.7 The Meiso no Mori Funeral Hall, Kakamigahara
Photo: Author

example is architect Toyo Ito's Municipal Funeral Hall of Meiso No Mori in Kakamigahara (Fig. 15.7), which opened in 2006. It consists of a curvaceous concrete roof that seems to float with such lightness—almost like bird wings that are spread in the air. The roof is supported by 12 columns, and one can climb it to get a view of the clear lake of the Gifu region. Literally, Meiso no Mori means "forest of meditation," a reference to the surrounding natural forest and meditation as internal contemplation and reflection. When commissioned for the project, Toyo Ito "was free to create a crematorium that would not be constrained by religious content" (Pallister 2015: 62). Here, the space is simultaneously secular and sacred, as religious content of any affiliation is stripped down and one is left with pure meditative spirituality and connection with the natural cycle of life and death. Though a crematorium is a place of grief and parting, Meiso no Mori creates a space in which, as Pallister aptly remarks, "death would not be grim, final and static," but, "part of a continual dance of movements, linked to and part of the air, the trees, the water and the wider natural world" (ibid). Water surrounds the hall and further reflects nature—hills and trees; it is calm and quiet and allows for a true meditation on the transitory nature of life. It is in meditation that we let go, breaking down the walls that surround us so that the gap between the subject (observer) and objects (observed) slowly disappears into emptiness as the ultimate expansion of inner-outer space.

As opposed to Miso no Mori, the second example of an edge-of-the-water scene is specifically affiliated with religious content—namely, Christianity. This is the Church on the Water by architect Tadao Ando in Yufutsu-gun, Tomamu on the island of Hokkaido, constructed in 1985 (Fig. 15.8). When presented with the task of building a church, Ando immediately thought of water so he would be able, "to make a scene of a crucifix standing still on a quiet, mirror-like lake surface…" (2014a: 140). Perhaps he also realized that due to the harsh weather of this northern island, water will manifest itself in all its possible states, e.g., fluid, ice, or snow. The church consists of two overlapping cubes; the larger is the chapel itself, accessed by walking under a glass/steel cube, and taking a spiral stairway. It is only upon entering the chapel (a bare, simple, straight line, concrete space) that the scene of the cross on the water is revealed—and it is striking.

In fact, the scene is a reinterpretation and re-manifestation of two cultural traditions, Western and Japanese. Namely, (1) the familiar decorations found in many churches worldwide—consisting of a rich array of images, statues, and figurines (of Jesus and others)—are replaced by the pure, transparent, and mirror-like surface of the water; thus, a scene that is traditionally context-specific is expanded and elevated to a universal image of nature (which, for the believer, I can presume, constitutes God's omnipresence); and, (2) Ando uses the Japanese technique of "borrowed scenery" (*shakkei* 借景), but changes its content, i.e., rather than a

Sacredness and Water in Contemporary Japanese Architecture **241**

FIGURE 15.8 The Technique of *Shakkei* utilized in the Church on the Water—a garden view is replaced with a 'Cross on Water'
Photo: Author

traditional garden that is viewed from the inside of the building (in the same way one looks at a painting on the wall), here it is a cross on water. But there is another visual layer here. In addition to the traditional iconography, the cross constitutes a pure minimalist image of a man on water, perhaps evoking in believers' hearts the famous image of Jesus walking on water.

Going back to the highly significant idea and concept of way, intriguing reinterpretations are manifested in a number of contemporary structures. For instance, the path of art-water-nature which was created in 2004 as part of the Chichu Museum (literally, "art museum inside the earth"), designed by architect Tadao Ando on Naoshima Island (in the Seto Inland Sea).[13] From the ticket office, the visitor walks up the road, reaching a natural pond on the left—a beautiful replica of Monet's garden of lilies at Giverny. The route continues, and Ando's signature walls emerge in sight; though utilizing concrete, a material so different from traditional wood (heavy and cold versus light and warm), it is remarkable how a Japanese "lightness" is still preserved. Through a small entrance, the visitor "falls" into a different realm consisting of alternating spaces of brightness and darkness. Inside, the visit is choreographed by attendants (ritual-like), which eventually leads to an off-white, empty, spacious room that exhibits Monet's "Water Lilies." I argue that the full meaning of the Japanese term *oku* 奥 (concentric circles going deeper and deeper spatially and/or, psychologically) is manifested here, beginning with the wide scenery of Seto Inland Sea—a garden dotted with islands—to a natural pond that imitates art, to water in a man-made work of art—water within water within water while one walks along a path. So it goes, deeper and deeper, eventually reaching emptiness, which resonates with Ando's expressed wish that one day the museum will, "eventually disappear into the landscape" (Pollock 2005: 122), illustrating the ancient Japanese philosophy of impermanence.[14]

One of the most remarkable examples of a relationship between water and the museum as sacred space is the Teshima Art Museum, designed by architects Rei Naito and Ryue Nishizawa in 2010 (Fig. 15.9). It is located on Teshima Island in Seto (Inland Sea), which, alongside Naoshima and Inushima, constitutes a floating museum of experimental art and architecture. The island is remote, echoing with numerous shrines and temples traditionally built on distant islands and in the depths of mountains. It is this separation from the main mundane that constitutes one of the characteristics of creating a sacred place (Geva 2012). Architect Fumihiko Maki refers to it, stating, "Inner space has a religious dimension, in that it suggests the direction in which the seat of a deity (*kami*) lies…the inner shrine is located deep in a mountain because it is believed that important things should remain hidden; a winding mountain trail therefore provides the only access" (2000: 157).

To reach the museum is a long journey consisting of a ferry and a climb up a long and steep road to the green hills of Mt. Myojin. The white, round-shaped structure, titled *bokei* (matrix) slowly unfolds with each step, consciously echoing the surrounding hills in curve and height (4 square meters, or about 13 feet). It symbolizes, as Lars Müller and Akiko Miki say, "a rebirth during a time of active revitalization for the island" (2011: 322). At the entrance, attendants monitor the number of people going inside, aiming at relative solitude and space for contemplation in one's heart/mind.[15] The small entrance was purposely designed (by Nishizawa) so that visitors enter one by one, and I wonder whether it culturally converses with

FIGURE 15.9 The Teshima Art Museum, Teshima Island, Seto Inland-Sea
Photo: Author

sixteenth-century Zen Buddhist tea-houses, which had a *nijiriguchi* ("crawling-in entrance"), through which visitors "crouched as a sign of humility as they go through" (Louis 2002: 107).

Once inside, one realizes the art exhibited inside. Drops and shiny beads of water emerge from holes in the floor and slide around, sometimes gathering at depressed areas in the floor to form a puddle. The characteristics of change, emptiness, and adaptability of water are manifested before one's eyes, as one wanders in the empty space or sits on the floor mesmerized by the movement of the drops. The ceiling has two large openings, through which light, rain, or wind can freely penetrate; this induces a typically Japanese state of blurred borders between inside and outside, open and closed, man-made designation of space and nature. Furthermore, sounds from afar (of the sea or trees outside) reverberate through the openings, while the light inside changes with the position of the sun. It evokes a Buddhist state of mindfulness to appreciate the tiny details of life (a droplet), and, I maintain, enables one to feel part of something bigger. I believe it is also related to *yugen*, an important Japanese concept of aesthetics, which refers to this profound and deep sense of beauty evoked in us, coupled with a realization of life's transiency. Upon exiting, the visitor is welcomed by open green grassland, with fantastic views of yet another form of water, the big blue sea.

By utilizing this strong Japanese motif of water coming up from below, people are (literally) drawn into the depths of Japanese geological and cultural roots. I contend that this sacred space constitutes a contemporary take on "nature-reverencing Shinto-shrine," which celebrates water as the embodiment of the organic facet of natural life: an inherent ability to change, adapt, and create endless forms of life. By exhibiting water as *art*, I believe the architects hint that both are essential to man, and, furthermore, that water's characteristics (adaptability, flexibility, etc.) are essential for man-made artistic creation. Indeed, "there are no boundaries between nature and art…it tells us something about being alive."[16] There is something primordial and basic, perhaps even a contemporary form of paganic ritual, about the way in which people experience feelings of humility, spiritual awakening, and reverence to nature and water as the most sacred for the planet and human lives! Indeed, the fact that the museum was constructed as part of a clean-up operation after an environmental crisis adds yet another layer of significance to the project. As Naito says, the project "comes into being…and goes back to nature as it is" (2016: 66).

Finally, another work by Tadao Ando that utilizes waterfalls to enhance transcendence is the Garden of Fine Arts, Kyoto (1994; Fig. 15.10). On one hand, it is a museum—a structure that exhibits art—but on the other hand, it is an open "garden" in which one admires the "plants" revealed to him along a path, only, in this case, the plants are actually a few selected

FIGURE 15.10 The Garden of Fine Arts, Kyoto
Photo: Author

masterpieces of world art (European, Chinese, and Japanese). Water accompanies the visitor throughout in the form of pools but, most importantly, as waterfalls at each bend of the path. Water takes the experience to yet higher levels of sacredness, reflection, and clarity. It simultaneously connects the aesthetics of the human sphere with nature and waterfalls, which are revered in Japan to this day. These waterfalls accompany the visitor visually, tangibly, and even auditorily—their cascading sounds mimic a waterfall in a Japanese garden. This constant reminder of falling water brings to mind the Zen saying, "not the stillness in stillness, but the stillness in movement is the real stillness" (Nitschke 1993: 238).

Some Concluding Remarks

Contemporary Japanese architecture constitutes, according to Nelson, "an ongoing process" (1996: 11), continuously subsisting between its traditional roots and modern contents. This creative and dynamic tension intensifies when it comes to traditional concepts of sacredness and attitudes toward nature, and in particular, to water. The examples presented here reveal an interesting gradient of "metaphorical significance" through which water evokes sacredness—namely, that the less a space/structure is "religious/profane" to begin with, the more intensive and versatile water's metaphorical significance becomes. Thus, *onsens* and tea-rooms, whose very essence is water, pronounce sacredness through a ritualistic act involving people's very bodies, either by soaking in it for purification or consuming it as tea (only to become *the* body). As for structures that are religious by definition (e.g., Water Temple, Church on Water, or Miso no Miro), water is an *added* component that broadens the space beyond its contextualized (man-made) religion, elevating it to wider circles of the natural world and the universe. Then we have the third type, which I find most intriguing—contemporary Japanese museums. Here, water is at its highest efficacy, evoking a state of wholeness and connection with nature, even to the extent that it is exhibited as the museum's centerpiece (e.g., Teshima museum). Indeed, from a Japanese aesthetic perspective, water (in nature) and art (in the human world) share a phenomenal characteristic—namely, the ability to transform, change, and constantly evolve, as a prerequisite to life itself. This brings us full circle back to Hiroshi Sambuichi's words with which we started this journey—that architecture as a form of art resembles a living plant, dependent on water, air, and sun. I also find that these contemporary architectural spaces constitute an aesthetic experience through which one fully senses a growing awareness and gratitude to nature, as it is, indeed, *sacred*.

Notes

1. Reproduced by permission from Architectural Record © from an interview with former Architectural Record editor in chief Robert Ivy (*Architectural Record*. May 2002). https://www.architecturalrecord.com/articles/12624-tadao-ando. Accessed September 2021.
2. Brownell. 2018. https://www.iconeye.com/architecture/future-50-hiroshi-sambuichi
3. Indeed, even the Japanese word for religion (*shukyou*) was dubbed only after the 1868 Meiji Restoration (Kramer 2013).
4. The "sacred" has received numerous definitions, from Rudolf Otto (1917), who suggested it is "a feeling of awe and mystery" (Rots 2014: 33), to Mircea Eliade, who saw it as standing in opposition to the "profane," a definition that is criticized now as inadequate to non-Western cultures; Aike P. Rots, for instance, claims that, "the 'religion-secular' dichotomy is increasingly problematized" (2014: 31).
5. Otowa Falls, located at the far end of Kiyomizu Temple (literally, "clear water"), is a living example of such a mutually enforcing relationship between temples and waterfalls.

6. Before the introduction of Western museums, sacred objects in Japan had been stored in "halls of myriad objects" (*homotsuden*); Suzuki calls them ambiguous spaces, "not wholly secular nor sacred" (2007: 130). Furthermore, reevaluations of the museum as a "non-secular cathedral" are beginning to be heard, as "culture is taking the role of religion" (Jencks 2000: 44).
7. Architect Hiroyasu Takasaki designed an *onsen* named *hotaru no yuya* ("Bathhouse of Fireflies") in Ogawa, Saitama (2015), wishing to "give everyone a sense of continuity of life, a peace of mind, and a hope for the future" (2015). Takasaki, Hiroyasu. "Bathhouse of Fireflies/Takasaki Architects." *Archdaily*. 2015. https://www.archdaily.com/777998/bathhouse-of-fireflies-takasaki-architects. Accessed September 2021.
8. Yoshioka, Tokujin. "Making Time Visible: Tokujin Yoshioka's Glass Tea House in Kyoto." *Yatzer*. 2015. https://www.yatzer.com/kou-an-glass-tea-housa-tokujin-yoshioka. Accessed September 2021.
9. *Sakaki* is etymologically related to *sakai*, meaning "a boundary" which "purifies areas and distinguishes holy places for Shinto gods" (Omura 2004: 180). Numerous Shinto rituals utilize *sakaki* branches, and its wood is believed to convey sacredness into the structure it becomes part of.
10. The concepts of way (*dao* 道) and "space in-between" (*ma* 間) are key to Chinese and Japanese philosophies and spatiality; Hiraia Isozaki says that, whereas the West "gave rise to absolutely fixed images of an homogenous and infinite continuum," in East Asia, "space was conceived as identical with the events of phenomena occurring in it" (1979: 13).
11. Simek, Peter. "Interview: Architect Tadao Ando on the Modern Art Museum of Fort Worth." *Dimagazine*. October 23, 2012. https://www.dmagazine.com/arts-entertainment/2012/10/interview-architect-tadao-ando-on-the-modern-art-museum-of-fort-worth/. Accessed September 2021.
12. In the 21st Century Museum of Contemporary Art in Kanazawa (SANAA architectural firm, 2004) water is utilized in as a "gate of mirror-clarity." Upon entrance, a transparent room with a pool installed allows visitors to look down through its transparent floor, seeing the people underneath; later, one reaches the bottom floor and looks up.
13. Other water projects on Naoshima Island aim at its reverence, such as "The Water" by architect Hiroshi Sambuichi; here, a pool is filled with water from the groundwater arteries.
14. This is an intriguing aspect of traditional Japanese architecture. Caroline Humphrey remarks that shrines were considered a renewable entity, reflecting the idea that it is a "temporary abode (*yorishiro*) of the deity who periodically visits the people" (2003: 92). Ise Shrine is the best instance of this concept, as it goes through a 20-year cycle of destruction and re-construction.
15. "Heart/mind" is a better rendering of the Japanese *kanji, kokoro* 心 (or *xin* in Chinese), as it does not separate the brain's thinking faculties and emotions (as opposed to Western vernacular).
16. Naito, Rei. "An interview with artist Rei-Naito." *Mazda*. March 16, 2021. www.mazda.com.au/beyond-the-drive/zoom-zoom-magazine—2021—issue-40-autumn/an-interview-with-artist-rei-naito. Accessed September 2021.

References

Ando, Tadao. *Tadao Ando: Process and Idea*. ToTo Publishing, 2014a.
———. *Tadao Ando: Naoshima*. Paris: Comité exécutif de l'exposition Paris Gauche, 2014b.
Angenp, Courtney. "Concept and Technique: How Traditional Japanese Architecture can contribute to Contemporary Sustainable Design Practices." *Environmental Studies Honors Papers* 10 (2013) pp. 1–118.
Buntrock, Dana. *Materials and Meaning in Contemporary Japanese Architecture: Tradition and Today*. New York: Routledge. 2010.
Durant, W. *The Story of Philosophy*. New York: Simon & Schuster, 1977.
Geva, Anat. *Frank Lloyd Wright's Sacred Architecture: Faith, Form and Building Technology*. New York: Routledge. 2012.
Grilli, Peter. *Pleasures of the Japanese Bath*. Colorado: Shambhala Publications, 1992.
Humphrey, Caroline and Piers Vitebsky. *Sacred Architecture*. London: Duncan Baird Publishers, 2003.
Isozaki, Arata. *Japan-ness in Architecture*. Massachusetts: The MIT Press, 2011.
Isozaki, Hiraia et al. *MA Space-Time in Japan*. New York: Cooper, 1979.
Jencks, Charles. "Black Box, White Cube. Ersatz Cathedral, Shopping Mall and Renta-culture." *The Art Newspaper* no. 109 (2000): 44–47.

Kasulis, P. Thomas. *Shinto: The Way Home*. Hawaii: University of Hawaii Press, 2004.

Kramer, Hand Martin. "How 'Religion' Came to be Translated as Shukyo: Shimaji Mokurai and the Appropriation of Religion in Early Meiji Japan." *Journal of the International Research Center for Japanese Studies* 25 (2013): 89–111.

Kuma, Kengo. *Anti-Object: The Dissolution and Disintegration of Architecture*. Tokyo: Chikuma Koubou, 2000.

Kuma, Kengo et al. *A Japanese Technique for Articulating Space*. Kyoto: Tankosha, 2010.

Lang, F. Michael. *Signs of the Holy One: Liturgy, Ritual, and Expression of the Sacred*. Ignatius, 2015.

Louis, Frédéric. *Japan Encyclopedia*. Harvard: Harvard University Press, 2002.

Maki, Fumihiko. *Nurturing Dreams: Collected Essays on Architecture and the City*, edited by Mark Mulligan. Massachusetts: MIT Press, 2000.

Müller, Lars and Akiko Miki. *Insular Insight: Where Art and Architecture Conspire with Nature. Naoshima, Teshima, Inujima*. Zurich: Lars Müller publishers, 2011.

Naito, Rei et al. *Teshima Art Museum*. Naoshima: Fukutake Foundation, 2016.

Nelson, K. John. *A Year in the Life of a Shinto Shrine*. Washington: University of Washington Press, 1996.

Nitschke, Gunter. *From Shinto to Ando: Studies in Architectural Anthropology in Japan*. New Jersey: Ernst & Sohn, 1993.

Omura, Hiroshi. "Trees, Forests and Religion in Japan." *Mountain Research and Development* 24, no. 2 (2004): 179–182.

Pallister, James. *Sacred Spaces: Contemporary Religious Architecture*. New York: Phaidon, 2015.

Parker, D. Josef. *Zen Buddhist Landscape Arts of Early Muromachi Japan (1336–1573)*. New York: SUNY Press, 1999.

Pollock, Naomi. "Tadao Ando Buries his Architecture at the Chichu Museum so Only the Voids Emerge from the Earth." *Architecture Record* 10, 2005.

Reader, Ian and J. George Tanabe. *Practically Religious: Worldly Benefits and the Common Religion of Japan*. Hawaii: University of Hawaii Press, 1998.

Rots, P. Aike. "The Rediscovery of 'Sacred Space' in Contemporary Japan: Intrinsic Quality or Discursive Strategy?" In *Rethinking 'Japanese Studies' from Practices in the Nordic Region*, edited by Jianhui Lui and Mayuko Sano. Kyoto: International Research Center for Japanese Studies, 2014.

Sakurai, Takutaro. "The Main Features and Characteristics of Japanese Folk Beliefs" in *The Sociology of Japanese Religion*, edited by K. Morioka et al. Leiden: Brill, 1968.

———. "The Expressive Dimensions of Folk Performing Arts: A Gebserian Approach to Kagura." *Intercultural Communication Studies* XXV, no. 3 (2016). pp. 259–274.

Suzuki, Y. "Temple as Museum, Buddha as Art: Horyuji's Kudara Kannon and Its Great Treasure Repository." *Cambridge* 52, (2007): 128–40.

Yiengpruksawan, Mimi. "The Phoenix Hall at Uji and the Symmetries of Replication." *The Art Bulletin* 77, no. 4 (1995): 647–672.

16
BAPTISTRIES IN MARCEL BREUER AND ASSOCIATES' AMERICAN CATHOLIC SACRED SPACES

Victoria M. Young

On March 7, 1953, Abbot Baldwin Dworschak of the Benedictine Abbey of Saint John the Baptist in Collegeville, Minnesota wrote to twelve of the world's leading architects, searching for a designer to complete a comprehensive plan for the expanding Abbey.[1] To be connected to their time and place, the brethren mandated modernism as the preferred architectural style and from this group of designers emerged the Hungarian-born, Bauhaus-trained designer Marcel Breuer. Working with the Benedictines, Breuer and his New York City-based design team planned a church that responded to reformed liturgical needs with an architectural expression of the present day (Fig. 16.1). Breuer's church was a success, both liturgically and architecturally, and it led to additional religious commissions including two Catholic buildings in the United States. In 1954 Prioress Edane Volk and the Benedictine sisters of Annunciation Priory outside Bismarck, North Dakota decided that their seven-year-old order needed a more suitable setting.[2] Aware of his ongoing work in Collegeville from publications and monastic connections, including Saint John's liturgical coordinator Frank Kacmarcik, they presented Breuer with their ideas and he agreed to design their convent, stating, "perhaps we might build a little jewel" (Koyama and Burns 1961, 362) (Fig. 16.2). Several years later, Kacmarcik also recommended Breuer's office to the parish of Saint Francis de Sales in Norton Shores, Michigan, a suburb of Muskegon. In this 1960s design, Breuer's firm employed their concept of a freestanding bell banner, as they had done at Saint John's and Annunciation, as inspiration for the building itself (Fig. 16.3). Although these are three different types of churches, a combination of monastic and parish at Saint John's, monastic only at Annunciation, and parish for Saint Francis, Breuer's team developed design characteristics common across the trio. With the use of reinforced concrete and other natural materials left raw and unadorned, Breuer and Associates shaped midcentury liturgical space. It included bell banners that announced these structures to the interiors fashioned around a renewed emphasis on the sacraments including baptism, penance, and the Eucharist. This essay focuses on the ritual of baptism and the design elements needed to sustain its increased importance in the midcentury Catholic church. Working with their patrons, Breuer and his associates created a baptistry typology that drew on reformed liturgical notions that brought the worshipper closer to all the sacraments, historic and contemporary architecture, and the significance of water.

DOI: 10.4324/9781003358824-22

FIGURE 16.1 Saint John's Abbey Church, Collegeville, Minnesota, 1953–1961.
Photograph by Shin Koyama. Courtesy of Welder Library, University of Mary

FIGURE 16.2 Annunciation Priory, Bismarck, North Dakota, 1954–1963.
Photographer unknown. Courtesy of the Benedictine Sisters of Annunciation Monastery, Bismarck, ND (Archives)

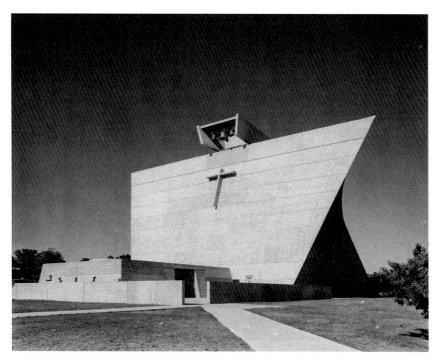

FIGURE 16.3 Saint Francis de Sales, Norton Shores, Michigan, 1961–1966.
Photograph by Hedrich-Blessing, HB-30662-G2. Courtesy of the Chicago History Museum, Hedrich-Blessing Collection

Water, Baptism, and the Baptistry

Water is the principal element of baptism, the first sacrament a Catholic receives and an initiation into the church and Christian life as one dies to original sin and rises to a new life with Christ. In the Bible Jesus explained that "No one can enter the kingdom of God without being born of water and the Spirit" (John 3:5). John baptized Jesus in the River Jordan (Mark 1:9). Jesus and his disciples baptized others in waters near Judea (John 3:22). During the crucifixion, water flowed from Jesus' side when it was pierced as a sign of his grace (John 19:34).

Water takes on many forms and is cleansing, purifying, and lifegiving in Catholic rituals. It can be dynamic or calm, shallow or deep, sprinkled or poured, and visible or covered. Water is transformative during the sacrament of baptism when it is either poured over the forehead of the initiate (baptism by affusion) or entered into as is done in baptism by full immersion. After the sacrament is complete, every time a Catholic worshipper enters a church they reconfirm their relationship with baptism as they dip their hands into the holy water found in stoups located near the entrances and bless themselves with it.[3]

The setting for baptism has changed over time. Early Christian baptism occurred in natural bodies of water, but by the fourth century CE builders constructed rooms specifically for the ritual in various shapes, most of which had a central plan. These baptistries, either attached to or separate from the main worship space in a church, held a baptismal font, the container of holy water necessary for the celebration of the sacrament.[4] Fonts or pools of water varied in their design, size, and location within the baptistry. The font serves two main functions according to liturgical design consultant, Regina Kuehn. "First, it *reveals* by its shape part of the truth about baptism. Second, the font *points* to the water" (Kuehn 1992, viii). Kuehn is referring to the baptismal font's role in conjunction with the entire baptistry as a symbolic womb of the church from "where Christians are reborn through water and the Holy Spirit" (*Book of Blessings* 1989, no. 1084). Images relating to these theological notions can also be found in these purpose-built spaces.

Creating a Baptistry Typology at the Mid-Twentieth Century

In the middle of the twentieth century decades of liturgical reform came together to create public worship that focused on an altar more conspicuously placed in the sanctuary so that all the laity could participate in the celebration of the Eucharist. Additionally, reformers sought engagement with all the sacraments on a regular basis, baptism and penance included. Pope Pius XII's 1947 encyclical *Mediator Dei* or "The Sacred Liturgy" codified these reforms and this necessitated change in the architectural settings of worship.[5] In this same year, the Holy See encouraged the German Catholic Bishops' Liturgical Commission to create specific architectural guidelines for church design. Composed by Father Theodore Klauser, the "Guiding Principles for the Design of Churches According to the Spirit of the Roman Liturgy" addressed all elements of the reformed liturgy, including baptism. The Benedictines of Saint John's Abbey published the principles in the December 1949 issue of their liturgical journal *Orate Fratres*. The Bishops lamented the lack of expression of the sacrament of baptism in present-day churches, either in the form of the baptistry or baptismal font, and presented a new model: "In the ideal church, this 'spring of baptism' (*fons*) would be given a monumental treatment and placed in a separate room near the entrance" (Busch 1949, 16). Saint John's own Father Cloud Meinberg's December 1961 essay, "The Baptistry and Other Spaces" published in *Worship* (formerly *Orate Fratres*), was important to the design team. Even though his essay postdates the completion of the Abbey church by a few months, it collected conversations the patron had with Breuer and his team during the design process, as it revealed the key elements of the mid-twentieth-century baptistry:

1. The sacraments of baptism and the Eucharist and their "physical functioning," as Meinberg put it, required distinct architectural spaces that should be adjacent to each other. The baptistry's placement should reveal the sacrament's meaning. This refers to its role as an entry point into the church, so a location near the building's entrance was important. It should connect to other sacraments with adjacencies, for example, confessionals for the sacrament of penance (reconciliation) could be nearby as it renewed baptismal grace. There should also be room in the baptistry for movement as part of the ceremonial nature of the ritual.
2. A freestanding font should be the focus of the baptistry. Its connection with the altar is of paramount importance.
3. Dignified design of the baptistry must reveal the character of baptism in all elements from architecture to art (Meinberg 1961, 537–539).

How did these requirements reveal themselves in Breuer and Associates' baptistry designs in the midcentury? And how do they adapt to the particular conditions of each of the three sites considered in this essay? Let's start by looking at the first design by the team, one that set the template for those that would follow, the baptistry at Saint John's Abbey Church.

Saint John's Abbey Church: A Baptistry Paradigm

Physical Functioning

Father Cloud and others called for a baptistry to be functional and symbolic. It should be located so that the worshipper encountered it each time they entered the church and proceeded to their seats in the sanctuary or nave. In the overall layout of the church, the baptistry and its font are part of what I have called the spiritual axis that ran from the bell banner through the baptistry on its way to the altar and abbot's throne (Fig. 16.1) (Young 2014, xvi–xvii). The baptismal font filled with holy water is the soul of the space. Its dignified design with appropriate imagery to support the importance of the sacrament is essential.

Breuer and Associates' 1956 design for the baptistry met the requirements of liturgical reforms as seen through Father Cloud's criteria and Breuer's version of midcentury modern architecture (Fig. 16.4). It is the first room one encounters upon entering the building through its northern doors under the bell banner.[6] Stairs on the east and west sides of the space lead to the parish chapel at the crypt level, thereby necessitating the inclusion of a baptistry in this monastic church. Breuer and his team provided ample space for the ritual of baptism, including seating on the east and west perimeter adjacent to the stairwell. The trapezoidal-shaped room features a coffered ceiling supported by two cruciform columns and walls of reinforced concrete. Those on the east and west sides are covered with a veneer of light gray granite in rectangular pieces that were quarried in nearby Cold Spring, Minnesota. The southern wall is comprised of darkly stained oak cabinets for storage and mechanicals as well as a central tripartite doorway of oak inset with copper which leads into the sanctuary. The

FIGURE 16.4 Saint John's Abbey Church Baptistry. Photograph by author

designers and client agreed on the placement of confessionals for the sacrament of penance immediately on either side of this doorway in the back of the sanctuary. They placed the baptistry at the center of the space with the font directly on the spiritual axis. Red brick was used on the floors throughout the space except for in the sunken area of the baptistry which features Cold Spring dark gray granite.

With a dual function of narthex and baptistry, the architects had to find a way to make baptism a focus of the space. Breuer and his associate Hamilton Smith, the lead architects for the project, created a space within a space. They inserted a central trapezoid with half-height walls around a depression in the floor with the baptismal font located at its center. Three steps lead down into this space on the north and south ends, aligned directly on the spiritual axis that unites the sacraments as preferred in the midcentury liturgical reform. The Benedictines requested that gates of simple oak wooden beams held by brass brackets be added on either end at the north and south openings.[7] Skylights provide direct light on the baptistry and its font in this rather dimly-lit space. Two holy water stoups of black Cold Spring granite attached on the upper portion of both sides of the sunken space are used by worshippers to recall baptism, as they bless themselves with holy water each time they enter the church. Tucked into the baptistry's interior walls are ambries where the necessary accessories for baptism are stored including oils, candle, vessel, garment, and salt.[8] The baptistry's architectural design and placement elevated the practical function of the space.

The Baptismal Font

The baptismal font anchors the space and its design and gave Breuer an opportunity to work as a sculptor, something he cherished.[9] He revised it several times, moving from a two-tiered rectangular structure to a circular one carved from a single piece of dark gray granite from nearby Cold Spring (Fig. 16.5). One workman from McGough Construction hollowed out the bowl with modern tools over eighteen days. The font's interior bowl has two parts filled with water of different depths. One part is the holy water storage area for baptism, hidden under a silver circular cover with a raised Y-shaped form on its surface, a sculptural piece designed by the architects.

Water makes this an appropriate place for the ritual of baptism. The water in the font basin is agitated by a single jet under the surface. Although the water has movement, which gives the space life and implies sound, there is no audible element. The water used in this font, and particularly the holy water inside the covered area of the inner basin, is sacred and so is its drainage. The Benedictines informed the architects in November 1959 that the "outer as well as inner basins will drain into the sacrarium system."[10] A sacrarium is a "special sink that is used for the reverent disposal of sacred substances. This sink has a cover, a basin, and a special pipe and drain that empty directly into the earth, rather than into the sewer system" (United States Conference of Catholic Bishops 2000, 236).

Dignified Design

Symbolically the space is simple but effective and worthy of the sacrament of baptism. The three steps down to the granite floor of the baptistry recall immersion baptism as done by the early church, as one walked down into and out of rivers to die and rise with Christ. Plants in planter boxes on the north and south ends symbolize life as does the simple but soundless agitation in the font's water. A lit candle during the ritual of baptism brings the presence of

FIGURE 16.5 Saint John's Abbey Baptismal Font. Photograph by author

Christ. The Abbey's namesake Saint John the Baptist, sculpted of bronze by the American sculptor Doris Caesar, stands ninety-six inches (almost 2.5 meters) tall and overlooks the sunken baptistry. The expressionistic, elongated figure extends a hand toward the baptismal font to encourage one's gaze in its direction. It highlights the importance of what happens here. Abbot Dworschak and Sub-Prior John Eidenschink visited Caesar in March of 1959 and viewed the finished clay model to approve it before she completed the cast in bronze.[11] Caesar shipped the sculpture to Collegeville in June of 1961, in time for Breuer to position it during a visit.[12] With the sculpture placed in its modernist setting, art and architecture came together to uphold the importance of baptism in this Catholic monastic and parish church. Unfortunately, the parish has moved out of the Abbey church and now the font is rarely used for baptism. But what happens if a monastic worship space never had a parish associated with it? How would the notion of a baptistry change from this archetype set at Saint John's? Our next case study reveals Breuer and Associates' solution to this programmatic situation in a chapel just south of Bismarck, North Dakota.

Our Lady of the Annunciation Chapel: A Symbolic Baptistry

Physical Functioning

The Priory of the Annunciation (1954–1963) featured two chapels for monastic and collegiate use that were set within a complex of an administrative, classroom, and dormitory space (see Fig. 16.2).[13] In the late 1960s with the completion of the College of Mary by Breuer's office, the chapels became even more heavily used as the student body increased. There was no associated parish and therefore a baptistry and baptismal font were not required.

FIGURE 16.6 Annunciation Priory Chapel Entrance Portico with Fountain. Photograph by Shin Koyama. Courtesy of the Benedictine Sisters of Annunciation Monastery, Bismarck, ND (Archives)

The symbolic importance of this sacrament would not be neglected in the design of the main chapel Our Lady of the Annunciation (1959–1963). A portico with a fountain marked the entry into the worship space and connected the user to baptism.

A spiritual axis of bell banner, fountain, confessionals, and altar organizes the sacred path of worship. A flagstone path moves past the banner toward the chapel's southern entrance portico with a fountain, the symbolic baptistry of Our Lady of the Annunciation (Fig. 16.6). Breuer and Smith employed midcentury modernist architectural values of engineered architecture paired with the use of materials in their natural states to define the chapel's aesthetic quality. There is no façade wall of the portico. Space is shaped by two walls of split rubble granite that run alongside the user on the east and west. The walls stop a few feet short of the entrance façade made of terracotta flue tiles set three feet (almost 1 meter) in front of full-height glass windows. Entry doors of gray with glass panels are inset into a white-painted concrete surround on the portico's north side. The floor is flagstone of rectilinear shapes and it slopes up six inches (15 centimeters) to meet the chapel's entry doors. Reinforced concrete for the ceiling is painted white and its formwork lines run perpendicular to the user walking into the building. Four can lights illuminate the portico, casting circular shadows on the ground in the dark hours of the day. The space is simple, unadorned, and purposeful in providing a place of welcome and recollection of one's sacramental entry into the Catholic church through baptism.

FIGURE 16.7 Annunciation Priory Fountain. Photograph by author

Fountain as Symbol of Font

A fountain is set nearly in the center of this portico and on the spiritual axis to the altar. It "symbolizes the sacrament of baptism" according to the architects and sisters.[14] Just over two feet (61 centimeters) tall, its base is a pentagon that twists out to a larger pentagon at the top whose sides each measure forty-two inches (almost 107 centimeters) (Fig. 16.7). The circular water basin's diameter is forty-eight inches (122 centimeter) with a depth of twelve (30.5 centimeters). A ring of jets inside the basin propels water six inches (15 centimeters) into the air before it returns to the surface.[15] Masons from Anderson, Guthrie and Carlson, Inc. of Bismarck, North Dakota fabricated the fountain of blue granite from the quarries near Lake Placid, New York. The granite is subdued in color, its blues and grays offset against tan tones that bring out the best in each other. The fountain has a coarse surface on its horizontal face while its angled sides are a bit rougher, as the surface texture was an artistic tool for the architects. This fountain is an aid to the memory of baptism. The architects and Benedictine sisters made sure, however, to include the holy water stoups necessary for the user to physically connect with the sacrament inside the chapel at all four of its entrance doors.[16]

Dignified Design

Distinguished design in the portico and fountain came from the use of materials left mainly in their natural state, the employment of symbolic form, and the incorporation of water. The Lake Placid blue granite complements the colors found in the local split rubble granite and flagstone. The painted concrete, glass, and terracotta flue tiles bring additional color and reflectivity to the space. The pentagonal star implied in the fountain symbolizes "time and nature" while the circular basin within it represents "eternal life."[17] It is the water in this fountain though that brings the strongest connection to baptism and the sacred. Not only is life represented in the agitation caused by the jets in the basin, but the sound of the fountain's water also commands a presence in the most powerful way. Sound is contained within the portico and coupled with the blustery North Dakota wind. It sets a backdrop of connection to nature and a higher power as one prepares to enter the chapel. Due to the exterior setting of an open portico acting as an *aide-mémoire* to baptism, the sound was an important part of the design paradigm with the building of Annunciation's symbolic baptistry. But what happens when sound is eliminated from the equation? How else might the power of baptism be conveyed? At the Church of Saint Francis de Sales, the symbolic presence of the Virgin Mary elevated baptism's importance for the Catholic parishioners.

Saint Francis de Sales: Parish Church Baptistry and the Virgin Mary

Physical Functioning

Connections from Kacmarcik, along with Breuer's now growing reputation as a religious designer, brought him to the awareness of Reverend Louis B. LaPres, pastor of the young community of Saint Francis de Sales in Norton Shores, Michigan. In need of a new church to house the growing parish, they commissioned Breuer's firm in June 1961 and construction lasted from 1964 to the celebration of the first Mass in December 1966. Here Breuer and associate Herbert Beckhard employed the banner form from Collegeville and Bismarck as the east wall of the building itself, rather than as a stand-alone structure. The east and west walls and the roof were each trapezoidal-shaped planes connected by hyperbolic paraboloid side walls on the north and south, all fashioned from reinforced concrete by the construction firm of M.A. Lombard of Chicago (see Fig. 16.3).[18]

As the banner form was now the façade of the church, the narthex with baptistry began Saint Francis de Sales' spiritual axis. One entered an exterior atrium with walls five feet six inches (1.7 meters) in height from the northeast and southeast corners, moving toward a low mastaba-like building of reinforced concrete rectangular in plan. Entrance doors on the north and south walls moved the user into this space that functioned as both a narthex and baptistry.

The use of the Egyptian mastaba as architectural inspiration is of interest here with regard to Breuer's career as it was the first time he used it. The Egyptians used the mastaba as a tomb and built them from mud brick or stone. Breuer loved the simplicity, size, and massiveness provided by the stone construction of Egyptian architecture in particular, and he found it a useful source for his innovative forms in reinforced concrete more than 4500 years later. In his preface to the 1964 book *Living Architecture: Egypt*, Breuer stated:

> Both cultures have a similar responsibility toward the material of construction. Both intend to create characteristic, basic and unmistakable expressions of their technology; both exploit the utmost function and the potential form of their available material.
> (Breuer in Ceneval 1964, 3–4)

Breuer so loved the structurally expressive and symbolic form of the mastaba that he employed it in many subsequent religious commissions. At Saint Francis de Sales the mastaba inspired form provided the space necessary for many functions. The architects located the trapezoidal-plan baptistry at the center of the western half of the room and sunk it three steps below grade around the baptismal font (Fig. 16.8). Half-height walls define a space within a space. The designers included holy water stoups on the exterior of these walls. On the main level of the narthex/baptistry, four confessionals surround the baptistry, two each on the north and south, giving the sacraments an adjacency called for by liturgical reform. The eastern half of this mastaba-inspired space went through several functional layouts with restrooms, preparatory rooms, and stairwells to the basement. The built structure included seating for fifty-six people for use during the ritual of baptism or while waiting for confession and a multipurpose parish room for the ushers, meetings, and processional assemblies.[19] The floors are waxed red brick except for the dark gray granite found in the baptistry depression. Fashioned of reinforced concrete throughout, the narthex/baptistry has thirteen-foot (almost 4.0 meters) tall ceilings with skylights above the baptistry and parish room. An eight-foot (almost 2.5 meters)

FIGURE 16.8 Saint Francis de Sales Baptistry with Baptismal Font, September 29, 1967. Photograph by Hedrich-Blessing, HB-30662-J2. Courtesy of the Chicago History Museum, Hedrich-Blessing Collection

258 Victoria M. Young

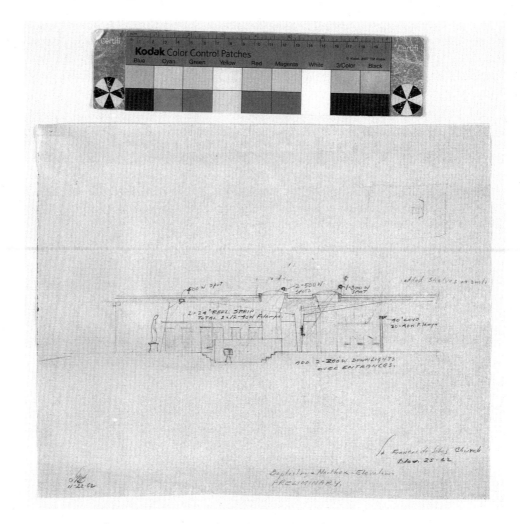

FIGURE 16.9 Preliminary Baptistry and Narthex Drawing for Saint Francis de Sales, November 1962. T248_001. Courtesy of Marcel Breuer Papers, Syracuse Collections Research Center, Syracuse University Libraries

wide center trapezoidal-shaped column supports the roof at the space's center. It created a surface on which a sculpture of the church's patron saint was placed years later. The back side of this column includes a niche for the holy oils cabinet. And just inside the entrance from the narthex/baptistry to the sanctuary, the designers included a sculpture of the Virgin Mary, seen at left in Figure 16.9. Mary is a unique addition to the spiritual axis here, a modification of the model layout of the Saint John's baptistry.

The Baptismal Font

After the completion of the building in 1966, a small circular baptismal font with a metal cover anchored the sunken baptistry. Its design is uninspired. Critics Donald Bruggink and Carl Droppers in their 1971 book, *When Faith Takes Form: Contemporary Churches of Architectural Integrity in America* (Bruggink and Droppers 1971, 52) noted that this font is also out of scale with its surroundings. The parish replaced this font over time with something more aesthetically and spatially appropriate and dignified—a large cube of black granite with a circular basin where a fountain slightly agitates the holy water. While the original font locked sound under its cover, the replacement allowed flowing water to act as a white noise calming agent as it helped to focus one's attention on the sacrament of baptism.

Dignified Design

Breuer's language of materials provided a noble architectural setting for baptism at Saint Francis de Sales. The three steps into and out of the space on the spiritual axis signify baptism by immersion, a connection to the historic church. Plants were added to emphasize life, the candle signifies Christ's presence, and light from the skylight connects the ritual to the heavens. Confessionals for the sacrament of penance on either side of the baptistry made this a place of renewal and cleansing. In 1998 the congregation added to the central column a sculpture by artist Wiktor Szostalo. It is a seven-foot (2.0 meters) tall stainless-steel image of the patron Saint Francis de Sales. As the parish reminded us in their fiftieth-anniversary booklet that year, "Baptism incorporates believers into the communion of saints who are invoked in the litany of the saints at the baptismal liturgy."[20] Including the patron saint is a reminder of the spiritual connection a Catholic has to the heavenly realm. And placing the baptistry in this location upon entry made it visible to the worshipper attending the weekly Mass.

But what about the Virgin Mary? Why is the sculpture of the Virgin at the entrance to the sanctuary important to our discussion of the baptistry here at Saint Francis de Sales? Muskegon artist and parish member Barbara Saint Denis completed the life-size bronze sculpture, *Mary, Mother of God*, in time for the church's opening in 1966.[21] Placed on a black granite base, the open stomach area of the sculpture is at eye level of the average human, and as the parish noted in its opening day press kit, "Through Mary's womb, the altar, Christ is viewed."[22] As Father LaPres explained: "Mary is the symbol of the Mother Church. ... Baptismal font, statue of the Mother of Jesus, and altar (which is the symbol of Christ) will stand in a true focal relationship."[23] Recall that the baptistry and font can be seen as a symbolic womb of the church. This insertion of the womb-less *Mary, the Mother of God* on the spiritual axis of Saint Francis de Sales required that the baptistry and font be close to it, to stand in for the womb and represent the place where Christians are reborn through baptism. This alignment of baptistry with confessionals, sculpture, and altar in some ways is the most powerful spiritual axis one could find in a parish church. And in those years after the Second Vatican Council (1962–1965) made liturgical reforms official church policy, it was essential that all the sacraments of the church find themselves front and center.

Conclusion

Over a little more than a ten-year period, Marcel Breuer and Associates designed three modern sacred spaces that upheld liturgical reforms and provided models for others across the world. Dozens of architectural and religious journals shared the philosophies behind the finished projects, the pillars of which involved using contemporary architectural forms to define spaces for all the sacraments to be fully present in the daily worshipper's life. In the baptistries for Saint John's Abbey Church, Our Lady of the Annunciation Chapel, and the Church of Saint Francis de Sales, patrons, architects, and artists united and created a paradigm for the mid-twentieth-century Catholic church in the baptistry's physical placement and functioning, its baptismal font design, and associated artwork. At the center of this all was water, and whether covered or open, still or agitated, it elevated sacred design in its role as the cleansing agent of deliverance and purification.

Notes

1. Abbot Baldwin Dworschak to selected architects, March 7, 1953. Box 2 Folder 13. Office of the Abbot. New Church and Monastery Building Records, 1952–1981 (bulk 1953–1962). St. John's Abbey (Collegeville, Minnesota).
2. "Annunciation Monastery: Heritage." Accessed February 25, 2022, https://www.annunciation-monastery.org/about/heritage/history.html.
3. Henri Leclercq, "Holy Water Fonts," *The Catholic Encyclopedia*. Accessed January 31, 2022, http://www.newadvent.org/cathen/07433a.htm.
4. A clergy member's blessing makes water holy. For more on the architectural settings of baptism see Davies 1962.
5. Pope Pius XII, "The Sacred Liturgy" part 195. Accessed September 20, 2021, https://www.vatican.va/content/pius-xii/en/encyclicals/documents/hf_p-xii_enc_20111947_mediator-dei.html.
6. For an image of the floor plan of Saint John's Abbey Church see "AD Classics: St. John's Abbey Church / Marcel Breuer." Note the baptistry at left (north). Accessed January 31, 2022, https://www.archdaily.com/255902/ad-classics-st-johns-abbey-church-marcel-breuer.
7. Hamilton Smith to Marcel Breuer and Associates, "Notes on the November 11–13, 1959 Visit to Saint John's Abbey," November 19, 1959. Image ID 58555-001 to 58555-004. Marcel Breuer Papers, Syracuse Collections Research Center, Syracuse University Libraries. Accessed September 15, 2021, https://breuer.syr.edu/xtf/view?docId=mets/85732.mets.xml;query=baptistry;brand=breuer.
8. Blessed salt is a sacramental of the Church, a material object ritually blessed by a priest to recall a sacrament in the Catholic church. It was given to those preparing for baptism up until the time of the Second Vatican Council (1962–1965). See Francis Mersham, "Salt," *The Catholic Encyclopedia*. Accessed September 29, 2021, https://www.newadvent.org/cathen/13403b.htm.
9. Isabelle Hyman, "Breuer and the Power of Concrete." Paper delivered June 22, 2002 at Saint John's Abbey. Hyman believed that Breuer's first calling was to be a sculptor. He completed only one public commission, *The Athlete*, a rectilinear human figure fashioned of gray Cold Spring granite installed in 1973 at Saint John's University outside the Warner Palaestra.
10. Hamilton Smith to Marcel Breuer and Associates, "Notes on the November 11–13, 1959 Visit to Saint John's Abbey", November 19, 1959. Image ID 58555-001 to 58555-004. Marcel Breuer Papers, Syracuse Collections Research Center, Syracuse University Libraries. Accessed September 15, 2021, https://breuer.syr.edu/xtf/view?docId=mets/85732.mets.xml;query=baptistry;brand=breuer.
11. Abbot Baldwin Dworschak to Doris Caesar, March 25, 1959. Box 1, Folder 1, Doris Caesar Papers, Special Collections Research Center, Syracuse University Libraries.
12. Doris Caesar to Abbot Baldwin Dworschak, undated handwritten note. Box 1, Folder 1, Doris Caesar Papers, Special Collections Research Center, Syracuse University Libraries.
13. For a site plan and tour of Annunciation Monastery see "A Self-Guided Tour of Breuer Architecture." Accessed February 16, 2022, https://issuu.com/umary/docs/breuer_walking_tour_.
14. Hamilton Smith, "Priory of the Annunciation Architects Description." September 1963: 7. Box 39, Folder 2D-8. Benedictine Sisters of Annunciation Monastery, Bismarck, ND (Archives).
15. For drawings of the fountain see "Granite Fountain at Main Entrance." Image ID T1282_004. Marcel Breuer Papers, Syracuse Collections Research Center, Syracuse University Libraries. Accessed September 15, 2021, https://breuer.syr.edu/xtf/view?docId=mets/49635.mets.xml;query=fountain;brand=breuer.
16. Holy water stoups near the entrance to a sacred space act as a sacramental for baptism. See Henri Leclercq, "Sacramentals," *The Catholic Encyclopedia*. Accessed January 31, 2022, http://www.newadvent.org/cathen/13292d.htm.
17. "University of Mary Walking Tour – Marcel Breuer Architecture." Accessed September 25, 2021, https://issuu.com/umary/docs/breuer_walking_tour_.
18. "Site Plan with Parking - Saint Francis de Sales." Image ID T1199_024. Marcel Breuer Papers, Syracuse Collections Research Center, Syracuse University. Accessed February 16, 2022, https://breuer.syr.edu/xtf/view?docId=mets/50056.mets.xml;query=;brand=breuer.

19. "Press Kit." Box 21, Reel 5729, Frame 1308. Marcel Breuer papers, 1920–1986. Archives of American Art, Smithsonian Institution. Accessed September 20, 2021, https://www.aaa.si.edu/collections/marcel-breuer-papers-5596/subseries-8-8-3/reel-5729-frames-1295-1323.
20. "A Self-Guided Tour: Saint Francis de Sales Church, Muskegon, Michigan." Accessed September 25, 2021, https://stfrancisns.org/photoalbums/self-guided-tour.
21. For an image of *Mary, Mother of God* please see "In Memoriam: Barbara Saint Denis." Accessed February 27, 2022, http://legalnews.com/muskegon/1471504.
22. "Press Kit." Box 21, Reel 5730, Frame 1310. Marcel Breuer papers, 1920–1986. Archives of American Art, Smithsonian Institution. Accessed September 20, 2021, https://www.aaa.si.edu/collections/marcel-breuer-papers-5596/subseries-8-8-3/reel-5729-frames-1295-1323.
23. "Bronze Model, Mary Mother of Jesus." Box 21, Reel 5729, Frame 1298. Marcel Breuer papers, 1920–1986. Archives of American Art, Smithsonian Institution. Accessed September 20, 2021, https://www.aaa.si.edu/collections/marcel-breuer-papers-5596/subseries-8-8-3/reel-5729-frames-1295-1323.

References

International Commission on English in the Liturgy. *Book of Blessings*. New York: Catholic Book Publishing Co., 1989.

Breuer, Marcel. *Preface to Living Architecture: Egyptian*, Jean Louis de Ceneval, 3–5. New York: Grosset & Dunlap, 1964.

Bruggink, Donald J. and Karl H. Droppers. *When Faith Takes Form: Contemporary Churches of Architectural Integrity in America*. Grand Rapids, MI: William B. Eerdmans, 1971.

Busch, William, trans. "Directives for the Building of a Church." *Orate Fratres* 24, no. 1 (December 1949): 9–18.

Davies, J. G. *The Architectural Setting of Baptism*. London: Barrie and Rockliff, 1962.

Koyama, Shin, and Anne Burns, O.S.B., "A Convent is Born." *American Benedictine Review* 12, no. 3 (1961): 361–368.

Kuehn, Regina. *A Place for Baptism*. Chicago: Liturgy Training Publications, 1992.

Meinberg, Father Cloud H. "The Baptistry and Other Spaces." *Worship* 35, no. 8 (August-September 1961): 536–549.

United States Conference of Catholic Bishops. Built of Living Stones. Washington, D.C., 2000.

Young, Victoria M. *Saint John's Abbey Church: Marcel Breuer and the Creation of a Modern Sacred Space*. Minneapolis: University of Minnesota Press, 2014.

17
STRENGTH IN WEAKNESS—DAOIST WATERS AND THE ARCHITECTURE OF THE XINJIN ZHI MUSEUM

Ariel Genadt

Daoism emerged in China as a philosophy in the sixth century BC and evolved into a religion, boasting temples and monasteries, under the Eastern Han Dynasty (AD 25–220) (Qiao 2015: 14). The Daoist scriptures overflow with mentions of water in all its phases, both as an environment for allegories and as a metaphor (Laozi & Mitchell 2006; Zhuangzi 1968). Therefore, one may be surprised to discover that buildings dedicated to Daoist rituals and prayer made only minor, if any, formal references to water. Meanwhile, ideas from Daoist philosophy permeated and informed Chinese garden design in close relation to their manifestations in Chinese landscape painting. Considering that until the twentieth century the distinction between architecture and garden design in China was unfettered by present-day disciplinary boundaries, a study of water in Daoist built form must then include both practices.

This chapter examines the challenges of integrating the Daoist philosophical understanding of water and the possible reasons for its formal absence in Daoist religious structures. It then demonstrates how current architecture might be inspired by water or use it expressively, by analyzing the Xinjin Zhi Museum (also known as Wisdom Art Museum), designed by Japanese architect Kuma Kengo and inaugurated in 2011 (Fig. 17.1).[1] The building is a gateway to the sacred Daoist site of Mount Laojun, southwest of Chengdu, Sichuan, China. The region's subtropical monsoon climate and the abundant water in its rivers, air, and notoriously cloudy skies, inspired the architect. Those aqueous features joined spiritual ideals to inform the design spatially, materially, and metaphorically. Rekindling the disciplinary freedom of old, the museum has a garden-like layout. Its envelope expresses the portrayal of water in Daoist philosophy as supple, weak, and yielding, while performing as a mediating agent between humans, heavens, and earth. My interpretations suggest connections between Kuma's references to water formations in his writings and the Daoist parables that use water's behavior to illustrate abstract concepts. They unfold the possibilities and difficulties of employing water architecturally.

DOI: 10.4324/9781003358824-23

FIGURE 17.1 Xinjin Zhi Museum - Aerial view from the west. Photo: © Jianan John Dai

Water in Daoism—Substance, Environment, and Contradictory Metaphor

The word Dao, meaning "way," was used by all schools of thought in China to designate the principles or methods, each believed to be correct for living as a society in harmony with nature. Daoist philosophers appropriated the term to mean "the totality of all things whatsoever," or the way of the world (Creel 1956: 140). They faced a significant challenge in conveying the spirit and meaning of Dao, which they contended "cannot be described in words or even comprehended by thought" (Creel 1956: 140). They thus resorted to parables featuring natural phenomena. Water was often used as a metaphor for Dao itself (Watts 1974: 41). Its multiple phases as amorphous vapor, liquid, or ice, offered a fertile terrain for sophisticated and sometimes contradictory images. As such, water is abundant in the foundational Daoist texts. The *Dao De Jing* ("Classic of the Way's Virtue") is dated to the sixth or fifth century BC and is credited to the sage Laozi. Laozi emphasizes water's conflicting attributes and changing appearances as a metaphor in three of the eighty-one verses that make up the *Dao De Jing* (Laozi & Mitchell 2006: §8, §15, §78). For example: "The supreme good is like water, which nourishes all things without trying to. It is content with the low places that people disdain. Thus, it is like the Dao" (Laozi & Mitchell 2006: §8).

In the other foundational Daoist text *Zhuangzi*—named after its author of the third century BC—the word water appears more than 70 times. In some instances, its properties are metaphors for virtues, such as lucidity, purity, and perfection:

> Water that is still gives back a clear image of beard and eyebrows; reposing in the water level, it offers a measure to the great carpenter. And if water in stillness possesses such clarity, how much more must pure spirit.
>
> *(Zhuangzi 1968: 142).*

In other instances, water is part of a rural, agrarian environment and can be a life-giving or life-threatening phenomenon with manifold manifestations: river (44 mentions); sea (38); ice (12); rain (9); flood (7); snow (4); mist (4); and cloud (3). Such diversity testifies to water's central role in the daily life of the time, while also posing challenges to understanding Daoist allegories since contradictions arise between water's erratic behaviors. There are also discrepancies between water's symbolic meanings and its capacity to regulate the flow of *qi* or *yuanqi* ("cloud-vapor")—the vital energy or breath believed to unite all things in the universe (Cheng 2000). For example, while Zhuangzi mentions still water as an image of virtue, stagnant water is considered inauspicious for a good flow of *qi*, according to the principles of Chinese geomancy—*fengshui*—that were widely observed. To ensure that flow, a site should have a constant supply of fresh water that is properly contained and drained (Eitel & Michell 1984: 40). To complicate matters further, water's duality and shape-shifting properties make its meaning inconsistent over time. Although water is considered a *yin* element (Zhuangzi 1968: 267), associated with the feminine, dark, cold, dead, earthly, and soft, its effects can be *yang* when it interacts with other elements, becoming vigorous, nourishing, and light-reflecting. Thus, water sometimes connotes weakness and at other times strength. It may be both transparent and turbid, uninterrupted and permeable, soft and hard, heavenly and abyssal. The challenge of using water as a building substance is that construction typically freezes materials in one state, delimiting them with frames and joints—actions that would deny water its impermanent nature.

Daoist Architecture and Chinese Gardens

The association of Daoism and built form appeared with the inception of Classical Daoism as a religion during the Han dynasty (202 BC–220 AD) (Qiao 2015: 32). Around that time, Daoism emerged as "a system of thought that comes to have deities and then spaces for contemplation of the Dao (Way), such as caves, or spaces for worship of those deities, both halls in monasteries and caves used in the manner of Buddhist worship spaces" (Steinhardt 2019: 255). Daoist buildings then evolved through several centuries, and the resulting array of structures may be categorized into classes. Among them, the palatial city style ranked highest; followed by the palatial monastery with looser layout regulations; and third, the courtyard house style—smaller in scale and situated in a landscaped setting (Qiao 2015: 33–35). The earliest form of the house style was the cave or grotto, ideal for ascetic communion with nature. Later, courtyard-style buildings appeared on mountaintops, overlooking the sea, or in garden or park settings. The layouts of these various complexes varied significantly, between the formal axial and symmetrical for the palatial class, and the informal, asymmetrical pavilions in courtyard/park settings (Qiao 2015: 33–38).

Although mountains were as sacred to Daoists as to Buddhists, and both preferred them as sites for temples and monasteries (Steinhardt 2019: 255), Daoist complexes may be distinguished by their careful integration into the topography and use of existing natural features. Taking advantage of the terrain, Daoist monasteries, included gardens at the back or sides of the main hall, joined by a winding footpath, along which one found pavilions, terraces, and pergolas (Qiao 2015: 32). This layout emphasized the role of a path as a meditative instrument. Springs, streams, and waterfalls situated along the path, enhanced the flow of *qi* and made it sensorially manifest. The most prominent extant examples of such nature-integrated architecture are located in Mount Wudang in Hubei Province, one of the four mountains sacred to Daoism (Steinhardt 2019: 255–257).

It is often difficult to distinguish between Daoist, Buddhist, and secular edifices since all three were assimilated to the monumental Chinese architectural styles of the place they were situated in (Steinhardt 2019: 259). They all shared volumetric layouts, proportions, and construction materials, namely, a stone or brick platform, a wood structure, brick walls, and a ceramic tiled roof (Qiao 2015: 38–39). Meanwhile, Daoist buildings' symbolic charges relied on the ornament, stone statuary, and stele inscribed with verses of wisdom. Symbolically, the use of masonry and stone artifacts was in tune with the religion's espousal of the tenets of longevity and immortality (Creel 1956: 142–143), but it was at odds with the water metaphors for flexibility and yielding. Meanwhile, Daoist frescoes depicted natural or ephemeral themes such as "the sun, moon, the wind, clouds, mountains, water, trees, rocks and mythological figures" (Qiao 2015: 32). Noteworthy external motifs related to water are the S-shaped fish finials on the roofs' top ridge, believed to protect the structure from fire (Mitchell & Wu 1998: 47). Similar to all Chinese monumental architecture, roofs were the chief mediators between heavens and earth, providing a seasonal reminder of the structure's position amid the natural water cycle. Hipped and gabled roofs comprised about one-half of the hall's height and symbolized its status. Glazed ceramic tiles formed the roof's complex curved surfaces that drained waters by way of an open waterfall at the gutter-less eaves' edge, turning the environmental phenomenon into a spectacle.

In parallel to the evolution of purposely built structures for Daoist worship, during the Han dynasty in the third century AD, private gardens began to express the Daoist view of nature. In contrast to the appropriation of landscape features as found in the monasteries, Chinese literati palaces and their extensive gardens boasted artificial ponds, streams, and waterfalls. Among many that existed in southeast China, the extant Lion's Grove Garden in Suzhou, built in 1342, is a prime example (Fig. 17.2). Those gardens' designs were inspired by the union of sensual materials and the spiritual world through the invisible *qi*. Designer and Chinese garden expert Maggie Keswick summed the experience as "Man stood between heaven and earth, united by the flow of essence of *qi*. Gardens were the place where people could experience the mysterious Dao" (Keswick 2003: 73).

Chinese garden design was not auxiliary to the design of buildings. Setting the grounds, layout, and position of each of the many structures in the garden was integral to the designer's task. This process was elaborated in the construction manual *Yuanye* ("The Craft of Gardens"), published in 1634. Its author, landscape painter and garden designer Ji Cheng (1582–ca. 1642) provided guidelines for the garden's various components, including the topography, ponds, rocks, and many built structures, though very little about plants and trees (Ji 1988: 66–74). Ji Cheng also formalized for the first time the method of "borrowed scenery"—*jie jing*—as a pillar of Chinese gardens (Ji 1988: 39–40, 45, 119–121). Thus, he writes, gazebos (*xie* or *jie,* "to borrow") "are made to borrow or take advantage of the scenery" (Ji 1988: 70); while pavilions (*ting*) are "a place for travelers to stop and rest…" (Ji 1988: 69). Connecting these structures are covered walkways, "curving with the form of the ground" (Ji 1988: 69–71).

FIGURE 17.2 The Lion Grove Garden 獅子林園, Suzhou, Jiangsu, China, was built in 1342. On the right: a grotto built of Taihu rocks; on the left: a gazebo on the central pond connected by a winding footpath. Photo: King of Hearts, 2017. CC BY-SA 4.0 <https://creativecommons.org/licenses/by-sa/4.0>, Wikimedia Commons

These were oriented in relation to the garden's water features and their reflections of the surroundings (Ji 1988: 120–121) (Fig. 17.2). As we shall see, the Xinjin Zhi Museum combines spaces, topographies, and "borrowed scenery" that conjure up those described by Ji Cheng.

Another concept informing garden design was *li*. The flow of *qi* is believed to be regulated by the principles of *li*, an order that is not mathematical or mechanical but rather akin to that of complex natural phenomena. "Li is asymmetrical, a non-repetitive and unregimented order which we find in the patterns of moving water, the forms of trees and clouds" (Watts 1974: 46). *Li* has been integrated into Chinese garden design with specific relation to Daoist water metaphors.

Three examples can be noted. First, porous, sculptural rocks were central constituents of the garden. *Taihushi* limestone rocks, excavated from the depths of Lake Tai near Suzhou, were particularly sought after (Ji 1988: 112–119) (Fig. 17.2). Their irregular water-induced erosion pattern is governed by *li*, and the carved-out mass incarnates Laozi's saying that "nothing in the world is weaker than water, but it has no better in overcoming the hard" (Laozi & Mitchell 2006: §78). In the design of the garden as a whole the *yang* rocks and *yin* water balance one another (Keswick, in Ji 1988: 19–20). The second example is found in paving pebbles or clay tiles laid in sinuous patterns that seem to obey a complex order (Ji 1988: 101–102). And third, the triangulated or polygonal pattern known as "cracked ice" appears occasionally in paving (Ji 1988: 101) and frequently in wood latticework, defining the threshold between the interior and the open-air (Fig. 17.3). The recurrence of this pattern in literati gardens may be related to Laozi's illustration of the ancient Masters' adaptability and

FIGURE 17.3 A wooden screen with a "cracked ice" pattern. Garden of the Master of the Nets 网师园, Suzhou Jiangzu, China, was built in 1140 and restored in 1785. Photo: © Ariel Genadt, 2017.

resilience: "They were careful as someone crossing an iced-over stream… Fluid as melting ice. Shapable as a block of wood. Receptive as a valley. Clear as a glass of water" (Laozi & Mitchell 2006: §15).

In applying these formal translations of *li*, garden designers inscribed the evasive and transformational essence of water in immutable artifacts, integrating it into material culture. This feat can also be identified in some patterns of *lòuchuāng* openwork inserted into garden walls, made of bricks or clay tiles spaced out to allow visitors to peek from one space of the garden onto another. Of the myriad patterns, the most symbolic of water is called *liúshuǐ wén* ("flowing water pattern") formed by superimposed semi-circles, and originally used to depict the sea on ancient Chinese maps.[2]

Water as "Conditions" in Kuma Kengo's Work

To illuminate architect Kuma Kengo's design for the Xinjin Zhi Museum (built 2010–2011), antecedent references to water in his architecture and writings will be examined. Kuma's interest in water as a building material stemmed from his research into the phenomenal and philosophical aspects of what he called "weak architecture," which consists in buildings that have been "broken into fragments" (Kuma 2005). In creating them, he seeks to soften the work's spatial presence, its monumentality, and "to bring nature back into architecture by

FIGURE 17.4 Guesthouse in Atami (1995) designed by Kengo Kuma. View of infinity edge pool towards the Pacific Ocean. Photo: © Mitsumasa Fujitsuka

breaking down natural materials into smaller particles… By particlizing material, we can allow light, wind, and sound to penetrate freely… we can unite the environment effectively with the people inside" (Bognár & Kuma 2009: 16–17). This intention aligns with the Daoist view of the unity of all things through *qi,* and its translation into garden design.

Since the mid-1990s, Kuma took on commissions in Japan's countryside, thereby reconnecting to its landscapes, natural materials, and regional craft. It was then that he became interested in using materials for their sensual, phenomenal qualities (Kuma 2009: 20–32). A turning point in that regard was the Water/Glass Guesthouse, perched on a cliff overlooking the Pacific Ocean in the hot spring town of Atami, Shizuoka Prefecture, Japan (1995) (Fig. 17.4). There, he first utilized water to convey an impression that the building is assimilated to atmospheric conditions, being visually ambiguous and seemingly evanescent. Describing the project, Kuma remarks:

> It is the strange nature of water that makes this experiment possible. Able to alternate easily between its solid, liquid, and gaseous states, water makes our attempts to categorize the world look foolish. Water is also an infinitely sensitive receptor, responding to the slightest changes in the environment.
>
> *(Kuma 2008: 38)*

This observation followed his reading of Leibnitz's idea that "matter is not composed of autonomous particles (i.e., objects) with absolute hardness; nor is it a fluid of absolute liquidity"

(Kuma 2008: 67). Kuma then attempted to mimic the particle/fluid quality of the ocean in a reflecting pool. Its appearance changes in response to passing clouds and wind, while its infinity edge visually connects the building to the sea.

He continued his pursuit of "particlizing" after his Guesthouse in Atami, aiming to transgress what he saw as a modern and postmodern obsession with "objects" that he defined as "a form of material existence distinct from its immediate environment" (Kuma 2008: 1). Inspired by water, he proposed "to create a *condition* that is as vague and ambiguous as drifting particles. The closest thing to such a condition is a rainbow… A certain relationship established between particles of water vapor, the sun and the observer… generates the phenomenon we call a rainbow" (Kuma 2000). As such, Kuma's conception of architecture implies an eventuality, rather than a certainty typically associated with built objects. While such determinate objects convey strength, conditions connote weakness, since their outcomes are uncertain. This positive concept of weakness, I argue, is the kind both Kuma and Laozi found in water—one that is apparent but conceals its actual strength. Although Kuma has never referred to Daoism explicitly, the design principles he developed boast clear affinities to Laozi's ideas.

Water and its related weather phenomena continued to inspire Kuma's designs, and he was lucid about the challenge to use them architecturally: "Natural elements, such as wind, rain, and fog are continuously changing in character and essence, [so] it is a difficult task to provide a single expression for such ambiguous entities" (Kuma, 1999: 94). Since 2005, his endeavors of translating water's contradictory phases into built "conditions" joined his desire to overcome binary oppositions such as "object" *or* "anti-object," whole *or* parts, particle *or* flow, building *or* environment. He became interested in revealing the relationships between those entities through movement (Kuma 2009: 44–50). His embrace of relative definitions over absolute ones echoes the idea of inter-permeation of *yin* and *yang*. Thereafter, Kuma aimed to change the perception of his buildings into ambiguous parts-and-whole entities, boasting what I have called elsewhere "discrete continuity" (Genadt 2021), and often mimicking complex organic orders, which in Daoist terms, follow *li*.

It is likely the implicit kinship between Daoist ideals and the design principles Kuma had applied in several buildings in Japan and China since 1995 that appealed to the Chinese developer Fantasia Group who commissioned him to design a museum dedicated to Daoist wisdom in 2008.

A Flow of Clay Particles

In designing the Xinjin Zhi Museum in Chengdu, China, Kuma faced the challenge of applying "particlization" to create "conditions" for a spatial experience that evokes the Dao. His response was a space defined by a helical circulation path that changes as one moves through its artificial topography. It may bring to mind and body the experience of Daoist courtyard-style monasteries or temples set in gardens and integrated into the landscape with informal asymmetrical layouts. This *parti* may have been inspired by the first chapter of the *Zhuangzi*, titled "Free and Easy Wandering" (Zhuangzi 1968: 29). It is expressed by the building's volumetric division and angling of the floors in plan and elevation (Figs. 17.5 and 17.6).

Xinjin Zhi Museum offers variations on traditional garden themes and components. Having crossed a small bridge over the still dark pool, one can begin the journey. From the lowest level, a path winds up via stairs and ramps that alter the climbing cadence like twisting mountain trails. It leads the visitor from darkness to light, between indoors and outdoors, through covered walkways, alternatively walled or veiled by screens, reminiscent of the gardens described

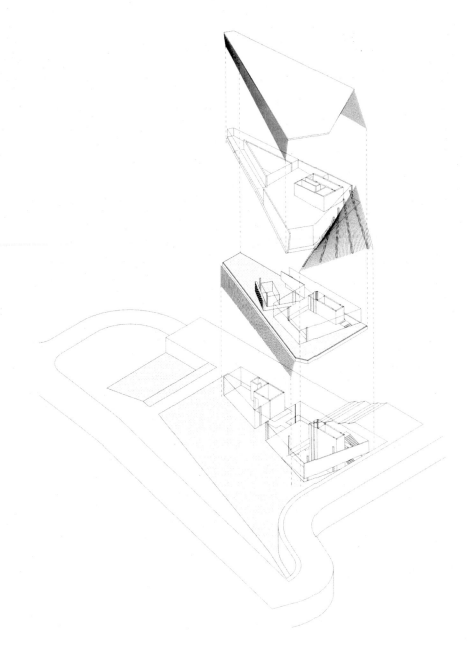

FIGURE 17.5 Xinjin Zhi Museum, axonometric drawing (exploded), showing water pools, internal circulation, and envelope of tiles. Drawing: © Kengo Kuma and Associates

by Ji Cheng. Along the way, one discovers a terrace, a patio, and a tea pavilion or gazebo that appears to be floating on a reflecting pool (Figs. 17.5, 17.6, and 17.7). The water surface's infinity edge creates visual contiguity between the "borrowed scenery" of verdant hills and the mirror in the foreground, similar to Kuma's Guesthouse in Atami of 1995.

The themes of fluidity and floatation are expressed in the external "particlized" envelope of clay tiles, delaminated from the frameless floor-to-ceiling low-emissivity glass panes that

FIGURE 17.6 Xinjin Zhi Museum, south elevation: angled floors hint at the internal circulation. Screens of suspended tiles in a wavy pattern (front) and retaining walls clad in tiles in the distance. Photo: © Daichi Ano.

make the interior weathertight (Fig. 17.6). Kuma tacitly associates the materiality of the envelope to the path's spiritual function, where he maintains:

> To describe the relationship between solid and fluid, we use onomatopoeia like *sarasara* (silky) or *nebaneba* (sticky) or *guruguru* (round and round)... In Buddhism, that condition is called *rin'ne*. *Guruguru* movement can recall *rin'ne*, or described environmentally, it can be understood as recycling.
>
> *(Kuma 2015: 53)*

FIGURE 17.7 Xinjin Zhi Museum, second level: tea pavilion, reflection pool, screen of tiles in a *liúshuǐ wén / seigaiha* pattern, and "borrowed scenery." Photo: © Erieta Attali

Thus, he links particles, fluids, and the circulation path in Xinjin Zhi with the concept of reincarnation, which has an equivalent in Zhuangzi's philosophy:

> The Way is without beginning or end, but things have their life and death—you cannot rely on their fulfillment. One moment empty, the next moment full—you cannot depend on their form… Decay, growth, fullness, and emptiness end and then begin again.
>
> (Zhuangzi 1968: 269)

At Xinjin Zhi, the architectural translation of *rin'ne* is encapsulated in the way clay particles appear to drift as if driven by invisible currents. The effect is achieved by weaving the tiles on an array of tensioned steel wires that seem to connect them like *qi*—a frozen potential of flow, a "condition." The resulting screen that envelops the path creates an image of material transformation between solids, particles, and fluids, especially when rain flows on the surface into the pool below.

Kuma's reference to "recycling" may also allude to the cosmological *wu xing* pentagram adopted by Daoism. It designates the five phases, or elements, of wood, metal, earth, water, and fire that are believed to regenerate one another (Mitchell & Wu 1998: 13). For example, earth overcomes water and produces metal; water overcomes fire and generates wood, and so forth. At Xinjin Zhi, four elements are readily visible: metal (steel columns and wires), water (reflecting pools), earth and fire (clay tiles). Tiles are also associated with water, as their original function is to channel precipitations from the sky to the earth. The absence of wood leaves the pentagram incomplete, provoking one's imagination. But the visitor may find the wood in the nearby mountain—the "borrowed scenery" to which the mirror pool reaches out (Figs. 17.1 and 17.7). This kind of intentional incompleteness in the design is related to the Chinese artistic principle *xushi,* which is composed of sinograms for "emptiness" and "substance." "When joined in a compound, *xushi,* they often refer to the ways in which the artist deals with those things in a poem or painting that are real and present to the reader or viewer (*shi*) and those things that are absent and left to the imagination (*xu*)" (Kuo 2015: 329).[3]

Xinjin Zhi does not reference any Daoist building components explicitly, except for clay tiles—reappropriated and deployed differently than in any traditional roofs. The *wu xing* phase change or the recycling Kuma mentioned can be observed in the four ways of laying and orienting the clay tiles. First, in the perimeter-retaining infrastructure, where tiles are placed vertically on edge, cemented to concrete walls that surround the entire site (Fig. 17.8). This is the heavy, earthbound, solid phase of clay. Second, at the building's underground level, an array of tiles vertically stacked and woven into an opaque partition, evoking compression and condensation (Fig. 17.9). Third, in the main elevations, the tiles that make up the envelope's external layer appear as "floating particles" or a mist-like "condition." Their function is both symbolic and climatic, shading the glass enclosure (Fig. 17.6). And fourth, tiles are laid flat and shelved horizontally into a rhomboid mesh of wires, forming an openwork in a *liúshuǐ wén* flowing water pattern (Figs. 17.7 and 17.9). This orderly arrangement is reserved for the tea pavilion, the place in the "garden" where one is invited to pause. Each of the four orientations evokes a distinct image of water: earthly and muddy, continuous and opaque, jittery and fuzzy, and still and calm.

The wavy lines traced by the envelope's tiles were inspired by the region's abundant precipitations, humidity, clouds, and rivers.[4] A hazy pattern found on one tile was magnified to the scale of the entire elevation and recreated by manually calibrating the tiles' spacing (Fig. 17.6). The drawing was then manually transcribed onto a Microsoft Excel spreadsheet

FIGURE 17.8 Xinjin Zhi Museum. The curved tensile screen on the east, opposite a tile-clad retaining wall. The discrete cloudy texture of each tile is apparent. Photo: © Daichi Ano.

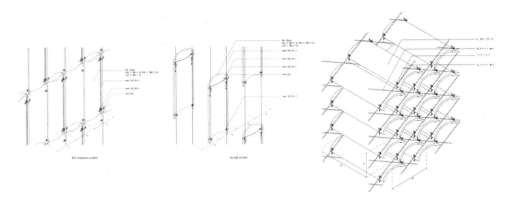

FIGURE 17.9 Xinjin Zhi Museum. Assembly details of clay tiles into screens, using steel cables. On the right: a *liúshuǐ wén / seigaiha* pattern. Drawing: © Kengo Kuma and Associates

that served as assembly instructions for the construction workers.[5] The pattern, which was freely drawn rather than using mathematical formulas or pure geometry, is akin to a complex order governed by *li*. Considering that the architect avoided digital parametric tools in favor of a painstaking analog process adds a layer of meaning to the envelope's expression of an assiduous pursuit of the Dao.

The still water pools at the lower and middle levels are balanced by the dynamism of the tile screen, which has two geometric variations: coplanar (tiles are on one plane), and a hyperbolic-paraboloid surface ruled by tensioned cables, perhaps alluding to the doubly curved surfaces of the *fei yan* ("flying swallow eaves") of old temples and gazebos (Figs. 17.2 and 17.8). However, the heft of traditional roofs is replaced by a delicate, lace-like textile, woven from steel threads, to which each perforated tile was hand-tied by four knots (Fig. 17.9). The *yin* frailty of this screen is multiplied when reflected in the dark-bottom pool, especially when the water ripples under a breeze. These various arrangements give the tile different metaphoric meanings, evoking the Daoist proverb on the interdependency of opposites: "The heavy is the root of the light. The unmoved is the source of all movement" (Laozi & Mitchell 2006: 26). The clay particles' levitation is contrasted and sustained by their earthliness, imbuing the whole with a sense of fragile equilibrium.

From the inside, the experience of the screened landscape evokes the openwork of literati gardens, with similar symbolism as the "cracked ice" pattern. It may feel like being enveloped by a cloud, through which the environment is alternatively revealed and concealed (Fig. 17.10). The effect can again be related to the painterly concept *xushi,* by which parts of the landscape are eclipsed, but still exists in the beholder's imagination.

Kuma recounts that his choice to utilize Chinese-made tiles was driven by the qualities he had identified years earlier in clay jars:

> I wanted to show the great potential of the earthy China… I learned from my father the beauty of a Shaoxing wine jar… ceramics are interesting because they are made of dirt… [they] have great power to reconnect humans… and the earth.
>
> *(Kuma 2014: 109–113)*

In other words, Kuma was interested in using local soil as a construction material and local craftsmanship to shape it, to both enable and express the building's rootedness in the place

FIGURE 17.10 Xinjin Zhi Museum. Main entrance over the reflective pool. The landscape is veiled by a screen of tiles. Photo: © Daichi Ano

and culture. To do so, he chose an artisanal production process: an open-air firing method, which transforms the red-brown tone of the soil into a misty anthracite hue with variegated patterns, highlighted in the final design as traces of the elements' metamorphosis (Kuma 2015: 54). Kuma drew inspiration from "the old farmhouse roof tiles around the area… In comparison [to the Japanese], the Chinese roof tiles are beautiful… they are thin and fragile, and uneven in color and size. … [They] are still baked in the open… using the local soil… Variations and raggedness are most lacking in architecture now" (Kuma 2014: 109–113). The unevenness that Kuma found in traditional tiles, and the way he projected these qualities onto the screen, echoes the Daoist symbolism of water-eroded rocks in Chinese gardens. In addition, he observed that the tiles in Sichuan were lighter than in other parts of China. Regional variations in tiles' shape and weight were likely a result of an adaptation over time to the specific wind loads they had to resist. Hence, suspending them was a way to express their climatic specificity.[6]

Can Architecture Reveal the Dao?

While Kuma's words disclose his interest in the earthly aspect of clay, his reference to the Shaoxing jar evokes Laozi's aphorism that calls one to imagine the space it delimits: "We join spokes together in a wheel, but it is the center hole that makes the wagon move. We shape clay into a pot, but it is the emptiness inside that holds whatever we want" (Laozi & Mitchell 2006: 11). Laozi's dialectics is paralleled at Xinjin Zhi in the relationship between the envelope and the experience of an architectural topography that is both wrapped around a void and contained within the natural environment. The tensioned steel-and-clay envelope may be likened to the clay pot. This materialization of flows and "conditions" elicits the ineffable spatial experience in one's mind. The envelope's components are expressive in and of themselves, but the relationship between them and the space they define is the most meaningful. Thus, they function both symbolically and as a medium for abstract ideals.

The envelope's spatial performance appears to be in harmony with the cycles of nature, thus, almost effortless. This condition is related to the Daoist ideal *wu wei*, "meaning 'no doing/effort/exertion.' It refers metaphorically to a state in which action is occurring even though the Subject is no longer exerting force" (Slingerland 2003: 29). For Laozi, water "nourishes all things without trying to... Thus, it is like the Dao" (Laozi & Mitchell 2006: §8). This has been interpreted as an allusion to *wu wei*—a state where one masters the Dao to a degree that its practice no longer requires effort or thought (Laozi & Mitchell 2006: viii, §38, §48). In this light, Xinjin Zhi's envelope's association with water can prompt one's attention to the virtues of that which merely appears to be effortless, having been achieved through total dedication.

To conclude, an architect aiming to relate to Daoist philosophy architecturally faces the challenges of conveying unrepresentable concepts. As we have seen, since it is difficult to pinpoint the unique characteristics of Daoist architecture as such, there is a limited formal and material inventory for reinterpretation. Kuma, therefore, relied on a selection of components, critically distilled from past implementations of philosophical principles in Chinese garden design, and also on the layout of nature-integrated religious structures. The sophistication of the result stems from this selective process and the translation of the contradictory aspects of water into a form that demonstrates the possibility of finding strength in weakness.

Kuma's inspiration from weather "conditions" and "particlization" is inscribed within a contemporary interest in architectural possibilities opened by physical and spatial parallels between atmospheric phenomena and climatically tuned habitation spaces. One thinks of the work of Icelandic-Danish artist Olafur Eliasson, or that of Japanese architect Ishigami Junya, as examples of pursuits of similar themes to those explored by Kuma in Xinjin Zhi. While these may indicate that some Daoist principles find footing in other contexts, they have received little attention in recent Chinese architecture. This may be an outcome of a construction culture that has been predicated by-and-large on masonry, and which continues today with Brutalist concrete, brick, and stone (Bologna 2020).

Meanwhile, the architectural expression of complex patterns inspired by nature appears to have another dimension in twenty-first-century China. It has been used to counter the anonymity and repetition that often resulted from the wholesale adoption of universal construction methods. Expressing these concerns, architects Wang Shu and Lu Wenyu, for example, have labored to combine pre-industrial materials including rammed earth, recycled bricks, roof tiles, and timber, with reinforced concrete and steel framing (Klanten & Elli 2021: 5–7). Wang has qualified these efforts as an attempt to reinstate "the Dao of Nature" into architecture and cities, in a physical and spiritual sense.[7] The common ground between Kuma's and Wang's design approaches can be noted in their respective buildings for the China Academy of Arts Xiangshan Campus in Hangzhou. There, in 2015, Kuma reapplied the tile suspension technique developed for Xinjin Zhi Museum (Kuma 2015). Meanwhile, Wang's work celebrates the heft that is part of masonry traditions, while Kuma's buildings champion the expression of weakness, in the Daoist sense. Other contemporary Chinese architects who share Kuma's interest in reinterpreting local craft and materials include Li Xiadong, Neri & Hu, Archi Union, and Zhu Pei, to name a few. Like the Xinjin Zhi Museum, their work stands out amid the prevailing urban development that has neglected important principles of

China's architectural heritage, in which inhabitants lived more harmoniously within their natural milieu and its abundant waters. Ultimately, in an age when Daoist rituals and sites have lost their meaning for the vast majority of Chinese people, architecture inspired by pre-industrial harmony can perhaps reconnect the secular and spiritual realms.

GLOSSARY

CHINESE NAMES AND TERMS

Dàodé jīng	道德經
Jì chéng	計成
Lǎo jūnshān	老君山
Lǎozi	老子
Tàihú shí	太湖石
Wǔdāng Shān	武當山
Xīnjīn zhī	新津 知
Yuán yě	园冶
Zhuāngzi	莊子
dào	道
fēiyán	飛簷
fēngshuǐ	風水
jièjǐng	借景
lǐ	理
liúshuǐ wén	流水纹
lòuchuāng	漏窗
wú wèi	無爲
wú xing	五行
xūshí	虛實
yuánqì	元氣

JAPANESE TERMS

rin'ne	輪廻
seigaiha	青海波

Notes

1. Japanese and Chinese person names are written in the surname—given name order.
2. The origin of the *liúshuǐ wén* (*seigaiha*—"blue sea wave"—in Japanese) cannot be asserted, but in both China and Japan, it seems to have originated in illustrations of poetic motifs on textiles (Jia & Zhao 2019), long before it was constructed using curved clay tiles (Neighbour Parent, Mary. "Seigaiha." *JAANUS*, 2003. http://www.aisf.or.jp/~jaanus/. Accessed March 31, 2022). I am grateful to Dr. Hua Zhengyang for identifying the Chinese reference.
3. I am grateful to Dr. Liu Linfan for the insight on *xushi*.
4. Information conveyed to me by the project architect Ko Minoru, Tokyo, November 2015.
5. Ibid.
6. Ibid.
7. Wang Shu, "To Listen to the Principles of Nature." Lecture delivered at the University of Pennsylvania School of Design, October 4, 2011. https://vimeo.com/30109234 - 18'40" Accessed: March 31, 2022.

References

Bognár, Botond, and Kengo Kuma. *Material Immaterial*. New York: Princeton Architectural Press, 2009.

Bologna, Alberto. *Chinese Brutalism Today: Concrete and Avant-garde Architecture*. Novato, Calif: ORO Editions, 2020.

Cheng, Chung-ying. "Qi (Ch'i): Vital Force." In *Encyclopedia of Chinese Philosophy*, edited by Antonio S. Cua. New York: Routledge, 2000, 615–617.

Creel, Herrlee Glessner. "What Is Taoism?" *Journal of the American Oriental Society, July - September, 1956*, 76, no. 3 (Jul. - Sep., 1956): 139–152.

Eitel, Ernest John, and John Michell. *Feng-Shui: The Science of Sacred Landscape in Old China*. 4th ed. London: Synergetic Press, 1984 (1873).

Genadt, Ariel. "Discrete Continuity in the Urban Architectures of H. Hara & K. Kuma." In *ACADIA 2020 Distributed Proximities: Proceedings of the 40th Annual Conference*. [S.l.]: ACADIA Publishing (2021): 420–423.

Ji, Cheng. *The Craft of Gardens*. New Haven: Yale University Press, 1988.

Jia, Xizeng and Qian Zhao. "Research on the Curved-Stream Pattern and the Falling-Flower-and-Flowing-Water Pattern," *Art & Design Research*, no. 3 (2019): 61–66.

Keswick, Maggie. *The Chinese Garden*. Cambridge, MA: Harvard University Press, 2003 (1978).

Klanten, Robert, and Elli Stuhler. *Beauty and the East*. Berlin: Gestalten, 2021.

Kuma, Kengo. *Kengo Kuma: Geometries of Nature*. Milano: L'ARCA, 1999.

———. "Dissolution of Objects and Evasion of the City," *JA The Japan Architect*, 38, Summer (2000): 58.

———. "Weak Architecture." In *GA Architect 19 Kengo Kuma*, edited by Yukio Futagawa, and Kengo Kuma. Tokyo: A.D.A. Edita, 2005, 8–15.

———. *Anti-object: The Dissolution and Disintegration of Architecture*. London: Architectural Association, 2008 (2000).

———. *Studies in Organic*. Tokyo: TOTO Shuppan, 2009.

———. *Boku no basho*. Tokyo: Daiwa Shobō, 2014. Unpublished translation by Hiromi Kawakami, 2016.

———. *Kuma Kengo: Onomatope kenchiku*. Tokyo: X-Knowledge, 2015. Unpublished translation by Sarah Lam, 2016.

Kuo, Jason C. "Emptiness-Substance: Xushi." In *A Companion to Chinese Art*, edited by Martin J. Powers, Katherine R. Tsiang, and Dana Arnold. Chichester: Wiley Blackwell, 2015, 329–348.

Laozi, and Stephen Mitchell. *Tao Te Ching: A New English Version*. New York: Harper Perennial, 2006.

Mitchell, C. Thomas, and Jiangmei Wu. *Living Design: The Daoist Way of Building*. New York: McGraw-Hill, 1998.

Qiao, Yun. *Taoist Buildings*. New York: CN Times Books, 2015.

Slingerland, Edward. *Effortless Action: Wu-Wei as Conceptual Metaphor and Spiritual Ideal in Early China*. Cary: Oxford University Press, 2003.

Steinhardt, Nancy Shatzman. *Chinese Architecture: A History*. Princeton: Princeton University Press, 2019.

Watts, Alan. *Tao - The Watercourse Way*. New York: Pantheon, 1974.

Zhuangzi. *The Complete Works of Chuang Tzu*. New York: Columbia University Press, 1968.

EPILOGUE

The Expression of Water in Virtual Sacred Architecture: The Case of a Virtual Baptism

Nesrine Mansour

This chapter examines the expression of water in virtual sacred architecture through the convergence of architecture, religion, and digital media. The last few decades marked a fast growth of technology, substantially with the emergence and spread of the internet in the 1990s. Digital technology became a significant component of quotidian activities, resulting in less dependency on the physical world and its constraints. Such changes enabled building new realms driven by unlimited imagination (Anders 2007) and my observed sense of blurriness between online and offline lives started to develop as both intertwined. New technological habits became even more prevalent throughout the COVID-19 global pandemic, which further promoted digital technologies with the increase of live-streaming and broadcasting in various aspects of life including rituals such as masses, sermons, and virtual baptisms (Lorea 2020). This chapter looks into the expression and use of water—in this case the holy water[1]—in virtual sacred architecture. It describes a Christian virtual baptism as an example of digital religious practices where sacred space, blessed and divine water, religion, and media all intersect.

Digital Religion and Virtual Sacred Architecture

New media platforms promoted the rise of digital spaces that introduced important changes in the practice of religion (Campbell 2010; Helland 2016; Højsgaard and Warburg 2005; Tsuria 2021; Wagner 2013). Scholars from various disciplines—mainly the humanities and social sciences—have developed a field of study called digital religion, where pioneering research and learning are conducted on religions, mostly Christianity, Islam, Judaism, Buddhism, and Hinduism in the digital realm, namely the Internet (Campbell 2012). Digital Religion is a structured and analytical inquiry that studies a variety of religious contexts and their use of emerging digital technologies. The manifested key research areas raise questions about the new definitions of religion while trying to understand identity, community, and rituals shaped by digital media (Campbell 2012; Campbell and Tsuria 2021; Hoover 2013). The intersection of media and religion is manifested through different formats, for example, cyber or online churches, religious radios, religious blogs, online prayers and rituals, online and virtual Bible studies, virtual pilgrimages, megachurches, televangelism (religious TV broadcasts), "god-casting," (podcast), and "god-blogging,"

FIGURE E.1 Digital Religion
Source: Author

(blogs) among others (Campbell 2010; Hill-Smith 2011; Helland 2016) (Fig. E.1). However, current scholarship on digital religion focuses largely on textual religious narratives, including scriptures and rituals as digital "spiritual" experiences. It pays little attention to the importance of visual and graphical representations including religious ambiance and its effects on spirituality. These visual effects could be expressed by means of photographs, drawings, paintings, computer illustrations, animations, video recording, or live streaming, as well as augmented and virtual reality (AR and VR). Implementing such visual techniques is important in conveying the experience of digital sacred architecture in addition to the text (Mansour 2019).

The literature demonstrates that religious spaces and their architecture possess theological and spiritual characteristics (Carroll 2003; Geva 2011; Jones 2000). This raises the question; how do such characteristics translate into the digital space? The Internet fosters the perception of the divine (Cobb 1999), and often, the move to cyberspace enables the valorization of inner spiritual perceptions similar to physical ones (Wertheim 2000). Digital Religion scholars believe in the importance of visual representations of sacred buildings and their attributes in the digital realm (Gelfgren and Hutchings 2014), yet very few informational inquiries, especially empirical ones were conducted (Mansour 2019). With the advancement of virtual environments and their graphic qualities, users of digital platforms like video games and virtual worlds are now able to experience full or partial immersions in digital worship experiences. Games like *Second Life*, *World of Warcraft* (WoW), and *Minecraft* are a few examples of online video games where players become worshipers communicating interactively via avatars. Such games belong to a category called Massively Multiplayer Online Games[2] (MMOG) where players have the ability to customize their characters with specific looks and qualities in order to engage in social interactions by joining guilds such as churches and temples (Chan and Vorderer 2006). *Second Life,* in particular, is an interactive virtual world that offers players or inhabitants a sense of geography and terrain (Bell 2008). In addition to being an online world, it has the capacity to offer visual expressions of spiritual inspiration where divine presence could be experienced (Kaburuan 2012). Numerous religious buildings found in virtual worlds like *Second Life or Sim City*, employ traditional and familiar architectural typologies of physical religious houses of worship (e.g., churches). In research on the virtual reconstruction of church architecture in *Second Life*, Gelfgren and Hutchings (2014) found that out of the 114 surveyed buildings, 81 were reminiscent of churches found in real life, and only 15 buildings were not characterized as a stereotype of a Christian church. The *Church of Fools*[3], currently named *St Pixels* Church of the Internet, is one of the first examples of online churches described as "a virtual space, designed using the kind of computer animation more commonly seen in games, but it looks and sounds like a traditional church. Wooden pews filled a stone hall, lined with pillars and lit by stained glass windows, with an altar at one end" (Hutchings 2015). These digital spaces aim to feel familiar, like community churches, and allure to worshipers who display physical limitations due to certain conditions such as sickness, disability, geographical difficulties, and sometimes the fear of being physically present in such sacred buildings (Hutchings 2015).

Religious or spiritual Websites and digital applications (especially ones belonging to the Christian faith) conventionally utilize a series of images and/or videos to portray existing buildings' architecture along with sacred features and religious symbols they comprise (e.g., sanctuary, chapel, prayer hall, baptismal fonts, etc.). Some applications adapted to be used on smartphones or tablets show a variety of digital still or animated illustrations, digital models, and renderings reconstructing sacred buildings as well as sacred Typology. The *Sanctuary application*[4], available both on phones and tablets, depicts a real-time three-dimensional interactive experience inside a virtual church. The users are able to virtually walk around the space of the sanctuary, sit to pray, and even light a candle using touch screen features that control the procession movement and actions. For the Muslim communities, *Muslim 3D*[5], formerly called *Mecca 3D*, represents a virtual world offering the possibility to experience and imagine being at the holy site, learning about the history, or engaging in a simulation of the pilgrimage of Hajj beforehand.

Another example of ceremonial Hindu worship of Puja or Pooja is the *Digital Durga Puja*[6] website created specifically for this ritual[7]. Devotees can receive blessings from the comfort of their homes, anywhere in the world, free from the constraints of physical space, geographical location, and time. Other games consider virtual worlds to display bigger varieties of designs since the players take on the role of designing their own worlds by the use of an expansive database of architectural elements and artifacts[8] (Bartle 2004) A *Second Life* player described their journey seeking a spiritual experience in the virtual world as follow:

> "So off we went in search of beautiful churches. I especially love stain glass windows and I am enchanted by religious art. We found Walsingham Church with its simple interiors, St Paul and its large stained-glass windows, the sweet gilt display of the blessed child at St George and the wondrous Basilica Cardinale. Basilica was stunning with stain glass, ornate alter and prayer pews for the patrons. I loved it here and we stayed [in the virtual world] for about an hour."[9]

(Figs. E.2, E.3).

FIGURE E.2 Basilica Cardinale interior space in Second Life
Source: https://www.flickr.com/photos/raftwetjewell/3175726270/in/photostream/

FIGURE E.3 Basilica Cardinale exterior view with rain in Second Life
Source: https://www.flickr.com/photos/raftwetjewell/3175726270/in/photostream/

Then they continue the journey with a visit to an art gallery while describing the virtual depiction of water

> "I wanted to see art. Cherry (another player) had sent a tip to Galerie Francane, so I arrived ready. Colorful psy (psychedelic) art and photographs lined the walls, but I was enchanted with the waterfall and river sculpture. Very spiritual with a reverence for nature and water. I loved it."[10]

(Figs. E.4, E.5).

FIGURE E.4 Art Galerie Francane in Second Life depicting photographs of water
Source: https://www.flickr.com/photos/raftwetjewell/3175726270/in/photostream/

FIGURE E.5 Art Galerie Francane in Second Life showcasing river and waterfall artwork
Source: https://www.flickr.com/photos/raftwetjewell/3175726270/in/photostream/

Virtual worlds may become an extension of the real one while the main difference manifests in the use of avatars and networked computers as means of interaction guided by real humans. Indeed, Cyberspace is defined as a place denoting spaces created by the Internet that becomes an extension of the physical one beyond the simple role of communication medium (Gibson 2004; Kalay and Marx 2005). The unlimited possibilities offered by virtual realities give these worlds distinct characteristics (Bell 2008). As such, virtual sacred architecture could be expressed through various media like still or animated images and digital models of buildings found in video games, mobile applications, and websites. This new digital virtuality permits the notion of three-dimensionality, interactivity, immersion, and multimedia phenomenon (Bermudez 1999).

In previous research on the intersection of sacred architecture and media, I focused on light as a prominent element of sacred architecture that contributes to the enhancement of spiritual experiences in virtual sacred architecture (Mansour 2022). In this study, I highlight holy water, which is another important element of sacred architecture that contributes to the spiritual and transcendent experience.

Water, Religion, and the Digital Realm

Water along with fire, earth, and air, constitute the four elements believed to construct the cosmos and represent the sacred associated with earth, heaven, and hell (Bermudez 2015; Eliade 1959; Geva 2011). Water embodies the energy of life and purity in its liquid state and is used for physical and spiritual purification. In Christianity, water becomes holy when it is blessed by a member of the ordained ministries of the church (Schmemann 1974). Holy water is used for blessings and particularly in baptisms as it symbolizes the purification of the body and soul. Used naturally in early Christianity, streaming from rivers and creeks, it did not require supplemental benediction. In classic antiquity, the placid water of baptismal fonts and stoups received blessings by the sign of the cross. Whether static or in motion, water incites the human spirit and is used both in ceremonial religious rituals and as a symbolic element of sacredness. Christianity, Islam, Judaism, and Hinduism consider water a symbol of life, a gift of God, used for purification and salvation. Purification seems to be a common characteristic of water across different religious beliefs and traditions. To purify is to free from material defilement, from guilt or moral blemish, and to grow and become pure and clean.[11] In Islam, God or Allah "sent down water from the sky upon you, that thereby he might purify you."[12] The Sunni Islamic law, Fiqh of the prophetic example (sunnah), has categorized the use and function of water into four categories, one of which is purification.[13] The Quran considers water to be not only the source of every living entity but the best mean by which people purify themselves before prayers (Ghabin 2020). The most sacred water in Islamic tradition bursts from Mecca's holy spring. For centuries, devoted Muslims believed that Zamzam water has the aptitude to cure diseases and alleviate hunger (Ghabin 2020). The Quran alluded to Zamzam in Surah Ibrahim Q14:37 when Abraham asked God to provide his offspring with fruit while they settled in a barren valley near his sacred house (Ghabin 2020). The veneration of water wells and springs like Zamzam is a common practice among North African and Middle Eastern religions, and Indian communities as they symbolize purification, aid fertility, and serve for ablution (Kreinath 2020). Sacred wells are also found in Judeo-Christian traditions. The city of Jerusalem was known to have the healing pool of Siloam and the pool of Bethesda believed to possess curative abilities due to angelic visits (Ray 2020). Since Genesis, water holds a central role in the *Torah*, which considers that the world was brought to life by God who created "an expanse in the midst of the water" (Phillips 2020). In past centuries, Jewish beliefs and rituals have always associated the sacred with water (Phillips 2020). *Mikvahs*, pools containing water emerging from natural sources (spring, rain, snow), were and still are commonly found in locations where Judaism is practiced. *Mikvahs* are designed specifically for immersion, according to Jewish laws (Silva 2007). Nowadays, *mikvahs* are found in synagogues or built-in Jewish centers to serve large Jewish communities (Phillips 2020). Similarly, Christian immersive baptisms serve as a purification ritual in addition to an acceptance ritual into the church.

In Hindu mythology, water is also perceived as the basis of life, and rivers are exemplified as removers of pollution possessing purifying powers (Singh 1994). Again, water is considered a purifying medium to "wash away sins," depending on its sanctity and cosmological attributions to Hindu mythologies (Singh 1994). Religious scriptures highlight and valorize the sanctity of water as it existed even before the earth was formed "Now the earth was formless and empty, darkness was over the surface of the deep, and the Spirit of God was hovering over the waters."[14] Eliade (1959, 188) has stated, "Water symbolizes the whole of potentiality: it is the *fons et origo*, the source of all possible existence … water symbolizes the primal substance from which all forms came and to which they will return."

Water is a common denominator across faiths, recognized and appreciated for its purification and holy characteristics. Still, the expression of water is not widely discussed in its virtual form and there are limited representations of it in virtual sacred spaces compared to the expression of light for example. Most of the use of water in virtual sacred architecture focuses on virtual baptismal functions/rituals.

Water, Baptism, and Baptistery

The divine baptismal water represents a multilayered experience by devotees. The water serves as an invitation into the church and the complete absolution plan of God starting from the creation (Bream 2020). Some passages of the Old Testament relate the water used for baptism to the crossing of the Red Sea, "That our ancestors were all under the cloud and they all passed through the sea."[15] Water symbolizes a clean dividing line between slavery and freedom, another evidence of its salvation quality (Thiry, Kamphoefner, and Bennett 1953). Baptism is a ritual through which a person receives the first sacrament to become a member of the church. It is an emblem of salvation, "Whoever believes and is baptized will be saved,"[16] and a representation of forgiveness of sins, "Peter replied 'repent and be baptized, every one of you, in the name of Jesus Christ for the forgiveness of your sins. And you will receive the

FIGURE E.6 Baptismal font for Christening
Source: https://commons.wikimedia.org/wiki/File:Amsoldingen_Kirche_Taufstein03384.jpg

gift of the Holy Spirit.'"[17] Thus, baptism is deemed to be an important passage to becoming an member of the Christian community.

Baptistries are important architectural features in churches since they serve as markers of the area where disciples receive the first sacrament (Jensen 2012). They are part of the church or built as separate buildings to accommodate the congregation witnessing the sacred ritual. The dominant feature standing in a Baptistery is a receptacle, typically a freestanding, stone structure containing baptismal water, and named the baptismal font (Jensen 2012). Baptismal fonts are not dictated by specific shapes or sizes (Fig. E.6). They are required to be made of impermeable materials capable of containing water and capacious to convey the importance of their sacramental function (Thiry, Kamphoefner, and Bennett 1953). These fonts could take multiple shapes, varying from round or elliptical, to polygonal (Fig. E.7). They generally display a protruded piece or ledge where baptismal accessories would stand.

FIGURE E.7 Baptismal font
Source: https://www.peakpx.com/573569/white-knitted-dress

Baptismal rituals shifted from sprinkling infants, witnessed in Catholic and Protestant churches, to full immersion of the body mainly of adults, seen in several evangelical churches (Klaver 2011). The question arises: how do the purifying and sacred characteristics of water translate when baptismal rituals are performed in virtual sacred architecture?

The Digital Sacred and Christian Baptism

Virtual environments may generate evocative perceptions despite their immaterial state (Bermudez 1999). Hence creating virtual realities possessing sacred properties offers unlimited possibilities for architectural styles and design options (Fig. E.8).

In video games and virtual worlds, where a great presence and variety of designs exist, game developers and artists are the main creators of these environments. In some instances, the players also become the architects of their individually designed virtual worlds. *Second Life Marketplace*[18] represents a virtual shopping database where *Second Life* residents are able to browse through millions of items, including landscape and home décor, fashion items, religious iconography, and accessories used for a myriad of religious rituals to name a few. Players use Linden Dollars, a virtual currency named after Linden Lab, the creator of the virtual game, to purchase any items needed for their newly created world. A quick search in the celebrations category of the marketplace using "baptism" as a keyword yields over one hundred items related to the ritual. Items range from a variety of baptismal fonts that differ in shape, size, and material (still or animated models that show water in them, sometimes showcasing a slight movement simulating the physical characteristics of water), baptismal accessories, blessing stoups, and fountains, to baptism certificates. The font's prices differ depending on the materials they are made of (e.g., wood, steel, stone) and the colors or patterns applied to them (e.g., black, blue, technicolored, native patterns, etc.) Some of the animated items even come with detailed instructions on how to use them. One example of a manual accompanying a baptismal font describes it as:

> "Beautifully designed baptism font perfect for baptism and christening. Marble and stone etched with the holy symbols important to the sacrament. Water; flowing, moving, and cleansing fill the font with a tiny glow. Oil container, candlestick, shawl, and Bible complete the alter. The sculpted design keeps it low prim while not sacrificing details. This baptismal font features three menu-driven animations for three people (mother, father, and priest)—ceremony, baptism, and celebrate. Touch the alter sides to get the

FIGURE E.8 Virtual Church with Baptismal Font
Source: http://bit.ly/2Z6sw6g

FIGURE E.9 Examples of Baptismal Fonts found in Second Life Marketplace
Source: https://marketplace.secondlife.com/p/DM-Mesh-Medieval-Baptismal-Font/4611913

menu for the animations or put out your own pose balls to create what you'd like. Included is a notecard reader with a notecard entitled 'Baptism.' Copy and paste what you would like said at your ceremony. Now touch the Bible, and you will see that your ceremony is repeated into local chat for all to hear. Anyone can touch the candlestick to receive a lighted candle to hold. Touch the urn to receive the priest bowl."[19]

For 300 Linden Dollars (equivalent to $0.93), residents can purchase a Medieval baptismal font "with a simple touch up/down lid to add a touch of realism and creating a convincing and realistic church environment. Mounted on a beautifully carved base, the font has an ageless beauty and feel suited to any style of church."[20] These fonts can be purchased for use by churches or individuals to place in their virtual homes or gardens (Fig. E.9). While visiting virtual churches in *Second Life,* one can come across a variety of baptismal fonts and blessed fountains filled with water. Some provide the possibility to be touched by the avatar's hands to receive sacred blessings. In some cases, similar baptismal fonts are found in virtual Hindu temples, like the Temple of Shiva. Those fonts are not used for the Christian function of baptism but for those entering the temple to wash their hands before meditating in front or in the middle of a great fire (Radde-Antweiler 2008). Other examples of water features like fountains (e.g., Moorish, and Arabic designs adorned with beautifully decorated tiles) can be found in other buildings, sacred and secular, some of them are virtual mosques. Sometimes they are mostly used for ornamentation purposes rather than purification as they were intended to be.

Since the emergence of the Internet, several churches have performed baptisms using digital tools. Some opted for the use of skype as the communication platform, while others chose social media like Facebook live or Youtube recordings as congregations attended and witnessed the rituals online (Dyer 2020). The first Internet baptism was performed in 2008 by the Flamingo Road Church[21] in Florida. The full ritual was streamed live on Youtube by the priest while the baptized was being immersed in their home bathtub filled with water.

Altspace VR[22] is a more recent example of a social virtual reality platform that was founded in 2013 and started functioning in 2015. People, using avatars, can engage in social activities through virtual reality headsets. Those activities range from meetups, educational and religious classes, live shows, and a variety of religious events (e.g., Bible study, meditation, Sunday services, baptisms) (Fig. E.10).

D.J. Soto is the bishop of a virtual reality church called "VR Church" (Virtual Reality Church) that takes place in Altspace VR. The vision of the church is to "cultivate loving spiritual communities across the metaverse."[23] VR Church represents a spiritual community

FIGURE E.10 Architecture graduate student (Jordano Hernandez) using Altspace VR to engage in a meditation session
Photo: Author

that exists in virtual reality where worshipers interact with each other using computer-generated environments. They believe that "church can be anywhere, anytime, and with anyone." One of their most shared church events is a virtual baptism that took place three years ago in the virtual world. Headlines of games and virtual reality articles read, "Watch in awe as a real pastor baptizes an anime girl in a video game"[24] with a picture of an avatar immersed in a baptismal pool. The ceremony shows a pool of water located in what looks like a garden of a Japanese religious temple surrounded by pink and white *Sakura* (cherry blossom) trees. The person being baptized, appears as the avatar of a girl with pink hair, and the priest starts the ceremony immersed in the outdoor basin filled with water while other avatars depict people witnessing the ceremony from different parts of the world. The water filling the pool shows slight undulations as the pastor moves their arms and body. The reflections of the *Sakura* trees are perceived on the surface of the water, while a few petals are transported with the small breeze to land on the surface. A water fountain placed on one side of the pool, attached to the wall of the temple, displays a continuous flow of water filling up the pool as the ceremony continues. The whole atmosphere seems eerie, especially with the addition of what seems like fog or smoke. The pastor starts the ritual by introducing the meaning of baptism, equating the immersion in the "virtual" water as being immersed in god's love and stating, "The water symbolizes the spiritual cells soaking in divine love bringing with it new life and forgiveness." He continues by emphasizing the actions taking place in the virtual space, being lowered into the water to eliminate old habits, regrets, guilts, and failures. The baptized person gets fully submerged into the water as their avatar while the pastor gives a blessing, "I baptize you in the name of the Father, the Son, and the Holy Spirit. Rise up again to signify your new life for your spiritual walk." The newly baptized cartoon girl with the pink hair expresses blood rushing through her head as she gets out of the water, commenting "I feel I am out of breath, like I just had an experience, even though I was just crouching for thirty seconds," while one of the audience members affirms the full submersion in the water. Suddenly the water disappears, leaving an empty pool behind, marking the baptism completion.

The video of the virtual baptism assumes the function of an introduction to a spiritual path where the digital water becomes the holy water of cyberspace. The sacred could embody anything expressed by the ritual's narrative. Seeing the object is to pierce into an embodied experience that goes beyond it. The architecture could represent the computer itself, with the software and the operating system as where we dive (Wertheim 2000). Thus, the holy water becomes part of the details contained in the sacred space.

This case study uncovers one of the very few existing examples describing the expression of water in virtual sacred architecture. It places the emphasis on the emerging phenomenon of digital religion and its virtual space design that so far was left to game designers and digital artists with little or non-existing sacred architectural features.

Conclusion

In the case study of virtual baptism, the intention was clearly stated. The immersion was carried out in front of witnesses with the presence of a priest as well as the audience watching online. This virtual baptism, like other real ones, captures the symbolic denotations present in the bible, immersion being one of them. The sophisticated level of interactivity in virtual reality environments offers a means to create sensation, perception, and reflection which are consistent with some elements of the true symbolism formula by Paul Avis, a priest and theologian (Avis 2013).

One could argue that a virtual representation of water, no matter how realistic it may look, is an inadequate substitution for the blessed and purifying qualities of real water used in such rites. However, empirical studies showed that an element like light has indeed an effect on the spiritual experience of worshipers in virtual sacred architecture (Mansour 2019). A bright virtual church containing religious iconography (i.e., stained glass, crucifix, altar, bible, candles) produced more positive emotions than dim/dark church with the absence of icons. Thus, sacred architecture attributes, including light and water, do affect the extent of spirituality in virtual spaces.

Numerous religious communities are now adopting digital technologies as theologically adequate to today's technophile society (Anderson 2021). Such practices have been in focus, especially during the COVID-19 global pandemic and the enthusiastic and rapid move toward the Metaverse, an online space that goes beyond the universe by the use of high-quality 3D graphics viewed in virtual and augmented realities. This poses a question for architects and designers: to what extent does the digital context facilitate the continuation of sacredness when translated from the real to the virtual, freed from fixed time and space? This is particularly applicable today as the world is still in the midst of a global pandemic and other threats that have severely altered our realities. The further the move toward the digital, the further the research discourse widens to ask: what is the role of the architect in designing virtual sacred architecture and its religious attributes in the digital realm?

Notes

1. Holiness refers to divinity. Holy water is considered blessed or divine water. The Editors of Encyclopedia Britannica. "Holy water." Encyclopedia Britannica, November 2019. https://www.britannica.com/topic/holy-water. Accessed February 2022.
2. Massively Multiplayer Online Games (MMOG) is a large-scale gaming communities connected together in online virtual environments (Chan and Vorderer 2006)
3. The Church of Fools is now called St Pixels, Church of the internet and was active on social media like Facebook and Twitter. http://www.stpixels.com. Accessed March 2022.
4. The Sanctuary App designed for iPads by RXM Design, LLC. https://apps.apple.com/us/app/the-sanctuary-app/id568865203. Accessed March 2022.
5. Muslim 3D, a Virtual World of Islam, application designed for iPads by BIGTECH GmbH. https://apps.apple.com/us/app/muslim-3d/id871225494. Accessed March 2022.
6. Digital Durga Puja. https://digitaldurgapuja.com/index.html Accessed January 2022.
7. Durga Puja is a ritual performed in south Asia mostly by Bengali Hindus in India and all around the world. It is a five-day celebration of "the victory of the goddess Durga over the evil buffalo demon Mahishasura." Cohen, Dylan. "Durga Puja." http://www.globalgivingresource.com/blog/durga-puja/ Accessed May 2022.

8. Second Life https://secondlife.com. Sim City https://www.ea.com/games/simcity. Minecraft https://www.minecraft.net/en-us. Accessed May 2022.
9. Rafeejewell. 2009. Basilica Cardinale in Second Life https://www.flickr.com/photos/raftwetjewell/3175726270/in/photostream/. Accessed March 2018.
10. Rafeejewell. 2009. River and Waterfall Artwork https://www.flickr.com/photos/raftwetjewell/3175725184/. Accessed October 2021.
11. Merriam-Webster. "Purify." https://www.merriam-webster.com/dictionary/purifying. Accessed March 2022.
12. "Surah Al-Anfal (The Spoils of War)," verse 11.
13. "Fiqh-us-Sunnah." Volume 1. https://www.iium.edu.my/deed/lawbase/fiqh_us_sunnah/vol1/fsn_vol1a.html. Accessed September 2021.
14. Genesis 1:2, The New International Version.
15. 1 Corinthians 10:1.
16. Mark 16:16.
17. Acts 2:38.
18. Second Life Marketplace, https://marketplace.secondlife.com. Accessed March 2022.
19. CUDA Baptism Font, Second Life Marketplace, https://marketplace.secondlife.com/p/CUDA-Baptism-Font/2731609. Accessed March 2022.
20. DM Mesh Medieval Baptismal Font, Second Life Marketplace, https://marketplace.secondlife.com/p/DM-Mesh-Medieval-Baptismal-Font/4611913. Accessed March 2022.
21. See Flamingo Road Church first internet baptism https://www.youtube.com/watch?v=qThUe1-RvXU Accessed March 2022.
22. Altspace VR https://altvr.com/. Accessed May 2022.
23. Virtual Reality Church, https://www.vrchurch.org. Accessed March 2022.
24. Patricia Hernandez, "Watch in awe as a real pastor baptizes an anime girl in a video game: Modern faith is complex." Polygon, May 20, 2019. https://www.polygon.com/2019/5/20/18632723/vr-chat-baptism-anime-girl-dj-soto. Accessed March 2022.

References

Anders, Peter. 2007. "Designing Mixed Reality: Principles, Projects and Practice." *Technoetic Arts* 6: 19–29.
Anderson, William H. U. 2021. *Technology and Theology*. Vernon Press.
Avis, Paul. 2013. *God and the Creative Imagination: Metaphor, Symbol and Myth in Religion and Theology*. Routledge.
Bartle, Richard A. 2004. *Designing Virtual Worlds*. New Riders.
Bell, Mark W. 2008. "Toward a Definition of 'Virtual Worlds'." *Journal For Virtual Worlds Research* 1: 2–5.
Bermudez, Julio. 1999. "Between Reality and Virtuality: Towards a New Consciousness." *Reframing Consciousness*: 16–21.
———. 2015. *Transcending Architecture: Contemporary Views on Sacred Space*. CUA Press.
Bream, Tyler. 2020. "Water Baptism: The Divine Drama." Doctoral Dissertation, United States–Virginia: Regent University.
Campbell, Heidi. 2010. *When Religion Meets New Media*. Routledge.
———. 2012. *Digital Religion: Understanding Religious Practice in New Media Worlds*. Routledge.
Campbell, Heidi, and Ruth Tsuria. 2021. *Digital Religion: Understanding Religious Practice in Digital Media*. Routledge & CRC Press. 2021.
Carroll, Thomas K. 2003. "Architecture and Spirituality." *Irish Theological Quarterly* 68 (1): 35–50.
Chan, Elaine, and Peter Vorderer. 2006. "Massively Multiplayer Online Games." In *Playing Video Games: Motives, Responses, and Consequences*, 77–88. Mahwah, NJ, US: Lawrence Erlbaum Associates Publishers.
Cobb, Jennifer J. 1999. "A Spiritual Experience of Cyberspace." *Technology in Society* 21 (4): 393–407.
Dyer, John. 2020. "Digital Baptisms: What We Can Learn from Online, Virtual, and Broadcast Practices." *John Dyer* (blog). April 18, 2020. https://j.hn/digital-baptisms-learn-from-online-virtual-and-broadcast-practices/.
Eliade, Mircea. 1959. *The Sacred and the Profane: The Nature of Religion*. Vol. 144. Houghton Mifflin Harcourt.

Gelfgren, Stefan, and Tim Hutchings. 2014. "The Virtual Construction of the Sacred–Representation and Fantasy in the Architecture of Second Life Churches." *Nordic Journal of Religion and Society* 27 (1): 59–73.

Geva, Anat. 2011. *Frank Lloyd Wright's Sacred Architecture: Faith, Form and Building Technology*. Routledge.

Ghabin, Ahmad. 2020. "THE WELL OF ZAMZAM." *Sacred Waters: A Cross-Cultural Compendium of Hallowed Springs and Holy Wells*. Routledge.

Gibson, William. 2004. *Neuromancer. 20th Anniversary Ed. William Gibson ; with a New Introduction by the Author ; with an Afterword by Jack Womack*. New York: Ace Books.

Helland, Christopher. 2016. "Digital Religion." In *Handbook of Religion and Society*, edited by David Yamane, 177–96. Handbooks of Sociology and Social Research. Cham: Springer International Publishing.

Hill-Smith, Connie. 2011. "Cyberpilgrimage: The (Virtual) Reality of Online Pilgrimage Experience." *Religion Compass* 5 (6): 236–46.

Højsgaard, Morten T., and Margit Warburg. 2005. *Religion and Cyberspace*. Psychology Press.

Hoover, Stewart. 2013. "Evolving Religion in the Digital Media." *Religion Across Media: From Early Antiquity to Late Modernity*, :169–84.

Hutchings, Tim. 2015. "Real Virtual Community." *Word & World* 35 (2): 151–161.

Jensen, Robin M. 2012. "Material and Documentary Evidence for the Practice of Early Christian Baptism." *Journal of Early Christian Studies* 20 (3): 371–405.

Jones, Lindsay. 2000. *The Hermeneutics of Sacred Architecture: Experience, Interpretation, Comparison*. Vol. 1. Harvard Univ Ctr for the.

Kaburuan, Emil. 2012. "Spiritual Enlightenment in Virtual Worlds. Designing a Religion Site in Second Life," PhD diss., National Cheng Kung University.

Kalay, Yehuda, and John Marx. 2005. "Architecture and the Internet: Designing Places in Cyberspace." *First Monday*, (0): 230–240.

Klaver, Miranda. 2011. "From Sprinkling to Immersion: Conversion and Baptism in Dutch Evangelicalism." *Ethnos: Journal of Anthropology* 76 (4): 469–88.

Kreinath, Jens. 2020. "Water Sanctuaries of Hatay, Turkey." *Sacred Waters: A Cross-Cultural Compendium of Hallowed Springs and Holy Wells* : 247–56.

Lorea, Carola Erika. 2020. "Religious Returns, Ritual Changes and Divinations on COVID-19." *Social Anthropology* 28(2): 307–308.

Mansour, Nesrine. 2019. "Virtually Sacred: Effect of Light on the Spiritual Experience in Virtual Sacred Architecture."

———. 2022. "The Holy Light of Cyberspace: Spiritual Experience in a Virtual Church." *Religions* 13 (2): 121.

Phillips, Robert. 2020. "A Higher Level of Immersion: A Contemporary Freshwater Mikvah Pool in Israel." In *Sacred Waters*, 213–19. Routledge.

Radde-Antweiler, Kerstin. 2008. "Virtual Religion. An Approach to a Religious and Ritual Topography of Second Life." *Online - Heidelberg Journal of Religions on the Internet* 3 (1): 174–211.

Ray, Celeste. 2020. *Holy Wells and Sacred Springs*. London: Routledge.

Schmemann, Alexander. 1974. *Of Water and the Spirit: A Liturgical Study of Baptism*. St Vladimir's Seminary Press.

Silva, Sonia Smith. 2007. "Total Immersion: A Mikvah Anthology. 2nd Revised Edition." *Women in Judaism* 5 (1): 1–3.

Singh, Rana P. B. 1994. "Water Symbolism and Sacred Landscape in Hinduism: A Study of Benares (Vārāṇasī) (Wassersymbolismus Und Heilige Landschaft Im Hinduismus: Eine Studie Aus Benares (Vārāṇasi))." *Erdkunde* 48 (3): 210–27.

Thiry, Paul, Henry L. Kamphoefner, and Richard M. Bennett. 1953. *Churches & temples*. Reinhold.

Tsuria, Ruth. 2021. "Digital Media: When God Becomes Everybody—The Blurring of Sacred and Profane." *Religions* 12 (2): 110.

Wagner, Rachel. 2013. "God in the Game: Cosmopolitanism and Religious Conflict in Videogames." *Journal of the American Academy of Religion* 81 (1): 249–61.

Wertheim, Margaret. 2000. *The Pearly Gates of Cyberspace: A History of Space from Dante to the Internet*. WW Norton & Company.

INDEX

Note: *Italicized* folios refers figures and with "n" notes in the text.

Ābānāgan (annual feast-day celebration) 194
Abaneri Chand Baori *145*
Abdali, A. S. 45
Adalaj, Gujarat: *Rudabai vaav* 149, *153*, 154, *157*, 158, 162n10
Adjaye, D. 126
Afenapa, A. 127n2; *Osun* 114
afra/apra (spillways) 135, 137–138
African American Church House 123–126
Agarwal, A. 133
agor (catchment area) 135, 136, *136*, *139*, 141
ahamkara (ego) 139
Ahmedabad, Gujarat: *Ambe maata vaav* 158; *Ashapura maata vaav*, Bapunagar 158, *160*; *Bai Harir vaav* 154, *155*, 158; *Khodiyar maata vaav* 158; Le Corbusier's buildings in 210, 211; *Maata Bhawani vaav* at Asarva 158, *159*; map of *149*; *Rudabai vaav* 149, *153*, 154, *157*, 158, 162n10; stepwells in 148–162; Tagore Memorial Theater in 204
Ahmedabad Textile Industry Research Association (ATIRA) 201–203
air 1, 4, 20; conditioning 219, 220, 225, 226; handling unit at the Unity House 217, 218, *221*; lotus pedestal 110; movement of water 91; narthex 26; pollution 226; preheating ventilation 224; sacredness of 283; ventilation supply 219; warm 216, 220; Zoroastrians preference of open-air sacrifice 186
Al Rashid Mosque, Edmonton, Alberta, Canada 29, 33–36, *33–36*
Altar Court *70*, 74–75, 77, 79–81, *80*
al-ʿĀbedīn, ʿAlī Zayn 191

Amarsagar lake, Jaisalmer: *agor* of 141; *beri* in the bed of *142*; gateway of *142*; pal of *137*, 139; statues of a horse and an elephant in *139*
Ambe maata vaav (Ahmedabad, Gujarat) 158
Amida Buddha 238
Anāhitā 183, 184, 185; gold diadem 186; high-relief of *188*; materializing sacred water 186–194; pilgrimage shrines 189–192, *190–192*; rituals and traditions 184; temples 192–194
Anand. M. R. 209
Ando, T. 237, 238; Church on the Water in Japan 3; Museum of Modern Art in Forth-Worth, Texas (design) 4
Annunciation Priory, Bismarck, North Dakota 247, *248*, 254–255
Archaeological Survey of India (ASI) 152, 155, 158
Architectural Consulting Engineers (ACE) 217, 218
Arəduuī Sūrā Anāhitā 183, 184, 189, 192
Artaxerxes II Mnemon 186, 187
Ashapura maata vaav, Bapunagar (Ahmedabad, Gujarat) 158, *160*
Atticus, H. 88, 91, 96n10; Nymphaeum of *89*, *90*
Aurelius, M. 88, 91

Bai Harir vaav (Ahmedabad, Gujarat) 154, *155*, 158
baori (stepwells) 135, 144–146, *145*; defined 144 *see also* stepwells (Ahmedabad, India)
baptism 4, 13–28, 249–250; Christian scriptural roots for 13–15; Loretto Christian Life Centre Chapel, Niagara Falls, Canada 17–20, *18–19*; Mary Mother of God Roman Catholic Church, Oakville, Ontario, Canada 20–24,

21–23; Orthodox Baptistery at Ravenna 15–17, *16*; sacraments of 250; scriptural roots for 13; St. Gabriel's Passionist Parish, North York, Ontario, Canada 24–28, *25–27*; transformative power of water 13–15; virtual baptism and 279–289 *see also* virtual baptism
baptismal font 249, 250; in Catholic Church architecture 15; for Christening 285, *285*; filled with holy water 251; marble 24; Mary Mother of God Roman Catholic Church in Oakville 20, *21*; Saint Francis de Sales, Norton Shores, Michigan 258–259; Saint John's Abbey Church, Collegeville, Minnesota 252; *Second Life Marketplace 287*; St. Gabriel's Passionist Church *26*; virtual church with *286*
baptistries 247–260; baptism and 249–250; Our Lady of the Annunciation Chapel 254–256; Parish Church Baptistry and the Virgin Mary 256–259; Saint Francis de Sales 256–259; Saint John's Abbey Church 251–253; typology at the mid-twentieth century 250; virtual baptism and 284–286; water and 249–250
Baragan, L. 3; design of home (Casa) in Mexico City 4
Beckhard, H. 256
Behrendt, K. A. 110n3
Beijing, China 101–102, 110n7
Benares 206–207
Bhagavata Purana 41, 44
Bhatt, P. M. 154
Bībī Shahrbānū at Mount Ṭabarak 189, 191–192; shrine of *192*
"bicultural identity" 88
black sacred spaces 119–126 *see also* sacred spaces
blessed salt 260n8
Bodies of Water: Posthuman Feminist Phenomenology (Neimanis) 161
Bombay 206, 207
Botta, M. 237; Holy Pope Giovanni XIII Church in Seriate, Italy (design) 4; Sant Giovanni Battista in Mongo, Switzerland (church design) 3, 4
Breuer, M. 247–260; *Living Architecture: Egypt* 256
British Raj 206
Brown, R. M. 116
Bruggink, D.: *When Faith Takes Form: Contemporary Churches of Architectural Integrity in America* 258
brush arbor *see* hush harbor, United States
Buddhism 98, 148, 165–177, 271, 279; in China 109; ice stupa, building of 168–170, *169*; Mahayana 98; ontological frameworks 171–173; patrons of 103; sacred architecture 170–171; Tibetan 102, 109; Vajrayana 110n7
Burgess, J. 155
Butcher, A. 172, 175

Caesar, D. 253
Čakčak ("drip drip") 189, 191–192
Canadian Islamic Centre *see* Al Rashid Mosque, Edmonton, Alberta, Canada
Canadian Shield 21
Carney, J.: "Little Things" 3
Caro, Y. 52, 53
Catholic rituals 249
central ravine 72, 74, *74–76*, 79
central valley 74–75, 79
chado ("Way of Tea") 236
Chaityana 44
chajja (projecting eaves) 47, 207, 212n4
chakra (wheel or discus) 139, 141
char baghs (four square gardens) 46–48, 50
chattri (memorials) 45–48, *46*, 50, 204, 212
Chinese gardens 264–267, 275
chorten (venerated stupa) *165*, 167, 170, 171, 173
Christian baptism 86, 115, 249; virtual baptism and 286–289
Christian Eschatology 13, 23
Church of Fools 281, 289n3
Civil Rights Movement 115
climate-adaptive design 167, 168, 174
climate change 161, 163n19, 165–177; adaptation 173–174, 176
Clitumnus River 84–85, *85*
commons 134, 138–139, 162, 165, 225
community 167, 201–205, 210, 279; African American 115; Al Rashid Mosque 35; Buddhist 174, 175; buy-in 167, 175; Christian 285; churches 281; control over natural resources 155; faith 15, 21, 23, 24, 26; festivals 194; industrialized modernity 209; integration 209; Japanese Canadian Cultural Centre (JCCC) 36; Jewish 63; local 149, 189; long-term intergenerational obligation 139; mikvah in 53, 54; mobilization 161–162; modern housing 203; multipurpose space at Noor Cultural Centre, North York, Ontario 37; Muslim 189; Muslim diaspora 32; nature and 134; Parsi in 205; in precolonial India 201; restoration of community lost in oppression and slavery 115; shared water resource 139; social activities and 33; spiritual 287; sustained engagement 161; water infrastructure 205; for white-collar workers 199
Cone, J. H. 115
Contemplation Court 126, *126*
Coomaraswamy, A. K. 108, 205
Cooper, L. 54, 63
COVID-19 279, 289
The Crisis of Global Modernity: Asian Traditions and a Sustainable Future (Duara) 161
Cunningham, A. 155
cyberspace 8, 280, 283, 288
cymbee 116

daēvas 184, 185, 194
dams 113; Bhakra-Nangal in Himachal Pradesh 208; construction of 174; frozen 168; as "modern temples" 161
Dan Ghati temple sculpture, Govardhan 42
Dao De Jing ("Classic of the Way's Virtue") 263
Daoist/Daoism 262–277; architecture and 264–267, 275–277; Chinese gardens and 264–267; clay particles 269–275; contradictory metaphor 263–264; environment 263–264; substance 263–264; water as "conditions" in Kuma Kengo's work 267–269; water in 263–264
darshan 45, 49, 206, 212n3
Day, S. 173
Daykin, A. 77
decorative architectural elements 138–144
Denis, B. 259
Deo, B. S. 45
design thinking 174, 176; climate-adaptive 167; ice stupa 168
dharmakaya (body of law) 102
Digital Durga Puja 281
digital realm 279–280; virtual baptism 283–284
digital religion *280*; virtual baptism and 279–283
digital sacred: architecture 280; virtual baptism and 286–289
Dioskoroi 71
Doshi, B. 199–212 *see also* Gujarat State Fertilizers Corporation
Droppers, C.: *When Faith Takes Form: Contemporary Churches of Architectural Integrity in America* 258
Duara, P. 163n20; *The Crisis of Global Modernity: Asian Traditions and a Sustainable Future* 161
DuBois, W.E.B. 125
Durga Puja 289n7
Dworschak, B. 247, 253

Earth 1–3, 20, 22, 24, 108, 178n3, 220, 225, 227, 265, 272, 276, 284; fertility of 71; power of 74; *qanats* 185; sacred community 26; temperature of 216
East Asia 98, 101, 245n10
Eastern Han Dynasty 262
Eastern Hill 73, 74
Eck, D. L. 162n1
Eidenschink, J. 253
Eight Pagodas 110n7
Elbaum, S. T. 55
Elchanan, I. 54
Eliade, M. 14, 48, 244n4, 284
epopteia 78, 82n2
euergetism 96n10
everyday religion 172
The Extraction of Hidden Waters (Karaji) 185

Fagg, B. 122–123
fei yan ("flying swallow eaves") 274
fire 1, 2, 20, 110, 272, 283, 287; altars 109; gods of 186; for *Pāw mahal* 193; temple 189
First African Baptist Church of Savannah, Georgia 123, *123*
First Unitarian Society of Madison, Madison, Wisconsin 220–228; auditorium, and fellowship hall, looking southeast *226*; green roof looking southwest *227*; interior view looking northwest toward pulpit *223*; site plan, showing existing complex and new addition *223*; view from northeast *222*
Fitzgerald, P. *183*
Frazier, E. F. 124
Fujimori, T. 235, 237

Gagné, K. 165, 171
Gandhara 105–106
Ganga 144, 148–149, 162n1, 211–212
Gangajal 144
garbhagriha 206, 212n3
Garden of Fine Arts, Kyoto 243, *243*
gardens *see* Chinese gardens; Paradise Garden at Aleppo
Gathas 184
gazdhars 135, 143–144; defined 143; of Taron Bharat Sangh *143*
Gelfgren, S. 281
geothermal systems and religious ethics 215–228; First Unitarian Society of Madison, Madison, Wisconsin 221–228, *222–223*, *226–227*; Unity Temple, Oak Park, Illinois *216–219*, 216–220, *221*
geysers (named "mouths of hell") 234
Gharsisar lake in Jaisalmer: agor of *136*; pal of *137*, 141
ghats (steps descending to water body) 41, 47, 49, 50, 136, 138, 139
Ghazni in East Afghanistan 98, 101–102
Ghosh, A. 163n19; *The Great Derangement* 161
Giovanni Battista in Mongo, Switzerland 3, 4
Goepper, R. 171
"Go Green, Go Organic" campaign 174
"good" waters 86
Gopal Sagar at Deeg 47
The Great Derangement (Ghosh) 161
Great Mosque of Cordoba 30
Greece 95, 96n10; Nymphaeum of Herodes Atticus and Regilla, Olympia 88, *89–90*, 91, 92 *see also* Samothrace, Greece
Grilli, P. 235
Guesthouse in Atami *268*, 269, 270
Gujarat 144; map of *199 see also* Adalaj, Gujarat; Ahmedabad, Gujarat; Patan, Gujarat
Gujarat State Fertilizers Corporation (GSFC) 199–212; community 201–205; parikrama, subsidiary shrines, and cantilevered

water-spouts *210*; resacralization of water imagery 210–212; sacred wells 205–209; secular water towers 205–209; temple *201*, 210–212; tower 201–205, 210–212; township plan *202*; water 201–205; water tower *200*, 201
Guruguru movement 271

Hadrian 87–88, 92, 94
Haibak Caves 108
halakhic [Jewish legal] 53, 54
Hall of Choral Dancers 75, 79, 80
Hamilakis, Y. 87
Hansiya, R. 45
Harboe, G. 220
hare (purification rites) 233, *234*
Harivamsa 41
"heart/mind" 245n15
Hebrew Bible 52
Herskovits, M. J. 124
Hieron 70, 79–81, 82n2
Himachal Pradesh, India 106–109, 208
Hinduism 5, 41, 48, 148, 152, 205, 279, 283
Histories of Herodotus of Halicarnassus 186
Hoffman, M. 53
holiness 52, 53, 61, 63, 86, 284, 289n1
Holy Trinity 15
al-Ḥosayn, Imam 191
hotaru no yuya ("Bathhouse of Fireflies") 245n7
Humphrey, C. 245n14
hush harbor, United States 118–119
Hutchings, T. 281
Hyman, I. 260n9
hymns 183–195; materializing sacred water 186–189; monumentalizing sacred water 189–194; naming sacred water 184; transmitting sacred water 184–186

Ice Stupa Project 168–170, *169*; limitations of 175–176; stakeholders 175; sustainability efforts 175 *see also* stupa
India 174, 209; 17th-century mosques 31; architectural history 211; art 205; British anxiety about architectural esthetics 207; civilization 133; culture 202; independence of 207; map of *167*, *199*; Nehru attempted to re-sacralize water infrastructure 208; precolonial 201, 205; religious traditions 209; river goddesses 207; rural habitats 146; of sacrality of water 148–149; stupas 108; temple architecture 144; water architecture, sacred typology of 144–146; water culture 134, 144; water harvesting systems 138 *see also* Kusum Sarovar, Govardhan, India
Indo-Aryans 184
Indus River 101, 103, 167
informing: decorative elements as tools of 138–141; garden design 266

Iran 194–195; Isfahan 30; Khorasan road in western 193; map of *183*; Persian *qanat* system 186; pre-Islamic 105; south-central 186
irrigation 139, 149, 152, 199; drip 26; in Gujarat 156; ice stupa 168, 172, 174, 175; infrastructure 175; landscaping 39
Islam 13, 30, 205; architectural developments under Islamic dynasties 144; cleansing and purification 205; Kusum Sarovar 47; mausoleum 48; in Persia 189; ritual washing 34; tombs in paradise gardens 46; water buildings 152
Island 71–72
Ito, T. 240
Izanagi (creator-deity) 234, 235

Jaffe, S. E. 55
Jain-Neubauer, J. 144, 163n23; *The Stepwells of Gujarat: In Art-historical Perspective* (Jain-Neubauer) 152
Japan 233–244; Chichu Museum 241; gardens 237; "island landscape" 234; Kou-An Glass Tea House 236, *236*; Municipal Funeral Hall of Meiso No Mori in Kakamigahara 240; religiosity 233; Teshima Art Museum 242; tsunamis/typhoons 234; Water Temple, on Awaji Island 237, *239*
Jerusalem 14, 284
Jesus Christ 14, 284; baptization in the River Jordan 14, 16–17, 249; turning water into wine 2
Jewish Orthodoxy 55
Jews 52–65; Kirshtein family 63; *mikvah* 53–54; Miller, D. 54–62; spiritual purification 53–54
jharokha 203–204, 212
Ji Cheng 265, 270
John the Baptist 14, 16, 247, 253
Jordan River 4, 14
Judea 14, 249

Kacmarcik, F. 247, 256
Kagan, M. 63
Kahn, Louis 203, 212
kami (mythic spirits and deities) 233, 242
Kaplan, R. 63
Karaji, A. B.: *The Extraction of Hidden Waters* 185
Kaviraj, K. 45
ke (healthy, mundane life, and work) 233–235
kegare (ill and polluted state) 233, 234
Kenrokuen Garden, Kanazawa *235*
Keswick, M. 265
Khodiyar maata vaav (Ahmedabad, Gujarat) 158
kilundu/kulundu 116
kinesthetic fulcrum 80
Kirshtein, A. 63
Kirshtein, S. 63
Kirshtein family 63
Kishori, R. 45

296 Index

Klapper, A. 54
Klauser, T. 250
Kosrow II 187
Kou-An Glass Tea House 236
Krishna 41–45, 48–49
Kubala Washatko Architects 215, 222
Kuehn, R. 249–250
Kuma, K. 234, 235, 239, 262, 267–269; guesthouse in Atami *268*; Xinjin Zhi Museum in China 5
Kumtura Caves 108
kund (tanks) 45–48, *47*, 151, 207; Gopal Sagar at Deeg 47; Narad Kund 44, 49; Ratna Kund 43, 49; Shyam Kund 49; at the Sun Temple complex in Modhera *151*; Uddhav Kund 44, *44*, 49 *see also* Kusum Sarovar, Govardhan, India
Kundvav at Kapadwanj 152
Kushan Empire 98, 101
Kusum Sarovar, Govardhan, India 41–50; *chattri* (memorials) 45–48; Dan Ghati temple sculpture *42*; *kund* (tanks) 45–48; 'Lambagaon' Gita Govinda, Kangra *43*; layout of *44*; *lila sthal* (places of divine play) 42–45; location of *42*; *parikrama* (pilgrimage) 48–49

Ladakh 101–102; artificial glacier in *169*; desert landscapes of *165*; ice stupa in *166*, 167; sacred landscape *166*
Lake Placid 255
Lakhani, H. 36
'Lambagaon' Gita Govinda, Kangra *43*
Laozi 266, 275, 276
LaPres, L. B. 256, 259
Larissa Nymphaeum, Argos 92, *92*, 94, 95; 3-D reconstruction of *93*; Hadrian statue from *94*; side-elevation reconstruction of *93*
Last Supper 17
Lautman, V.: *The Vanishing Stepwells of India* 145
Le Corbusier 203, 204, 209–211; water spout on Sanskar Kendra *211*
LEED certification 224, 226
Lehmann, K. 77
Lesches, S. Z.: *Understanding Mikvah: An Overview of Mikvah Construction* 54
Leviticus 11:36 52
Leviticus 15:16 13
li 266, 267
lila sthal (places of divine play) 42–45
Linden Dollars (virtual currency) 286
Linden Lab 286
linga 45, 210, 211–212, 212n6
Linrothe, R. 170
Lion Grove Garden, Suzhou, Jiangsu, China 266
"Little Things" (Carney) 3
liúshuǐ wén (*seigaiha*—"blue sea wave") 267, 277n2

Living Architecture: Egypt (Breuer) 256
Livingston, M. 162n5; *Steps to Water: The Ancient Stepwells of India* 151, 152
living water 14, 17, 24, 52, 53, 65 *see also* water
Lord Vishnu 139
Loretto Christian Life Centre Chapel, Niagara Falls, Canada 17–20, *18–19*
lotus ceilings 106–109
lotus pedestals 98–101
Louis, "Sammy" 63
Lu Wenyu 276

Maata Bhawani vaav at Asarva (Ahmedabad, Gujarat) 158, *159*
Madan, T.N. 209
Madhya Pradesh 144
"*Mahatmas*" (great souls) 143
Mahayana Buddhism 98 *see also* Buddhism
makaras 205
Maki, F. 242
Mami Wata 116–117
Manasi Ganga at Govardhan 45, *46*, 49, 50
mandapa 204, 209
marble bull *89*
Marks, R. "Moby" 63
Mary Mother of God Roman Catholic Church, Oakville, Ontario, Canada 20–24, *21–23*
Massively Multiplayer Online Games (MMOG) 280–281, 289n2
material culture 2, 5, 6, 87, 102, 267
materializing sacred water 186–189
McGough Construction 252
Mecca 3D 281
Meiso no Mori Funeral Hall, Kakamigahara *240*
Memorial to the Soil Chapel, Wisconsin 4
Miki, A. 242
mikvah 4, 53–54, 58–62, *62*, *64*, 284; communal 63; construction and regulations 57; defined 52; in Judaism 6; Kirshtein family 63; Kirshtein Family 63–64; private 54, 63; structures 56
mikvaot 52, 55–58
Mikveh Yehuda 54
Miller, D. 54–62; do-it-yourself (DIY) manuals 53, 55–58; floorplan for a bathroom with a mikvah *64*; floor plans for mikvaot hidden *60*; illustration for Jewish family *61*; illustrations for hidden mikvaot *60*; illustrations for luxurious mikvah rooms *62*; illustrations for mikvaot in disguise *59*; *mikvaot* 55–58, 62; *The Secret of the Jew: His Life - His Family* 55, 56, 58, 61–62; *Seyfer Miḵyeh Yiśroel* 55
Mills, M. 174
Minecraft 280
Ming dynasty 102, *102*
Mishra, A. 133–146
misogi (waterfall purification) 234
Mitchell, H. H. 125

Miθra 184
Mogao Cave 285 in Dunhuang, China 106
Mongol-Yuan 102
monumentalizing sacred water 189–194
monumental relief sculptures 187
Moriyama, R. 36
mosques 154, 158, 207; Al Rashid Mosque, Edmonton, Alberta, Canada 29, 33–36, *33–36*; Canada 29–39; diaspora 32–33; Great Mosque of Cordoba 30; historical designs 30–32; Umayyad Great Mosque in Aleppo 30
Mount Kronos 91
Mount Laojun 262
Mount Wudang in Hubei Province 265
Mukut Mukharvind Temple 45
Müller, L. 242
muqannis 185
Muslim 3D 281
Muslims 30, 32–33, 36, 39, 152, 194, 284
Muslim Sultans 152
myesis 78
mysteria 71, 78

naga sadhus 139
Nahid Temple, Kangavar *193*, 193–194
Naito, R. 242
naming sacred water 184
Nandy, A. 209
Naoshima Island 245n13
Naqš-e Rostam (northwest of Persepolis) 187, 193; Narseh Investiture Scene *188*
Narad Kund 44, 49
Narain, S. 133
Narseh (Persian king) 187
National Museum of African American History and Culture, Washington, D.C. *126*
The Natural House (Wright) 219
Negro Spirituals 115
Nehru, J. 161, 199, 205, 208
Neimanis, A. 163n21; *Bodies of Water: Posthuman Feminist Phenomenology* 161
Nelson, A. F. 118, 119
Nelson, K. J. 244
nestha 135, 137, 138
New Testament 2, 13
Nishizawa, R. 242
Noor Cultural Centre, North York, Ontario, Canada 36–38, *37–38*
Northern Wei dynasty 106
Nussbaum, M. 217
Nymphaeum of Herodes Atticus and Regilla, Olympia 88, *89–90*, 91
nymphaion 96n7

Od, Y. 103
Odeion 96n10
Ohrmazd 184, 187, 189
Ohrmazd Zaraθuštra (Zarathustra) 184

Old Testament 13, 284
Olokun Temple, Nigeria 117, *118*; ancestral shrines 119–123
Orate Fratres 250
Orthodox Baptistery at Ravenna 15–17, *16*
Osun (Afenapa) 114
Osun River in Osogbo, Nigeria 114
Otowa Falls 244n5
Ottawa Muslim Association Mosque in Ottawa 35
Otto, R. 244n4
Our Lady of the Annunciation Chapel 254–256; Annunciation Priory Chapel Entrance Portico with Fountain *254–255*; dignified design 255–256; fountain as symbol of font 255; physical functioning 253–254
Owomoyela, O. 113–114

padam (lotus) 139
pal (dike) 135, 136; of the Amarsagar lake in Jaisalmer 136–137, *137*, 139; Gharsisar 141
Paradise Garden at Aleppo 30
Parikh, R. 210
Parish Church Baptistry and the Virgin Mary 256–259
parti 269
particlizing 268–270, 276
Patan, Gujarat: *Rani Ki Vav in* 145
Patna New Capital Water Tower, Patna, Bihar, India *208*
Pāw mahal 193
Peregrinus 91
Phyang Village in Ladakh, map of India depicting *167*
Pīr-e Bānū Pars (Lady of Pars) 189, 192; entrance to the pilgrimage site *190*
Pīr-e Sabz (Green Shrine) 189, 191; interior of *191*
Pliny the Younger 84
Polybius 185
ponds 41, 136, 141; architects and sanctifiers of 143–144; artificial 265; *gazdhars* 135; Govardhan 42; rainwater stored in 133; stepped 151; wedding 144
Pope Pius XII 250
Porphyry 189
pradikshina (ritual circumambulation) 205, 210
Priory of the Annunciation *254–255*, 254–256
Propylon of Ptolemy II 72, *72–73*, 76, 78
pugri (turban) 144
Puja 281
Pulesi Temple 110n7
purification 86, 235, 244, 287; holiness and 284; physical cleansing 30, 31, 39, 77; rituals/rites 4, 49, 53–54, 98–101, 110, 116, 205–206, 233, 234; salvation and 283; waterfall 234
Pursiful, D. J. 116

qanats (gravity-flow tunnel-wells) 185; cross-section of *185*; Persian *186*; wedding 186
qi 264–266, 268, 272
Qing dynasty 110n7
Queen's stepwell in Patan, stepped corridor *150*, 152, *153*
Qur'an 30, 284

Raboteau, A. J. 124–125
Raj, M. 204
Rajasthan 6, 41, 134, 135, 138, 141, 144
Ramayana 211
Rani ka Vav (Queen's Stepwell), Patan, Gujarat, India *145*, 206
Rashedi, S. H. *186*
Ratna Kund 43, 49
Ray, C. 114
Red Sea 284
religion 117, 120, 124–125, 143, 148, 173, 174, 239, 244; Abrahamic 13; *Anāhitā* 194; Classical Daoism 264; culture and 176; desert 29; digital 279–283, *280*; Eurocentric 124; everyday 172; Jewish 61; lived ancient 95, 96n3; longevity and immortality 265; polarizing affiliation 175; Roman 85–87; vernacular 233, 234; virtual baptism 283–284
remembering, decorative elements as means of 141–143
resacralization of water imagery 210–212
Richardson, H. H. 220
Rimpoche, C. 174
Rinpoche, Drikung Kyabgon Chetsang 170
River Jordan 115, 249
Roman Empire 84; map of *88*; religion 85–87; water-displays 87–95; waterscapes 84–95
Romanus, V. 84
Rosenberg, Y. Y. 54
Rotunda of Arsinoe II 79
Rudabai vaav, Adalaj, Ahmedabad 149, *153*, 154, *157*, 158, 162n10

Saarinen, E.: MIT Chapel (design) 3
Sabarmati Riverfront Development Project 163
Sacrament of Reconciliation 23
sacrarium 252
sacred architecture, Buddhism 170–171
sacred landscape 41, 71, 78, 81, 88, 122, *166*; defined 119; Olokun Temple 117
sacredness/sacrality 6, 71, 84–95, 148–162; constructed 119; decline of stepwells as sources of water 155–156; defined 244n4; functionality of stepwell 149–151; inhabitation in *Stepwells of Ahmedabad* 156–160; secular 162; of the stepwell 151–154; stepwells in the urban realm 160–162; of water and place 113–127; of water in the Indian Subcontinent 148–149; women and stepwells 154
Sacred Rock 77

sacred spaces: black 119–126; secular and 72; virtual 284
sacred typology of Indian water architecture 144–146
sacred verticality 110n4
sacred water: materializing 186–189; monumentalizing 189–194; naming 184; transmitting 184–186
sacred wells 205–209, 284 *see also* ponds
Saint Francis de Sales, Norton Shores, Michigan *249*, 256–259; baptismal font *257*, 258–259; dignified design 259; physical functioning 256–258
Saint John's Abbey Church, Collegeville, Minnesota *248*, *251*, 251–253, *253*; baptismal font 252, *253*; dignified design 252–253; physical functioning 251–252
sakaki 237, 245n9
Sakura trees 288
Sambuichi, H. 2, 233, 244, 245n13
Samothrace, Greece 69–82; architectural shape of water 74–75; central valley 74–75; digital model of the sanctuary's Eastern Hill *73*; entrance to the sanctuary 72–74; the Gods 71–72; the Island 71–72; map of *69*; restored plan of the sanctuary *70*; retaining walls of Central Ravine *75*; water 71–72; water and sacred experience in sanctuary 78–81; water in, around, and through buildings 76–78
Sanctuary of the Great Gods on the Greek island of Samothrace, Greece 69, *69*, *70*, 72, *74*, 78, 81
Sanctuary of Zeus at Olympia *89*; Regilla 88
Sanskar Kala Kendra 211
Sarabhai, V. 201–202
Schuler, M. 224
SC Johnson Administration Building in Racine, Wisconsin 219
Second Life Marketplace 280–281, 286; Art Galerie Francane in *282–283*; Basilica Cardinale exterior view with rain in *282*; Basilica Cardinale interior space in *282*
Second Vatican Council 259
secular water towers 205–209
sensorial artifacts 87, 91, 95
sensorial assemblage 87
sensory experience 85–87
sensory turn/approach 87
shakkei (borrowed scenery) 240, *241*
shakti (female power) 212
Shaktidevi Temple at Chatrari, Himachal Pradesh, India *109*
shankh (conch) 139
Shey whitewashed 102–104, *103–104*
shikhara 210, 211
Shyama Kuti 49
Shyam Kund 49
Shyam Sagar (Alwar, Rajasthan) 138

Simore, N.: "Take Me to the Water" 115
Singh, B. 50
Singh, R. 208
siropa (robe of honor) 144
Smee, S. 123
Smith, H. 252
society, architects and sanctifiers of 143–144
Solanki dynasty 162n7
Soloveitchik, C. 63
songs, water 115–116
South Asia 101
Spənta Ārmaiti (earth) 184
spirits, water 116–117
spiritual beliefs 124
spiritual cleansing 14, 100
spiritual purification 39, 53–54, 283 *see also* purification
spirituals 115, 118, 124
Steps to Water: The Ancient Stepwells of India (Livingston) 151, 152
stepwells (Ahmedabad, India): decline as sources of water 155–156; functionality of 149–151; sacrality of 151–154; in urban realm 160–162; women and 154
Stepwells of Ahmedabad 156–160, 162, 163n16, 163n22
The Stepwells of Gujarat: In Art-historical Perspective (Jain-Neubauer) 152
St. Gabriel's Passionist Parish, North York, Ontario, Canada 24–28, *25–27*
stupa 98–110; Beijing 101–102; Gandhara 105–106; Ghazni 101–102; Himachal 106–109; Ladakh 101–102; lotus ceilings 106–109; lotus pedestals 98–101; purification rites 98–101; Shey whitewashed 102–104, *103–104*; Tapa Sardar 98–101; water vessels as reliquaries 105–106; Yungang 106–109 *see also* Ice Stupa Project
Stupa 7 100, *100*
Suraj Mal 45, 46, 48, *48*
Suryakund (Sun Temple complex in Modhera) *151*, 152
Szostalo, W. 259

Tagore Memorial Theater (Ahmedabad, Gujarat) 204
taihushi 266
Taj Mahal in Agra, India 2
Takasaki, H. 245n7
"Take Me to the Water" (Simore) 115
talaab 134, *135*
Tapa Sardar 98–101
Ṭāq-e Bostān 187
Taron Bharat Sangh, *gazdhars* of *143*
tayammum 30
Telushkin, N. 55
Temple, F. C. 207, *208*

temples *201*, 210–212; *Anāhitā* 192–194; dams as modern temples 161; Dan Ghati temple sculpture *42*; fire 189; Mukut Mukharvind Temple 45; Nahid Temple, Kangavar *193*, 193–194; Olokun Temple, Nigeria 117, *118*, 119–123; Pulesi Temple 110n7; Shaktidevi Temple at Chatrari, Himachal Pradesh, India *109*; Uddhav Bihari *44*; Unity Temple, Oak Park, Illinois 216–220; Zeus Temple 91
Teshima Art Museum, Teshima Island, Seto Inland-Sea *242*
Thales of Miletus 3
Theatral Circle 78
thronosis 78
Tibetan Buddhism 102, 109 *see also* Buddhism
tirthas 162n1
toko-no-ma (a niche, "gap") 236
Torah 53, 284
torii gate of Itsukushima shrine *238*
tower 201–205, 210–212
Traditional Ecological Knowledge (TEK) 133–134
transformative power of water 13–15
transmitting sacred water 184–186
Trojan War 71
tsatsas 101–102, *102*, 109
Tucci, G. 102
21st Century Museum of Contemporary Art in Kanazawa 245n12

uchimizu (sprinkling water on pavements) 234
Udayamati (queen) 206
Uddhav Bihari temple *44*
Uddhav Kund 44, *44*, 49
Umayyad Great Mosque in Aleppo 30
Unitarian Universalist Association 215, 220
United States: hush harbor 118–119
Unity Temple, Oak Park, Illinois 216–220; geothermal HVAC system *219*; heating and ventilating system *217*; interior looking south toward pulpit *218*; second-floor plan for mechanical ductwork *221*; west front *216*
Unity Temple Restoration Foundation 217
upaya (skillful means) 236

Vajrayana Buddhism 110n7 *see also* Buddhism
The Vanishing Stepwells of India (Lautman) 145
Vergil: *Aeneid* 85
Verus, L. 88
Vestal Virgins 85
virtual baptism 279–289; baptism and 284–286; baptistery and 284–286; Christian baptism and 286–289; digital realm 283–284; digital religion 279–283; digital sacred and 286–289; religion 283–284; virtual sacred architecture 279–283; water 283–286 *see also* baptism

virtual sacred architecture 279–283
Vishnu Purana 41 *see also* Ramayana
Vitti, P. 95
Volk, E. 247

Wangchuk, S. 168
Wang Shu 276
water 85–87, 201–205; architects and sanctifiers of 143–144; architectural shape of 74–75; baptistries and 249–250; harvesting 133; in, around, and through buildings in Somathrace 76–78; Japanese mythology 3; management, "shifting the paradigm" 146; materiality of 1; physical and psychological threshold 4; role of 3; and sacred experience in sanctuary Somathrace 78–81; sacredness of 1, 3; as sacred placemaking 117–119, sanctification processes of 136–138; songs 115–116; spirits 116–117; stewardship 227; strength of 2; tower *200*, 201, *204*; transformative power of 13–15; as universal solvent 86; veneration 86; vessels as reliquaries 105–106; virtual baptism 283–286 *see also* purification
water culture 133–146; sanctification processes of water bodies 136–138; sanctifying role of decorative architectural elements 138–144; stepwells, sacred typology of Indian water architecture 144–146
waterscapes 84
Water Sensitive Urban Design (WSUD) 146
Weber, D. 222
When Faith Takes Form: Contemporary Churches of Architectural Integrity in America (Bruggink and Droppers) 258
Williams, G. B. 207
Wittet, G. 207
women 152, *171*, 192; exclusion of lower castes and menstruating 139; fertility 139; married 53; *mikvaot* 56; prayer balcony 35; purification of 4; ritualistic routines of 149; saints 189; and stepwells 154; washroom and *wudu* 35
wooden stupa model from Saspotse, Ladakh *105*
World of Warcraft (WoW) 280
Wright, F. L. 2, 215–228; *The Natural House* 219; Steel Cathedral in New York City 4; Taliesin Unity Chapel in Wisconsin (design) 3
wudu 4–5, 29–39; at the Al Rashid Mosque, Edmonton, Alberta, Canada 33–36, *33–36*; in contemporary diaspora mosques 32–33; designs in historical mosques 30–32; at the Noor Cultural Centre, North York, Ontario, Canada 36–38, *37–38*

Xinjin Zhi Museum 262; aerial view from the northwest *263*
xushi 272, 274

yazatas 184
Yazdegerd III 189
ye dharma 102
Yom Kippur (Day of Atonement) 63
Yoshioka, T. 236
yuanqi ("cloud-vapor") 264
Yuanye ("The Craft of Gardens") 265
Yungang Cave 106–109

Zamzam water 284
Zanskar 170, 171; sacred landscape *166*
Zen Buddhism 236, 244 *see also* Buddhism
Zeus Temple 91
Zhuangzi 264
ziyārat-nāme 191
Zoroastrian/Zoroastrianism 183, 184, 292; belief 183; deities 194; liturgy 184; Nahid Temple 194; *qanat* 186; sanctuary conversion 189; shrines 189; visitors at Pīr-e Sabz 191

Simore, N.: "Take Me to the Water" 115
Singh, B. 50
Singh, R. 208
siropa (robe of honor) 144
Smee, S. 123
Smith, H. 252
society, architects and sanctifiers of 143–144
Solanki dynasty 162n7
Soloveitchik, C. 63
songs, water 115–116
South Asia 101
Spəntā Ārmaiti (earth) 184
spirits, water 116–117
spiritual beliefs 124
spiritual cleansing 14, 100
spiritual purification 39, 53–54, 283 *see also* purification
spirituals 115, 118, 124
Steps to Water: The Ancient Stepwells of India (Livingston) 151, 152
stepwells (Ahmedabad, India): decline as sources of water 155–156; functionality of 149–151; sacrality of 151–154; in urban realm 160–162; women and 154
Stepwells of Ahmedabad 156–160, 162, 163n16, 163n22
The Stepwells of Gujarat: In Art-historical Perspective (Jain-Neubauer) 152
St. Gabriel's Passionist Parish, North York, Ontario, Canada 24–28, *25–27*
stupa 98–110; Beijing 101–102; Gandhara 105–106; Ghazni 101–102; Himachal 106–109; Ladakh 101–102; lotus ceilings 106–109; lotus pedestals 98–101; purification rites 98–101; Shey whitewashed 102–104, *103–104*; Tapa Sardar 98–101; water vessels as reliquaries 105–106; Yungang 106–109 *see also* Ice Stupa Project
Stupa 7 100, *100*
Suraj Mal 45, 46, 48, *48*
Suryakund (Sun Temple complex in Modhera) *151*, 152
Szostalo, W. 259

Tagore Memorial Theater (Ahmedabad, Gujarat) 204
taihushi 266
Taj Mahal in Agra, India 2
Takasaki, H. 245n7
"Take Me to the Water" (Simore) 115
talaab 134, *135*
Tapa Sardar 98–101
Ṭāq-e Bostān 187
Taron Bharat Sangh, *gazdhars* of *143*
tayammum 30
Telushkin, N. 55
Temple, F. C. 207, *208*

temples *201*, 210–212; *Anāhitā* 192–194; dams as modern temples 161; Dan Ghati temple sculpture *42*; fire 189; Mukut Mukharvind Temple 45; Nahid Temple, Kangavar *193*, 193–194; Olokun Temple, Nigeria 117, *118*, 119–123; Pulesi Temple 110n7; Shaktidevi Temple at Chatrari, Himachal Pradesh, India *109*; Uddhav Bihari *44*; Unity Temple, Oak Park, Illinois 216–220; Zeus Temple 91
Teshima Art Museum, Teshima Island, Seto Inland-Sea *242*
Thales of Miletus 3
Theatral Circle 78
thronosis 78
Tibetan Buddhism 102, 109 *see also* Buddhism
tirthas 162n1
toko-no-ma (a niche, "gap") 236
Torah 53, 284
torii gate of Itsukushima shrine *238*
tower 201–205, 210–212
Traditional Ecological Knowledge (TEK) 133–134
transformative power of water 13–15
transmitting sacred water 184–186
Trojan War 71
tsatsas 101–102, *102*, 109
Tucci, G. 102
21st Century Museum of Contemporary Art in Kanazawa 245n12

uchimizu (sprinkling water on pavements) 234
Udayamati (queen) 206
Uddhav Bihari temple *44*
Uddhav Kund 44, *44*, 49
Umayyad Great Mosque in Aleppo 30
Unitarian Universalist Association 215, 220
United States: hush harbor 118–119
Unity Temple, Oak Park, Illinois 216–220; geothermal HVAC system *219*; heating and ventilating system *217*; interior looking south toward pulpit *218*; second-floor plan for mechanical ductwork *221*; west front *216*
Unity Temple Restoration Foundation 217
upaya (skillful means) 236

Vajrayana Buddhism 110n7 *see also* Buddhism
The Vanishing Stepwells of India (Lautman) 145
Vergil: *Aeneid* 85
Verus, L. 88
Vestal Virgins 85
virtual baptism 279–289; baptism and 284–286; baptistery and 284–286; Christian baptism and 286–289; digital realm 283–284; digital religion 279–283; digital sacred and 286–289; religion 283–284; virtual sacred architecture 279–283; water 283–286 *see also* baptism

virtual sacred architecture 279–283
Vishnu Purana 41 *see also Ramayana*
Vitti, P. 95
Volk, E. 247

Wangchuk, S. 168
Wang Shu 276
water 85–87, 201–205; architects and sanctifiers of 143–144; architectural shape of 74–75; baptistries and 249–250; harvesting 133; in, around, and through buildings in Somathrace 76–78; Japanese mythology 3; management, "shifting the paradigm" 146; materiality of 1; physical and psychological threshold 4; role of 3; and sacred experience in sanctuary Somathrace 78–81; sacredness of 1, 3; as sacred placemaking 117–119; sanctification processes of 136–138; songs 115–116; spirits 116–117; stewardship 227; strength of 2; tower *200*, 201, *204*; transformative power of 13–15; as universal solvent 86, veneration 86; vessels as reliquaries 105–106; virtual baptism 283–286 *see also* purification
water culture 133–146; sanctification processes of water bodies 136–138; sanctifying role of decorative architectural elements 138–144; stepwells, sacred typology of Indian water architecture 144–146
waterscapes 84
Water Sensitive Urban Design (WSUD) 146
Weber, D. 222
When Faith Takes Form: Contemporary Churches of Architectural Integrity in America (Bruggink and Droppers) 258
Williams, G. B. 207
Wittet, G. 207
women 152, *171*, 192; exclusion of lower castes and menstruating 139; fertility 139; married 53; *mikvaot* 56; prayer balcony 35; purification of 4; ritualistic routines of 149; saints 189; and stepwells 154; washroom and *wudu* 35
wooden stupa model from Saspotse, Ladakh *105*
World of Warcraft (WoW) 280
Wright, F. L. 2, 215–228; *The Natural House* 219; Steel Cathedral in New York City 4; Taliesin Unity Chapel in Wisconsin (design) 3
wudu 4–5, 29–39; at the Al Rashid Mosque, Edmonton, Alberta, Canada 33–36, *33–36*; in contemporary diaspora mosques 32–33; designs in historical mosques 30–32; at the Noor Cultural Centre, North York, Ontario, Canada 36–38, *37–38*

Xinjin Zhi Museum 262; aerial view from the northwest *263*
xushi 272, 274

yazatas 184
Yazdegerd III 189
ye dharma 102
Yom Kippur (Day of Atonement) 63
Yoshioka, T. 236
yuanqi ("cloud-vapor") 264
Yuanye ("The Craft of Gardens") 265
Yungang Cave 106–109

Zamzam water 284
Zanskar 170, 171; sacred landscape *166*
Zen Buddhism 236, 244 *see also* Buddhism
Zeus Temple 91
Zhuangzi 264
ziyārat-nāme 191
Zoroastrian/Zoroastrianism 183, 184, 292; belief 183; deities 194; liturgy 184; Nahid Temple 194; *qanat* 186; sanctuary conversion 189; shrines 189; vistitors at Pīr-e Sabz 191